Cambridge Intellectual Property and Information Law

:onomic potential has rapidly expanded, intellectual property has become
t of front-rank legal importance. *Cambridge Intellectual Property Rights and
tion Law* is a series of monograph studies of major current issues in
:ual property. Each volume contains a mix of international, European,
ative and national law, making this a highly significant series for practi-
judges and academic researchers in many countries.

Series editor

William R. Cornish
*Emeritus Herchel Smith Professor of Intellectual Property Law,
University of Cambridge*

Lionel Bently
*Herchel Smith Professor of Intellectual Property Law, University of
Cambridge*

Advisory editors

François Dessemontet
Professor of Law, University of Lausanne

Paul Goldstein
Professor of Law, Stanford University

The Rt Hon. Sir Robin Jacob
Court of Appeal, England

books in the series can be found at the end of this volume.

Relocating the Law of Geogra[

As its [
a subje[
Inform[
intelle[
compa[
tioners[

There is considerable variation in the [
forms of legal protection for valuable [
Champagne, Colombian coffee and I[
products are increasingly important for p[
makers, the international legal regime [
remains unclear.

Adopting a historical approach, D[
regulating these valuable geographical d[
intellectual property law. He traces t[
indications as a distinct category while i[
ing feature of the link between region[
origin. The research addresses long-star[
plicity of regimes operating in this ar[
between product and place and its cu[
definition; the varying scope of prote[
geographical indications ought to be tr[
trade marks.

DEV GANGJEE is a lecturer in intellect[
of Law, London School of Economics[
the Oxford Intellectual Property Resea[
IP Osgoode, Osgoode Hall Law Scho[
Munich Intellectual Property Law Ce[

A list o[

Relocating the Law of Geographical Indications

Dev Gangjee

CAMBRIDGE
UNIVERSITY PRESS

CAMBRIDGE UNIVERSITY PRESS
Cambridge, New York, Melbourne, Madrid, Cape Town,
Singapore, São Paulo, Delhi, Mexico City

Cambridge University Press
The Edinburgh Building, Cambridge CB2 8RU, UK

Published in the United States of America by
Cambridge University Press, New York

www.cambridge.org
Information on this title: www.cambridge.org/9780521192026

© Dev Gangjee 2012

This publication is in copyright. Subject to statutory exception
and to the provisions of relevant collective licensing agreements,
no reproduction of any part may take place without
the written permission of Cambridge University Press.

First published 2012

Printed in the United Kingdom at the University Press, Cambridge

A catalogue record for this publication is available from the British Library

Library of Congress Cataloging-in-Publication Data

Gangjee, Dev.
   Relocating the law of geographical indications / Dev Gangjee.
     p. cm. – (Cambridge intellectual property and information law; 15)
   Includes bibliographical references and index.
   ISBN 978-0-521-19202-6
   1. Marks of origin.   2. Intellectual property (International law)   3. Agreement
on Trade-Related Aspects of Intellectual Property Rights (1994)   I. Title.
II. Series.
   K1562.G36 2012
   346.04′8–dc23

2011035580

ISBN 978-0-521-19202-6 Hardback

Cambridge University Press has no responsibility for the persistence or
accuracy of URLs for external or third-party internet websites referred to
in this publication, and does not guarantee that any content on such
websites is, or will remain, accurate or appropriate.

Table of contents

Acknowledgments	*page* vii
List of abbreviations	ix
Table of cases	xi

1.	**Introduction: locating geographical indications**	**1**
	1. The mess: conceptual, institutional and epistemic	2
	2. Controversies and interests	8
	3. Contribution and organisation	14

Part I

2.	**The Indication of Source – Paris and Madrid**	**21**
	1. Introduction	21
	2. The Paris Convention	23
	2.1 The Indication of Source	27
	2.2 The scope of protection: Articles 9 and 10	41
	2.3 Alternative possibilities?	52
	3. The Madrid Agreement	65
	3.1 The scope of protection: Article 1	65
	3.2 Generic terms: Article 4	68
	4. Conclusion	74
3.	**The Appellation of Origin in France**	**77**
	1. The significance of the French experience	77
	2. The role of origin in wine regulation	80
	3. A geology of *terroir*	83
	4. Phylloxera and fraud	93
	5. From the AO to the AOC	96
	5.1 The Law of 1905	98
	5.2 The Law of 1919	102
	5.3 The Laws of 1935 and 1947	108
	6. Doing things differently: Germany and the UK	115
	7. Conclusion	124

vi   Table of contents

4. The Appellation of Origin in the Lisbon Agreement   127
1.   Introduction   127
2.   The Appellation of Origin: Article 2   130
 2.1   *The link between product and place*   137
 2.2   *Natural and human influences*   141
 2.3   *Geographical denomination*   143
 2.4   *Reputation*   145
3.   International registration and its effects   146
 3.1   *Process of registration*   147
 3.2   *Consequences of registration*   152
4.   The scope of protection: Article 3   157
 4.1   *Nominate categories of prohibited uses*   158
 4.2   *The general prohibition against usurpation or imitation*   162
 4.3   *Absolute protection*   172
5.   Conclusion   177

Part II

5. TRIPS today   183
1.   Introduction   183
2.   An outline of Articles 22 to 24   185
3.   Pathways to TRIPS   191
 3.1   *TRIPS as compromise(d)*   192
 3.2   *The WIPO negotiations*   195
 3.3   *Compromise and its consequences*   199
4.   The definition of a GI: Article 22.1   213
 4.1   *The sign*   215
 4.2   *The goods*   216
 4.3   *Region of origin*   218
 4.4   *The link between product and place*   223
5.   The scope of protection: one definition, yet
      two levels   237
6.   Generic status   244
7.   The relationship between GIs and trade marks   255
 7.1   *The language of trumps: FITFIR*   257
 7.2   *Parma ham and the inequities of FITFIR*   259
 7.3   *Descriptive fair use and co-existence*   261
8.   Conclusion   262

6. TRIPS tomorrow?   265
1.   The significance of contemporary debates   265
2.   Extending Article 23 to all products   266
3.   Normative arguments in favour of extension   275
4.   International registration and its effects   288
5.   Conclusion   295

7. Conclusions – relocating geographical indications   297

Bibliography   303
Index   332

Acknowledgments

It's always nice to begin on a happy note. The manuscript in your hands began life as a doctoral dissertation at Oxford a decade ago and has amassed a mountain of debts in its meanderings. As my supervisor, Michael Spence was a wonderful role model. If this book has asked any of the right questions, it owes much to the clarity of his approach to legal puzzles. David Vaver, both as thesis examiner and mentor, has been unfailingly generous in sharing insights and providing opportunities not just for myself but for an entire generation of research students at Oxford. Lionel Bently was the other reason for a memorable and rewarding doctoral defence. As will become evident, his approach to historically informed legal scholarship has greatly influenced my own. These three were (ex officio) compelled to read earlier versions of this hefty manuscript, but others nobly volunteered to do so. Heartfelt thanks to Delphine Marie-Vivien, Barton Beebe and Dwijen Rangnekar for their perceptive comments and suggestions. More general gratitude is reserved for Justin Hughes and Latha Nair, fellow travellers in the wilderness of geographical indications research. David Higgins is a wonderful colleague and the Indiana Jones of archives, from whom I have learned much. I am also indebted to my colleagues at the LSE Law Department. It continues to be an intellectually rich, stimulating and collegial environment in which to be an academic. The conceptual approaches adopted here were influenced by the work of LSE colleagues and friends.

A number of institutions have generously supported this project over the years and I am deeply indebted to them. My doctoral research was funded by a Rhodes scholarship and St Catherine's College was a wonderful home during this time. Without the amazing resources of the Bodleian library system and the LSE's British Library of Political & Economic Science, the interdisciplinary research would not have been possible. The World Intellectual Property Organization librarians deserve special mention for patiently posting me materials on request, while also scanning archival materials for me. May their digitisation efforts flourish and prosper. The Oxford Intellectual Property Research Centre gave me the opportunity to present this research at various stages, as did Cardozo, NYU, Chicago-Kent, Munich Intellectual Property Law Centre and Cambridge. Part I in particular has benefitted greatly as a result. My efforts at transcending linguistic limitations were ably assisted by the translations of Martin Ilmer, Bahne Seivers, Cesar Ramirez-Montes, Amelie Labbe and Essi Maglo. General untidiness was tackled by the keen eyed and measured approach of Serena Kern, a wonderful research assistant at the final stages. Cambridge University Press has been an absolute pleasure to work with. Kim Hughes was the perfect blend of friendliness and firm deadlines, while Kate Ollerenshaw has considerably improved the manuscript with impeccable and thoughtful copy editing.

At the end of all things and the beginning of others, there are the steadfast presences. My love and gratitude to Deepa, Zahid and Kabir, for more than will fit in a library of acknowledgments; to Nikita, whose intellect, integrity and love have been the lights which guided me to the end of this project; and to Adil, who constantly reminds me that there is so much more to the world than research – like rubber ducks, stories about bears or chewable books.

Abbreviations

AIPPI	Association Internationale pour la Protection de la Propriété Industrielle
Annuaire	Annuaire de l'Association Internationale pour la Protection de la Propriété Industrielle
AO	Appellation of Origin or *Appellation d'Origine*
AOC	Controlled Appellation of Origin or *Appellation d'Origine Contrôlée*
BIRPI	Bureaux Internationaux Réunis pour la Protection de la Propriété Intellectuelle
BGH	Bundesgerichtshof
CAP	Common Agricultural Policy
CTM	Community Trade Mark
EC	European Community
ECJ	Court of Justice of the European Union (formerly European Court of Justice)
ECtHR	European Court of Human Rights
EIPR	European Intellectual Property Review
ETMR	European Trade Mark Reports
FAO	Food and Agriculture Organisation
FSR	Fleet Street Reports
FTA	Free Trade Agreement
GATT	General Agreement on Tariffs and Trade
GC	General Court of the ECJ (formerly Court of First Instance)
GI	Geographical Indication
GRUR	Gewerblicher Rechtsschutz und Urheberrecht
IGO	Indication of Geographical Origin
IIC	International Review of Intellectual Property and Competition Law
INAO	Institut National des Appellations d'Origine
INTA	International Trade Mark Association
IP	Intellectual Property

x   List of abbreviations

IPQ	Intellectual Property Quarterly
IS	Indication of Source
JWIP	Journal of World Intellectual Property
Lisbon Agreement	Lisbon Agreement for the Protection of Appellations of Origin and their International Registration 1958
Madrid Agreement	Madrid Agreement for the Repression of False or Deceptive Indications of Source on Goods 1891
OHIM	Office of Harmonisation for the Internal Market
Paris Convention	Paris Convention for the Protection of Industrial Property of 1883
PDO	Protected Designation of Origin
PGI	Protected Geographical Indication
PP	Parliamentary Papers
RPC	Reports of Patent Cases
SC	Supreme Court
SCT	WIPO Standing Committee on the Law of Trademarks, Industrial Designs and Geographical Indications
TCE	Traditional Cultural Expression
TFEU	Treaty on the Functioning of the European Union
TK	Traditional Knowledge
TMR	Trade Mark Reporter
TRIPS	Agreement on Trade-Related Aspects of Intellectual Property Rights
TTAB	Trade Mark Trial and Appeal Board (US)
UWG	Gesetz gegen den unlauteren Wettbewerb
WIPO	World Intellectual Property Organization
WTO	World Trade Organization

Table of cases

Australia

Beringer Blass Wine Estates v. *GIC* [2002] 70 ALD 27 (FCA) *page* 107–8
Comité Interprofessionnel des Vins de Côtes de Provence and INAO v. *Bryce and Another* [1996] 69 FCR 450   241
Comité Interprofessionnel du Vin de Champagne v. *N.L. Burton Pty Ltd* [1981] 38 ALR 664 (FCA)   44
Penola High School v. *Geographical Indications Committee* [2001] AATA 844   107
Ross & Veronica Lawrence [2005] ATMO 69 (21 November 2005)   242
Thomson v. *B. Seppelt & Sons Ltd* [1925] 37 CLR 305 (HCA)   84

Austria

'*Saunders Whisky*' [1989] 20 IIC 543 (Oberster Gerichtshof, Austria, 1987)   159

Belgium

'*Paris Perfume*' [1963] *Industrial Property* 225 (Brussels CA, 17 November 1961)   51
Comité Interprofessionnel du Vin de Champagne v. *Simon*, CFI Namur, Belgium (Criminal Division), 24 January 2007 (unreported)   163

Canada

Consorzio del Prosciutto di Parma v. *Maple Leaf Meats Inc* [2001] 2 FC 536 (Federal Court of Canada, Trial Division)   261
Consorzio del Prosciutto di Parma v. *Maple Leaf Meats* [2002] FCA 169   261
Maple Leaf Foods Inc v. *Consorzio Del Prosciutto Di Parma* [2009] FC 1035   261

xii   Table of cases

France

Bravay et Autres v. *Syndicat des Propriétaires Viticulteurs de Châteauneuf-du-Pape et Autres* [1935] *Propriété Industrielle* 76 (Cour de Cassation, 21 November 1933)   110

Chambre Syndicale des Fabricants de Dentelles et Passementeries de la Haute-Loire v. *Gouteyron et Jérôme* [1931] *Propriété Industrielle* 188 (Le Puy-en-Velay Civil Court, 19 February1931)   111

Chapin et Cie v. *Le Syndicat du Commerce des Vins de Champagne* [1893] *Propriété Industrielle* 111 (Court of Appeal, Paris 1st Chamber, 18 November 1892)   97

Institut National des Appellations d'Origine v. *Yves Saint Laurent* [1994] EIPR D74 (Court of Appeal, Paris 1993)   123

Kronenbourg Breweries v. *Budějovický Budvar Narodni Podnik* (RG 2002/04572) (Tribunal de Grande Instance of Strasbourg, 30 June 2004)   140

Societe Empresa del Tabaco Cubatabaco v. *Aramis Inc & Ors* (Court of Appeal, Paris 4th Chamber, Reg No. 1998/10814, 17 May 2000)   169

Syndicat du Commerce des Vins de Champagne v. *Ackerman Laurance* [1892] *Propriété Industrielle* 145 (Angers, Court of Appeal, 15 December 1891)   97

Syndicat Général des Vignerons de la Champagne Viticole Délimitée v. *Syndicat Régional des Vignerons de Champagne* [1928] *Propriété Industrielle* 183   105

Syndicat Viticole de Sauternes et de Barsac v. *Chaumel et Autres* [1935] *Propriété Industrielle* 76 (Court of Appeal, Bordeaux, 19 February 1934)   110

Tea Board of India v. *Jean-Luc Dusong* (Paris, Court of Appeal, 4th Chamber, Reg No. 05/20050, 22 November 2006   123, 169

Veuve Rodiès v. *Société Civile d'Yquem et Autres* [1931] *Propriété Industrielle* 230 (Cour de Cassation, 4–6 June 1931)   110

Germany

'*A Champagne among Mineral Waters*' [1988] IIC 682 (BGH)   123

Bocksbeutelflasche [1971] GRUR 313 (BGH)   216

'*Get Champagne, Pay for Sparkling Wine*' [2002] 33 IIC 990 (BGH)   166

Rügenwalder Teewurst [1956] GRUR 270 (BGH)   117

'*Scotch Whisky*' [1970] IIC 402 (BGH)   119

Shamrock Trade Mark [1986] FSR 271 (BGH)   27

Hungary

Anheuser Busch Inc v. *Budějovický Budvar Národní Podnik* [2009] IIC 353 (Hungary SC, 21 March 2007)   156

Table of cases   xiii

Anheuser Busch Inc v. *Budějovický Budvar Národní Podnik* [2009] IIC 357 (Hungary SC, 28 March 2007)   156

Israel

Budweiser I [1991] IIC 255 (Israel SC, 1990)   154
Budweiser II [1994] IIC 589 (Israel SC, 1992)   155
Budweiser III [1997] IIC 596 (Israel SC, 1997)   156
The Citrus Division of the Plant Production and Marketing Board v. *Israel Commissioner of Patents and Trade Marks* [2007] 1011/05, Appeal Board (Jerusalem), 12 July 2007)   212

Italy

'Budweiser' [2003] IIC 676 (Corte Suprema di Cassazione, 2002)   139
Pilsen Urquell v. *Industrie Poretti SpA* [1998] ETMR 168 (Corte Suprema di Cassazione, 1996)   139, 153, 209

New Zealand

Anheuser-Busch Inc v. *Budweiser Budvar National Corporation* [2003] 1 NZLR 472 (CA)   160
Comité Interprofessionnel du Vin de Champagne v. *Wineworths Group Ltd* [1991] 2 NZLR 432 (Wellington HC)   84
Wineworths Group Ltd v. *Comité Interprofessionnelle du Vin de Champagne* [1991] 23 IPR 435 (CA NZ)   44

Portugal

Budějovický Budvar Národí Podnik v. *Anheuser Busch Inc* [2002] ETMR 96 (Supremo Tribunal De Justiça, 2001)   161
Budweiser, Civil Court of Lisbon, 13 Chamber, 3rd Section, Case 7906 (Unreported, 8 March 1995)   140

South Africa

Bergkelder Bpk v. *Vredendal Koöp Wynmakery* [2006] SCA 8 (RSA)   28

Sweden

Anheuser-Busch Inc v. *Budějovický Budvar Národni Podnik and Ors* [2006] ETMR 77 (Swedish SC)   161

Switzerland

Anheuser-Busch Inc v. *Budějovický Budvar Národni Podnik* [2001] ETMR 7   12

xiv Table of cases

United Kingdom

A. G. Spalding & Brothers v. *A. W. Gamage Ltd* [1915] 32 RPC 273 (HL)   39, 120

Biogen Inc v *Medeva plc* [1997] RPC 1 (HL)   78

Budějovický Budvar Národní Podnik v. *Anheuser Busch* [2009] EWCA Civ 1022   130

Chocosuisse Union des Fabricants Suisse de Chocolat v. *Cadbury Ltd* [1998] RPC 117 (Ch D)   122–3, 207, 220

Chocosuisse Union des Fabricants Suisses de Chocolat v. *Cadbury Ltd* [1999] RPC 826 (CA)   122, 220

Consorzio del Prosciutto di Parma v. *Asda Stores Limited and Others* [2001] UKHL 7; [2002] FSR 3   11, 226

Diageo v. *Intercontinental Brands* [2010] EWHC 17 (Ch); [2010] ETMR 17 (Vodka)   120, 220

Diageo North America v. *Intercontinental Brands* [2010] EWCA Civ 920   220

Erven Warnink BV v. *J. Townend & Sons (Hull) Ltd* [1979] FSR 397 (HL)   121

H. P. Bulmer Ltd and Showerings Ltd v. *J. Bollinger and Champagne Lanson Pere et Fils* [1977] 2 CMLR 625 (Champagne Ciders and Champagne Perry)   120–1

J. Bollinger v. *Costa Brava Wine Co Ltd* [1960] Ch 262   120–1

J. Bollinger v. *Costa Brava Wine Co Ltd* [1961] 1 All ER 561 (Ch D)   84

John Walker & Sons Limited v. *Henry Ost and Co Ltd* [1970] FSR 63   6

L' Oréal SA and others v. *Bellure NV and others* [2007] EWCA Civ 968   58, 120

L'Oréal SA and others v. *Bellure NV and others* [2010] EWCA Civ 535   172

Magnolia Metal Company's Trade-Marks, In Re [1897] 2 Ch 371 (CA)   45

Northern Foods Plc v. *DEFRA, Melton Mowbray Pork Pie Association* [2005] EWHC 2971 (Admin) (Melton Mowbray Pork Pie)   222

Perry v. *Truefitt* (1842) 6 Beav 66   44, 120

R (on the application of Northern Foods Plc) v. *Secretary of State for the Environment, Food and Rural Affairs* [2006] EWCA Civ 337   222

Reckitt & Colman Products Ltd v. *Borden Inc* [1990] RPC 341 (HL)   120

Union Syndicate's Application [1922] 39 RPC 346   31

Vine Products Ltd v. *Mackenzie & Co Ltd (No.3)* [1967] FSR 402 (Ch D)   253

United States

Bacardi & Co Ltd, In re 48 USPQ 2d 1031 (TTAB 1997)   243

Bronco Wine Co v. *Jolly* 129 Cal App 4th 988 (2005); Cert. denied 126 S Ct 1169 (Mem) (2006)   205

Table of cases   xv

Cheney Bros v. *Doris Silk Corp* 35 F2d 279 (2d Cir 1929)   171

Community of Roquefort v. *William Faehndrich* 303 F2d 494 (1962)   111

Consorzio del Prosciutto di Parma v. *Parma Sausage Products* 23 USPQ 2d 1894 (1992 TTAB); 1992 WL 233379 (TTAB)   259

Cooperativa Produttori Latte e Fontina Valle D'Acosta, In re 230 USPQ 131 (TTAB 1986) (Fontina cheese)   250

Delaware and Hudson Canal Company v. *Clark* 80 US 311 (1871)   41

Douglas and others v. *Newark Cheese Co* 274 NYS 406 (1934)   111

Federal Trade Commission v. *Gratz* 253 US 421 (1920)   55

French Republic v. *Saratoga Vichy Co* 191 US 427 (1903) (Vichy spring water)   250

Hanover Star Milling v. *Metcalf* 240 US 403 (1916)   27

Institut Nat'l Des Appellations D'Origine v. *Vinters Int'l Co* 958 F 2d 1574 (Fed Cir 1992) (Chablis for wine)   250

International News Service v. *Associated Press* 248 US 215 (1918)   171

K. P. Permanent Make-Up Inc v. *Lasting Impression Inc* 543 US 111 (2004)   262

Louis Vuitton Malletier v. *Haute Diggity Dog* 507 F 3d 252 (4th Cir 2007)   167

Lucasfilm Ltd v. *High Frontier* 227 USPQ 967 (DDC 1985)   253

Moseley v. *Victoria's Secret Catalogue Inc* 123 S Ct 1115 (2003)   166

Richemond, In re 131 USPQ 441 (TTAB 1961)   51

Salem China Co, In re 157 USPQ 600 (TTAB 1968)   59, 159

Schweizerische Kaeseunion Bern v. *Saul Starck Inc* 293 NYS 816 (1937) (Swiss cheese)   250

Scotch Whisky Association v. *Barton Distilling Company* 489 F 2d 809 (7th Cir 1973)   44

Tea Board of India v. *The Republic of Tea Inc* 80 USPQ 2d 1881 (TTAB 2006)   27, 250

Two Pesos Inc v. *Taco Cabana Inc* 505 US 763 (1992)   164

United Drug Co v. *Theodore Rectanus Co* 248 US 90 (1918)   257

European Union & ECtHR

Abadia Retuerta, SA v. *OHIM* (T-237/08) 11 May 2010 (CFI)   241

Alberto Severi v. *Regione Emilia-Romagna* (C–446/07) [2009] ECR I-8041; [2009] ETMR 64   12, 245

American Clothing Associates v. *OHIM* (C-202/08 P) [2009] ECR I-6933; [2010] ETMR 3   276

Amrut Distilleries Ltd v. *OHIM* (R 635/2005–1) 1st BoA, 26 September 2005   243

Anheuser-Busch Inc v. *Portugal* [2007] ETMR 24 (ECHR Grand Chamber)   227

xvi Table of cases

Apple and Pear Development Council v. *KJ Lewis Ltd* (C-222/82) [1983] ECR 4083   202

Bavaria NV, Bavaria Italia Srl v. *Bayerischer Brauerbund eV* (C-343/07) [2009] ECR I-5491; [2009] ETMR 61 (Bavaria)   230, 246, 252–3

Bayerischer Brauerbund eV v. *Bavaria NV* (C-120/08) [2011] ETMR 11 (Bavaria)   225

Belgium v. *Spain* (C-388/95) [2000] ECR I-3123; [2000] ETMR 999 ('Rioja II')   209

Björnekulla Fruktindustrier AB v. *Procordia Food AB* (C-371/02) [2004] ECR I-5791; [2004] ETMR 69   251

Budějovický Budvar Národni Podnik v. *OHIM* (Joined Cases T-53/04 to T-56/04, T-58/04 and T-59/04) [2007] ECR II-57 (CFI)   174

Budějovický Budvar Národni Podnik v. *OHIM* (Joined cases T-225/06, T-255/06, T-257/06 & T-309/06) [2008] ECR II-3555 (CFI)   144

Budějovický Budvar Národni Podnik v. *Rudolf Ammersin GmbH* (C-478/07) [2009] ECR I-7721; [2009] ETMR 65 (ECJ Grand Chamber)   14, 144

Canadane Cheese Trading v. *Hellenic Republic* (C-317/95) [1997] ECR I-4681 (AG)   91, 207, 245

Commission of the European Communities v. *Federal Republic of Germany* (C-132/05) [2008] ECR I-957; [2008] ETMR 32 (Parmesan)   46, 161, 246, 254

Commission of the European Communities v. *Federal Republic of Germany* (C-12/74) [1975] ECR 181 (Sekt/Winebrand)   165, 227

Commission of the European Communities v. *Republic of Ireland* (C-249/81) [1982] ECR 4005   227

Consorzio del Prosciutto di Parma v. *Asda Stores Ltd and Hygrade Foods Ltd* (C-108/01) [2003] ECR I-5121; [2004] ETMR 23 (Proscuitto di Parma)   209

Criminal Proceedings against Karl Prantl (C-16/83) [1984] ECR 1299   216

Etablissements Delhaize Frères et Compagnie Le Lion SA v. *Promalvin SA* (C-47/90) [1992] ECR I-3669 ('Rioja I')   210

Exportur SA v. *LOR SA and Confiserie du Tech SA* (C-3/91) [1992] ECR I-5529 (Touron Alicante and Touron Jijona)   165–6, 228

Federal Republic of Germany and Kingdom of Denmark v. *Commission of the European Communities* (C-465/02 & C-466/02) [2005] ECR I-9115; [2006] ETMR 16, (AGO) (Feta)   28, 219–21, 245, 254

Gerolsteiner Brunnen & Co v. *Putsch* (C-100/02) [2004] ECR I-691; [2004] ETMR 40 (ECJ)   262

Intel Corp Inc v. *C. P. M. United Kingdom Ltd* (C-252/07) [2008] ECR I-8823; [2009] ETMR 13   167

Table of cases   xvii

Ivivi Pty Ltd (R 130/2009–2) OHIM 2nd BoA, 9 June 2009   242

L'Oréal SA v. *Bellure NV* (C-487/07) [2009] ECR I-5185; [2009] ETMR
   55   166

Molkerei Grossbraunshain & Ors v. *Commission of the European Communities* (C-447/98 P) [2002] ETMR 55 (Altenberger cheese)   222

Philips Electronics NV v. *Remington Consumer Products Ltd* (C-299/99)
   [2002] ECR I-5475; [2002] ETMR 81   27

Ravil SARL v. *Bellon Import SARL* (C-469/00) [2003] ECR I-5053;
   [2004] ETMR 22 at [49] (ECJ) ('Grana Padano')   209–10

Regione autonoma Friuli-Venezia Giulia v. *Ministero delle Politiche Agricole e Forestali* (C-347/03) [2005] ECR I-3785 (Tokaj)   202, 240

Reh Kendermann GmbH Weinkellerei (R 822/2010–2) OHIM 2nd BoA,
   27 September 2010   242

René Barbier SA v. *OHIM* (R 1220/2000–2) 2nd BoA, 11 December
   2002   243

S. A. Cnl-Sucal NV v. *Hag G. F. A. G.* (C-10/89) (1990) 3 CMLR
   571   164

S. M. W. Winzersekt GmbH v. *Land Rheinland-Pfalz* (C-306/93) [1995] 2
   CMLR 718   159

Schutzverband gegen Unwesen in der Wirtschaft eV v. *Warsteiner Brauerei*
   (C-312/98) [2000] ECR I-9187   3

WTO and GATT

GATT Panel Report *Japan – Customs L   es, Taxes and Labelling Practices on Imported Wines and Alcoholic Beverages* 10 November 1987 (BISD 34S/83)   193

WTO Panel Report, *European Communities – Protection of Trademarks and Geographical Indications for Agricultural Products and Foodstuffs*, 15 March 2005 (WT/DS174/R)   11, 190, 226, 261

1 Introduction: locating geographical indications

This book is concerned with the origins of Geographical Indications (GI) protection and the process by which they have emerged as a distinct category of subject matter within international Intellectual Property (IP) law. It sets out to locate GIs within the 'webs of significance' spun across the legal discourse of a century, by pursuing two interrelated questions:

(1) Under what circumstances were signs which indicate the geographical origin of products incorporated within international IP law?
(2) What can this usefully tell us about the present international regime governing their use and misuse?

These questions are important because the law in this area is a mess. In fact, it has been spectacularly messy for over a century. Despite the popularity of wines from Champagne, Colombian coffee, Darjeeling tea and other such regional products,[1] the nature, scope and institutional forms of protection available vary considerably across jurisdictions. Notwithstanding a century of harmonisation efforts, a consensual basis for granting rights to a particular group to use a geographical designation and the extent to which third parties should be excluded continues to prove elusive. This state of affairs is undesirable since an ever-expanding range of stakeholders – producers, consumers and policy makers – have an interest in the regulation of these signs. The debates grind on, generating abundant heat but far less light. The TRIPS Agreement[2] has emerged as the site where these arguments coalesce, during attempts

---

[1] For the purposes of this book, regional or local products are those where the region of origin has added significance in the marketplace. See A. Tregear, 'What is a "Typical Local Food"? An Examination of Territorial Identity in Foods Based on Development Initiatives in the Agrifood And Rural Sectors', Centre for Rural Economy, Working Paper 58 (January 2001), 1. While the usage is most commonly found in the agricultural foodstuffs and beverages sectors, it extends beyond this to include crafts, textiles and other sectors.

[2] Agreement on Trade-Related Aspects of Intellectual Property Rights, 15 April 1994, in the Marrakesh Agreement Establishing the World Trade Organization, Annex 1C (1994) 33 ILM 1125, 1197 (hereafter, TRIPS).

2   Introduction: locating geographical indications

to clarify its existing provisions or reform its architecture. Although there are several points of disagreement, a central puzzle relates to the differential treatment sought for GIs by their proponents. These geographical signs appear functionally analogous to trade marks, a more familiar category of subject matter protected by IP law. Both categories signal the (commercial or geographical) origin of goods in the marketplace and sustain valuable reputations. Granting exclusive rights over such signs ensures uncluttered signalling in the marketplace, with consumers as well as legitimate producers benefiting from this. Yet despite the apparent similarities, advocates of GI protection seek enhanced international standards, which would proscribe a broader range of uses by third parties. The epistemic basis for this differential treatment rests upon the claim that a distinctive or unique link exists between a certain category of products and their regions of origin. The most influential articulation of this link is encapsulated in *terroir*, an expression associated with the French wine industry. However, the international reference point is found in Article 22.1 of TRIPS:

Geographical indications are, for the purposes of this Agreement, *indications which identify* a good as originating in the territory of a Member, or a region or locality in that territory, where a given *quality, reputation or other characteristic* of the good is *essentially attributable to its geographical origin* (emphasis added).

This link between product, producers and place therefore grounds attempts to carve out a distinct niche for GIs within the IP canon. In the following pages, the functional significance of this link is unpacked as it fluctuates over several decades. It is only by first locating the historical basis of GI protection that we can meaningfully evaluate contemporary attempts to relocate GI protection. These attempts either awkwardly straddle distinct epistemic paradigms or occasionally generate entirely new normative accounts that cannot readily be integrated within the current framework.

1.   The mess: conceptual, institutional and epistemic

Having set out the central axis of enquiry, it is necessary to expand upon the initial diagnosis in order to more fully appreciate the task that lies ahead. Let us begin by making some sense of the mess we are in, disentangling its component strands along the way. The muddle is primarily conceptual and relates to the identification of appropriate subject matter. An unmistakeable symptom is the terminological diversity in this area. Several categories of signs are conventionally understood to fit within the broad heading of 'GIs' as a category of IP. With due apologies

The mess 3

for the servings of alphabet soup, the list begins chronologically with the Indication of Source (IS) explored further in Chapter 2. It then incorporates the Appellation of Origin (AO) and its inspiration, the French *Appellation d'Origine Contrôlée* (AOC) reviewed in Chapters 3 and 4. Subsequently Chapters 5 and 6 consider the EU's Protected Designation of Origin (PDO) and Protected Geographical Indication (PGI), the World Intellectual Property Organization (WIPO) attempt at establishing the Geographical Indication (GI), followed by the TRIPS definition of the GI already introduced above. This is only a limited selection of the major contenders. The most comprehensive WTO survey of national laws to date identifies twenty-three distinct national definitions applied in this area.[3] It is recognised that because 'of the diverse ways in which the protection of [GIs] has evolved under national laws, there is no generally accepted terminology' in this area.[4] This is in marked contrast to the other domains of IP. 'The protection of GIs, unlike that of patents or trade marks, is not an IP system whose variants, which are more or less similar – or at least comparable – to each other, are applied throughout the world'.[5] The lack of a common conceptual framework leads to co-ordination difficulties,[6] with one commentator suggesting that we are 'confronted with a tower of Babel'.[7] According to Norma Dawson, throughout the twentieth century GIs have been 'an intellectual property right in the making surrounded by a complex debate lacking common terminology'.[8] Opposing sides therefore tend to talk past one another during international negotiations. The judiciary has joined this concerned chorus on occasion, with Advocate General Jacobs noting that 'the terminology used in this area itself risks being a fruitful source of confusion'.[9] Since these terms usually originate within the context of specific multilateral treaty

---

[3] See Annex B to the WTO, 'Review under Article 24.2 of the Application of the Provisions of the Section of the TRIPS Agreement on Geographical Indications', 24 November 2003 (IP/C/W/253/Rev.1).

[4] G. B. Dinwoodie, W. O. Hennessey and S. Perlmutter, *International Intellectual Property Law and Policy* (Lexisnexis, New Jersey 2001), 315. See also C. M. Correa, *Trade Related Aspects of Intellectual Property Rights: A Commentary on the TRIPS Agreement* (Oxford University Press 2007), 211 ('There are few areas of [IP] law where definitions are as diverse as in the area of [GIs]').

[5] A. Jokuti, 'Where is the What if the What is in Why? A Rough Guide to the Maze of Geographical Indications' [2009] EIPR 118.

[6] F. Gevers, 'Topical Issues in the Protection of Geographical Indications', October 1997 (WIPO/GEO/EGR/97/5), 2 (also referring to GIs as the 'sleeping beauty' of IP on this basis).

[7] M. Ficsor, 'Challenges to the Lisbon System', 31 October 2008 (WIPO/GEO/LIS/08/4), [5].

[8] N. Dawson, 'Locating Geographical Indications: Perspectives from English Law' (2000) 90 TMR 590.

[9] *Schutzverband gegen Unwesen in der Wirtschaft eV* v. *Warsteiner Brauerei* (C-312/98) [2000] ECR I-9187, [2] (AGO).

4   Introduction: locating geographical indications

obligations, the WTO Secretariat navigates this minefield by adopting the neutral terminology of Indications of Geographical Origin (IGOs) as a common denominator.[10] The Secretariat's umbrella term is adopted for the duration of this book, where *the IGO refers to a category of sign denoting the geographical origin of the associated product and that category has previously figured within the IP discourse,* making it relevant for our purposes. It is hoped that this will avoid the artificial backward projection of the GI in TRIPS onto categories which are not functional analogues.

The preceding paragraph suggests that the only reliable functional baseline for IGOs is that they operate as signs indicating geographical origin in the marketplace. Yet this also lays the foundations for a variety of additional messages to be communicated. For instance, are they signs which indicate (1) merely a product's origin, (2) its reputation associated with a specific origin, (3) its distinctive qualities associated with origin, or (4) its unique qualities that are reliant upon origin? Once we add time and space into the mix, matters get more complicated. What if a sign fulfils one of these functions, but only in a particular jurisdiction? Should we pre-emptively reserve its ability to do so elsewhere? It is evident that this terminological diversity corresponds to divergent expectations about the communicative work these signs are supposed to do and the ensuing scope of protection. There is a general understanding of what we mean by the 'protection' of such signs,[11] but on what basis should we define its scope?

Geographical designations, like many other forms of identifier, also touch a wide variety of interests and sensitivities that range from our most basic territorial instincts to more sophisticated conceptions of market and cultural justice. While the misuse of geographical attributions may offend many feelings, only certain types of such misuse are sanctioned by the law.[12]

Identifying suitably qualified signs, types of undesirable misuses and proportionate legal responses has proven enduringly divisive. There is a narrow consensus around the proposition that the use of a geographical sign will be prohibited where it results in consumers being misled or confused as regards the origin or qualities of the product. But beyond this, to what extent should any geographical reference on a product

---

[10] WTO, 'Review under Article 24.2', [6].

[11] J. Audier, 'Protection of Geographical Indications in France and Protection of French Geographical Indications in Other Countries', October 1997 (WIPO/GEO/EGR/97/8 Rev), 7 ('Protection is a term with several meanings and there are many reasons for it. Generally speaking, protection means "right to use" a geographical name ... Protection also means a right to prevent illegal use of geographical names').

[12] WIPO, *Report of the Second WIPO Internet Domain Name Process – The Recognition of Rights and the Use of Names in the Internet Domain System* (3 September 2001), [205].

by third parties be deemed illicit? The ambiguity leaves a number of unsettled controversies in its wake. Should only Greek producers be allowed to make Feta? Should French producers have exclusive rights to the use of Champagne, overriding the protests of Californian and Australian wine-makers? To what extent do we protect GIs from developing countries – regional specialities consisting of coffees and crafts, toys and textiles? Whose interests do we accommodate in these balancing acts? As we will see in Chapter 4, the categories of misuse under consideration can be parsed into: (1) misleading or confusing uses; (2) allusive uses which relate to other types of harm, such as third party use leading to the erosion of the distinctiveness of an IGO, or the tarnishment of its reputation; (3) misappropriation or 'free riding' on another's efforts; and (4) 'absolute' protection, which *presumes that any use* of a geographical sign by those based outside the eponymous region ought to be prohibited. One line can be drawn between the first category (universally accepted) and the other three (which remain controversial). Another demarcates the first three (where audience perceptions matter) from the fourth (more formalistic and less context sensitive in its approach). This suggests the need for an overarching enquiry. How are we to decide these questions of scope? What are the epistemic frameworks – the background benchmarks for separating true from false claims – that operate in this area?

The tentative terminology and epistemic uncertainty also leads to an assortment of institutional arrangements at the national level. Since a number of different legal regimes encompass origin marking for disparate reasons, this adds yet another layer of complexity. WIPO notes that the variety of different legal concepts surrounding GIs 'were developed in accordance with different national legal traditions and within a framework of specific historical and economic conditions'.[13] Given the variety of forms of protection in this area, which institutional configurations are optimal? A long-standing obstacle to harmonisation efforts has therefore been 'the diversity of various national concepts. [GIs] are addressed in laws concerning unfair competition, trade marks, advertising and labelling, foods and health, as well as in special regulations'.[14]

---

[13] WIPO, 'Document SCT/6/3 Rev. on Geographical Indications: Historical Background, Nature of Rights, Existing Systems for Protection and Obtaining Protection in Other Countries', 2 April 2002 (SCT/8/4), 4.

[14] A. Conrad, 'The Protection of Geographical Indications in the TRIPS Agreement' (1996) 86 TMR 11, 14. For other surveys of the legislative variety, see A. Devletian, 'The Protection of Appellations of Origin and Indications of Source' (1968) *Industrial Property* 107, 111–13; O'Connor & Co, *Geographical Indications and TRIPS: 10 Years Later ... Part II – Protection of Geographical Indications in 160 Countries around the World* (Report commissioned for European Commission (DG Trade) 2007).

6   Introduction: locating geographical indications

If the expectation is for IP rights to be bureaucratically channelled through an Intellectual Property Office or Patent Office at the national level, IGOs – even those formally recognised as categories of IP – are sometimes lodged elsewhere.[15] GIs are defined and regulated by the Consumer Code in France,[16] registered as protected names by the Department for the Environment, Food and Rural Affairs (DEFRA) in the UK[17] and have been governed by aspects of Agricultural Law in Switzerland.[18] For several decades revenue laws have played a significant role in this area.[19] Surveys indicate that IGO protection 'is provided through a variety of laws and regulations, including laws against unfair competition, fair trade practices laws, marketing and labelling laws, consumer protection laws, laws for the protection of appellations or origin and national and regional registration systems for geographical indications'.[20] An explanation for the existence of multiple, often over-lapping forms of protection is offered in Chapter 2, which recovers the origins of this heterogeneity. In response, there are periodic attempts to tidy up this profusion into analytically useful categories:

The first [category] relates to laws focusing on business practices. Typically, the issue at stake in legal proceedings regarding the use of a [GI] under such laws is not whether the GI as such is eligible for protection but, rather, whether a specific act involving the use of a GI has contravened the general standards contained in laws covering unfair competition, consumer protection, trade descriptions, food standards etc. The second category concerns protection through trade mark law ... On the one hand, protection may be provided against the registration and use of GIs as trade marks. On the other hand, protection may be provided through collective, guarantee or certification marks. In contrast to the general means of protection of the first and second

---

[15] I. Kireeva and B. O'Connor, 'Geographical Indications and the TRIPS Agreement: What Protection is Provided to Geographical Indications in WTO Members?' (2010) 13 JWIP 275, 284 ('In some EC member states such as Italy, Spain, Greece, Ireland and Finland, the competent authorities are the Ministries of Agriculture, which have a principal role [along] with the European Commission in verifying applications').

[16] Arts. L 115–1 to L 115–33 of the Code de la Consommation.

[17] See www.defra.gov.uk/food-farm/food/protected-names/.

[18] See Art. 63 of the Federal Law on Agriculture adopted on 29 April 1998. For the French text, see WTO, 'Main Dedicated Intellectual Property Laws and Regulations Notified Center Art. 63.2 of the Agreement', 7 July 2003 (IP/N/1/CHE/G/6). See also F. Brand, 'Protection of Geographical Indications: The Experience of Switzerland', 18 November 2003 (WIPO/GEO/DEL/03/3).

[19] Legislation would often define such regional products with an eye to duties based on origin marking. For example Scotch whisky was initially defined by statute in s. 24 of the Finance Act 1933 and subsequently in s. 243(1)(b) of the Customs and Excise Act 1952. See *John Walker & Sons Limited* v. *Henry Ost and Co Ltd* [1970] FSR 63, 67.

[20] WIPO, 'Protection of Geographical Indications: General Introduction, International Protection and Recent Developments', June 2001 (WIPO/GEO/CIS/01/1), [28].

The mess 7

categories, the third category of protection concerns means specifically dedicated to the protection of GIs. Some of these means provide *sui generis* protection for GIs that relate to products with specifically defined characteristics or methods of production; other means apply without such specific definitions.[21]

It is worth mentioning that each technique selected 'reflects a particular approach to reconciling the various interests engaged by GI protection that may suit the particular needs of a specific community, but may not deliver identical outcomes to the different legal means used in other jurisdictions'.[22] To this terminological jumble, epistemic ambiguity and variety of legal instruments, we must add the relative obscurity of this area of the law. It has been referred to as 'the untended patch of the [IP] garden',[23] having a tangled and 'cobweb like texture'[24] and an area 'long considered to be exclusively of interest to some few wine and cheese producing countries and, besides that, to be that kind of intellectual property nobody really understood and therefore to be left to a handful of specialists'.[25] There is a sense that 'the conceptual underpinnings of GIs have not been rigorously examined'.[26] The heterogeneity of concepts and forms coupled with scholarly neglect also precipitates a more fundamental question. GIs continue to be regarded by some as offshoots of consumer protection law, tools of agricultural policy or aspects of food quality regulation and therefore a questionable presence within IP regimes. There are some who challenge the inclusion of such subject matter within the recognised categories of IP. The question is most directly posed by Stephen Stern but is also taken up by other commentators.[27] It is a fair question to ask and one that this book sets

---

[21] D. De Sousa, 'Protection of Geographical Indications under the TRIPS Agreement and Related Work of the World Trade Organization (WTO)', November 2001 (WIPO/GEO/MVD/01/2), 4–5.

[22] A. Taubman, 'The Way Ahead: Developing International Protection for Geographical Indications: Thinking Locally, Acting Globally', November 2001 (WIPO/GEO/MVD/01/9), 10. Unsurprisingly, the institutional form adopted depends on the underlying subject matter interest. See G. R. d'Imperio, 'Protection of the Geographical Indications in Latin America', November 2001 (WIPO/GEO/MVD/01/5), 2 ('Thus, whereas in some countries protection is granted . . . for viticultural and agricultural products, in others the economic interest . . . has led to protection being given to non-agricultural products such as mineral waters, beers, porcelains and semi-precious stones').

[23] B. O'Connor, *The Law of Geographical Indications* (Cameron May, London 2004), 21.

[24] Jokuti, 'A Rough Guide to the Maze', 118.

[25] WIPO, 'International Protection of Geographical Indications: The Present Situation and Prospects for Future Developments', 1 September 1999 (WIPO/GEO/CPT/99/1), [1].

[26] K. Raustiala and S. R. Munzer, 'The Global Struggle over Geographical Indications' (2007) 18 *European Journal of International Law* 337, 339–40.

[27] S. Stern, 'Are GIs IP' [2007] EIPR 39. See also J. Belson, *Certification Marks* (Sweet and Maxwell, London 2002), 23; W. van Caenegem, 'Registered Geographical Indications: Between Rural Policy and Intellectual Property – Part II' (2003)

8   Introduction: locating geographical indications

out to answer. IP rights are fundamentally exclusionary and need clear justifications because they affect 'what [people] may do, how they may speak, and how they may earn a living'.[28] Otherwise they remain vulnerable to allegations of protectionism and the selective favouring of certain interests. Such allegations do make frequent appearances during the international deliberations on this topic.

2.   Controversies and interests

If the conceptual and institutional ambiguity provides the fuel, it is the actual or potential value of IGOs that sparks off controversies. 'The economic and political significance of [GIs] has been growing in recent years as the use of distinctive or quality signs has promoted the demand for products of a specific geographical origin'.[29] While value is usually measured in economic terms within the context of international trade negotiations, their heritage value or value as vectors of rural development is gaining in prominence. Cumulatively, these raise the stakes and the 'debate about [GIs] has proven to be intractable, ill-defined, and at times passionate'.[30] The sensitivities surrounding the current regime in TRIPS stem from the growing 'recognition of the commercial significance of [GIs], in particular in respect of agricultural and food products, for exporting countries that may rely upon the added value that [they] may bestow'.[31] For that reason, IGO protection is situated within the framework of international trade strategies and constraints.[32] To take

---

6 JWIP 861, 874; E. Meltzer, 'Geographical Indications: Point of View of Governments', 30 June 2003 (WIPO/GEO/SFO/03/3), [12]; J. Hughes, 'Champagne, Feta, and Bourbon – The Spirited Debate about Geographical Indications' (2006) 58 *Hastings Law Journal* 299, 331–4. H. Ilbert and M. Petit, 'Are Geographical Indications a Valid Property Right? Global Trends and Challenges' (2009) 27 *Development Policy Review* 503. For a response to Stern, see D. Rangnekar, 'The Intellectual Properties of Geography' [2009] EIPR 537.

[28] J. Waldron, 'From Authors to Copiers: Individual Rights and Social Values in Intellectual Property' (1993) 68 *Chicago–Kent Law Review* 841, 887.

[29] Communication from New Zealand, 'Geographical Indications and the Art. 24.2 Review', 18 September 2000 (IP/C/W/205), [3].

[30] Taubman, 'The Way Ahead', 2; See also L. Bendekgey and C. Mead, 'International Protection of Appellations of Origin and Other Geographical Indications' (1992) 82 TMR 765; L. Beresford, 'Trade Marks and Geographical Indications 101: What Trade Mark Owners Should Know' (2008) 1 *Landslide* 19 ('One of the most controversial subjects facing the IP world today is the treatment of [GIs]').

[31] De Sousa, 'Protection of Geographical Indications under the TRIPS Agreement', 2.

[32] W. van Caenegem, 'Registered GIs: Intellectual Property, Agricultural Policy and International Trade' [2004] EIPR 170; A. F. R. de Almeida, 'The TRIPS Agreement, the Bilateral Agreements Concerning Geographical Indications and the Philosophy of the WTO' [2005] EIPR 150; T. Josling, 'The War on *Terroir*: Geographical Indications as a Transatlantic Trade Conflict' (2006) 57 *Journal of Agricultural Economics* 337.

Controversies and interests

one example, the major part of the annual production of Darjeeling tea is exported,[33] which underlines the need for an international regime regulating the misuse of such designations. An important factor here is the territorial nature of IP rights. IGOs may be recognised within the legal system of their 'home' country,[34] but recognition and protection is confined to that national jurisdiction.[35] Bilateral treaties and international conventions are adopted to work around this limitation, by establishing minimum standards of protection or reserving the use of certain terms identified in lists exchanged between signatories. The awareness of this value and the desire for greater international protection has drawn a number of new participants into these debates, beyond a core group of European countries with experience in this area. As we will see in Chapter 6, over one hundred WTO Members now support proposals to increase the international scope of protection and institutional recognition for GIs. 'Behind these negotiations is an increasing perception that localisation of the signified source of products is associated with increased value and reach into global markets. In effect, export-focussed producers learn to act globally by thinking locally. This has increased the sense of what is at stake in the identification and protection of [GIs]'.[36] Meanwhile the additional values associated with GI protection are being explored in earnest. 'The importance of GIs in Asia, however, goes beyond trade and commerce. It has to be understood in the wider context of protecting and preserving intellectual property pertaining to traditional cultures, assets, and production methods in some of the world's oldest human settlements. GIs ... can serve key development objectives'.[37] The entry of these new players, many of whom are from the Global South, has resulted in the absorption of new interests, arguments and dynamics into the existing stock.[38] This opens up the space to fundamentally reassess the basis as well as techniques for GI protection, as newer entrants will need

---

[33] N. K. Das, 'Protection of Darjeeling Tea', 3 July 2003 (WIPO/GEO/SFO/03/8), [26].

[34] For the duration of this book, 'home country' is shorthand for the state or legal jurisdiction within which the GI's region of origin is located.

[35] A. Kamperman Sanders, 'Incentives for Protection of Cultural Expression: Art, Trade and Geographical Indications' (2010) 13 JWIP 81, 84.

[36] Taubman, 'The Way Ahead', 7.

[37] S. Wagle, 'Protection of Geographical Indications and Human Development: Economic and Social Benefits to Developing Countries', November 2003 (WIPO/GEO/DEL/03/7), 3.

[38] Ilbert and Petit, 'Are Geographical Indications a Valid Property Right?', 516; S. Escudero, 'International Protection of Geographical Indications and Developing Countries' Working Paper No. 10, South Centre (July 2001); D. Rangnekar, 'Protecting Indications of Geographical Origin in Asia: Legal and Practical Issues to Resolve', in R. Meléndez-Ortiz and P. Roffe (eds.), *Intellectual Property and Sustainable Development: Development Agendas in a Changing World* (Edward Elgar, Cheltenham 2009), 273.

10   Introduction: locating geographical indications

to adapt or even fundamentally reinvent European *sui generis* GI models.[39] For instance, they may have a greater interest in crafts and textiles, alongside agricultural products and alcoholic beverages, or the nature of state involvement in the process of recognition and protection may differ.

If one side of the story celebrates the growing interest in GIs within the TRIPS membership, it is matched by a counter-narrative of concern, if not downright hostility, directed towards *sui generis* GI protection systems. The opposition stems from the apparent prioritising of GI producers' interests over others within these systems. In particular, the interests of trade mark registrants or those who use geographical terms in a generic manner appear to be threatened. Under certain conditions, geographical signs can be registered as individually owned trade marks, which could result in conflicting claims over the use of the same sign in a given jurisdiction.[40] If subsequently recognised GIs are allowed to trump prior trade mark rights, this endangers established proprietary interests.[41] Opponents also wish to preserve the freedom to use a geographical term in a generic manner, to designate a type of product irrespective of its place of origin. There is broad agreement that cheddar is the generic expression for a kind of cheese, while there is vigorous international disagreement about the status of Feta or Parmesan.[42] Much turns on the legal status of these expressions, as illustrated in a statement by the Director of the Grocery Manufacturer's Association (GMA) of America before the US House of Representatives, during a series of formal hearings on international GI protection.

[Even] the loss of one name (e.g., parmesan) could represent hundreds of millions of dollars to GMA member companies. Companies would be forced to repackage products, and, more importantly, re-educate consumers through re-branding campaigns. GMA is concerned that the very companies that created the value in many goods may be forced [to] renounce their claim on these

---

[39] M-C. Wang, 'The Asian Consciousness and Interests in Geographical Indications' (2006) 96 TMR 906; D. Marie-Vivien, 'The Role of the State in the Protection of Geographical Indications: From Disengagement in France/Europe to Significant Involvement in India' (2010) 13 JWIP 121.

[40] D. Gangjee, 'Quibbling Siblings: Conflicts between Trade Marks and Geographical Indications' (2007) 82 *Chicago–Kent Law Review* 1253.

[41] J. Phillips and I. Simon, 'Geographical Indications: The Biggest Threat to Trade Marks?' *Marques Newsletter* (Spring 2004), 2; H. Harte-Bavendamm, 'Geographical Indications and Trade Marks: Harmony or Conflict?', September 1999 (WIPO/GEO/CPT/99/6); WIPO, 'Possible Solutions for Conflicts between Trade Marks and Geographical Indications and for Conflicts between Homonymous Geographical Indications', 8 June 2000 (SCT/5/3).

[42] See Chapter 5, Section 6 for further details.

Controversies and interests

products. The products in question are no longer source identifiers since they have become known as a type or style of product...[43]

These threats to established trade marks and generic usage were identified during the Uruguay Round leading up to the formation of the TRIPS GI provisions.[44] As Chapter 2 documents, they were initially flagged up in the late nineteenth century and remain very much part of the conversation today. In many cases, these concerns are well founded and they cannot be ignored. The following pages will reveal, that there are several problematic claims and assumptions found within *sui generis* GI protection systems. However, the response by those opposing *sui generis* GI protection is not without its own biases and oversimplifications.

The response has two broad components. Taking into account the conceptual ambiguity surrounding GIs, opponents argue that these geographical signs can be better accommodated within the registered trade mark system, primarily as certification or collective marks. Since this more 'rational' and widely accepted model is available, they are often dismissive of *sui generis* GI protection, tending towards a caricature of protectionism in their critiques. The US has taken up the vanguard in recommending that since GIs and trade marks share a functional equivalence, the former category should be merged within the latter. Thus GIs 'can be viewed as a subset of trade marks. [They] serve the same functions as trade marks, because like trade marks they are: 1) source-identifiers, 2) guarantees of quality, and 3) valuable business interests'.[45] The US argues that 'both aim to prevent consumers from being misled or confused as to whether the goods they buy possess the anticipated qualities and characteristics'.[46] This functional similarity has been appreciated elsewhere as well. In *Parma* v. *Asda*, the House of Lords, as it then was, stated that the purpose of GI protection 'is twofold. It is intended both to protect producers of the products from unfair competition and to protect consumers from being misled by the application to products of false or misleading descriptions'.[47]

---

[43] Prepared statement of Sarah Thorn, Director of International Trade, Grocery Manufacturers of America in Hearings before the Committee on Agriculture, House of Representatives on the Status of the World Trade Organization Negotiations on Agriculture, (108–5) 108th Congress (2003) 273, 276.

[44] See, e.g., GATT, 'Minutes of Negotiating Group of 12–14 July 1989', 12 September 1989 (MTN.GNG/NG11/14), [56]–[57], [61], [62].

[45] See USPTO, 'Geographical Indication Protection in the United States', available at www.uspto.gov/web/offices/dcom/olia/globalip/pdf/gi_system.pdf.

[46] EC – Protection of Trademarks and Geographical Indications for Agricultural Products and Foodstuffs, First Submission of the United States, 23 April 2004 (WT/DS174 and 290), [132].

[47] *Consorzio del Prosciutto di Parma* v. *Asda Stores Limited and Others* [2001] UKHL 7; [2002] FSR 3, [58] (Lord Scott of Foscote).

12   Introduction: locating geographical indications

Lord Scott noted that there is 'an obvious similarity of purpose shared by trade marks and [European PDOs]'.[48] Similarly, the Swiss Federal Court of Justice has observed that the 'function both of trade mark protection and of protection for appellations of origin is to ensure the distinguishing function of the designation and to prevent mistaken attributions – whether regarding the manufacturer or the place of origin'.[49] More recently, the ECJ has noted that the EU's IGO registration system 'meets both the requirements of consumer protection ... and the need to maintain fair competition between producers'.[50]

As *sui generis* GI protection has proved controversial and GIs share an apparent functional equivalence with trade marks, international lobbying efforts have intensified to absorb these collectively used signs within the trade mark regime, via certification or collective trade marks.[51] The US actively subsumes GI protection under trade mark law within the framework of a series of bilateral trade agreements.[52] Alongside this proposed amalgamation, opponents also contend that a *sui generis* GI regime committed to strong standards of protection can largely be explained on the basis of protectionism. If trade mark systems can do the job, what else explains the existence of independent regimes favouring GI collectives? Therefore some commentators have concluded that GIs are a protectionist device for European regional producer collectives and agricultural models.[53] Seen as an act of resistance by

---

[48] Ibid., [100].

[49] *Anheuser-Busch Inc* v. *Budějovický Budvar Narodni Podnik* [2001] ETMR 7, [82] (Swiss FC).

[50] *Alberto Severi* v. *Regione Emilia-Romagna* (C–446/07) [2009] ECR I-8041; [2009] ETMR 64, [53] (ECJ).

[51] See, e.g., the USPTO position, available at www.uspto.gov/ip/global/geographical/index.jsp; Statement of Jon W. Dudas, Deputy Director, US Patent and Trade Mark Office in Hearings before the Committee on Agriculture, House of Representatives on the Status of the World Trade Organization Negotiations on Agriculture, (108–5) 108th Congress (2003) 349; Communication from the US, 'Suggested Method for Domestic Recognition of Geographical Indications for WTO Members', 11 March 1999 (IP/C/W/134); WIPO, 'Report to the 7th Session of the SCT', 27 May 2002 (SCT/7/4), [33].

[52] A list of US FTAs is available at www.ustr.gov/trade-agreements/free-trade-agreements.

[53] See e.g., J. Armistead, 'Whose Cheese Is It Anyway? Correctly Slicing the European Regulation Concerning Protections for Geographic Indications' (2000) 10 *Transnational Law & Contemporary Problems* 303, 318; D. B. Shalov, 'Will the European Union Prove to be Lactose Intolerant? (2004) 11 *Cardozo Journal of International and Comparative Law* 1099, fn 8; L. B. Nieuwveld, 'Is This Really about What We Call Our Food or Something Else? The WTO Food Name Case over the Protection of Geographical Indications' (2007) 41 *International Lawyer* 891; T. Broude, 'Taking "Trade and Culture" Seriously: Geographical Indications and Cultural Protection in WTO Law' (2005) 26 *University of Pennsylvania Journal of International Economic Law* 623, 655 ('More broadly, like other forms of agricultural protectionism, GIs may be construed as necessary for the preservation of the farm culture of production in general').

Controversies and interests

the local against the global, 'the desire to maintain what is local is considered by many to be ... perhaps protectionist'.[54] By denying the use of feta as a generic term, those who claim Feta as a protected term are insulating themselves against generic competitors using the same designation. It must be recalled that GI protection does not prevent others from manufacturing a white cheese in brine that tastes broadly similar. They simply cannot describe it as Feta, but this could impede the signalling of substitutability. GIs are portrayed as the objects of realpolitik gambits with favourable trade outcomes, rather than nuances of intellectual property doctrine, informing negotiating positions.[55] 'Although *terroir* and a claim for a unique communications function for [GIs] is the European Union's public rhetoric ... [the] European Commission has a simpler goal: control of geographic words for their evocative value in the marketplace. The monopoly rents available from exclusive control of this evocative value drive the EU position in the debates.'[56] There is some evidence to support these misgivings, such as the greater emphasis being placed on GIs in response to declining market shares for European wines as they are outperformed by competitors from the Americas, Australia and South Africa.[57] Yet collapsing GI regimes into a functional equivalent (or even a poor cousin) of trade mark law, whilst restricting the explanations for the existence of *sui generis* systems to mere protectionism is an unsustainable generalisation.

The critique of *sui generis* GI protection in turn provokes a counterresponse, which is based on the understanding that the overlap between GIs and trade marks is only partial. This challenges the premise of the registered trade mark system being a complete functional substitute. To a certain extent, GI protection is attuned to protecting consumer interests and protecting legitimate producers against unfair competitive practices in the marketplace. However, this is only the starting point.

---

[54] M. Echols, *Geographical Indications for Food Products: International Legal and Regulatory Perspectives* (Kluwer, Alphen aan den Rijn 2008), 3.

[55] S. Stern, 'Geographical Indications and Trade Marks: Conflicts and Possible Resolutions', 13 June 2003 (WIPO/GEO/SFO/03/13), [4].

[56] Hughes, 'Champagne, Feta, and Bourbon', 305.

[57] The crisis is acknowledged in Recital 2 of Council Regulation (EC) No 479/2008 of 29 April 2008 on the Common Organisation of the Market in Wine [2008] OJ L148/1 ('Wine consumption in the Community has been steadily diminishing and the volume of wine exported from the Community since 1996 has been increasing at a much slower rate than the respective imports. This has led to a deterioration of the balance between supply and demand which in turn puts producers' prices and incomes under pressure'). See also M. Torsen, 'Apples and Oranges (and Wine): Why the International Conversation Regarding Geographical Indications is at a Standstill' (2005) 87 *Journal of the Patent and Trade Mark Office Society* 31, 40–5.

14   Introduction: locating geographical indications

GIs (usually those towards the AO end of the spectrum) differ in that they implicate a collective interest as opposed to a private commercial interest; they signal the associated product's link to a specific geographical origin and the degree of 'quasi-public' or state involvement in their recognition is greater.[58] These features of form and function facilitate a range of distinct policy agendas.

There are multiple objectives behind the protection of GIs: first, protection of consumers against fraud; second, protection of the producer of the good; third, territorial, local, regional and rural development; and, fourth, conservation of the biological resources, biodiversity and cultural diversity.[59]

Chapter 6 considers the extent to which GIs regimes are designed differently, to deliver on distinct goals and priorities. In alluding to this difference, the legal literature resorts to the language of 'ideological schisms',[60] 'fundamental, philosophical confict[s]',[61] the existence of 'very divergent system of laws and bodies of belief'[62] and 'profound cultural differences'.[63] Yet the differences have never been satisfactorily worked out. A genealogy of today's GI, as a distinct conceptual category, has never been attempted.

3.   Contribution and organisation

How has the GI come to mean what it does and function in the way that it does? In retracing the construction of this distinct category of subject matter within international IP law, this book seeks to bring the current controversies within the TRIPS Agreement into focus. It is impossible to make sense of the TRIPS Agreement without appreciating its inheritance. Given the conceptual and terminological ambiguity, the mapping metaphor was hard to resist in a work on geographical signs.

---

[58] See respectively, *Budějovický Budvar Narodni Podnik* v. *Rudolf Ammersin GmbH* (C-478/07) [2009] ECR I-7721; [2009] ETMR 65, [82] (AG Ruiz-Jarabo Colomer); M. Agdomar, 'Removing the Greek from Feta and Adding Korbel to Champagne: The Paradox of Geographical Indications in International Law' (2008) 18 *Fordham IP Media and Entertainment Law Journal* 541, 577; OECD, Appellations of Origin and Geographical Indications in OECD Member Countries: Economic and Legal Implications (COM/AGR/APM/TD/WP(2000)15/FINAL), 10.

[59] Marie-Vivien, 'The Role of the State', 121.

[60] Torsen, 'Apples and Oranges (and Wine)', 32.

[61] INTA Resolution, Protection of Geographical Indications and Trademarks, 24 September 1997.

[62] L. A. Lindquist, 'Champagne or Champagne? An Examination of US Failure to Comply with the Geographical Provision of the TRIPS Agreement' (1999) 27 *Georgia Journal of International and Comparative Law* 309, 312.

[63] Ilbert and Petit, 'Are Geographical Indications a Valid Property Right?', 503.

Contribution and organisation 15

However, the accompanying baggage proved too burdensome.[64] It was abandoned in favour of an analysis of relational legal categories such as the IS, AO and GI as Weberian ideal types, i.e. conceptual and not normative ideals. The relativistic conceptual analysis is aided by an attempted genealogy, or perhaps geology, of GIs. There is an obsession with TRIPS in contemporary scholarship, as if it were a self-contained code, but it is only the tip of the iceberg. Apart from exposing the contingencies of this multilateral agreement and recovering the transitions between the categories leading up to it, this approach also reveals the existence of at least two intersecting epistemic frameworks in this area. Put simply, do we protect signs on the basis of ensuring their communicative coherence (communicative logic) or do we universally reserve the use of signs for a certain group because we value the underlying product associated with the sign for its link to a specific place (*terroir* logic)? The two logics overlap, as communicative logic at the national level – when the IGO is recognised in the home jurisdiction – often shades into *terroir* logic at the international. For this reason, international protection was chosen as the appropriate level of analysis, since the interaction between divergent national approaches generates epistemic churn. The analysis concludes by suggesting that alongside a careful re-evaluation of the subjects of the law (consumers *and* producers), we may need to reconsider the manner in which its objects (signs *and* regional products) are constituted. This historical approach was also adopted to showcase the limitations of the thin version of neoclassical law and economics that otherwise occupies the theoretical foreground. It is descriptively inaccurate or simply silent on several doctrinal aspects of international GI protection, whereas its normative prescriptions presume a considerable overlap with the goals of trade mark protection. There is far more to GIs than this account acknowledges – law's constitutive influence and legitimating functions, the choice between prioritising production or consumption as the privileged site for definitional purposes, the opposing forces of homogenisation and distinction in a globalising world, attributing authorship to nature, a defence of place, the liberal individualism underpinning much of modern IP law juxtaposed against the collective or associational ideals associated with AOs, the evolving relationship between market and state, and even notions of authenticity in the face of mimesis.

---

[64] Maps tend to simplify and distort. They also suggest neat boundaries and disciplined, exclusive categories, while the research here suggests that continuity and overlaps are far more prevalent in this area.

16   Introduction: locating geographical indications

The advantage of the historical approach adopted here is that it casts new light on familiar questions, enabling us to reformulate them more meaningfully in the process. It also opens up a menu of interpretative options in some situations, while revealing the basis for existing constraints in others. The archival research directly addresses the following questions:

(1) Why is there such an abundance of terminology as well as overlapping regimes of protection in this area?
(2) How did the notion of a link between product and place arise (and to what extent does it recognise people)?
(3) Why does the European GI registration system have two distinct definitions but only one level of protection?
(4) Why does the TRIPS definition refer to qualities, characteristics or reputation as three alternative means to link product to place?
(5) Is there an explanation for the two distinct levels of protection in Articles 22 and 23 of TRIPS?
(6) How should we determine generic status?
(7) More generally, to what extent is GI protection distinct from the goals of trade mark law?

Since GIs have been insufficiently unpacked to date, this book sets out to provide a framework for thinking about this area. It tends towards theoretical explanations rather than theoretical justifications, to the extent that such delineations are possible. It is ambitious of necessity, seeking out the (many) gaps in explanations and awkward silences in the literature. Much that is interesting lies in the detail. A related purpose of this book is bibliographical. It is time we moved beyond the endless descriptive regurgitation of international treaties that has become a permanent fixture of the legal scholarship in this area, when there are far more interesting avenues of research to be pursued.

The organisation follows a broadly historical trajectory and Part I is concerned with origins. Any response to the question of whether GIs are a form of IP must begin by addressing the puzzle of the inclusion of the IS within the Paris Convention of 1883. What was a sign which merely indicates geographical origin doing within an industrial property convention? Where was the valuable intangible that we associate with IP protection? Revisiting the history of the IS in both the Paris Convention and the Madrid Agreement is instructive because (1) it accounts for the swarm of disparate institutional mechanisms regulating origin marking; (2) it reveals a collectively generated reputation to be the valuable intangible that is the object of the industrial property right; (3) while identifying the conceptual and pragmatic reasons for treating these signs as a category distinct from trade marks. Of particular interest to IP scholars will be the exploration of alternative possibilities, unfair competition prevention and collective mark protection, considered within the Paris Convention. The Madrid Agreement is also of interest since it marks the transition from the IS to the AO, officially incorporating *terroir* logic for the first time.

Having introduced the notion of a special link between certain types of products and their regions of origin, Chapter 3 explores wine as the paradigmatic subject matter for IGO protection, which sets the initial benchmarks and boundaries for the subject matter template. *Terroir* is a crucial ingredient in the processes of legitimation whereby IGOs are treated as a discrete category of protected signs. Its origins and influences are unpacked in some detail. Given the specific contingencies of the French national experience, the chapter concludes by asking whether the story of wine should become the story for all GIs. The Lisbon Agreement is the subject of Chapter 4. It documents attempts to expand the subject matter bubble beyond products of the vine to incorporate agricultural products and even crafts. In the process, the link between product and place is reconfigured to recognise the contribution of culture, or human factors, alongside nature. Yet compromises that affect the coherence of certain claims are made in the process of establishing a more abstract definition. The chapter also looks closely at the workings of this Agreement and its interpretation by various national courts. Finally, it disentangles the various categories of purported misuses of geographical signs by third parties, underlining the exceptional nature of 'absolute' protection. This tier cannot be justified according to principles conventionally found in unfair competition doctrine and based upon communicative logic.

In Part II of this book, the focus shifts to the present, which perches precariously upon the past. The TRIPS Agreement contains the current framework for the international protection of GIs and Chapter 5 tries to make sense of its provisions. It provides an account of the shape and form of contemporary rules, identifying and explaining the significance of the compromises which have been papered over. TRIPS reflects the equivocation between an unfair competition derived communicative paradigm and the *terroir* paradigm. Following this, it considers the extent to which prescriptive attempts to relocate or reinvent the basis for GI protection can build upon historic foundations, informed by unfair competition logic and dependent upon the meaning of the sign. The present and future rest on the past, which remains poorly understood. By establishing continuities with Part I, Chapter 5 identifies and unpacks the unfinished business that distorts the TRIPS architecture. The

18   Introduction: locating geographical indications

analysis is rounded off in Chapter 6, with a review of contemporary debates before the TRIPS Council and some speculation about their epistemic significance. The newer arguments in support of the extension of Article 23 or the establishment of a multilateral register have the potential to recognise regional products as an additional object of GI protection, alongside the sign. Chapter 7 concludes by selectively re-emphasising the insights gleaned. Finally, some notes on housekeeping. All translations are the author's unless otherwise indicated. Internal citations are omitted in quotations. Spellings have been standardised for ease of perusal (e.g., 'trademark' being replaced by 'trade mark'). All internet references are valid as of 31 May 2011.

Part I

2 The Indication of Source – Paris and Madrid

1. Introduction

How were signs indicating geographical origin conceived of as suitable subject matter for IP law? This is the thematic line of enquiry developed across the first part of this book. Although present negotiating positions have deep historical roots, much has been forgotten. Prior to 1994, three multilateral agreements administered by the World Intellectual Property Organization (WIPO) addressed the protection of geographical signs. They set the parameters for subsequent negotiations while introducing two very different definitional visions of subject matter – the Indication of Source (IS), corresponding to a minimalist regulation of truth telling, and the Appellation of Origin (AO), embedded in more elaborate, registration-based architecture. Part I of this book retraces the journey from the IS to the AO. The key debates driving the transition are as follows: should these geographical signs constitute a distinct category within the IP canon? Consequently, should the scope of protection depend upon the message they convey to particular audiences, or should they be protected regardless of semantic reception because they are valued for other reasons? The responses to these questions determine both the form and scope of protection granted.

Chapter 2 takes up the story of the IS and investigates the following puzzle. A number of regulatory regimes have an interest in truthful origin marking, including penal regimes preventing fraud, rules of origin regimes for tariff classification purposes and phytosanitary regimes. So why was a simple indication of geographical origin folded within a system regulating the use of valuable intangibles? Under what circumstances did the language of property make an appearance in legal discourse? The founding of the Paris Convention for the Protection of Industrial Property in 1883[1] is the starting point for this investigation.

---

[1] Paris Convention for the Protection of Industrial Property, 20 March 1883 as revised at Stockholm on 14 July 1967, 828 UNTS 305 (1972), (hereafter, the Paris Convention). All WIPO treaties are also available at www.wipo.int/treaties/en/.

22   The Indication of Source

This instrument introduced both the IS and AO, although it regulates only the former. It prohibits the use of false indications of source, with an emphasis on border measures such as seizure by customs authorities or simply barring the entry of imports. It is closely followed by the Madrid Agreement for the Repression of False or Deceptive Indications of Source on Goods of 1891.[2] This treaty extends the scope of protection for the IS. More significantly, it affords higher levels of protection for products of the vine and signals the transition from the IS to the AO. In the process, the Madrid Agreement affords the first glimpses of the conceptual realignments leading up to the Lisbon Agreement for the Protection of Appellations of Origin and their International Registration of 1958.[3] The third of the WIPO treaties, considered in Chapter 4, establishes an international registration system for AOs and provides for property-like standards of protection by moving beyond protection contingent on harmful conduct, such as misleading uses.

A close study of these international agreements offers up a rich yield of insights because developments in this area have traditionally been driven by a top down approach. The 'international legal rules associated with the protection of geographical indications do not derive their authority from longstanding or widespread presence of analogous rules within national laws prior to signature of the TRIPS Agreement in 1994, such that these international rules could be considered to reflect general principles of law'.[4] These agreements established an institutional setting where different models of Indications of Geographical Origin (IGOs) protection were proposed and resisted. Terminological and conceptual apparatus have crystallised across a century of international treaty negotiations, shaping the legal discourse in this area. Yet contemporary scholarship introduces these formative instruments as preliminaries to the main event, something to be skimmed over for the sake of completeness. Such token acknowledgment is based on their perceived irrelevance in a post-TRIPS world, the lack of enforcement mechanisms or, for the more specialised agreements, the modest numbers of signatories.[5]

---

[2] Madrid Agreement for the Repression of False or Deceptive Indications of Source on Goods, 14 April 1891, 828 UNTS 389 (1972), (hereafter, the Madrid Agreement).
[3] Lisbon Agreement for the Protection of Appellations of Origin and their International Registration, 31 October 1958, 923 UNTS 205 (1974), (hereafter, the Lisbon Agreement).
[4] WIPO, 'The Definition of Geographical Indications', 1 October 2002 (SCT/9/4), [3].
[5] E.g., L. A. Lindquist, 'Champagne or Champagne? An Examination of U.S. Failure to Comply with the Geographical Provisions of the TRIPS Agreement' (1999) 27 *Georgia Journal of International and Comparative Law* 309, 314–15; M. Blakeney, 'Geographical Indications and Trade' (2000) 6 *International Trade Law and Regulation* 48, 52; R. Harle, 'AIPPI and the Appellations of Origin, Indications of Source and Geographical

Unfortunately, this dismissal overlooks their decisive contribution in framing the current regime. These treaties provided the rubric for debating the terms on which IGOs ought to be the subject matter of IP law. Revisiting the *travaux préparatoires* reveals why key concepts and opposing views settled into such durable patterns. While preventing blatantly deceptive conduct has traditionally grounded arguments, there are repeated attempts to protect a commercially valuable reputation even in the absence of confusion or deception.[6] Excavating the early framing devices, analogies, justifications and their critiques, as well as associated institutional apparatus, exposes the process by which IGOs emerge as distinct subject matter. This focus does not indicate a desire to bracket legal discourse in this book, as is evident from the interdisciplinary vantage points adopted for studying wine production in Chapter 3. Instead this approach seeks to clarify the manner in which the various iterations of IGOs have functioned in IP discourse by looking at particular operational categories over the course of a century.

2.   The Paris Convention

The Paris Convention was concluded in 1883 and revised several times during the twentieth century.[7] It remains an early landmark in international intellectual or industrial property[8] protection for its principles of national treatment for foreigners,[9] priority afforded to proprietors of

---

Indications', in AIPPI, *1897–1997 Centennial Edition* (AIPPI Foundation, Basle 1997), 255, 257; X-T. N. Nguyen, 'Nationalizing Trade Marks: A New International Trade Mark Jurisprudence?' (2004) 39 *Wake Forest Law Review* 729, 758–60; M. Torsen, 'Apples and Oranges (and Wine): Why the International Conversation Regarding Geographical Indications is at a Standstill' (2005) 87 *Journal of the Patent and Trade Mark Office Society* 31, 34–6.

[6] Depending on the jurisdiction and context, deception is usually treated as distinct from a misleading or confusing use. It may require an additional element, such as establishing intent to deceive (focusing on the defendant's mental state) or a measurable impact on consumer behaviour, in the sense that the deception will influence a purchase decision (focusing on the effect).

[7] Revisions at Brussels on 14 December 1900, Washington on 2 June 1911, The Hague on 6 November 1925, London on 2 June 1934, Lisbon on 31 October 1958 and Stockholm on 14 July 1967; and as amended on 28 September 1979.

[8] 'Intellectual property' and 'industrial property' are used interchangeably throughout this work, depending upon the historical materials being considered. Conventionally, the former is seen as the umbrella term which absorbed both 'literary property' and 'industrial property'. See WIPO *Introduction to Intellectual Property – Theory and Practice* (Kluwer Law International, London 1997), 3; Cf. J. Hughes, 'Notes on the Origin of Intellectual Property: Revised Conclusions and New Sources', Cardozo Legal Studies Research Paper No. 265 (11 July 2009).

[9] Art. 2.

24   The Indication of Source

registered intellectual property rights within the folds of its membership[10] and minimum substantive standards of protection.[11] It is additionally significant for establishing the Bureaux Internationaux Réunis
pour la Protection de la Propriété Intellectuelle (BIRPI), which would
consolidate technical expertise and influence international rule setting
as the predecessor to WIPO.[12] Prior to TRIPS, this convention was
the big tent of international IP regulation and has attracted an impressive
number of signatories over the years.[13] However, a well-recognised
limitation is the variable implementation of its substantive standards
at the national level. The Convention leaves 'considerable freedom
to the countries of the Union to legislate on questions of industrial
property according to their interests or preferences'.[14] It also lacks an
effective dispute settlement mechanism to resolve complaints of non-
compliance.[15] Perhaps most significantly, to contemporary observers the
GI provisions seem to lack bite.[16] Despite these deficiencies, the Paris
Convention is our springboard because of its taxonomic implications.
It formally recognises the existence of the IS as a separate category
within the international classification of industrial property. Those with
an unhurried view of this area concur that it was 'in the course of the
years ... closely following 1880 that we saw the development of the
principle of protecting that which is now agreed should be referred
to as geographical indications'.[17] Writing in the early decades of multilateral intellectual property protection, Stephen Ladas noted that prior
'to the Convention of 1883, few countries protected indications of origin
by their domestic law, and the remedies for the repression of false

[10] Art. 4(A)(1).
[11] For our purposes, the relevant provisions are: Art. 1 (definition of industrial property);
Art. 9 (sanctions including seizure on importation); Art. 10 (proscription against false
indications); Art. 10*bis* (unfair competition) and Art. 10*ter* (standing to initiate
proceedings and remedies).
[12] BIRPI, *L'Union Internationale pour la Protection de la Propriété Industrielle – Sa Fondation et
son Développement* (Bureau de l'Union, Berne 1933), 127–48.
[13] Presently, it has 173 Contracting Parties. See www.wipo.int/treaties/en/ip/paris/.
[14] G. H. C. Bodenhausen, *Guide to the Application of the Paris Convention for the Protection of
Industrial Property* (Bureau de l'Union, Geneva 1968), 15.
[15] While Art. 28 stipulates that disputes over the interpretation or application of the
convention may be brought before the International Court of Justice (ICJ), it also
clarifies that signatories can choose not to be bound by this provision. There is no
record of any such proceeding being brought before the ICJ to date.
[16] WIPO, 'The Need for a New Treaty and its Possible Contents', 9 April 1990 (GEO/CE/
I/2) [18]; W. Moran, 'Rural Space as Intellectual Property' (1993) 12 *Political Geography*
263, 268 (The 'protection offered by the Paris Convention is relatively weak');
Lindquist, 'Champagne or Champagne?', 315 (Prior 'to the TRIPS Agreement,
geographical indications received little international protection').
[17] Harle, 'AIPPI and the Appellations of Origin', 255.

The Paris Convention

indications of origin were very inadequate, [being] recognized and regulated in most of the countries about the same time by national and international legislation'.[18]

The international recognition of GIs in effect begins with the definition of 'Industrial Property' in Article 1(2) of the Paris Convention, which refers to both the IS and the AO[19] alongside more familiar categories:

The protection of industrial property has as its object patents, utility models, industrial designs, trade marks, service marks, trade names, indications of source or appellations of origin, and the repression of unfair competition.

The very process of accommodation within the broad parameters of industrial property provides us with two valuable insights. First, it introduces the controversial distinction between natural and manufactured products.[20] As we will see over the course of Part I, this marks an important boundary when accounting for the ontological independence and scope of GI protection. Since GIs have routinely been associated with wines, spirits, agricultural products and foodstuffs, Article 1(3) expressly refers to 'agricultural and extractive' industries:

Industrial property shall be understood in the broadest sense and shall apply not only to industry and commerce proper, but likewise to agricultural and extractive industries and to all manufactured or natural products, for example, wines, grain, tobacco leaf, fruit, cattle, minerals, mineral waters, beer, flowers and flour.

Agricultural products (and wines in particular) were mentioned during the initial Paris negotiations[21] and included in the Protocol to the final treaty of 1883. To formalise the inclusion, this particular provision was introduced during the Washington conference in 1911 and further amended at The Hague conference in 1925 to take account of specific examples of agricultural industries. Supporters of the amendments included those directly affected by the question of whether 'industrial' property rights could apply in the context of 'natural' products and explains Cuba's request for tobacco leaves to be included in the illustrative list.[22] Alongside the question of whether natural products were

---

[18] S. P. Ladas, *The International Protection of Industrial Property* (Harvard University Press, Cambridge MA 1930), 658–9.

[19] The AO was added after The Hague revision conference in 1925. For attempts to distinguish between the two categories, see Chapter 4.

[20] The analysis here does not subscribe to or naturalise such binary distinctions. It merely traces their deployment in these formative debates.

[21] Actes de la Conférence Internationale pour la Protection de la Propriété Industrielle (Ministère des Affaires Etrangères, Impr. Nationale, Paris 1880), 32–3, (hereafter, Actes de Paris).

[22] See Actes de la Conférence de la Haye (Bureau International de l'Union, Berne 1926), 535, (hereafter, Actes de la Haye).

26   The Indication of Source

covered, the desire for clarification related to experiences with French national legislation regulating the marking of products.[23] The influential penal legislation of 1824,[24] designed to repress fraudulent marking, was interpreted to apply to manufactured articles (*'objet fabriqué'*) alone.[25] Some French courts had initially ruled that this law did not apply to marks on 'natural' products, which were left to find shelter under *concurrence déloyale*, the prohibition against unfair competition within French delict doctrine.[26] In particular, there had been some debate about whether wine was a natural or manufactured product. Therefore clarifying that industrial property rights could exist in the context of 'all manufactured or natural products' was deemed necessary.

The listing of IP categories in the Convention also affords us a second insight, which is derived from attempts to situate the IS within the broader genus of unfair competition prevention during these deliberations. For instance, at The Hague conference, when considering the enumerated categories in the definition, the Italian delegate suggested that false indications of provenance could be incorporated within the broader grouping of unfair competition.[27] Again subsequent discussions refer to a proposal from Poland to amalgamate the protection of trade marks, trade names and indications of source more logically under the repression of unfair competition.[28] Although this particular tidying up exercise was unsuccessful, it introduces the notion that the regulation of place names had been consistently located within the broader family of unfair competition prevention regimes. As we see towards the end of this chapter, the illumination from this genealogical insight is muted, because the unfair competition family is both vast and varied. Determining when conduct between competitors should be legally recognised as unfair remains contested territory and IGOs need to be carefully situated within this family. Recurrent references to unfair competition do, however, provide us with clues as to the valuable intangible sought to be protected and why the IS was included within the taxonomy of industrial property law to begin with.

---

[23] Ibid., 536.

[24] Loi du 28 juillet 1824 Relative aux Altérations ou Suppositions de Noms dans les Produits Fabriques (1825) 7 *Bulletin des Lois* No. 19, 65, (hereafter Law of 1824). Reproduced in E. Calmels, *De la Propriété et de la Contrefaçon* (Cosse, Paris 1856), 838–9. For an English translation, see C. E. Coddington, *A Digest of the Law of Trade Marks* (Ward and Peloubet, New York 1878), 380–1.

[25] N. Olszak, *Droit des Appellations d'Origine et Indications de Provenance* (TEC & DOC, Paris 2001), 35.

[26] L. Jaton, *La Répression des Fausses Indications de Provenance et les Conventions Internationales* (Librairie Générale de Droit et de Jurisprudence, Paris 1926), 25.

[27] Actes de la Haye, 412.   [28] Ibid., 535.

The Paris Convention 27

2.1 The Indication of Source

While 'indication of source' is used in Articles 1(2) and 10 of the Paris Convention and throughout the Madrid Agreement, neither instrument supplies a definition. One may be inferred from Article 1(1) of the Madrid Agreement, which states that all goods 'bearing a false or deceptive indication by which ... [a Union country], or a place situated therein, is directly or indirectly indicated as being the country or place of origin shall be seized on importation into any of the said countries'. An IS therefore refers to a country, or region within it, as being the place of origin of a product. WIPO's suggested definition is an 'expression or sign used to indicate that a product or service originates in a country, region or specified place'.[29]

The emphasis is on geographical origin, as opposed to the commercial origin or trade source of the product, traditionally considered to be the communicative domain of a trade mark.[30] Examples include the name of a place on a product, or expressions such as 'Product of Papua New Guinea' or 'Made in Macedonia'. An 'indication' is a fairly broad signifier, covering place names such as 'Darjeeling' associated with a tea growing region in Eastern India,[31] iconic images such as the Bird's Nest stadium, Sphinx or Shamrock,[32] or it may even be a distinctive barrel[33]

---

[29] S. 1(b) of the WIPO Model Law for Developing Countries on Appellations of Origin and Indications of Source, (WIPO, Geneva 1975). See also: WIPO, 'Introduction to Geographical Indications and Recent Developments in WIPO', 12 June 2003 (WIPO/ GEO/SFO/03/1), [4] ('Consequently an indication of source can be defined as an indication referring to a country, or to a place in that country, as being the country or place of origin of a product').

[30] For trade marks, see, e.g., *Hanover Star Milling* v. *Metcalf* 240 US 403, 412 (1916) ('The primary and proper function of a trade mark is to identify the origin or ownership of the article to which it is affixed. Where a party has been in the habit of labeling his goods with a distinctive mark, so that purchasers recognize goods thus marked as being of his production, others are debarred from applying the same mark to goods of the same description'); *Philips Electronics NV* v. *Remington Consumer Products Ltd* (C-299/99) [2002] ECR 1-5475; [2002] ETMR 81 (ECJ) (The 'essential function of a trade mark is to guarantee the identity of the origin of the marked product to the consumer or end-user by enabling him, without any possibility of confusion, to distinguish the product or service from others which have another origin, [thereby offering] a guarantee that all the goods or services bearing it have originated under the control of a single undertaking which is responsible for their quality').

[31] *Tea Board of India* v. *The Republic of Tea Inc* 80 USPQ 2d 1881 (TTAB 2006).

[32] *Shamrock Trade Mark* [1986] FSR 271 (BGH). It was used by the defendant as a mark to indicate Irish origin in collective national promotions between Ireland and Germany.

[33] The barrels for the wines of Bordeaux were entitled to a special form and dimensions, so as to remain distinctive. W. van Caenegem, 'Registered Geographical Indications: Between Rural Policy and Intellectual Property – Part II' (2003) 6 JWIP 861, 862. He further argues that these larger barrels gave the wine producers entitled to their exclusive use an anti-competitive advantage, as the wine travelled better and freight charges, imposed per barrel, were reduced.

28   The Indication of Source

or bottle shape.[34] In principle, any symbol used on materials associated with the sale of a product and which communicates a specific geographical origin for that product should qualify. Regarding the area indicated, this could be a country, region, city or town or even smaller unit. Thus the ontological question of identifying which signs are indications of source is answered by drawing on principles first developed in the context of trade mark law.[35] The algorithm for this relies upon the communicative function of the sign – does it indicate the geographical origin of the product to the relevant audience?

Having established this algorithm for the IS, most commentators move swiftly onwards. Yet this raises more doubts than it resolves. If an IS merely indicates the place of origin or production, then why should it be included under the ambit of industrial property? After all, there are other bodies of law concerned with truth-telling on labels. Professor Audier asserts that an IS indicates 'the "origin" of the goods or the products for customs purposes'[36] while Advocate-General Colomer opined during the European *Feta* litigation that the IS has more relevance for the purposes of consumer protection.[37] What emerges from the historical records is that not only did these diverse regimes overlap with the IS in terms of subject matter, they were operationally deployed to prevent the use of misleading indications of geographical origin and acknowledged as a means of satisfying Paris Convention obligations. In 1902 one of the leading treatises identifies the following array of responses to the IS protection requirement under the Paris Convention: for Germany it is the law against unfair competition of 1896, supplemented by the trade mark legislation of 1894; Austria lacks any specific laws but is considering their enactment; Belgium relies on its Penal Code, as do Italy and the Netherlands; Brazil's response is found in the trade mark law of 1897, including detailed provisions for seizure by

---

[34] *Bergkelder Bpk* v. *Vredendal Koöp Wynmakery* [2006] SCA 8 (RSA), [2]. Here the South African Supreme Court was critical of German producers' attempts to protect the shape of the infamous 'goat's pouch' (*Bocksbeutel*) as an indication of origin despite longstanding usage by Italian and Portuguese wine makers.

[35] L. Bently, 'The Making of Modern Trade Marks Law: The Construction of the Legal Concept of Trade Mark (1860–80)', in L. Bently, Jane C. Ginsburg, Jennifer Davis (eds.) *Trade Marks and Brands: An Interdisciplinary Critique* (Cambridge University Press, 2008), 3, 28.

[36] J. Audier, 'Protection of Geographical Indications in France and Protection of French Geographical Indications in Other Countries', October 1997 (WIPO/GEO/EGR/97/8 Rev), 3.

[37] See *Federal Republic of Germany and Kingdom of Denmark* v. *Commission of the European Communities* (C-465/02 & C-466/02) [2005] ECR I-9115, [70] (The 'safeguarding of so-called simple indications of source is not based on the protection of industrial and commercial property, but rather, where applicable, on the protection of consumers').

The Paris Convention

customs authorities; Spain has bespoke ordinances prohibiting fraudulent marking for specific products; Britain relies on the penal provisions of the Merchandise Marks regime supplemented by customs regulations; Russia draws upon customs rules and procedures to regulate origin marks; Japan, Norway, the Dominican Republic, Serbia and Tunisia apparently do not have any relevant laws and so on.[38] This diversity continues to flourish in subsequent inventories. Approximately three decades after the advent of the Paris Convention, an official survey of forty jurisdictions for the British Parliament once again revealed the range of laws that apparently satisfied the obligation in Article 10.[39] A further survey of the laws of forty-two countries in 1913 indicates that despite many being signatories of the Paris Convention, few dedicated regimes were in place for preventing the sale or importation of products bearing false indications of origin.[40] This is evident once again in BIRPI's synoptic table of legislation from 1925, where penal laws directed at fraud, civil actions in tort or delict, revenue legislation, embryonic unfair competition regimes, trade and merchandise mark statutes, customs regulations and bespoke legislation prohibiting misleading labelling on specific products, such as hops or cotton textiles, all picked up this slack.[41]

It is particularly striking that customs rules and regulations find frequent mentions, since this underlines the outward looking or international trade-related concerns surrounding IS protection. Furthermore, each of these regimes represented a distinct configuration of consumer, general public, legitimate producer and competitor interests. This would determine the parties who could initiate legal proceedings (defrauded consumers, wronged individual producers, representative producer associations); the nature of proceedings (civil, criminal, administrative); the remedies available (injunctions, damages, imprisonment) as well as the important question of who would bear the costs (individual traders, public prosecutors, customs authorities). In these early iterations IGO protection gambits are scattered across a variety of legislative and institutional settings. To take one example, while the tort of (extended) passing off is widely considered to be the common law's primary response to IGO

---

[38] M. Pelletier and E. Vidal-Naquet, *La Convention d'Union pour la Protection de la Propriété Industrielle du 20 Mars 1883* (Larose & Forcel, Paris 1902), 258–62.

[39] Reports from His Majesty's Representatives Abroad on the Laws in Force in the Principal Foreign Countries to Prevent the Sale or Importation of Goods *Bearing a False Indication of Origin* 86 PP 739 [Cd 5531] (1911).

[40] B. Singer, *Trade Mark Laws of the World and Unfair Trade* (Hammond Press, Chicago IL 1913), 602–18.

[41] Actes de la Haye, 150–9.

30   The Indication of Source

protection,[42] it is significantly predated by the series of penal Merchandise Marks Acts dating back to 1862. Archival research into the regulation of trade descriptions under this regime, including descriptions of geographical origin, reveals reputed regional products and familiar legal issues.[43] Yet as a result of this morphological diversity, the IS no longer matches up to the expectations of modern IP doctrine. In differentiating between the IS and AO at the Lisbon Revision Conference, BIRPI suggested that the use of false indications was prevented under the consumer protection remit of unfair competition regulation.[44] It also emphasised the mandatory nature of source or origin marking on products for export purposes, in contrast to optional AO status which appeared to be a more deserving candidate for IP protection.[45] All this merely amplifies the enigma: why was simple geographical origin marking included within an intellectual property convention in the first place?

In the remainder of this chapter, a response to this question is developed along the following lines. The first move is to identify the valuable intangible that was the object of protection. The unambiguous answer from legal discourse is that it corresponds to the reputation surrounding certain famous regional products. However, that reputation was atypical in that it was collectively generated and accreted around a geographically descriptive term. The incorporation of such terms within the registered trade mark system proved challenging as that system was designed around individual proprietors using distinctive signs. Meanwhile other categories of identifiers, such as trade names, existed outside of these early trade mark registration systems. Therefore by the late nineteenth century, parallels are frequently drawn between trade names and indications of origin. Both these categories, along with unregistered trade marks, were protected via an array of legal regimes directed at preventing unfair competition between market participants,[46] often where the result was to disadvantage the consuming public. Since a reputation protection agenda was grafted on to a number of existing legal instruments, with miscellaneous objectives and institutional configurations, this valuable intangible drifts out of focus in subsequent

---

[42] See Chapter 3.
[43] See D. Higgins and D. Gangjee, '"Trick or Treat?" The Misrepresentation of American Beef Exports in Britain during the Late Nineteenth Century' (2010) 11 *Enterprise and Society* 203.
[44] See Actes de la Conférence de Lisbonne (Bureau de l'Union, Geneva 1963), 771, (hereafter, Actes de Lisbonne).
[45] Ibid., 772.
[46] C. Wadlow, *The Law of Passing Off: Unfair Competition by Misrepresentation*, 3rd edn (Sweet & Maxwell, London 2004), 61 (These regimes included 'various combinations of civil, criminal and administrative law').

analyses of the IS. To the extent that a common platform did exist across these regimes, it was the prevention of misleading marking. While the prevention of false labelling was initially a promising banner under which to rally support and had potential at the national level, a geographical sign gives rise to its own discrete set of concerns where international protection is sought. Put simply, meaning is slippery and while a sign may indicate a specific origin and quality in its 'home' jurisdiction, there is no guarantee that these referents stay fastened as the sign crosses into new markets. A name which is considered geographical in one context may also be used fancifully (e.g. AMAZON.COM), generically (dijon mustard or cheddar cheese) or allusively (a 'Thai Restaurant' in London). Formal geographical names (i.e. corresponding to a place on a map) on products do not always communicate an eponymous origin for those products. At this stage the fraud prevention argument starts to lose traction.

Additionally, origin marking was the subject of intense debates in the context of free trade during this period.[47] National or imperial origin marks[48] were seen as vectors for furthering non-tariff preference setting agendas and thus in tension with free trade commitments. Finally, with the growth in international trade and changing consumer preferences, the very notion of certain products having a single and neatly circumscribed origin began to unravel. Where raw materials were sourced separately from the place of processing, or a product consisted of an ensemble of disparately sourced constituent parts, a rigid approach to origin marking became increasingly undesirable. For these reasons the protection of a valuable collective reputation was possible via the regulation of origin marking, but only up to a point, since origin marking itself was situated at the intersection of broader debates.

We therefore commence with a review of the evidence that, analogous to the logic of trade mark protection, a collectively generated reputation formed the basis for including the IS within the Paris Convention. An important preliminary issue to address is the reason for selecting this international instrument as our starting point. While it is futile to search

---

[47] For background to the free trade debates, see J. V. Nye, 'The Myth of Free-Trade Britain and Fortress France: Tariffs and Trade in the Nineteenth Century' (1991) 51 *Journal of Economic History* 23; M. Flandreau and O. Accominotti, 'Does Bilateralism Promote Trade? Nineteenth Century Liberalization Revisited', CEPR Discussion Paper No. 5423 (2005). On the implications for food exports, see A. Nützenadel, 'A Green International? Food Markets and Transnational Politics, c.1850–1914', in A. Nützenadel and F. Trentmann (eds.), *Food and Globalization: Consumption, Markets and Politics in the Modern World* (Berg, Oxford and New York 2008), 153.

[48] Cf. *Union Syndicate's Application* [1922] 39 RPC 346 (considering the French UNIS Mark); Report of the Imperial Economic Committee, 13 PP 799 [Cm 2493] (1925) (considering the British Empire Mark).

32   The Indication of Source

for a definitive originary moment, the institution of the Paris Union is nevertheless a preferred point at which to begin this story. The practice of geographical origin marking on products significantly predates the time at which these marks become relevant for intellectual property doctrine. There are references to the 'fact that for centuries all kinds of products have been normally designated by a geographical name [honey from Attica, Bohemian or Waterford crystal, Champagne sparkling wine, Iran Caviar, Ceylon tea, etc.]'.[49] Louis Jaton traces this back to the markings on Chinese porcelain and Roman pottery, which guaranteed good craftsmanship as well provided proof of source.[50] Others suggest that historically, 'the identification of a product's geographic source has been a favoured method of product designation'.[51] Michael Blakeney asserts that geographical origin marking was an established practice since, prior to the industrial revolution, goods which 'entered international trade were primary products, such as minerals and agricultural produce and simple manufactured goods, such as pottery and woven fabrics'.[52] Therefore geographical signs are considered to be one of the earliest methods of distinguishing between products,[53] as illustrated by the Greek swords of Calcide used to equip Alexander's armies on their march eastwards[54] or by references to the practice in Roman times of marking 'the names of makers, or of places and towns where [lamps] were fabricated'.[55] Reputed regional products were perceived as having a superior quality that resulted either from natural geographic advantages or locally situated manufacturing skills. 'Roquefort' cheese is one such example which took the name of the small town in Aveyron, France where it was first produced. Literary references suggest that cheese from the region was known in ancient Rome while legal recognition is traced to the law passed by the Parliament of Toulouse on 31 August 1666, reserving the right to use the name exclusively for cheese cured in the natural caves at Roquefort.[56]

---

[49] Audier, 'Protection of Geographical Indications in France', 2.

[50] Jaton, *Répression des Fausses Indications*, 1–4.

[51] L. Bendekgey and C. H. Mead, 'International Protection of Appellations of Origin and Other Geographic Indications' (1992) 82 TMR 765.

[52] Blakeney, 'Geographical Indications and Trade', 48–9.

[53] H. Harte-Bavendamm, 'Geographical Indications and Trade Marks: Harmony or Conflict?', 1 September 1999 (WIPO/GEO/CPT/99/6), 2; M. Blakeney, 'Proposals for the International Regulation of Geographical Indications' (2001) 4 JWIP 629.

[54] L. de Javier, 'Appellations of Origin in the Viticultural Sector: The Vision of the Wine Producers', November 2001 (WIPO/GEO/MVD/01/3), 3.

[55] E. Rogers, 'Some Historical Matters Concerning Trade Marks' (1910) 9 *Michigan Law Review* 29, 30–1.

[56] L. W. Pollack, '"Roquefort" – An Example of Multiple Protection for a Designation of Regional Origin under the Lanham Act' (1962) 52 TMR 755.

The Paris Convention   33

These geographical designations were viewed as warranties of quality by purchasers, while producers from the region wished to protect commercially valuable reputations, giving rise to the need for regulating the truthful application of such origin signs. The difference is that when it comes to the accompanying institutional frameworks, these marking systems were often facets of larger guild structures situated in specific locales[57] or monitored by officially sanctioned regulators,[58] which emphasises the obligatory nature and policing dimensions of such marks.[59] By contrast, two crucial dimensions which modern intellectual property doctrine emphasises are the voluntary nature of marking[60] in addition to the proprietary nature of rights obtained.[61]

There is additional evidence to suggest that, despite these antecedents, the Paris Convention represents a fundamental conceptual shift in thinking about such signs, since the IS provisions were crafted with a specific template in mind. Contemporary sources confirm the French influence upon the draft text of the *Projet d'une Union Internationale pour la Protection de la Propriété Industrielle*, circulated by the French government along with the invitation to the initial Paris conference.[62] In particular, Article 19 of the French Law of 1857[63] is perceived as the inspiration for the draft Article 6 during the initial Paris negotiations. This draft contained the proposed prohibition against false indications of source

---

[57] Jaton, *Répression des Fausses Indications*, 3.

[58] P. B. Hutt, 'Government Regulation of the Integrity of the Food Supply' (1984) 4 *Annual Review of Nutrition* 1.

[59] On the tracing of liability and general policing functions of guild marks, as opposed to advertising the wares of individual traders, see F. I. Schechter, *The Historical Foundations of the Law Relating to Trade Marks* (Columbia University Press, New York 1925), 38–63.

[60] Jaton, *Répression des Fausses Indications*, 5; M. Amar, 'Des Marques Collectives' [1901] *Annuaire* 112, 112–13.

[61] Michael Spence describes an intellectual property right as 'a right: (i) that can be treated as property; (ii) to control particular uses; (iii) of a specified type of intangible asset'. He clarifies that the object of ownership is the legal right, not necessarily the intangible asset itself. See M. Spence, *Intellectual Property* (Oxford University Press, 2007), 12–16. Furthermore, specific attributes are ascribed to proprietary rights. E.g., within the common law tradition, a proprietary right relates to those interests which (1) can be alienated; (2) die when their object perishes or is lost without trace; (3) until then can be asserted against an indefinite number of people; (4) provides a degree of insulation for the protected interest against bankruptcy. F. H. Lawson and B. Rudden, *Law of Property*, 3rd edn, (Oxford University Press, 2002), 14.

[62] Ladas, *International Protection of Industrial Property*, 61–8; For the text of the Draft Project that formed the nucleus for discussions, see Actes de Paris, 23, 26–9. The foundational work of the Congress of 1878 is described in J. Bozérian, *La Convention Internationale du 20 mars 1883 pour la Protection de la Propriété Industrielle* (impr. de C. Pariset, Paris 1885), 6–8.

[63] Loi sur les Marques de Fabrique et de Commerce, du 23 Juin 1857, (hereafter, Law of 1857). Reproduced with an English translation in Reports Relative to Legislation in Foreign Countries on the Subject of Trade Marks 54 PP 585 (C. 596) (1872) 32–47.

34   The Indication of Source

and was eventually enacted as Articles 9 and 10.[64] The Law of 1857 had established one of the earliest modern trade mark registration systems and provided for relatively potent remedies where a registered trade mark was forged or fraudulently used. At the domestic level, this included seizure of the offending products within France under Article 14, while inaccurately labelled goods from abroad either entering French ports or in transit through them were liable to be seized by customs authorities under Article 19. While the Law of 1857 was primarily concerned with registered trade marks, Article 19 also prohibited the misleading use of a French place of manufacture.[65]

This legislation built on the foundations established by the Law of 1824, which penalised the misleading use of trade names. The 1824 legislation, targeting the fraudulent use of a manufacturer's trade name (*nom commercial*)[66] or place of production (*nom de localité* or *nom de lieu*), in turn supplemented the general penalties against fraud in Article 423 of the Code Pénal of 1810. The unpleasant aftertaste left by the repressive guilds of the *ancien regime* had ensured that pre-existing privileges had been swept away by the French Revolution. Yet having no regulation at all proved chaotic and these laws represent early attempts at reintroducing some order. According to Article 1 of the Law of 1824:

Whosoever shall either affix, or make appear by addition, retrenchment or by any alteration, upon manufactured articles, the name of a manufacturer other than he who is the producer, or the name of a manufactory other than that where said articles were made, or finally, *the name of a place other than that of the manufacture*, shall be punished by the penalties specified in Article 423 of the Penal Code,

---

[64] Pelletier and Vidal-Naquet, *La Convention d'Union pour la Protection de la Propriété Industrielle*, 266 ('*Au point de vue des fausses indications de provenance, la Convention d'Union a édicté des règles qui trouvent leur origine dans l'article 19 de la loi française de 1857*'); L. Donzel, *Commentaire et Critique de la Convention Internationale du 20 Mars 1883* (Marchal & Billard, Paris 1891), 266–9.

[65] This meant that misleading uses of foreign place names were initially beyond the scope of Art. 19. The Law of 1857, like other national laws at the time, discriminated between rights available to nationals and foreigners. It would only regulate the use of marks falsely indicating French manufacturers or French origin. For an excellent background to the preferential treatment of nationals and the issue of reciprocity, see P. Duguid, 'French Connections: The International Propagation of Trade Marks in the Nineteenth Century' (2009) 10 *Enterprise & Society* 3.

[66] A person's trade name was conventionally their own personal name or the adopted name of the business under which they were trading. Where this indication was used in commercial dealings but not registered as a trade mark, it was categorised as a trade name and protected against certain harmful uses by unauthorised third parties. See M. de Marafy, *Grand Dictionnaire International de la Propriété Industrielle*, Vol. 6, (Chevailier-Marescq et cie, Paris 1892), 194–5; D. M. Kerly, *The Law of Trade Marks, Trade Name and Merchandise Marks* (Sweet & Maxwell, London 1894), 392–3.

The Paris Convention   35

without prejudice to a decree for damages if there be occasion therefore. Every merchant, factor or retailer, whosoever, shall be liable to an action when he shall knowingly have exposed for sale, or put in circulation objects marked with fictitious or altered names (emphasis added).[67]

The *travaux* for the Law of 1824 make it abundantly clear that, just as an individual's trading name could acquire a commercially valuable reputation, so could the name of a place associated with a particular product.[68] When the statement of reasons was discussed in the Chamber of Deputies, there is reference to the notion that: '*Il est des villes de fabrique dont les produits ont aussi une réputation qu'on peut appeler collective, et c'est encore une propriété*' ('There are some manufacturing towns whose products have a reputation that may be referred to as collective, and this is still property').[69] The point is illustrated using the reputed fabrics from Louviers and Sedan,[70] where the manufacturers had an interest in preventing the inaccurate use of these geographical designations on cloth produced elsewhere. Preventing false marking would avert the twofold disadvantages of exposing honest producers to discredit and misleading purchasers.[71] These concerns, relating to the defence of a collective reputation for a product from a specific region and affecting all legitimate producers located there, are regularly aired during the passage of this legislation.[72]

Once this legislation was operationalised, the process of identifying the authentic place of origin raised additional important issues, since it was to be the standard for separating legitimate from illegitimate uses. First, producers or manufacturers legitimately based in the designated place were all entitled to advertise the geographical name on their products, especially where the place had acquired a reputation for particular products such as Champagne or Bordeaux for wines. Second, despite being collective stakeholders, each of these producers in their *individual capacity* was entitled to intervene in prosecutions against those based outside the region and falsely using the designation as this *collective goodwill did not exist in a legally recognisable form*.[73] Third, the name of a

---

[67] The translation is by Coddington, *Digest of the law of Trademarks*, 380–1.

[68] Reproduced in the Appendix to E. Pouillet, *Traité des Marques de Fabrique et de la Concurrence Déloyale en tous Genres*, 2nd edn, (Marchal & Billard, Paris 1883), 805–17.

[69] Ibid., 805–6.

[70] For the history of the luxury wool and linen trades centred in French towns including Sedan, Louviers and Elbeuf that are mentioned in the legislative record, see W. M. Reddy, *The Rise of Market Culture: The Textile Trade and French Society, 1750–1900* (Cambridge University Press, 1984). For around two centuries, the expensive *drap de Sedan* was the fabric of choice for European nobility and high ranking bureaucrats.

[71] Pouillet, *Traité des Marques de Fabrique*, 806.   [72] Ibid., 808–9, 812–13.

[73] Calmels, *De la Propriété et de la Contrefaçon*, 265–6.

36   The Indication of Source

place did not necessarily have to map on to the official names of administrative units. It included the names of vineyards or wine producing territories such as *maisons, crus* or *domaines*.[74] Fourth, how was the genuine place of origin identified for products whose fabrication was spread across different locales? While it was ultimately a question of fact to be determined by the trial court, the French judiciary initially struggled with wine production disputes. Was origin defined as the place where the grapes were harvested, or the place where the grapes were pressed, fermented and the wine ultimately produced? Each was considered an important facet of the process of creation.[75] Fifth, defining the outer limits of the circle of producers by delimiting a town or region also proved controversial in some cases. For instance there is some discussion of whether the medieval town walls should form the official limits, despite the town spilling out beyond them over time. Once again this was a question of fact to be determined in the context of a given dispute,[76] but the enquiry would focus on whether products from the penumbral regions had the same manufacturing techniques and quality that gave those from the core their reputation, or had been sanctioned by long-standing practice.[77] Yet the outer limits in the last two situations were clearly set out: if a use was likely to create misleading impressions in the minds of purchasers, then it would not be tolerated. These principles, despite being developed in the context of a penal law regulating fraud, were also directed at creating and managing boundaries around collective reputations for regional products.[78] Commentators evaluating the IS in the Paris Convention therefore drew on extant French national legislation and acknowledged this reputational kernel within the IS.[79]

Reverting to the preliminary Paris conference of 1880, there are clues that the protection of producer interests in a commercial reputation

---

[74] Pouillet, *Traité des Marques de Fabrique*, 386–7.   [75] Ibid., 389–90.
[76] Marafy, *Grand Dictionnaire International*, Vol. 6, 2.
[77] Pouillet, *Traité des Marques de Fabrique*, 388–9.
[78] A-J. Gastambide, *Traité Théorique et Pratique des Contrefaçons en Tous Genres* (Legrand et Descauriet, Paris 1837), 458 ('*En effet, la provenance des marchandises n'est pas chose indifférente dans le commerce. Telle localité est renommée pour ses draps, telle autre pour sa coutellerie, etc.; cette bonne réputation est la propriété de la ville ou de la contrée qui a su l'acquérir, elle est la propriété de tous les fabricans établis dans celle contrée ou dans cette ville*').
[79] Bozérian, *La Convention Internationale*, 44–6. Bozérian was elected President at the Conference of 1880 and an active participant during the deliberations. He acknowledged that while the draft Art. 6 was based on Art. 19 of the Law of 1857, the ultimate form of Art. 10 did not go far enough because of opposition during the Conference. See also Donzel, *Commentaire et Critique de la Convention Internationale*, 48–9, 268–9; Pelletier and Vidal-Naquet, *La Convention d'Union pour la Protection de la Propriété Industrielle*, 258–67.

The Paris Convention

was an independent concern. The draft Article 6 referred to both trade marks and indications of source, suggesting that their misuse raised similar concerns:

Any product illicitly bearing the trade mark of a manufacturer or trader established in one of the Union countries, or an indication of source of that country, will be prohibited from entry into all other Contracting States, excluded from transit and warehouses, and may be subject to seizure followed, if necessary, by legal action.[80]

Although WIPO's translations equate indications of source with *indications de provenance*,[81] this fails to accurately represent the underlying concept of provenance. Ladas suggests that 'source' does not capture the more holistic sense of geographical origin that *provenance* has in French.[82] While origin is pared down and simply indicates the geographical source of a product, *indications de provenance* conveys a sense of place conventionally associated with certain products.[83] Since this distinction proved to be unsustainably nuanced, subsequent negotiations glossed over it and equated provenance with origin to overcome translation difficulties.[84]

More direct support for reputation protection can be found in the Conference Proceedings of 1880, during discussions of the draft Article 6. The Hungarian delegate questioned the inclusion of false indications of provenance in the draft treaty, suggesting that such concerns are better accommodated under penal law and not industrial property.[85] The Portuguese delegate responded that retaining such a provision was essential as misleading use of geographical indications was particularly injurious, leading to widespread counterfeiting.[86] The corollary was that the regional reputation was an attractive target for dishonest traders thereby unfairly harming legitimate traders' interests, implicit in the French delegate's example of a reputed regional product like Champagne

---

[80] Actes de Paris, 27 (*'Tout produit portant illicitement soit la marque d'un fabricant ou d'un commerçant établi dans l'un des pays de l'Union, soit une indication de provenance dudit pays, sera prohibé à l'entrée dans tous les autres Etats contractants, exclu du transit et de l'entrepôt, et pourra être l'objet d'une saisie suivie, s'il y a lieu, d'une action en justice'*).

[81] For translations of the various iterations of the Paris Convention, see WIPO, *The Paris Convention for the Protection of Industrial Property From 1883–1983* (WIPO, Geneva 1983), 215–23, (hereafter *Paris 1883 to 1983*).

[82] S. P. Ladas, *Patents, Trademarks and Related Rights: National and International Protection* (Harvard University Press, Cambridge MA 1975), 1574.

[83] L. Berard and P. Marchenay, *From Localized Products to Geographical Indications: Awareness and Action* (Centre national de la recherche scientifique, Bourg-en-Bresse 2008), 10 (Provenance implies 'to issue from a place', while for source it is merely 'to be from a place').

[84] Actes de la Haye, 535; Actes de Lisbonne, 796.   [85] Actes de Paris, 64.

[86] Ibid., 65.

38 The Indication of Source

where this was known to occur.[87] Well-known indications of geographical origin were particularly vulnerable targets in the context of international trade, as evinced by the desire to equip *producers with the legal means to defend their interests*.[88] If external rivals could misrepresent their products to be what they were not, this would harm the sales and reputation of honest producers. Revisiting early common law authorities, Mark McKenna reminds us that the established notions of unfair competition at the time put legitimate producers' interests at the core, with consumer protection being used as a limitation device to help define those situations in which competitive conduct would be unfair.[89] The relevant law around this period was therefore incidentally about consumer protection.

While the argument that the IS was more relevant for consumer protection did occasionally resurface at subsequent revision conferences,[90] this exchange emphasises the intertwined reasoning of protecting the intangible value associated with a reputation by preventing fraud and finds resonances within the evolution of trade mark law. Taking the British experience as a comparison, Brad Sherman and Lionel Bently have pointed out that the principal objections to trade marks being included within the intellectual property canon were that while the law of patents or copyright was concerned with the creation and protection of intangible artefacts, trade marks merely sought to prevent falsehoods and were more akin to the criminal law prevention of forgery or fraud.[91] The underlying goodwill that trade marks symbolised gradually

[87] Ibid. ('*Il y a des contrefacteurs qui vendent a l'étranger du vin qualifie de Champagne, par exemple, et qui mettent sur les bouteilles, pour mieux tromper l'acheteur: M. Martin, négociant, à Reims. Or, il n'y a pas à Reims de marchand de vin de Champagne du nom de Martin. De telle sorte que la fraude demeurerait impunie, si l'on ne pouvait pas faire saisir les bouteilles comme portant une fausse indication de provenance*').

[88] Ibid., 63 (according to the Portuguese delegate: '*De plus, elle pourra rendre des services importants en prévenant ceux dont les produits seront contrefaits; en un mot, elle aidera celui qui aura la volonté de défendre ses intérêts*').

[89] M. P. McKenna, 'The Normative Foundations of Trade Mark Law' (2007) 82 *Notre Dame Law Review* 1839. This reasoning would also subsequently be made explicit within the framework of the Madrid Agreement. See Actes de Lisbonne, 792.

[90] Conférence Internationale de l'Union pour la Protection de la Propriété Industrielle (Imprimerie Héritiers Botta, Rome 1886), 118–19, 125, (hereafter, Conférence de Rome) (The Italian delegate argued that this was the concern of consumer protection and penal laws would prevent this sort of dishonest behaviour); Procès-Verbaux de la Conférence de Madrid de 1890 de l'Union pour la Protection de la Propriété Industrielle (Impr. Jent et Reinert, Berne 1892), 84–5, (hereafter, Actes de Madrid) (similarly grounded opposition to the proposed Madrid Agreement).

[91] B. Sherman and L. Bently, *The Making of Modern Intellectual Property Law: The British Experience, 1760–1911* (Cambridge University Press, 1999), 167–72. See also E. Lloyd, 'On the Law of Trade Marks: Nature of the Right to Use a Trade Mark (I)' (1860–1) 5 *Solicitor's Journal and Reporter* 486, 486–7.

The Paris Convention   39

came to be seen as the object of intangible property[92] and, in the British case, the impetus to label this as property arose from the need to attain injunctive relief.[93]

The result was that the IS and trade mark were perceived to share similar justifications for protection. The very first volume of the AIPPI's yearbook (1897) includes a comparative survey of IS legislation. The objectives identified were the protection of domestic consumers against deception concerning the nature and quality of the goods, the protection of all producers belonging to the region reputed for the product as well as the protection of both domestic industry and honest foreign producers against foreign fraudsters.[94] In 1898, Philippe Dunant observed that the usurpation of reputed indications of provenance was a favoured method of unscrupulous traders, in a manner similar to the misleading adoption of trade marks. A key difference was that clearly defined private rights could not be brought to bear in these cases, so actions in general tort or delict were resorted to,[95] where the focus was on the defendant's wrongful conduct instead. Similarly, Joanny Pey asserted that there were cities, regions or countries whose products had collectively gained a reputation and the law should protect this reputation by granting proprietary rights over it.[96] One commentator, writing in 1907, goes so far as to state that once the basis of rights to marks used in commerce has been established, there is no point in making any additional comments for geographical indications of source.[97] Regulating their use protects both consumers who rely on them to indicate origin and quality truthfully, as well as legitimate producers who would otherwise experience a diversion of customers through unfair competition.[98] Therefore by the close of the nineteenth century, indications of source were

---

[92] Lord Parker's statement preferring property in goodwill as opposed to property in the mark or get up itself is considered authoritative. See *Spalding & Brothers* v. *A. W. Gamage Ltd* [1915] 32 RPC 273, 284 (HL).

[93] Sherman and Bently, *The Making of Modern Intellectual Property Law*, 196–9. See also L. Bently, 'From Communication to Thing: Historical Aspects of the Conceptualisation of Trade Marks as Property', in G. Dinwoodie and M. Janis (eds.), *Trade Mark Law and Theory: A Handbook of Contemporary Research* (Edward Elgar, Cheltenham 2008), 3.

[94] J. F. Iselin, 'Des Indications de Provenance' [1897] *Annuaire* 266, 279.

[95] P. Dunant, *Traité des Marques de Fabrique et de Commerce, des Indications de Provenance et des Mentions de Récompenses Industrielles en Suisse, Comprenant l'Étude du Droit Comparé et du Droit International* (Ch. Eggimann, Geneva 1898), 443.

[96] J. Pey, 'Protection des Marques Communales, Regionales, Nationales' [1901] *Annuaire* 119.

[97] L. di Franco, *Le Indicazioni di Provenienza dei Prodotti* (Cavotta, Naples 1907), 31–2.

[98] Ibid., 13–14.

40   The Indication of Source

placed in the conceptual category of unregistered designation protection, alongside trade names.[99] As Ladas put it:

> Trade marks are only one means of distinguishing the goods of one producer from those of another and generally, of protecting advantageous business relations. This end may also be served by the trade name of a producer, by the indication of the place of origin of his products or by any other distinctive badge.[100]

Ladas elaborates on the nature of this protection, as the 'common right to use the name of a place ... by all the producers, manufacturers, or traders of that place, and the right of these persons to exclude others from the use of the same name'.[101]

Having considered the evidence that the IS was included within the Paris Convention on the basis of collective reputation protection, it is useful to also consider why it was excluded from registered trade mark protection of the time, despite apparent similarities in communicative functions and the nature of the intangible interest. The IS differs from a standard trade mark in two significant respects: (1) there is a collective interest in its availability as well as use by those from the designated place, and (2) by definition, it involves the use of a geographical sign, considered *prima facie* descriptive and thus unsuitable subject matter under internationally accepted trade mark registration rules. Each of these aspects made these signs effectively unregistrable as regular trade marks.

Early trade mark registration systems, including those of Britain,[102] the United States[103] and (to a more qualified extent) France,[104] prohibited the registration of geographical terms per se. Writing at the close of the nineteenth century, Arthur Greeley, an Assistant Commissioner of Patents in the US, could confidently state that names 'indicting locality of origin are in very few countries admitted to registration as trade

---

[99] Donzel, *Commentaire et Critique de la Convention Internationale*, 48–9; G. D. Cushing, 'On Certain Cases Analogous to Trade Marks' (1891) 4 *Harvard Law Review* 321, 325–6; P. Roubier, *Le Droit de la Propriété Industrielle*, Vol. 2 (Editions du Recueil Sirey, Paris 1954), 487, 753.

[100] Ladas, *Patents, Trademarks and Related Rights*, 36.   [101] Ibid., 658.

[102] See s. 10 of the Patents, Designs and Trade Marks Act 1888, 51 and 52 Vict, ch. 50. This strictly excluded geographical names from registrability, regardless of the manner in which they were understood by the relevant public.

[103] R. Brauneis and R. E. Schechter, 'Geographic Trade Marks and the Protection of Competitor Communication' (2006) 96 TMR 782, 783 ('Under the dominant interpretation of the Trade Marks Act of 1905, no brand name that consisted of a geographic term could ever be registered as a trade mark, no matter how remote and obscure the place, on the ground that all place names should remain available for use by all competitors').

[104] Pouillet, *Traité des Marques de Fabrique*, 76–7. A geographical sign could be claimed by an individual in modified form or as part of a more complex mark, so long as the simple geographical sign was left available to others.

marks, it being a generally accepted principle that any person has the right to mark goods produced or sold by him with the name of the place of their production'.[105] The geographical nature of the sign in turn contributed to the collective interest puzzle. If *exclusive* use by a single trader was the precondition for a sign becoming distinctive and therefore deemed worthy of registered protection, how would a shifting cloud of collective users be accommodated? Trade mark doctrines such as acquired distinctiveness or secondary meaning, where the relevant public is taught that a descriptive term has come to indicate a particular trade source for specific goods, would not be of any assistance, since there were multiple users to begin with. There was also a countervailing interest to keep geographical signs accessible to other legitimate producers in future. 'Could such phrases, as "Pennsylvania wheat", "Kentucky hemp", "Virginia tobacco" or "Sea Island cotton" be protected as trade marks; could anyone prevent all others from using them, or from selling articles produced in the districts they describe under those appellations, it would greatly embarrass trade, and secure exclusive rights to individuals in that which is the common right of many'.[106] Greeley concludes: 'The name of the locality of origin of goods is not in most countries registrable as a trade mark under the law as being descriptive, as well as being a mark which might rightfully be used by others'.[107] This principle of exclusion would find a place in the Paris Convention as part of Article 6*quinquies*(B), which states that trade marks may be denied registration or invalidated 'when they are devoid of any distinctive character, or consist exclusively of signs or indications which may serve, in trade, to designate the kind, quality, quantity, intended purpose, value, *place of origin*, of the goods' (emphasis added). Therefore revisiting the history of the IS proves instructive because it begins to account for the swarm of disparate institutional mechanisms claiming to regulate origin marking and reveals a collectively generated reputation to be the valuable intangible that is the object of the industrial property right while identifying the conceptual and pragmatic reasons for treating them as a distinct category from trade marks.

2.2   The scope of protection: Articles 9 and 10

In the preceding paragraphs we have identified the work the IS was implicitly understood to do. It not only communicated origin, but for

---

[105] A. P. Greeley, *Foreign Patent and Trade Mark Laws: A Comparative Study* (John Byrne & Co, Washington DC 1899), 134.

[106] *Delaware and Hudson Canal Company* v. *Clark* 80 US 311, 324 (1871).

[107] Greeley, *Foreign Patent and Trade Mark Laws*, 160.

42   The Indication of Source

certain reputed regional products such as the wines of Bordeaux or the cutlery of Sheffield, a reputation for quality rode upon this origin reference. To protect this reputation, reserving the use of this geographical term to those based within the eponymous region and strictly preventing its use by external rivals was the initial approach adopted at the Paris negotiations. This proved unsuccessful and the Convention provisions provide for an unexceptional level of protection. These standards can be satisfied by a number of different legal regimes which regulate labelling and are in principle available in most jurisdictions. Nonetheless it has taken a sustained effort to reach even these modest levels of protection under Article 10, a measure of the controversy surrounding GI protection from its inception.

Retracing these debates around the scope of protection is illuminating for the cracks and fissures revealed at the time when foundations were being laid in this area. The Paris Convention currently prohibits the use of a false indication of source in the following terms:

Article 10

(1) The provisions of [Article 9] shall apply in cases of direct or indirect use of a false indication of the source of the goods or the identity of the producer, manufacturer or merchant.
(2) Any producer, manufacturer or merchant, whether a natural person or a legal entity, engaged in the production or manufacture of or trade in such goods and established either in the locality falsely indicated as the source, or in the region where such locality is situated, or in the country falsely indicated, or in the country where the false indication of source is used, shall in any case be deemed an interested party.

Here Article 9 is referenced since it outlines potential remedies for trade marks and trade name infringements. According to the current version of Article 9, goods in respect of which a false indication of source is used have to be (1) seized upon importation, (2) seized in the country where the false indication has been affixed, (3) seized within the country of importation, if they make it past customs, (4) barred from importation, or (5) subject to other actions and remedies available in such cases to nationals under the law of the country in question.[108] However, goods in transit through a Union country are not affected by this treaty

---

[108] Art. 9 states

(1) All goods unlawfully bearing a trade mark or trade name shall be seized on importation into those countries of the Union where such mark or trade name is entitled to legal protection.
(2) Seizure shall likewise be effected in the country where the unlawful affixation occurred or in the country into which the goods were imported.

The Paris Convention   43

obligation. On the question of who can initiate proceedings, seizure shall take place at the request of the public prosecutor, any other competent authority or any interested party (Article 9(3)). As seen above, an interested party is defined in Article 10(2) to include legitimate producers, manufacturers or merchants of the relevant goods from the place falsely indicated. Since the interest in a geographical designation is collective,[109] Article 10*ter* allows federations and associations representing the interests of producers to take action, provided that these associations are recognised by the laws of Union countries and actions by such collective activities are permitted by national law.[110]

For Article 10, the key question is this – when is the use of an IS considered to be false? Ladas proposed a two-step test for this.[111] First ask whether the putative geographical sign on the product is actually understood by the relevant public[112] to be an indication of geographical source. Then one simply tests for whether the product actually originates in the indicated place. Evaluating the geographical import of a term 'depends solely on the understanding among the general public and the legal interpretation in the country in which protection is provided. It is these that determine whether a geographical indication is a protected indication of source or an unrestricted generic name or a fantasy

---

(3) Seizure shall take place at the request of the public prosecutor, or any other competent authority, or any interested party, whether a natural person or a legal entity, in conformity with the domestic legislation of each country.

(4) The authorities shall not be bound to effect seizure of goods in transit.

(5) If the legislation of a country does not permit seizure on importation, seizure shall be replaced by prohibition of importation or by seizure inside the country.

(6) If the legislation of a country permits neither seizure on importation nor prohibition of importation nor seizure inside the country, then, until such time as the legislation is modified accordingly, these measures shall be replaced by the actions and remedies available in such cases to nationals under the law of such country.

[109] Bodenhausen, *Guide to the Application of the Paris Convention*, 140 ('The difficulty in these cases is that a geographical indication is generally not privately owned, so that contrary to the situation which prevails regarding trade marks ... there is no owner or other person obviously competent to object to the use of false geographical indications').

[110] It is significant because of the general principle that a claimant needs to establish a legally recognised interest which is threatened, as a prerequisite. It was difficult for representative trade associations – not in the business of actually selling any products – to establish *locus standi* on this basis.

[111] Ladas, *Patents, Trademarks and Related Rights*, 1581.

[112] There have been occasional attempts to flesh out this 'public'. See, e.g., WIPO Director General's Memorandum, 'Basic Proposals – Supplement to PR/DC/3', 30 August 1979 (PR/DC/4), [37] ('The misleading effect must exist in respect of "the public," which, in this case, probably means the average consumer, a person considering buying or buying the goods in question with an average knowledge of geography and paying average attention to the possible connection of the said goods with a given country').

44   The Indication of Source

designation'.[113] Consumer expectations would need to be betrayed in some sense to trigger this prohibition. If consumers do expect the product to originate from the designated place, then falsehood is determined by a simple binary test. If the products do not originate from there, the test is satisfied.[114] An illustration, which directly refers to Article 10, is found in a US decision concerning Scotch whisky.[115] The defendant in Panama produced and marketed 'Blended Scotch Whisky', a combination of Scotch malts and locally produced spirits. The district court found this to be in violation of the relevant provisions of both US trade mark law and the Paris Convention as a false designation suggesting Scottish origin for the entire product.

Furthermore, where an expression retains its geographical connotations, general consumer protection legislation, tort law or administrative regimes scrutinising labelling standards – i.e. legal regimes geared towards preventing unfair competition and often indirectly concerned with intellectual property protection – would also prohibit this type of use.[116] French Champagne producers unsuccessfully resorted to s. 52 of the Australian Trade Practices Act 1974 in a situation where Champagne was being used in advertisements for wine imported from countries other than France. Since champagne was considered generic in Australia and not an indication of geographical source, such use was neither misleading nor deceptive.[117] By contrast, celebratory corks would have popped after a New Zealand decision which held that the use of Champagne by Australian producers violated s. 9 of the Fair Trading Act 1986.[118] This prohibits misleading or deceptive conduct and the arguments demonstrating passing off[119]

---

[113] R. Knaak, 'The Protection of Geographical Indications According to the TRIPS Agreement', in F-K Beier and G Schricker (eds.), *From GATT to TRIPS – The Agreement on Trade-Related Aspects of Intellectual Property Rights* IIC Studies, Vol. 18, (Weinheim, New York 1996), 117, 120.

[114] L. Baeumer, 'Protection of Geographical Indications under WIPO Treaties and Questions Concerning the Relationship between those Treaties and the TRIPS Agreement', October 1997 (WIPO/GEO/EGR/97/1 Rev), [24] ('As regards the term "false indication," this is an indication which does not correspond to the facts, namely, an indication to a geographical area for products not originating in that area').

[115] *Scotch Whisky Association v. Barton Distilling Company* 489 F 2d 809 (7th Cir. 1973).

[116] See 'Laws Focusing on Business Practises', in WTO, 'Review under Article 24.2 of the Application of the Provisions of the Section of the TRIPS Agreement on Geographical Indications', 24 November 2003 (IP/C/W/253/Rev.1), 6–9.

[117] *Comité Interprofessionnel Du Vin De Champagne v. N. L. Burton Pty Ltd* [1981] 38 ALR 664 (FCA).

[118] *Wineworths Group Ltd v. Comité Interprofessionnelle du Vin de Champagne* (1991) 23 IPR 435 (CA NZ).

[119] The archetypical wrongful conduct in the common law tort of passing off is that a 'man is not to sell his goods under the pretence that they are the goods of another man'. *Perry v. Truefitt* (1842) 6 Beav 66, 73 (Lord Langdale, MR). In *Wineworths* the misleading

The Paris Convention   45

established that there had been misleading use in this case. Thus the form and procedure of IS protection varies depending upon the regimes available in a given jurisdiction. Its effectiveness ultimately hinges upon the semantic reception of the designation in the country of dispute. Will it be understood as indicating the place of origin for the product in question? If not, the aggrieved group of producers have no remedy, even though they believe their reputation is being otherwise misappropriated or misused.

Bearing these limitations in mind, the present incarnation of Article 10 appears somewhat underwhelming to GI proponents. To more fully appreciate the achievements it represents we must undo several layers of amending surgery and study its original face in the text of 1883. As seen previously, the draft Article 6 had introduced an apparently strict prohibition against any illicit use of an IS, but when should the use of a geographical term be considered illicit? For proponents of IS protection, any 'literally false' use of geographical designations was to be presumptively forbidden. This bright line rule became the Holy Grail for those in favour of strong international IS protection.[120] It can be parsed as follows:

(1) If a product bears the indication of geographical origin 'X';
(2) But is in fact not produced in 'X';
(3) Such use should be strictly prohibited.

Here the 'literally false' label is a misnomer, because the objective was to reserve the use of the IGO to those based in 'X', regardless of the manner in which any particular audience actually understood the use of the indication. It would take over a century of international negotiations before something like this was finally achieved in Article 23 of TRIPS, which is considered in Part II of this book. It is unsurprising that such an approach proved unpalatable because it gives undue importance to mere existence on a map as opposed to the manner in which the sign is perceived. An early case exemplifying the antagonism to such a formalistic approach is *Magnolia's Trade Mark Application* for metal products, where the UK trade mark statute excluded the registration of geographical terms.[121] It was established that relatively obscure towns in the United States were named 'Magnolia' and the central issue before the Court of Appeal was to determine the standard for identifying a geographical term. It held that if the primary significance of the mark was

---

use was the suggestion that Australian and French Champagne are qualitatively indistinguishable, making this a member of the family of 'extended' passing off decisions.

[120] See, e.g., Actes de la Haye, 471 (French Proposal suggesting that this rule should apply provided the term was not generic in the 'home' country); WIPO, 'Report Adopted by the Committee of Experts', 15 November 1974 (TAO/I/ 8), [35].

[121] *In Re Magnolia Metal Company's Trade-Marks* [1897] 2 Ch 371 (CA).

46   The Indication of Source

not geographical to the intended (British) audience, it could be registered. Similar concerns surfaced at the Paris Conference of 1880, where the debate turned on whether the scope of protection should be provisional, depending on the meaning conveyed by the sign under dispute.

On 10 November 1880, the Swedish delegate, with considerable foresight, acknowledged that the scope of protection for the IS was a 'delicate' matter. Referring to a dispute between Sweden and Britain concerning the use of 'Lancashire', Sweden considered it to be generic for metal manufactured by a particular process. The situation was resolved by including 'Sweden' after 'Lancashire' on the metal, to clarify that it was used in the generic and not geographical sense.[122] This raises the issue of whether generic use is illicit use. The Court of Justice for the European Union (ECJ) has helpfully described the process of this semantic shift in the following manner:

[A] geographical designation could, over time and through use, become a generic name in the sense that consumers cease to regard it as an indication of the geographical origin of the product, and come to regard it only as an indication of a certain type of product. That shift in meaning occurred for instance in the case of the designations 'Camembert' and 'Brie'.[123]

Here the sign in question no longer has origin salience, instead referring to the general category of product. Therefore if the basis for protecting a GI is to preserve its ability to communicate the product's origin, generic usage is fatal to this ability. Generic status continues to be intensely disputed territory and was controversial during the formative Paris negotiations. The Norwegian delegate considered champagne to be a generic term for a process of manufacture, similar to eau de Cologne,[124] while the President for the session clarified that the purpose of the draft Article 6 was to capture false (i.e. misleading) and therefore illicit indications (*'l'indication mensongère de provenance, et dans le mot illicitement'*) and not prevent the use of generic expressions such as Russian leather, velvet from Utrecht or eau de Cologne which were general descriptions in the public domain.[125] Alongside the generic use of formerly geographical terms, the Swiss representative referred to the inveterate practices of traders who made inaccurate uses of place names, leading to question marks over the practical enforceability of any such legal prohibition.[126] The Belgian delegate conceded the tension between the competing viewpoints, by recognising the moral heft of the proposed article and chastising such

---

[122] Actes de Paris, 85.
[123] *Commission of the European Communities* v. *Federal Republic of Germany* (C-132/05) [2008] ECR-I 957; [2008] ETMR 32, [36] ('Parmesan').
[124] Actes de Paris, 86.   [125] Ibid., 88.   [126] Ibid., 84–5.

The Paris Convention 47

literally false uses as blameworthy, yet stating that the inertia of inveterate trade practices was too great to be halted.[127] Around this period, there is evidence to suggest that the interests of domestic sectoral lobbies in being allowed to make loose usage of foreign geographical terms was considered potentially as imperative as protecting consumer interests in honest labelling.[128] Finally, there was determined opposition to the mandatory prohibition against entry into a country in the draft Article 6, especially since customs authorities would be the arbiters for deciding whether an IS was false. The delegates from the Netherlands and Italy were concerned about this enforcement mechanism, especially in the absence of any judicial determination on infringement, while the Russian representative expressed concerns about the additional burden which would fall upon customs officials to verify the legality of marks.[129] Representatives from Switzerland, Turkey and Venezuela[130] were also concerned by the possibility that goods in transit could be held up on these grounds, which would presumably affect their transportation service sectors. This supports the argument made through this book that, despite the prominence given to doctrinal developments in the literature, international GI protection was negotiated within a broader network of international trade concerns right from the start.

As a result of these misgivings, what emerged was a highly qualified prohibition. The original official text of Article 10 read as follows:

The provisions of [Article 9] shall apply to any goods which falsely bear as an indication of source the name of a specified locality, when such indication *is joined to a trade name of a fictitious character or used with fraudulent intention.*
Any manufacturer or trader engaged in the manufacture of or trade in such goods and established in the locality falsely indicated as the source shall be deemed an interested party (emphasis added).[131]

It was thus restricted to rare cases of blatant, compound fraud thereby rendering it effectively superfluous as this was invariably covered by criminal law or other labelling laws. In light of the stated need to

---

[127] Ibid., 88 (*'Trouve la disposition très morale, mais bien difficile à mettre en pratique. Il faut, en effet, reconnaître qu'un nombre considérable de produits portent une indication mensongère de lieu de provenance. Il considère qu'il est dangereux de vouloir entrer en lutte avec des habitudes, des usages, certainement mauvais et blâmables, mais absolument invétérés, et qu'en agissant ainsi, on compromettrait le succès de la Convention, car il n'y a aucun Gouvernement qui puisse s'engager sérieusement à exécuter les dispositions de l'article 6'*).

[128] See Ladas, *Patents, Trademarks and Related Rights*, 40; T. Trinchieri, 'Moyens d'Obtenir de Nouvelles Adhésions, Particulièrement l'Adhésion de l'Italie à l'Arrangement de Madrid sur les Fausses Indications de Provenance' [1902] *Annuaire* 17 (identifying this as the basis for Italian opposition to joining Madrid).

[129] Actes de Paris, 79–80.   [130] Ibid., 81–2, 82–3, 87.

[131] The English translation of the original text is provided in *Paris 1883 to 1983*, 216.

48   The Indication of Source

preserve 'inveterate trade practices' and generic use, Article 10 had emerged as a cautious compromise. The example of compound fraud suggested is the illicit use of 'Bernard, a manufacturer of watches in Geneva' when neither is there any such Bernard, nor are the watches produced in Geneva.[132] An alternative to the fictitious trade name was to otherwise prove fraudulent intention, which posed a high evidentiary threshold. The focus thus remains on identifying undeniably blameworthy conduct, rather than on the possible effects of the sign upon its audience. The original Article 10 did not cover a situation where an IS by itself was used misleadingly. Similarly, Article 9 was watered down, stating that goods bearing false marks or indications *may* be seized on importation, depending on whether each Union signatory thought it appropriate and provided for it in national legislation.[133]

Dissatisfaction with the enfeebled text of Article 10 swiftly surfaced and proposals for amendment were made as early as 1886, at the first revision conference in Rome. The French representative sought to clarify the relationship between Articles 9 and 10, so that seizure (where possible) was not just restricted to the 'home' country, i.e. the country containing the place falsely indicated, but could be effected in any Member.[134] The Belgian delegation desired reassurances that traders placing orders from abroad and making a request for the products to be marked with the trader's country of residence should not be held liable on the basis of a fraudulent intention.[135] The example given was of an English manufacturer who orders rifles from Liège in Belgium, but asks for them to bear his own name and place of business.[136] Both these proposals once again allude to the complex web of international trade flows surrounding GI protection debates and the diverse interests affected by Article 10. Yet surprisingly one of the earliest proposals for substantive reform came from Great Britain, not usually visible at the forefront of GI protection campaigns. Britain proposed to drop the fraudulent trade name requirement from Article 10 and simply require that every product which unlawfully carried a false indication of source could be seized upon importation in all contracting countries.[137]

---

[132] Actes de Paris, 100–2.

[133] Seizure would only become mandatory at the Washington conference, in the sense that where the mechanisms for seizure already existed in national laws, a Member would be obliged to operationalise this. See Actes de la Conférence de Washington (Bureau de l'Union, Berne 1911), 302–3, (hereafter, Actes de Washington).

[134] Conférence de Rome, 12–13.   [135] Ibid., 91.   [136] Ibid., 121

[137] Conférence de Rome, 92 ('*Tout produit portant illicitement une indication mensongère de provenance pourra être saisi à l'importation dans tous les pays contractants*').

The Paris Convention 49

This was subject to the proviso that generic names, determined as such by a court in the country where a dispute arose, could still be used freely.[138]

This uncharacteristic zeal has its origins in correspondence between the Cutler's Company of Sheffield, the Foreign Office and the Board of Trade between 1884 and 1886.[139] The complaint of the Cutler's company was that hardware, and more specifically cutlery such as knives, falsely bearing the indication 'Sheffield' were appearing in France and Germany.[140] For various reasons including reciprocity requirements in national laws and the desire for generating a single international rule, existing national regimes were considered inadequate to address this. The additional false trade name requirement in the original Article 10 made it effectively useless in situations where producers in Germany were stamping 'Sheffield' alone on their products.[141] The Cutler's company was sufficiently concerned by the fraudulent use of Sheffield that it sent two representatives to attend the Rome conference.[142] Thus the introductory background to the British proposal mentions the fraudulent use of Sheffield, as well as the familiar two-pronged assault on the reputation of the locality falsely implicated as well as injury to consumers, who are misled into purchases on the basis of that reputation.[143] Concerns about preserving generic use were addressed, since national courts retained the authority to decide whether a term was generic. There is also overt reference to the need for rights of communities to be recognised and protected within the Paris framework.[144] This theme is picked up during the discussions by M. Nicolas of France, where he endorsed the view that manufacturers in towns can acquire a reputation

---

[138] Ibid., ('*Les tribunaux de chaque pays auront a décider quelles sont les appellations, qui, a raison de leur caractère générique, échappent aux présentes dispositions*').

[139] Papers relative to Conference at Rome on Industrial Property; Correspondence relating to Fraudulent Use of Trade Marks 60 PP 413 [C.4837] (1886), (hereafter, Rome Correspondence).

[140] See the Letters and Enclosures from the Cutlers' Company outlining the complaint to the Foreign Office, who in turn corresponded with the Board of Trade, Rome Correspondence, 1–2.

[141] The ambition was therefore to remove the additional false trade name requirement. See the letter from the Board of Trade to the Foreign Office, 4 April 1885, ibid., 5.

[142] The Board of Trade appointed Mr Henry Reader Lack, Comptroller-General of Patents, Designs and Trade Marks to be the delegate of Great Britain. He was accompanied Mr Charles Belk, the Master Cutler of the Sheffield Cutlers' Company and Mr Herbert Hughes, Secretary of the Sheffield Chamber of Commerce, to assist him in securing the proposed amendments. They were joined by Mr Bergne, Superintendent of the Treaty Department, of the Foreign Office. Rome Correspondence, 14–15.

[143] Conférence de Rome, 92–3.

[144] Ibid., 93 ('*La Convention de 1883 consacre les droits des individus. Consacrons dans cette Conférence des droits plus étendus, ceux des communautés, qui étant composées de plusieurs individus, sont à plus forte raison dignes d'être protégées*').

50   The Indication of Source

through centuries of honest toil and this subsequently belongs to the community of manufacturers, in a similar manner to the protection of individual trading reputations.[145] The Tunisian delegate, M. Pelletier, further endorsed the legitimacy of protecting town or city names by equating them with the protection of individual names.[146] An emerging consensus therefore supported the protection of collective local or regional reputations through the vector of the IS.

However, this conceptualisation did not circulate unopposed. According to M. Monzilli, the Italian delegate, these amendment proposals did not relate to the protection of industrial property. On the one hand, enhanced restrictions on origin marking could strengthen protectionism and enable parochial programmes favouring the products of national industry, since all marks of geographical origin and not just reputed ones were being protected. He asked why relative unknowns such as hats from Sheffield or buttons from Paris were included within the ambit of this proposal designed to protect collective reputations. His second criticism was that such rules were designed to protect consumers and defending their interests alone did not justify their inclusion within an industrial property convention.[147] Such frauds were considered criminal acts and best dealt with under criminal law.[148] Despite opposition from Italy the amendment proposal was ultimately passed,[149] but to little avail, since the acts signed at the conference of Rome were not subsequently ratified by Union countries.[150] Yet preparatory work on this issue was not entirely squandered. In the next Section, we see that this initiative ultimately contributed to the formation of the Madrid Agreement but Article 10 itself remained unchanged, and it would continue to be criticised for its limited scope.[151]

No significant changes were made until the Lisbon conference of 1958, where BIRPI proposed that Article 10 prohibit importation of 'any product which bears *directly or indirectly* a *false or misleading* indication of origin' (emphasis added).[152] Use which is misleading without

---

[145] Ibid., 117 ('*Cômme les fabricants, les villes, telles que Sheffield, Paris, ont aussi un nom, une réputation, acquis par des siècles de travail honnête et glorieux; ce nom appartient à la collectivité des fabricants de ces villes, il a le même droit à la protection que celui des particuliers*').
[146] Ibid., 118.   [147] Ibid., 116–17.   [148] Ibid., 119.   [149] Ibid., 120–1.
[150] Ladas, *Patents, Trademarks and Related Rights*, 74–5.
[151] The limitations were significant: seizure was not mandatory but only optional; the proscription was limited to names of a specified locality; this false IS needed to be joined with a fictitious trade name or used with fraudulent intention; and Art. 10 only applied to indications appearing on the product itself. WIPO, 'Present Situation and Possible New Solutions', 28 June 1974 (TAO/I/2), [14]–[22].
[152] Actes de Lisbonne, 777–9.

The Paris Convention   51

being strictly false would include the prominent mention of 'Milan' on fashionable shirts produced in Milan, Michigan.[153] Due to the dubious objection by South Africa that 'misleading' was a vague standard and would be applied differently by national courts, the specific proposal failed to pass.[154] However, some progress was achieved as (1) the prohibition now covered direct or indirect use of a false indication; and (2) the additional 'fictitious or fraudulent trade name' requirement was at long last dropped. For illustrations of the direct use of a false indication, the reader is invited to consider the allure of Paris on perfumes produced outside the French capital. A fragrance producer based in Brussels, although formerly resident in Paris for many years, was disentitled to the use of 'Paris' in its trading name as it would be construed as a misleading use concerning a city reputed for its perfumery.[155] Malodorous uses of Paris by those based elsewhere rankled sensibilities in the decisions of the Industrial Property Department of Brazil on 6 December 1966 ('*Principe de Paris*') and the Supreme Court of the Canton of Zurich on 16 May 1949.[156] In the US, 'Maid in Paris' for perfume was held to be geographically deceptive and thus unsuitable as a trade mark, as it would materially affect the purchasing decision of consumers.[157] By contrast, the notion of an indirect false indication still requires the target audience to consider the sign as a geographical indication (and not a fanciful or generic term) but covers a broader spectrum of insinuations. Professor Beier provides several examples of this from German case law, such as the image of the Cologne Cathedral used on goods from outside of Cologne, the use of a British Coat of Arms or foreign flags on goods which are made in Germany and the use of Cyrillic characters on Vodka not made in Russia.[158]

The scope of Article 10 can therefore be recapitulated as follows: while it no longer requires an additional fraudulent trade name to be triggered, (1) the indication in question (whether word or device, direct or indirect) must be understood by the relevant consumers to indicate the geographical origin of the product; and (2) the product does not in

---

[153] WIPO, 'The Need for a New Treaty and its Possible Contents', [13] (use is misleading while not literally false, where two 'areas in different countries have the same name but only one of those areas is internationally known for particular products').

[154] Actes de Lisbonne, 788.

[155] *Paris Perfume* [1963] *Industrial Property* 225 (Brussels CA, 17 November 1961).

[156] Cited by A. Devletian, 'The Protection of Appellations of Origin and Indications of Source' (1968) *Industrial Property* 107, 114–15.

[157] *In re Richemond* 131 USPQ 441 (TTAB 1961).

[158] F-K. Beier, 'The Protection of Indications of Geographical Origin in the Federal Republic of Germany', in H. C. Jehoram (ed.), *Protection of Geographic Denominations of Goods and Services* (Sijthoff & Noordhoff, Netherlands 1980), 11, 28.

52   The Indication of Source

fact originate in that region. The desire to preserve truthful commercial communication still beats strongly at the heart of such protection. The uphill struggle to achieve even these moderate levels of protection is a reminder of the contingency of a sign's geographical message and the perceived magnitude of the trading interests at stake for negotiators. Controversy is no stranger to early IGO protection debates.

2.3   Alternative possibilities?

The Paris Convention contains two further sets of provisions which generated conversations about IGO protection but were subsequently marginalised.[159] It proscribes conduct amounting to unfair competition and mandates that all its members accept collective marks within the fold of registered trade mark protection. These provisions are worth considering, since this book sets out to challenge the view that contemporary GI protection, as a distinct regime within IP law, has an essential or natural form. The early experimentation with alternative avenues is also worth recalling since each of these options continues to surface in contemporary debates. We therefore briefly consider their viability as workarounds to the limitations faced by the IS, while reinforcing the insight that a collective reputation was the intangible at stake in the IS debates.

2.3.1   Unfair Competition Prevention under Article 10bis

When considering the definition of industrial property earlier in this chapter, we noted that prohibitions on false designations of manufacturing, trading or geographical origin were occasionally gathered together under the umbrella category of unfair competition prevention. This reflects a position adopted under several national regimes: 'Most countries take the view that protection for geographical indications of source including appellations of origin falls in the area of unfair competition'.[160] In European jurisdictions in particular, there is an enduring view that the rules governing indications of origin are a subset of this broader

---

[159] A third possibility is Art. 6ter, whose purpose is to protect armorial bearings, flags and other state emblems of the signatories to the Paris Convention as well as official signs and hallmarks indicating control and warranty. While there are registrations for state hallmarks or official signs indicating control and warranty, there does not seem to be much scope for IGO protection. See WIPO, 'Article 6ter of the Paris Convention: Legal and Administrative Aspects', 14 October 2003 (SCT/5/3), [10]–[12]; Bodenhausen, *Guide to the Application of the Paris Convention*, 94–103.

[160] F-K. Beier, 'The Contribution of AIPPI to the Development of International Protection against Unfair Competition', in AIPPI *1897–1997 Centennial Edition* (AIPPI Foundation, Basle 1997), 299, 309.

The Paris Convention   53

category.[161] Once again this highlights the initial parallel trajectories of trade mark and IGO protection. Just as trade marks had been situated within the broader field of unfair competition prevention,[162] IS protection was initially conceived of in similar terms.[163] What's more, TRIPS includes an overt reference to the unfair competition provisions of the Paris Convention, when setting out the scope of GI protection.[164] Yet a question left unasked is this: what is the significance of suggesting that, like trade mark law, the IS was also considered to belong to the family of rules preventing unfair competition? Additionally, since Article 10 has proved relatively toothless, does Article 10*bis* contain greater potential for the protection of IGOs? In developing a response, we begin by considering the text of Article 10*bis*:

(1) The countries of the Union are bound to assure to nationals of such countries effective protection against unfair competition.

(2) Any act of competition contrary to honest practices in industrial or commercial matters constitutes an act of unfair competition.

(3) The following in particular shall be prohibited:

    1. all acts of such a nature as to create confusion by any means whatever with the establishment, the goods, or the industrial or commercial activities, of a competitor;

    2. false allegations in the course of trade of such a nature as to discredit the establishment, the goods, or the industrial or commercial activities, of a competitor;

---

[161] See M. Dufourmantelle, *De la Concurrence déloyale à l'aide de fausses indications sur la provenance des produits* (impr. de Berger-Levrault, Nancy 1895); E. Ulmer, 'Unfair Competition Law in the European Economic Community' [1973] IIC 188, 199–200; F. Henning-Bodewig and G. Schricker, 'New Initiatives for the Harmonisation of Unfair Competition Law in Europe' [2002] EIPR 271, 273; C. Wadlow, 'Unfair Competition in Community Law – Part 1: The Age of the "Classical Model"' [2006] EIPR 433, 440.

[162] O. R. Mitchell, 'Unfair Competition' (1896) 10 *Harvard Law Review* 275, 275 ('Logically speaking, the fact is that Unfair Competition is properly a generic title, of which trade mark is a specific division'); E. Rogers, 'Industrial Property' (1929) 27 *Michigan Law Review* 491, 497 ('Unfair competition, or better, unfair trading seems to us to be the genus – trade mark infringement, passing off, false indications of geographical origin, false trade descriptions . . . seem to be merely species of the genus').

[163] Actes de la Conférence Réunie a Londres (Bureau de l'Union, Berne 1934) 423, (hereafter, Actes de Londres) (according to the Italian delegate, the similarity was evident although the responses varied: '*Les marques, les indications de provenance et la répression de la concurrence déloyale sont, affirma-t-elle, des instruments destinés à protéger la bonne foi et à faciliter l'industrie et le commerce. Leurs rapports sont communs et leur action est souvent parallèle; seule la réglementation est différente*').

[164] Art. 22.2(b) stipulates that 'Members shall provide the legal means for interested parties to prevent . . . any use which constitutes an act of unfair competition within the meaning of Article 10*bis* of the Paris Convention (1967)'.

54   The Indication of Source

3. indications or allegations the use of which in the course of trade is liable to mislead the public as to the nature, the manufacturing process, the characteristics, the suitability for their purpose, or the quantity, of the goods.

At first glance, Article 10*bis*(2) appears broad enough to cover not just using another's sign so as to create misrepresentations as to origin, but possibly even pure misappropriation or free riding in the absence of any misrepresentation.[165] Therefore two lines of enquiry are pursued: (1) What is the substantive prescriptive content of Article 10*bis*, which is then obligatory to translate into national law? (2) To what extent does it specifically refer to signs indicating geographical origin?

In attempting to unpack the content of unfair competition, we are swiftly ushered into a hall of mirrors, for this legal category varies considerably in form and effect across jurisdictions. However, the sentiment is easily grasped:

The law of unfair competition has developed in part also in response to a general feeling that the honest and fair-dealing merchant is entitled to the fruits of his skill and industry, and must be protected against loss caused by fraudulent and unfair methods used by business rivals. It is a recognition by the courts of the duty to be honest and fair in all relations of business life ... The gradual judicial development of this doctrine is an embodiment of the principles of sound common sense, business morality, although it involves nice discriminations between what may and what may not be done in honourable business rivalry.[166]

One experienced commentator emphasises the scrutiny of marketplace conduct as its object.

Despite all their differences, all European countries have developed mechanisms based on the principle of fairness to control commercial activities. The fact that details are disputed ... does not affect the basic common conviction that market conduct should be fair in the interests of all market participants and that there must be some rules to secure this fairness.[167]

---

[165] This is controversial conduct in intellectual property debates. P. Drahos, 'Introduction', in P. Drahos and R. Mayne (eds.), *Global Intellectual Property Rights: Knowledge, Access and Development* (Palgrave MacMillan, New York 2002), 3–4 ('A free rider is a person who takes the benefit of an economic activity without contributing to the costs needed to generate that benefit. In the case of intellectual property, the free rider takes the benefit of information [or goodwill for commercial signs] for which the costs ... have been met by the producer'). For criticisms of the unreflexive impulse to prevent free riding, see M. A. Lemley, 'Property, Intellectual Property, and Free Riding' (2005) 83 *Texas Law Review* 1031; D. Gangjee and R. Burrell, 'Because You're Worth It: *L'Oréal* and the Prohibition on Free Riding' (2010) 73 *Modern Law Review* 282.

[166] H. D. Nims, *The Law of Unfair Business Competition* (Baker, Voorhis & Co, New York 1909), iii–iv.

[167] F. Henning-Bodewig, *Unfair Competition Law: European Union and Member States* (Kluwer Law International, The Hague 2006), xv.

The Paris Convention   55

At various points of time, the following types of marketplace misconduct have been included within its capacious remit:

(1) causing confusion with respect to another's enterprise or activities;
(2) misleading the public about one's own or another's goods;
(3) discrediting another's enterprise or activities;
(4) damaging goodwill or reputation through non-confusing associ-
     ations (e.g. dilution by blurring);
(4) unauthorised appropriation of secret or confidential commercial
     information;
(5) enticement of a competitor's employees;
(6) inducing breach of contract;
(7) bribery;
(8) misappropriation or pure free riding upon another's investment;
(9) false claims to testimonials of merit;
(10) intimidation or obstruction in the course of business dealings;
(11) unfair advertising including intrusive, misleading and comparative
     advertising;
(12) slavish imitation; and
(13) exploitative sales promotions.[168]

For greater analytical clarity, Michael Spence suggests that from an
intellectual property perspective, unfair competition consists of three
intersecting categories of norms against misrepresentation, denigration
and misappropriation.[169] These categories are not static, inviting a
flexible response. Justice Brandeis concluded almost a century ago that
any 'enumeration, however comprehensive, of existing methods of
unfair competition must necessarily prove incomplete, as with new
conditions constantly arising novel unfair methods would be devised
and developed'.[170]
Even this preliminary survey suggests the following three points.
First, a glance at the list reveals that some types of misconduct have
little to do with intellectual property, being more appropriately located
within the domains of contract, tort, consumer protection or criminal

---

[168] WIPO, *Model Provisions on Protection against Unfair Competition: Articles and Notes*
(WIPO Publication No 832, Geneva 1996); K. Misegades, 'The Scope of the Law of
Unfair Competition' (1932) 14 *Journal of the Patent and Trademark Office Society* 763,
764–5; WIPO, *Protection against Unfair Competition: Analysis of the Present World
Situation* (WIPO Publication No. 725(E), Geneva 1994), 48, 54–60; T. Alkin,
'Should there be a Tort of 'Unfair Competition' in English Law?' (2008) 3 *Journal of
Intellectual Property Law and Practice* 48, 49.
[169] Spence, *Intellectual Property*, 37.
[170] *Federal Trade Commission* v. *Gratz*, 253 US 421, 437 (1920).

56   The Indication of Source

law. While some argue that the infringement of nominate branches such as copyright or trade marks are also considered to be acts of unfair competition, in turn proposed as the backdrop to all IP protection,[171] certain categories of misconduct do not relate to property at all and the overlap with IP is only partial.[172] Therefore it is unsurprising that both the theoretical underpinnings for this general prohibition[173] and the institutional expression in individual jurisdictions diverge in significant ways. Usually the formal distinction is made between jurisdictions (1) where protection is based on specific legislation, such as the German Gesetz gegen den unlauteren Wettbewerb (UWG);[174] (2) where protection is based on general tort or delict and results in civil liability, such as Articles 1382 and 1383 of the French Civil Code;[175] and finally (3) where a hybrid approach is adopted.[176] Second, in light of the divergent approaches, there is considerable uncertainty as to the most appropriate configuration for reconciling competitor, consumer and general public interests within this legal category. While a tort regime will require the precondition of correlative obligations and rights between competitors, a statutory regime might better accommodate general consumer interests and independently accord consumers (or their representatives) the necessary legal standing to initiate proceedings. These differences have meant that unfair competition harmonisation has a particularly troubled history, even within the European context.[177] Conceptual tension remains as to the relationship between producer and consumer interests that are

---

[171] Ladas, *Patents, Trademarks and Related Rights*, 1675; Sanders, *Unfair Competition Law*, 8.

[172] Bodenhausen, *Guide to the Application of the Paris Convention*, 20, 23.

[173] Four overlapping theories, including *prima facie* tort theory based on conduct causing injury, are identified by Wadlow, *The Law of Passing Off*, 37. From an intellectual property perspective, see also R. M. Hilty, 'The Law against Unfair Competition and its Interfaces', in R. M. Hilty and F. Henning-Bodewig (eds.), *Law Against Unfair Competition: Towards a New Paradigm in Europe?* (Springer, Berlin and New York 2007), 1, 19 (suggesting the protection of investments against misappropriation, where otherwise the result would be a market failure); A. Kamperman Sanders, *Unfair Competition Law* (Clarendon Press, Oxford 1997) (arguing for an unjust enrichment or restitutionary basis).

[174] The most famous version is the Gesetz gegen den unlauteren Wettbewerb (UWG) of 7 June 1909 [1909] RGBl 499, (hereafter, UWG 1909). The law was substantially amended in 2004. On the new law see F. Henning-Bodewig, 'A New Act against Unfair Competition in Germany' [2005] IIC 421.

[175] A. Tunc, 'Unfair Competition – French and European Approaches' (1974–5) 1 *Monash University Law Review* 34.

[176] WIPO, *Protection against Unfair Competition*, 19–21; Sanders, *Unfair Competition Law*, 6, 23; Ladas, *Patents, Trademarks and Related Rights*, 1693–6.

[177] C. Wadlow, 'Unfair Competition in Community Law - Part II: Harmonization becomes Gridlocked' [2006] EIPR 469.

The Paris Convention 57

served by unfair competition law.[178] While these interests often coincide, they also diverge on particular issues and the protection of producer or even competitor interests in isolation can no longer be the principal organising concept for any harmonisation project.[179] Third, the issue of 'where the line should be drawn between fair competition and unacceptable competitive behaviour has created abundant debate and literature'.[180] Does comparative advertising provide useful information about product substitutability to prospective purchasers or allow indolent competitors to boost their image by aligning themselves with market leaders? Does the non-confusing yet 'slavish' imitation of a product, after the expiry of any patent or design protection, drive down prices and improve quality in the marketplace or merely free ride on the efforts of the creator? If we build on the efforts of others in order to learn, innovate and compete more effectively,[181] then when should copying or referencing be proscribed? It is evident that norms of acceptable commercial behaviour are context sensitive and 'the world is as divided now as it has been throughout the [twentieth] century over how far it is legitimate to extend civil obligations which inevitably inhibit the freedom of traders to compete in the course of competition'.[182]

This synopsis makes it clear that since the content of unfair competition diverges at the national level, Article 10*bis* cannot afford to set out a broad mandatory norm. Instead it delegates the task of fleshing out this category to the courts of a Paris Union country where a dispute arises. While some countries have expansive notions of what counts as unfair competition, others are more modest so it is difficult to make generalisations. At its

---

[178] F. Henning-Bodewig, 'International Unfair Competition Law', in R. M. Hilty and F. Henning-Bodewig (eds.), *Law Against Unfair Competition: Towards a New Paradigm in Europe?* (Springer, Berlin 2007), 53, 57; R. W. De Vrey, *Towards a European Unfair Competition Law: A Clash between Legal Families* (Martinus Nijhoff, The Hague 2006), 15, 45–8; P. J. Kaufmann, *Passing off and Misappropriation: An Economic and Legal Analysis of the Law of Unfair Competition in the United States and Continental Europe IIC Studies*, Vol. 9 (Max Planck, Munich 1986), 8.

[179] Wadlow, 'Unfair Competition in Community Law - Part I', 441 ('By [1973] there was widespread agreement that the Franco-German "classical model" of unfair competition law, defined solely by reference to the interests of competitors *inter se*, required revision to take into account the interests of consumers and other market participants').

[180] M. Hopperger and M. Senftleben, 'Protection against Unfair Competition at the International Level – The Paris Convention, the 1996 Model Provisions and the Current Work of WIPO', in R. M. Hilty and F. Henning-Bodewig (eds.), *Law against Unfair Competetion: Towards a New Paradigm in Europe* (Springer, Berlin 2007), 61.

[181] M. Boon, *In Praise of Copying* (Harvard University Press, Cambridge MA 2010); R. Tushnet, 'Copy this Essay: How Fair Use Doctrine Harms Free Speech and How Copying Serves It' (2004) 114 *Yale Law Journal* 546.

[182] W. R. Cornish, 'Genevan Bootstraps' [1997] EIPR 336.

58   The Indication of Source

most prescriptive, Article 10*bis*(2) provides an inductive methodology for determining when conduct is unfair. For instance, Christopher Wadlow suggests that the conduct scrutinised is limited to that between competitors; the standard of fairness is not based on abstract ethical precepts but instead rests on pragmatic considerations; and the prohibited conduct must fall foul of consistent practices of fair trading, as they are actually observed in the relevant market, instead of pious aspirational statements of good behaviour.[183]

The identification of a relatively slender core obligation is borne out by the drafting history. The substantive national treatment obligation in Article 10*bis*(1) was introduced in 1900 and has remained largely unchanged,[184] with the addition at the Washington Revision Conference of 'effective protection'.[185] At the Washington conference, the British proposal to enumerate a list of non-exhaustive, yet commonly proscribed activities was objected to on the basis that it could end up excluding other forms of misconduct.[186] The open ended definition of unfair competition as being 'contrary to honest practices in industrial or commercial matters' contained in Article 10*bis*(2) was first introduced at The Hague revision conference in 1925, along with the first two examples of such undesirable conduct in Article 10*bis*(3), i.e. acts likely to confuse, as well as false allegations which discredit. The debates surrounding the two specific examples reveal that they were included precisely because common agreement could be reached on them, while a broadly inclusive, albeit vague, definition was also desirable.[187] However, amendment proposals which expressly included indications of geographical origin within Article 10*bis* did not succeed.[188] To summarise, given the pre-existing national divergences, Article 10*bis* does not mandate that all signatories to the convention must adopt broad norms against unfair competition, despite occasional unconvincing attempts to argue otherwise.[189] Attempts to introduce provisions specifically relating to IS protection did not succeed. Instead this provision 'establishes a flexible, open minimum standard of protection against unfair competition ...

---

[183] Wadlow, *The Law of Passing Off*, 61–4.

[184] For the initial French proposal on *concurrence déloyale* and its final adoption, see Actes de la Conférence de Bruxelles 1897 et 1900 (Bureau de l'Union, Berne 1901), 140, 164, 411, (hereafter, Actes de Bruxelles).

[185] Actes de Washington, 255.   [186] Ibid., 105, 254, 305.

[187] Reviewed by Wadlow, *The Law of Passing Off*, 81–7.

[188] Such as the French and Italian proposals. See Actes de la Haye, 349–50.

[189] C. Gielen, 'WIPO and Unfair Competition' [1997] EIPR 78 (suggesting that the wide ranging WIPO Model Provisions are 'intended to give effect to [Art. 10*bis*] obligations'); *L'Oréal SA and others* v. *Bellure NV and others* [2007] EWCA Civ 968 [135]–[161].

The Paris Convention   59

Its implementation into national law is allowed to reflect the different traditions and historical sources of unfair competition law'.[190]

One final possibility remains to be considered. On a superficial reading, the proscription against indications likely to mislead the public in the third paragraph of Article 10*bis*(3) could be mobilised for IS protection purposes. Yet here too there are obstacles. For our purposes, the spectral presence in the third paragraph of Article 10*bis*(3) is of interest. At the Lisbon conference in 1958, Austria proposed the additional third paragraph which addressed 'indications or allegations, liable to mislead the public into error as to the nature, (including the mode of manufacture), *origin*, characteristics, usefulness or price of the products' (emphasis added).[191] The US then cast a single opposing vote in the plenary session of the conference and the reference to 'origin' was deleted.[192] This had the effect of curtailing the application of the prohibition against misleading uses in Article 10*bis*(3), to exclude misleading IS situations.[193] Since Article 10*bis* is now incorporated within the GI provisions of TRIPS via Article 22.2(b), it generates considerable ambiguity. Does Article 22 of TRIPS read in the missing 'origin' by implication? An alternate possibility is that since many GIs raise expectations about the nature, manufacturing process or characteristics of the goods, misleading consumers on these grounds ought to be actionable.[194] Once again this treaty obligation is easily satisfied through the availability of general fraud or consumer protection legislation. In conclusion, this brief detour into Article 10*bis* showcases yet again the ontological similarities between trade marks, indications of geographical source and other commercial indications, since the misuse of such signs is considered to be an aspect of unfair competition. Both consumer protection and reputation protection are designated the desirable outcomes. For reasons outlined above it is also unlikely that Article 10*bis* has additional resources to offer for those seeking strong international norms for GI protection.

---

[190] Hopperger and Senftleben, 'Protection against Unfair Competition at the International Level', 63.

[191] Actes de Lisbonne, 711, 725.   [192] Ibid., 790.

[193] It has been suggested that this was a deliberate move to check an expansive international GI protection regime. See J. T. McCarthy and V. Colby Devitt, 'Protection of Geographical Denominations: Domestic and International' (1979) 69 TMR 199, 203.

[194] R. W. Benson, 'Toward a New Treaty for the Protection of Geographical Indications' [1978] *Industrial Property* 127, 131 (considering misleading uses as to quality under Art. 10*bis*). For an example of the application of this principle, see *In re Salem China Co*, 157 USPQ 600 (TTAB 1968) (The Board upheld the trade mark examiner's rejection of AMERICAN LIMOGES on the basis that while it may not mislead as to origin, it would be deceptive as to quality suggesting an equivalence with the French porcelain).

60   The Indication of Source

2.3.2   Collective marks under Article 7bis

This chapter argues that the motivation for including the IS within the Paris Convention was to protect a valuable collective reputation. To that extent the IS debates shared overlapping rationales with registered trade mark protection. Yet recognising a collective interest in a geographical term proved difficult for registration systems that only recognised signs indicating distinctive or individual trade sources. By contrast, the Paris Convention expressly refers to the obligation to recognise collective marks in Article 7*bis*. This provision is of respectable vintage and was first introduced into the text in 1911 in a substantially recognisable form,[195] making it all the more surprising that it remains unexplored. If part of the problem was that the IS could not plug in to registered trade mark systems, here was a way to make it fit. The relative invisibility of Article 7*bis* is a puzzle worth investigating.

According to a recent comprehensive survey of national trade mark registration practices, collective marks are widely protected at the national and regional levels.[196] Synthesising these results, WIPO describes a collective mark, a form of club membership, as follows:

[S]igns which serve to distinguish the goods or services of the association which is the proprietor of the mark from those of other undertakings. The main feature of a collective mark is that it is used as an indication to the relevant public that *goods or services originate from a member of a particular association*. Additional features may include common quality or accuracy, *geographical origin* or other characteristics set by the association (emphasis added).[197]

At this stage, it is helpful to distinguish between collective and certification marks, since they will be considered in greater detail in Part II of this book. A certification mark may be said to constitute:

[A] sign which is used or intended to be used to distinguish goods or services dealt with or provided in the course of trade and certified by the proprietor of the certification mark in relation to origin, material, mode of manufacture of goods or performance of services, quality, accuracy or other characteristics, from other goods or services dealt with or provided in the course of trade but no so certified.[198]

---

[195] Actes de la Washington, 253 (discussion and adoption), 304 (report of the Commission), 333 (final text).

[196] WIPO, 'Summary of Replies to the Questionnaire on Trade Mark Law and Practice (SCT/11/6)', 25 January 2010 (WIPO/STrad/INF/1 Rev), 36–8.

[197] WIPO, 'Technical and Procedural Aspects Relating to the Registration of Certification and Collective Marks', 15 February 2010 (SCT/23/3), [11].

[198] Ibid., [15].

The Paris Convention 61

Certification marks are not specifically regulated by the international treaties, but the ubiquity of the collective mark can be traced to the relevant Paris Convention obligation to recognise them in national legislation.

In relevant part, Article 7*bis* states:

> The countries of the Union undertake to accept for filing and to protect collective marks belonging to associations the existence of which is not contrary to the law of the country of origin, even if such associations do not possess an industrial or commercial establishment.

While substantial concessions were made to national legal orders when determining the terms on which collective marks would be acknowledged,[199] this category has been internationally recognised for approximately a century. One of the conditions for membership within the collectivity can be a geographical origin requirement and there is evidence that, from its inception, the collective mark was seriously considered as a vehicle for achieving IS protection goals.

Along with collective marks, 'regional marks' are first mentioned in a Belgian proposal at Madrid in 1890 to amend the draft Agreement for the Repression of False Indications of Source.[200] At the subsequent revision negotiations in Brussels, a separate project for the registration of '*Marques d'Origine Collectives*' was proposed by BIRPI.[201] Here collective marks of origin, at the scale of both country as well as region, were considered in some detail. For the former, examples were drawn from German and French 'national brand' experiences,[202] while for regional marks the city of Lyon's municipal marking of textiles was the template. Issues arising during these deliberations included the question of who would be best placed to apply for such national or regional marks (national governments, local government representatives from the region in question or private producer collectives), whether recognition as well as protection in the country of origin should

---

[199] Under Art. 7*bis*(2) and (3) each country shall determine the particular conditions under which a collective mark shall be protected and may refuse protection if the mark is contrary to the public interest. Nevertheless, protection shall not be refused to any association which is lawful in the country of origin, on the ground that such association is not established in the country where protection is sought or is not constituted according to the law of the latter country.

[200] Actes de Madrid, 64 (proposed as draft Art. 3*bis*: '*Les marques régionales, municipales ou collectives seront protégées au même titre que les marques individuelles*').

[201] Actes de la Bruxelles, 69–81.

[202] For a study of the 'Unis France' mark, see Études Générales, 'Un Exemple de Marque Collective la Marque «Unis-France»' [1934] *Propriété Industrielle* 191.

62   The Indication of Source

be a precondition and the question of whether the scheme should only incorporate figurative or otherwise distinctive marks,[203] thereby avoiding the problem of having to register geographical word marks considered to be descriptive subject matter. Belgium raised additional concerns directed at the ability of communities – otherwise lacking legally recognised standing – to file for such marks, as well as the degree of oversight required so that such group marks continued to represent a certain standard of quality.[204]

The adoption of a separate agreement on collective marks of origin failed to crystallise and the conference voted instead to treat collective marks in a manner similar to regular trade marks under Article 6.[205] Therefore BIRPI's proposal for the 1911 conference at Washington began by reminding the Union that it had long been a concern that the protection was required for *inter alia* collective marks intended to ensure that products originated in a region or determined place.[206] As we have seen, the solution finally adopted in Article 7*bis* was to streamline all collective marks into the regular workflow of trade mark registration systems. Throughout this period regional origin marks, as a prominent category of collective marks,[207] continued to be discussed. The possibilities are considered in two comprehensive studies published by the Association Internationale pour la Protection de la Propriété Industrielle (AIPPI) in 1901. Moise Amar was 'of the opinion that the system of collective marks ... relating to particular areas would provide a solution to the difficulties arising from the mere protection of a place name'.[208] Pey went even further: 'Undoubtedly, great strides have been made as regards the indication of origin, an issue that relates so closely to that of collective marks, you can almost say that the discussions which led the former may apply to the latter'.[209] A comprehensive international review

---

[203] Contemporary examples would include the ducal crown image accompanying Prosciutto di Parma and the stylised profile of the female tea picker on Darjeeling tea.
[204] Actes de Bruxelles, 91–2.   [205] Ibid., 288–9.
[206] Actes de la Washington, 51–2 ('*On se préoccupe depuis longtemps de la protection des marques collectives destinées à garantir que certains produits sont originaires d'une région ou d'un centre déterminés, ou bien fabriqués ou mis en vente par les membres d'un certain groupement'*).
[207] Other categories included marks indicating minimum standards of quality, membership in professional associations or those indicating trade union membership. For a fascinating study of this last category and the obstacles to integration within mainstream trade mark law, see S. Ricketson, 'The *Union Label* Case: An Early Australian IP Story', in A.T. Kenyon, M. Richardson and S. Ricketson (eds.), *Landmarks in Australian Intellectual Property Law* (Cambridge University Press, Melbourne 2009), 15.
[208] Amar, 'Des Marques Collectives', 115 (author's translation).
[209] Pey, 'Protection des Marques Communales, Regionales, Nationales', 119 (author's translation).

The Paris Convention

of collective marks in 1934 concludes that not only were such marks an excellent instrument for appellation of origin protection, their collective use by producers to indicate regional origin was one of the principal motivations for instituting such marks in the first place.[210] So despite the promising start, why did this option fail to materialise?

There are two plausible responses to this question. The first relates to the incomplete incorporation of collective marks within trade mark registration systems. For a start, the process of incorporation was both sluggish and irregular, so registrability remained uncertain for decades after 1911.[211] The Hague Convention records the lament that as of 1925, at least thirteen Union countries still did not have provisions for registering collective marks.[212] Merely introducing an obligation to assimilate such group marks within a system designed around individual trade marks raised a host of additional complications. There was the fundamental hurdle of the distinctiveness test as the basis for registrability. If distinctiveness meant the ability to distinguish the goods of the registered proprietor from those of others, by indicating an individual trade source for the goods, a geographical collective mark by definition would fail this test. Even if the geographical collective mark could be registered, the applicant association might have to disclaim any exclusive use to the geographical term.[213] If others based in the region but not members of the association could continue to use the geographical sign, how effective would it prove as a guarantee?

Another obstacle was that for a regular trade mark, the applicant was expected to indicate on the application the classes of goods the mark would be applied to. For collective marks simply indicating national origin across a vast range of goods (such as the German Eagle mark), this would prove difficult. Additionally, what counted as use made of the collective mark in the course of trade in order to keep the registration alive? There was no clear consensus on whether use by the members of the association was sufficient, instead of the default rule of use by the proprietor.[214] Furthermore, in situations where an IS was

---

[210] Études Générales, 'La Marque Collective' [1934] *Propriété Industrielle*, 31–2 ('*La marque collective est, dans ce domaine, un instrument excellent, car elle se prête fort bien à être utilisée à titre d'appellation d'origine, par le fait qu'elle n'est mise qu'à la disposition des membres de la collectivité. Aussi fut-il souvent soutenu naguère que la fonction d'indication de provenance était la seule raison d'être de la marque collective*').

[211] Ibid., 39. See also Jaton, *Répression des Fausses Indications*, 60–1; Roubier, *Le Droit de la Propriété Industrielle*, 647.

[212] Actes de la Haye, 248–9.   [213] Actes de Bruxelles, 282–3.

[214] Études Générales, 'La Marque Collective', 36. See also Études Générales, 'La Marque Collective (Part II)' [1934] *Propriété Industrielle* 64, 64–5.

64   The Indication of Source

misleadingly used, actions for damages might be unobtainable due to the requirement for injury to be proved. While individual members might lose out on sales, a representative association might struggle to establish any relevant loss suffered by it.[215]

Thus paying lip service to the acceptance of collective marks within the trade mark fold was all very well, but the devil was in the detail. Their viability as an alternative form of IS protection was also affected by a second set of questions pertaining to the message communicated by such marks. Collective marks of origin were broad enough to include national (or even imperial) marks and there were concerns that state owned national marks would be the focus of protectionist agendas. Impediments to free trade could be achieved via campaigns to encourage the purchasing of domestically produced goods, or as the basis to boycott foreign products instead.[216] Another concern, which partially explains the persistent British opposition to collective mark proposals, related to the absence of any mechanism for ensuring that inspection procedures were in place, such that these marks continued to signify reliable quality.[217] It would take only a few unscrupulous members producing substandard products to destroy the ability of the collective mark to function as a useful guarantee of origin or quality and there was no safeguard against this internal fraud. Finally, if a collective mark was to indicate clearly defined geographical origin, specifying a boundary for this region was necessary and procedures to do so would vary at the national level. There was no consistent set of rules to delineate the region of origin.[218] When aggregated, these factors led to the narrowing of possibilities for international protection and would greatly delay meaningful options for place name protection within the registered trade mark system. Yet during these formative debates, the discussions surrounding Article 7*bis* reinforces the insight that the defence of a collectively established reputation was the prompt for international IS protection.

---

[215] Études Générales, 'De la Protection Internationale des Marques d'Origine' [1896] *Propriété Industrielle* 21, 24.

[216] Roubier, *Le Droit de la Propriété Industrielle*, 653–8; Études Générales, 'La Marque Collective', 32; Pey, 'Protection des Marques Communales, Regionales, Nationale', 121–2.

[217] Actes de Madrid, 125–6; Papers and Correspondence relative to Conference at Madrid on Industrial Property and Merchandise Marks 67 PP 725 [C. 6023] (1890), 40; Papers and Correspondence relative to Conference at Brussels on Industrial Property and Merchandise Marks 92 PP 155 [C. 9014] (1898), 54.

[218] Amar, 'Des Marques Collectives', 115–16; Pey, 'Protection des Marques Communales, Regionales, Nationales', 124.

3. The Madrid Agreement

This chapter concludes with a review of the Madrid Agreement for the Repression of False or Deceptive Indications of Source on Goods of 1891. By the end of the nineteenth century, the limitations of protection premised on the communicative content of a sign became acutely obvious to IS proponents and these limitations persist to date. If the test for infringement turns on whether prospective purchasers are confused or misled, it cannot apply where the sign in question is considered generic for a category (as champagne is in the US), where the relevant public are unfamiliar with the original home country product (such as traditional Bangladeshi textiles replicated externally and sold on the Australian market) or where the use of the sign is qualified to avoid falsely indicating origin (such as 'Swiss Champagne' or 'Roquefort-style cheese'). The vector of the AO and its undergirding *terroir* logic are subsequently mobilised in response to the limits of a truth-telling model. The Madrid Agreement is interesting because it represents the beginning of this transition.

3.1 The scope of protection: Article 1

The Madrid Agreement was established under Article 19 of the Paris Convention, which allows for special agreements within its membership. It was born out of dissatisfaction with the original Article 10 of the Paris Convention, almost before the ink was dry. While the intention was to protect 'celebrated goods' manufactured in a place well known for them,[219] it has not quite proved the runaway success that was initially hoped for, with membership currently at thirty-five contracting parties.[220] Yet deliberations under its aegis reveal a fascinating series of epistemic shifts in the basis for GI protection. The French and British proposals at the Rome Conference of 1886 to extend the scope of Article 10[221] were consolidated into a new compromise by prohibiting all false indications of origin, provided the courts of each member could determine which expressions were generic. Based on this, a draft agreement was presented for discussion at the Madrid conference of 1890. The aspiration was to reach beyond the 'false and fraudulent requirement' and prevent false or distorting indications in any form.[222] While this ambition met with

---

[219] M. Ostertag, 'International Unions for the Protection of Industrial, Literary and Artistic Property' (1926) 25 *Michigan Law Review* 107, 115.

[220] See www.wipo.int/treaties/en/ip/madrid/.

[221] See respectively Conférence de Rome, 12–13, 92–3.

[222] Actes de Madrid, 11 ('*[I]l s'agit maintenant d'atteindre toutes les fausses indications de provenance, quelle que soit la forme sous laquelle elles se produisent*').

66   The Indication of Source

limited success, it remains significant for introducing special provisions for wines, the archetypal subject matter of *sui generis* GI protection. The notion was formally introduced that certain products possess a special and possibly even unique link to their place of origin. This proved influential in not only shaping TRIPS standards but continues to buttress present day proposals favouring the extension of GI protection.

The Madrid Agreement improves upon the Paris Convention in a number of ways. Compared to the restrictive original text of Article 10, the Madrid Agreement addresses a broader range of misleading conduct:

Article 1(1)
All goods bearing a *false or deceptive* indication by which one of the countries to which this Agreement applies, or a place situated therein, is *directly or indirectly* indicated as being the country or place of origin *shall be seized on importation* into any of the said countries (emphasis added).

By jettisoning the additional fraudulent trade name requirement of Article 10, this represented significant advances, albeit only where both the importing country and home country were signatories. Other improvements which were part of the original text of Article 1[223] included the mandatory seizure requirement, the absence of a strict requirement to prove harm or injury resulting from the use of the false indication[224] and the coverage of direct or indirect indications.[225] The sense in which 'indirect indications' was included is subsequently clarified in light of the Brazilian delegate's concerns about designations such as the 'wax of carnauba'. Being a vegetable wax from the carnauba fan palm tree, it is not a direct or literal place name, yet it was suggested that the product was 'indissolubly linked'[226] to its origins in a very specific region, namely the north eastern savannahs of Brazil. Such indirect indications of origin would therefore be included within the scope of protected signs. Finally, the expression '*fallacieuse*' was introduced at the Lisbon conference in 1958.[227] Although the WIPO text translates '*fausse ou fallacieuse*' into 'false or deceptive',[228] 'false or misleading' would be more accurate.[229] To test for the presence of misleading use, the decision maker usually

---

[223] For the original text and an English translation, see Arrangement between Great Britain, Spain, France, Switzerland and Tunis for Prevention of False Indications of Origin on Goods, Madrid, April 1891 Treaty Series No. 13 [C. 6818] (1892).

[224] Considered at Actes de Madrid, 77, 85.   [225] Ibid., 11.

[226] Actes de Londres, 424.   [227] Actes de Lisbonne, 792–3.

[228] Madrid Agreement for the Repression of False or Deceptive Indications of Source on Goods 14 April 1891, 828 UNTS 389 (1972) (WIPO Publication No. 261), 3.

[229] In common law jurisdictions, deception has historical resonances with a mental intention requirement and emphasis on the defendant's conduct, harking back to the tort of deceit.

looks to the effect of the sign's use on the relevant public, even if the defendant is using it innocently. This prohibition also applies to signs that mislead by suggestion and insinuation, such as the use of a particular language or image of a famous national monument, rather than directly using a false place name.[230]

Despite these improvements, for proponents of enhanced place name protection the intrinsic limitations of this model are all too evident. Ultimately, the prohibition still relies on the trigger of consumers being misled as to the origin of the product. Therefore Britain could claim that it gave complete effect to Madrid obligations since its customs regulations, while prohibiting goods marked with misleading indications, would permit the use of 'Cape Port' or 'Swiss Champagne'. In such cases the 'indication of origin consists in the precise mention of the locality from which the goods come' and based on such labels, none would be misled as to the locality from which these products originated.[231]

The other paragraphs of Articles 1 and 2 clarify the situations in which the seizure of infringing goods, or a prohibition on their importation, can be requested in a manner similar to Article 9 of the Paris Convention. Under Article 2, customs authorities constitute the front line and are obliged to seize misleadingly marked goods. The alternative is a demand for seizure from the public prosecutor or other competent authority and they can do so either *ex officio* or at the request of injured parties. There is no mandatory provision enabling injured parties to directly approach customs authorities and, on this, Madrid is less responsive than the present Paris provisions. There is a revealing concession in Article 3 that permits the application of the name or address of the seller on goods of foreign origin, on condition that the place of manufacture is also clearly indicated. During the negotiations, M. Morisseau of Belgium was quick to point out that evolving commercial practices must be kept in mind when regulating origin marking. It was common for manufacturers and retailers to be separate entities and he provided the example of an established trader 'F. M.' in Brussels importing independently manufactured US stoves or other cast iron products. If the product was stamped with 'F. M. of Brussels' on his request, while being shipped from the US,

---

[230] Actes de Lisbonne, 792 ('*Afin d'éviter tout doute et d'éliminer la difficulté de reconnaître l'intention trompeuse, il y aurait lieu d'ajouter tout simplement a l'article premier – ainsi qu'aux autres articles – l'expression <<fallacieuse>> aux termes <<fausse indication>>. Cette dernière se rapporte inexactement a un lieu déterminé de production, tandis que la première peut se rapporter a une indication d'origine fictive utilisée comme indication de provenance, ou a toute autre indication qui pourrait être considérée de provenance*').

[231] Actes de Bruxelles, 303; Report on Unfair Competition, Particularly in Relation to False Marks and Indications [1922] *League of Nations Official Journal* 625, 627.

68   The Indication of Source

it could fall foul of the Madrid provisions. Yet customers would know that the product had been manufactured abroad and would interpret the Belgian trader's mark as an indication that he had selected the product and was willing to sell it under his trading name. Article 3 emerges as a compromise to allow such marking provided the place of manufacture or production is also indicated.

An additional innovation is found in Article 3*bis*, which expands the range of contexts in which misleading uses will be recognised:

[Signatories] undertake to prohibit the use, in connection with the sale or display or offering for sale of any goods, of all indications in the nature of publicity capable of deceiving the public as to the source of the goods, and appearing on signs, advertisements, invoices, wine lists, business letters or papers, or any other commercial communication.

This extends the scope of protection to other informative material associated with the product and was introduced at the London conference.[232] As a result of these provisions, protection against infringing uses was considerably strengthened when compared synchronically with the Paris Convention. Yet the ambition of countries such as France to prevent any literally false use of geographical names was threatened by an exception permitting generic uses.

3.2   Generic terms: Article 4

The compromise at the core of the Madrid Agreement is revealed in Article 4, which states that:

The courts of each country shall decide what appellations, on account of their generic character, do not fall within the provisions of this Agreement, regional appellations concerning the source of products of the vine being, however, excluded from the reservation specified by this Article.

Thus if a national court decides that a particular term has become generic (e.g., dijon mustard), its use on products from places other than the place bearing that name is not considered misleading under Article 1. However, viticultural products are excluded from this judicial scrutiny and their designations are *de jure* inoculated. The general provision in Article 4 is predictable, the issue of generic use having been considered extensively during the Paris negotiations. For our purposes, of far greater interest is the exceptional status for products of the vine.

The original draft of this provision contained a straightforward rule exempting all generic expressions from Article 1 scrutiny and was passed

---

[232] Actes de Londres, 201.

The Madrid Agreement

by the delegates, whereupon the Portuguese delegate proposed an additional rider to this rule.[233] M. De Oliveira Martins recommended that *all agricultural products* should be excluded as they could never become merely descriptive of a type or class. He distinguished between industrial or manufactured products such as eau de Cologne or Russian leather which were susceptible to the vagaries of genericide as they could be reproduced anywhere and, by contrast, agricultural products such as the wines of Bordeaux, which were *uniquely* causally linked to the climate and *terroir* of a particular region. Designations for such products could never legitimately be used in a generic sense.[234]

It is therefore on 8 April 1890 that *terroir* makes its appearance in multilateral IGO negotiations. This term encapsulates the epistemic shift from the IS to the AO by suggesting that certain products are uniquely, or at least distinctively, linked to specific regions and it is unpacked further in the next two chapters. At the negotiations, the immediate response to this claim was that like any other term, designations for agricultural products can also become generic through ordinary linguistic usage, while the artificial freezing of meaning necessitated by this exception would hamper accurate judicial determinations of context specific connotations.[235] The implications of this disagreement have profound significance. In effect, one approach advocated that legal protection should track consumer and trade understanding to determine whether the contested use was permissible. The methodology adopted called for an interpretation of the sign's meaning to a local audience in the country of dispute. The opposing point of view sought to fix a designation's 'true' significance through geographical fingerprinting in the home country, based on the inimitable link shared between the referent product and a distinct place. Once this was established, the focus shifted to scrutinising the conduct of an external imitator using

---

[233] Actes de Madrid, 82.

[234] Ibid., 87 ('*Le terme caractère générique, employé dans cet article, s'applique à des produits de nature tout à fait différente. Les dénominations telles que eau de Cologne, cuir de Russie, etc. comprennent, il est vrai, des noms de localités ou de pays; mais l'emploi de noms géographiques a une portée tout autre quand ils servent à désigner des produits industriels que quand ils s'appliquent à des produits agricoles, comme par exemple dans la dénomination vin de Bordeaux. Dans le premier cas, la dénomination est de nature abstraite; dans l'autre, elle désigne spécialement un produit qui ne peut être obtenu que dans une contrée déterminée. Les dénominations de produits agricoles, dont la contrefaçon est générale, correspondent toujours à des conditions particulières de climat et de terroir qui ne sauraient être changées ni transportées*'). See also L. Lacour, *Des Fausses Indications de Provenance: Contribution à L'étude de la Propriété Industrielle en Droit Français* (Rousseau, Paris 1904), 15–17.

[235] Put forward by the delegates from Sweden and Norway and the delegate from Britain respectively, Actes de Madrid, 87–8; See also Papers and Correspondence relative to Conference at Madrid (1890), 39.

70   The Indication of Source

the term generically on a similar product. Since it was not the 'real' thing, this use must be wrongful regardless of what consumers might think. At this stage M. Pelletier of France intervened to bridge the widening epistemic gap, restricting the special category status to viticultural products alone. Wine itself was not an unmediated agricultural product and required an additional transformative human intervention. Pelletier's reasoning is Delphic at best but implies that preventing adulteration at the stage of human involvement, possibly under the guise of generic use, was the basis for the immunity for wines.[236] In this manner the exceptional category was narrowed from all agricultural products to viticultural products and subsequently passed.

Given the relatively brief prelude to Article 4 and its abrupt adoption, even a charitable reading suggests that it is an amalgam forged out of compromise. The underlying tensions continued to simmer and would erupt in debates at subsequent negotiations. These discussions generated not just heat but light as well, since attempts to expand or contract the scope of Article 4 created a forum for debating the idea of a special link between product and place. This established the groundwork for the Lisbon Agreement, nearly seven decades later. For a start, the 'special link' or *terroir* reasoning as the basis for an exceptional category is gradually entrenched. During the Brussels negotiations in 1900, Pelletier again acknowledged that generic usage for the names of manufactured articles such as suede gloves was acceptable, but 'nature' itself placed limits upon such use for viticultural products.[237] According to Oliveira Martins, it was the pragmatic need for compromise that reduced the category of all agricultural products having a unique link to the place of origin to that of wines alone.[238] It was therefore only a matter of time before (ultimately unsuccessful) proposals reappeared to extend the exceptional category to all products possessing this link. In the process, attempts were made to articulate criteria for identifying members of the category for which wine is the exemplar.

At the Washington negotiations in 1911, France proposed an addition to Article 4, immunising against genericide all products which had their natural qualities related to geographically specific conditions of soil and

---

[236] Actes de Madrid, 88 (*'Cette dénomination s'applique en effet aux produits qui sont créés par les seules forces de la nature, sans que le travail de l'homme ait fait subir une transformation qui en ferait des produits manufacturés. La restriction qu'on propose d'apporter au droit d'appréciation des tribunaux se justifierait mieux en faveur des produits qui, originairement agricoles, sont fréquemment frelatés après avoir été rendus utilisables par des manipulations industrielles. La proposition de M. le délégué du Portugal gagnerait à être restreinte aux produits vinicoles, auxquels la fraude s'attaque souvent'*).
[237] Actes de Bruxelles, 268.   [238] Ibid., 271.

climate.[239] An essentialised and deterministic version of nature takes centre stage here. A more nuanced modification was introduced at The Hague in 1925, where BIRPI tackled the binary distinction between natural and manufactured by proposing a continuum. While for some (initially) natural produce the manufacturing process largely determined quality, for others the influence of climate and terrain was predominant. Products that derived their 'characteristic qualities' (i.e. distinctive features) from the influence of climate and terrain as opposed to manufacturing techniques were entitled to absolute rights to protection, in a manner akin to wine appellations and should be exempt from generic status.[240] This continuum would be incorporated into national regimes which gave special status to *terroir* products. Jaton sets out the manner in which French law differentiates between products with and without a natural influence. Under this approach, it was necessary to establish the extent to which human intervention was required in the fabrication process, to determine which category a product belonged to. He goes on to suggest that extractive products such as marble, oils and coal, wines, mineral waters, beer, certain types of cheese and spirits would be broadly 'natural' products in this sense.[241] However, at the international negotiations, this classificatory approach to *terroir* products was opposed on the basis of its vagueness and subjectivity.[242]

Despite regular rebuffs, attempts to enlarge this exceptional category beyond wines continued until Lisbon in 1958. At this conference, BIRPI's proposal for Article 4 refers to products whose natural qualities depend on soil and climate and whose characteristic features have been identified as such by competent authorities in the country of origin, thereby introducing the additional criterion of institutional recognition.[243] A Portuguese suggestion reframes the natural inputs by adopting the more holistic language of products influenced by local environmental or ecological conditions,[244] while clearly identifying wine as being within the class of such products.[245] Finally, a Czechoslovakian proposal refers to regional appellations for products deriving their natural qualities from the soil and climate as well as human experience, skill and local

---

[239] Actes de Washington, 218 ('*De même ne seront pas comprises dans ladite réserve les appellations régionales de provenance de tous autres produits tenant leurs qualités nature lies du sol ou du climat*').

[240] Actes de la Haye, 312.   [241] Jaton, *Répression des Fausses Indications*, 24–38.

[242] Actes de la Haye, 365 (Germany); Actes de Lisbonne 800 (Denmark), 803 (Sweden).

[243] Actes de Lisbonne, 797.

[244] Ibid., 807 ('*La Délégation du Portugal proposa de remplacer, dans l'alinéa 1, les mots ". . . tirant leurs qualités naturelles du sol et du climat" par ". . . tirant leurs qualités naturelles des facteurs mésologiques locaux"*').

[245] Ibid., 809.

72   The Indication of Source

manufacturing traditions. It mentions mineral water, viticultural products, beer, cheese and traditional crafts as examples.[246] This proposal signals the re-emergence of the subject, as the agency of regional producers is acknowledged alongside natural conditions. This dimension of human input has increased in prominence over the years and will be explored further in the next two chapters. The Czechoslovakian delegation was also an ardent supporter of expansion beyond wines and persistently appealed for the inclusion of mineral water and beers, including those of Pilsen and Ceske Budejovice, on the basis of *terroir* parallels.[247] There are references to local varieties of yeasts, barley, hops, water and localised atmospheric conditions, which are unique to particular regions. Yet not only did expansion attempts fail, several Members continued to express reservations about the exceptional status of wine per se.[248]

The debates circulating around the exception to generic status also made it possible to consider related 'special treatment' arguments under Article 4. One of these focused on the problem of definition and the need for institutional mechanisms at the national level to identify appropriate *terroir* products that would benefit from exceptional treatment under Article 4. As early as 1911, there were proposals for a two-stage process, initially involving recognition at the national level – via legislation or decrees, judicial or administrative decisions – as a precondition to benefitting from the special exemption. These clearly identified and geographically delimited designations should then be forwarded to BIRPI, which would subsequently notify other countries.[249] Spain had previously complained that since the production region in the home country often did not coincide with the administrative boundaries suggested by the name – Havana tobacco came from a broad hinterland around the city, while Manila tobacco came from other neighbouring islands – it would be useful to have an authoritative home country determination as the benchmark.[250] If successful, this would have established an international notification system in the early years of the twentieth century. Then again, the prerequisite for legally binding

---

[246] Ibid., 804, 809 ('*[L]es appellations régionales d'origine des produits tirant leurs qualités naturelles du sol, du climat et du travail humain qui sont reconnues comme caractéristiques par l'autorité compétente du pays d'origine, comme des eaux minérales, des produits vinicoles et des brasseries, des fromages et des produits de mains-d'œuvre traditionnelles, n'étant pas comprises dans la réserve spécifiée par cet article*').

[247] Actes de Washington, 292–3; Actes de la Haye, 365, 480–1; Actes de Londres, 296–7; Actes de Lisbonne, 804.

[248] Actes de Lisbonne, 801 (Italy), 802 (UK), 808 (Japan).

[249] Actes de Washington, 99–100, 218; Actes de la Haye, 312.

[250] Actes de Bruxelles, 261–2.

delimitation implied some form of systematic recognition or a national registration system. It proved too onerous for some members of the Madrid Agreement.[251]

Apart from delimitation and notification, the second possibility discussed was an additional prohibition to prevent qualified uses such as 'Champagne style' or 'Swiss Champagne'. Ladas suggests that use with qualifiers such as 'imitation Champagne', 'Champagne style' or 'Champagne type' would fall within the prohibition against indirectly misleading indications of source in Article 1 of the Madrid Agreement.[252] Yet this interpretation is unlikely based on the drafting history. Precisely these qualified uses were sought to be explicitly brought within the scope of infringement at subsequent conferences, without success. For instance, in 1934 there was a proposal from BIRPI for an additional Article 4(2):

Les fausses indications de provenance de produits vinicoles ne cessent pas de tomber sous le coup des mesures indiquées dans les articles précédents si elles sont accompagnées d'une périphrase destinée à leur donner un caractère générique (façon, genre, type, etc) ou du véritable lieu d'origine. (The false indications of origin for viticultural products do not cease to fall within the scope of the measures outlined in the previous articles if they are accompanied by a circumlocution designed to give them a generic character (method, genre, type etc.) or the true place of origin).[253]

For proponents of qualified uses, these labelling techniques made it clear that the designation was being used generically (style, type) or the true origin was specified so it was not misleading (Australian Burgundy). However, opponents were concerned about two types of resultant harms. First, qualified uses such as 'Swiss Champagne' would merely entrench the generic usage of champagne by itself and preventing generic use in the case of wines was precisely the object of Article 4. This problem was further exacerbated by 'style' or 'type' situations, suggesting a *terroir* product could be reproduced anywhere with fidelity, thereby encouraging the slide into genericide. Second, the assumption that a qualified use would not be misleading did not always hold. The purchaser's interpretation of the label would depend on the relative size and prominence of 'imitation' or 'method' when compared with 'Champagne', while the tendency of purchasers would be to focus on the prominent appellation.[254] Once again no such amendment to Article 4 was possible, but today we find an almost identical provision in Article 23.1 of TRIPS.

---

[251] See e.g., Actes de Lisbonne, 808 (Switzerland), 810 (Germany).
[252] Ladas, *Patents, Trademarks and Related Rights*, 1586–7.
[253] Actes de Londres, 202. See also Actes de Bruxelles, 262–73; Actes de Lisbonne, 798.
[254] Actes de Londres, 201–2; Actes de Lisbonne, 798, 855.

74   The Indication of Source

This gives us a better sense of the underlying motivations for this provision, not to mention the gestation period involved. It also underlines the value of these formative instruments. Only through a detailed study of the largely forgotten IS can one better appreciate the emergence of the AO, with its potential for manoeuvring around specific obstacles arising in the course of late nineteenth and early twentieth century debates.

A final insight worth flagging up from these foundational debates is the vigorous disagreement and nuanced positioning between European factions, especially since present GI debates are often collapsed into monolithic Old World versus New World contests. During this period there was a spectrum of opinion within representative associations of manufacturers or legal experts such as the AIPPI and the International Chamber of Commerce. Each of the revision conference proceedings contains a summary of resolutions and proposals by these organisations on issues including the scope of IS protection and generic use. At the risk of generalising, over time there is support for the enhanced protection of *terroir* products and a demand for effective proscriptions against misleading use but generic use remains divisive.[255] A detailed account of the various national interests and positions is provided in Part III of a study on the Madrid Agreement in 1920.[256] Far more striking is the distance between the positions of official European delegations, such as the fairly sharp exchanges between the delegation of Spain and those of France and Portugal,[257] or the fact that it would take IS provisions being incorporated into the Treaty of Versailles to bring Germany around to accepting enhanced protection for wine appellations.[258] We will return to these rifts between European approaches in Part II, as it explains the compromised final form of the definition of a GI in the TRIPS Agreement.

4.   Conclusion

The history of the foundational legal discourse in this area reveals much that is useful. For a start, we identify a compelling answer to the related questions of whether the IS was an appropriate fit within the category of

---

[255] See, e.g., Actes de la Haye, 105–6; Actes de Lisbonne, 963–5, 970.
[256] Études Générales, 'La Question des Fausses Indications de Provenance et l'Arrangement de Madrid' [1920] *Propriété Industrielle* 18, (Part I), 31 (Part II), 40 (Part III), 53 (Part IV).
[257] Actes de Bruxelles, 262–73.
[258] Arts. 274 and 275, Treaty of Versailles (28 June 1919). For details, see Études Générales, 'La Question des Fausses Indications de Provenance', 53–5; Wadlow, *The Law of Passing Off*, 73–6.

Conclusion   75

IP and why. According to the participants in these discussions and based on contemporary understandings, as a sign indicating geographical origin the IS was also capable of supporting a collectively generated reputation. The valuable intangible that we must seek at the centre of any IP regime is thus identified. Ensuring clear channels of communication for such signs, by suppressing fraudulent or misleading uses, would benefit the general consuming public as well as honest producers. There are traces of this impulse to protect location specific reputation in the formation of international norms for collective marks, as well as unfair competition prevention. This epistemic logic also neatly maps on to that of contemporaneous trade mark doctrine. However, the collective dimension to this valuable reputation would prove to be an enduring obstacle, particularly at the stage of defining entitlements. Trade mark doctrine had developed around the legal requirement of distinctiveness, or the ability to indicate a single trade source as the basis for distinction on the marketplace. Accommodating a fluid group of users, as opposed to a specific commercial entity, ran against the grain. This is possibly yet another symptom of the liberal individualism bias in modern intellectual property law, where recognising the group or collective has proved challenging.[259] In this case, the effect was to redirect these signs away from trade mark law, into the choppy waters of unfair competition prevention.

Of necessity, the IS was grafted onto a range of laws organised around the prevention of false labelling, but differing greatly in institutional form and teleological aspirations. Besides the conceptual clutter this generated, origin marking was itself subject to competing fields of interests. Finally, the IS was conceived very much with an eye to international protection and influenced by trade across jurisdictional boundaries. Since meaning was fluid and signifiers could gain new connotations over space and time (including through generic use or qualified use), such contingent protection was deemed unsatisfactory. While the IS represented a simplified link between product and place of origin, *terroir*

---

[259] Property rights in intangibles are usually granted on the basis of creation, where the individual is the primary creator, the creative output is inevitably commoditised and its market value is predominantly recognised. This view is now being challenged. WIPO, 'The Protection of Traditional Knowledge: Revised Objectives and Principles', 22 January 2010 (WIPO/GRTKF/IC/16/5 Prov), Annex 3 ('The protection of [TK] should aim to ... recognize the holistic nature of traditional knowledge and its intrinsic value, including its social, spiritual, economic, intellectual, scientific, ecological, technological, commercial, educational and cultural value, and acknowledge that traditional knowledge systems are frameworks of ongoing innovation and distinctive intellectual and creative life that are fundamentally important for indigenous and local communities and have equal scientific value as other knowledge systems').

suggested that certain products were anchored more tightly to their origins, thereby strengthening opposition to use by outsiders. At this stage the communicative logic supporting IS protection, that is shared with trade mark law, is layered over with *terroir* logic. As we see in the next chapter, the regulatory regimes that emerged around the AO were concerned with far more than just IP protection, but it is important to remember that reputation protection continues to be an essential ingredient. What does change is the procedure for defining the circle of those entitled to the use of the sign, as well as the basis for defining the subject matter and scope of protection. These begin to diverge from standard approaches under trade mark or unfair competition law. *Terroir* logic is used to justify the creation of a distinct category of legally protected signs and the AO, representing version two in the convoluted journey towards the GI in TRIPS, is unpacked across the rest of Part I. Predictably enough, there's a lot about wine in the following pages.

3   The Appellation of Origin in France

1.   The significance of the French experience

Terroir is a crucial ingredient in the processes of legitimation whereby IGOs are treated as a discrete category of protected signs. The previous chapter suggests that there are progressively more specialised functions for geographical designations associated with products: (1) Signs which are technically geographical (they correspond to a place on a map) may not always signify that the product originated there. Instead they may be perceived as fanciful, allusive or generic designations. 'Great Snoring' is the name of a village in the UK but is unlikely to be regarded as a geographical designation by consumers. (2) All signs which do signify the product's origin fit within the overarching category of the IS. The ubiquitous 'Made in China' is an example. (3) For a subset of such products, the origin message is the cue for associations of repute, based on subjective perceptions of quality. Here it is helpful to adopt the terminology of German unfair competition law, where the 'qualified IS' is a sign deemed worthy of protection, on the basis of a reputational link between product and place.[1] At this stage, the qualified IS functions analogously to a trade mark, bearing in mind the geographical descriptiveness and collective interest aspects impeding its assimilation within conventional trade mark law. Preserving the clarity of the origin signal is important to both purchasers and legitimate producers, with reputation protection as a desirable side-effect. (4) For an even more select sub-set, the logic of *terroir* structures the relationship between product and place, where the qualities of the goods are uniquely or distinctively determined by the place of origin. Following through on this logic, the 'real thing' is inimitable elsewhere and its use by outsiders should be strictly

---

[1] F-K. Beier, 'The Need for Protection of Indications of Source and Appellations of Origin in the Common Market' [1977] *Industrial Property* 152, 159 (describing qualified indications of source as those where the 'link between quality and geographical area ... cannot be proved objectively, but nevertheless exists because it is recognised by the trade').

78   The Appellation of Origin in France

prohibited. By definition, claims of equivalence are simply not true and will inevitably misappropriate the reputation of the original. It is therefore within this fourth category that the divergences between a trade mark and a GI are most apparent. Since Chapter 4 considers the Lisbon Agreement, which in turn is designed around the *Appellation d'Origine* (AO), this bridging chapter sets out to unpack this controversial linkage. It reviews the process by which the connection between product, place and people was initially configured and then reconfigured over the twentieth century in France. A richer account of the emergence of *terroir* and its subsequent institutional expression is indispensable if we wish to engage with contemporary claims supporting the distinct ontological status of GIs. The reader is therefore invited on a detour on the history of French wine regulation.

Lest the sober minded question this Bacchanalian diversion, it has been noted that certain archetypes, or perhaps ideal types, provide much of the scaffolding for the subject matter categories of modern IP law. Mechanical and chemical inventions have historically formed the kernel for the patent system, which raises all sorts of awkward conceptual questions when the system encounters computer software or biotechnological inventions.[2] Similarly, for trade marks registration, visual signs consisting of words and figurative devices have formed the paradigmatic subject matter. Attempts to register scents, sounds, tastes, textures and movements as trade marks have given rise to both adjectival and substantive law concerns.[3] Brad Sherman and Lionel Bently draw attention to the long term influence of subject matter models, whereby 'the shape that intellectual property law took, as well as the way this mode of organisation was explained were strongly influenced by the particular type of subject matter that was protected and the way in which that subject matter was interpreted'.[4] In the case of the AO, wine has long been considered the archetypal subject matter and legislative

---

[2] *Biogen Inc* v. *Medeva plc* [1997] RPC 1, 31–2 (HL) (Lord Mustill refers to 'the mechanical and chemical inventions to which so much of traditional patent law relates'); B. Sherman, 'Regulating Access and Use of Genetic Resources: Intellectual Property and Biodiscovery' (2003) EIPR 301 ('Given that the rules and principles of patent law largely developed in response to mechanical and chemical inventions, a lot of energy was also spent on adapting the existing framework to accommodate biotechnological inventions'). Cf. A. Pottage and B. Sherman, *Figures of Invention: A History of Modern Patent Law* (Oxford University Press, 2010).

[3] WIPO, 'New Types of Marks', 1 September 2006 (SCT/16/2), [3] ('The types of signs that are nowadays considered as being capable of constituting a trade mark have expanded beyond words or figurative devices').

[4] B. Sherman and L. Bently, *The Making of Modern Intellectual Property Law: The British Experience, 1760–1911* (Cambridge University Press, 1999), 142.

The significance of the French experience

experiments in France influenced wine regulation in its Southern European neighbours, went on to shape the European Union's wine labelling system, would serve as a foil to the geographical demarcation of wine regions in the New World and gradually extended to other product categories such as cheese. Teachings from French national experiences have informed EU GI policy for agricultural products and foodstuffs, while reinforcing arguments for enhancing the scope of GI protection at international debates.[5]

Since the French model serves as a reference point, Warren Moran reminds us of its potential limitations:

The justifiability of appellation systems [as distinct regimes] depends on the validity of their assumptions, the most important of which is that the character (sometimes defined as quality) of the product derives from the physical and human environment in which it is produced. While at first sight this statement seems like a truism, its truth really depends on the extent that the various components that give agricultural products character and quality are irrevocably tied to territory. Could a product with exactly the same characteristics be produced in a different locality?[6]

Furthermore, if wine occupies the core, craft products hover on the periphery of GI law, with doubts being expressed about their inclusion. So if the French wine appellation system has shaped *sui generis* GI law, different approaches to *terroir* have in turn shaped the French regime. The transformations in the manner in which place has been represented and then legally recognised are revealed most strikingly in the transition

---

[5] C. Foulkes (ed.), *Larousse Encyclopedia of Wine*, 2nd edn, (Hamlyn, London 2001), 130 (The French system forms the prototype for European national laws and 'impregnates the European Community (EC) Wine régime'); E. Barham, 'Translating Terroir: The Global Challenge of French AOC Labeling' (2003) 19 *Journal of Rural Studies* 127, 128 ('The AOC system is the oldest of the European label of origin systems and is widely regarded as the most strict and thoroughgoing of its kind. It is, in this sense, a model of reference for origin labelled products. The system is guided by the concept of "terroir"'); O. Brouwer, 'Community Protection of Geographical Indications and Specific Character as a Means of Enhancing Foodstuffs Quality' (1991) 28 *Common Market Law Review* 615, 618 (For details on the original French proposal to establish the European registered GI system for agricultural products and foodstuffs); B. Lehman, 'Intellectual Property under the Clinton Administration' (1993–4) 27 *George Washington Journal of International Law and Economics* 395, 409 (attributing the TRIPS GI provisions to 'strong French interest in appellations such as Champagne, Burgundy, and Chablis'). Lisbon Assembly, 'Report of the Twenty Third Session', 29 September 2008 (LI/A/23/2), [7] ('The protection of appellations of origin was a subject that was of particular importance for France').

[6] W. Moran, 'Rural Space as Intellectual Property' (1993) 12 *Political Geography* 263, 266–7. Cf. G. Teil, 'The French Wine "Appellations d'Origine Contrôlée" and the Virtues of Suspicion' (2010) 13 JWIP 253 (reviewing criticism of the appellation system within France, on the basis that it is unhelpful in making differentiations based on quality).

80   The Appellation of Origin in France

from the *Appellation d'Origine* to the *Appellation d'Origine Contrôlée* (AOC), which is the major thematic focus of this chapter.

2.   The role of origin in wine regulation

In Chapter 2 we witnessed the emergence of *terroir* as an anchor in multilateral debates. According to its advocates, the distinctive geographical influences of a region combine to imprint themselves on suitably receptive 'natural' products. Strategically, this logic functions to insulate these signs. Within this paradigm, they are shielded against the semantic storms and commercial cross winds which otherwise buffet wine designations, weakening their geographical signification. Consumer understanding of the indication is no longer the yardstick of true beliefs, for while we may be deluded into believing that imitations are perfect copies (champagne-style wine or Australian champagne), this ought to yield to the higher epistemic benchmark – certain products are irreproducible elsewhere, due to the special link between authentic product and unparalleled place. Origin is therefore a proxy for quality and wine exemplifies this product category. The 'concept of geographical indications relies on the assumption, almost universally accepted today in the wine industry, that different environments produce different wine grapes and, thus, wines of different characteristics . . . As a region or a producer gains repute as a source of a distinct and desirable product, imitations appear and the battle against fraud begins'.[7]

The linkages between origin and quality are not recent, being traced back to ancient Greek and Roman efforts at wine regulation. 'The connection between geography and quality had become a widely accepted belief, if not to say myth, by the nineteenth century, and is still the gospel of enophiles'.[8] Preventing origin fraud is therefore considered an important facet of preventing wine fraud more generally, with the overarching regulatory goal being to ensure quality. Since a deterministic understanding of *terroir* and the biophysical influences of place had surfaced early in the history of international GI protection, the aim of this chapter is to follow the twists and turns of its fortunes in France. Just how much authorship was attributed to 'nature'? Put differently, was geographical origin per se a sufficient proxy for the purposes of guaranteeing product quality? If wine epitomises the category of agricultural products whose

---

[7] M. Maher, 'On Vino Veritas? Clarifying the Use of Geographic References on American Wine Labels' (2001) 89 *California Law Review* 1881, 1884.

[8] L. A. Loubère, *The Wine Revolution in France – The Twentieth Century* (Princeton University Press, 1990), 114.

The role of origin in wine regulation

characteristics and qualities are uniquely shaped by '*conditions particulières de climat et de terroir*', to what extent is a regulatory regime based on guaranteeing geographical origin alone satisfactory? In addressing these questions, it helps to first outline the functions of origin marking in the wine industry more generally, in order to highlight the distinct inflections *terroir* brings to this otherwise familiar requirement.

The grapes of *vitis vinifera* have been subjected to legal regulation for a considerable period. This regulation often includes rules requiring truthful origin marking, satisfying a cluster of policy objectives in the process. Wine markets have been internationalised for some time, with taxation being predictably premised on accurate source identification. An oft-cited example is the sixty-two customs points along the Rhine in the fourteenth century, requiring wines traversing this route to be suitably marked with indications of origin.[9] In tracing the commercial fortunes of fortified Port wine, the significance of origin marking is again noteworthy. Paul Duguid observes that Portuguese trade benefitted from the fluctuating fortunes of the Anglo-French relationship. Since Port wine was favoured with preferential duties during the eighteenth and nineteenth centuries, British customs officials were careful to verify origin on this account.[10] Others provide additional illustrations of such taxes targeting either exports or imports, with the goal occasionally being to discourage exports by taxing them heavily.[11]

Apart from the relevance of origin labelling for revenue generation and attempts to control trade flows, another key theme is the persistence of fraud. The response was to ensure truthful origin marking. A characteristic feature of the international wine trade was the distances involved in transactions, which encouraged merchants to transform wines of an inferior quality into those of an apparently superior quality or 'revive' wines after a long ocean voyage.[12] In medieval England, food and drink quality was regulated by a melange of city ordinances as well as by Parliament. A proclamation was issued in 1419, requiring that wine from one 'geographical area must be so labelled and could not be mixed with another'.[13] Since origin was perceived as a proxy for quality, there

---

[9] H. Johnson, *The Story of Wine* (Mitchell Beasley, London 1989), 120.

[10] P. Duguid, 'Networks and Knowledge: The Beginning and End of the Port Commodity Chain, 1703–1860' (2005) 78 *Business History Review* 453.

[11] K. Andrerson, D. Norman and G. Wittwer, 'Globalisation and the World's Wine Markets: Overview', CIES Discussion Paper No. 143, Adelaide University (2002), 3.

[12] This included the addition of Turnsol or the juice of elderberries. T. Unwin, *Wine and the Vine: An Historical Geography of Viticulture and the Wine Trade* (Routledge, London 1991), 241–4, 276–7.

[13] P. B. Hutt and P. B. Hutt II, 'A History of Government Regulation of Adulteration and Misbranding of Food' (1984) 39 *Food, Drug, Cosmetic Law Journal* 2, 16.

82 The Appellation of Origin in France

are references to a league of wine makers being established in Rioja to set rules to control wine production collectively and establish quality zones as early as 1560.[14] A similar case in point is the initiative of Medici Grand Duke, Cosimo III of Florence, who issued an edict in 1716 establishing geographic delimitations for Tuscan wine grape-growing regions, most notably Chianti, Carmignano and Pomino. This restricted the use of these regional names exclusively to wine originating in the delimited regions.[15] Similarly, those involved in the Port commodity chain grappled with fraud in the eighteenth and nineteenth century.[16] Reverting to the English market for alcoholic beverages, by the beginning of the nineteenth century the beverages that appeared in advertisements were generally distinguished by regions, including Edinburgh ales, French Cognac, Champagne, Sherry and Port. Based on archival research, Duguid establishes that 'the trade press regularly protested advertisements for alcohol that, through either cupidity or stupidity, made false claims of origin'.[17] Therefore a legal guarantee of origin is often situated within a well-established narrative of combating fraud.

It is also worth remembering that some of these initiatives created the space for more questionable agendas. A primary concern here is rent-seeking.[18] 'The essential characteristic of all wine demarcations based on the territorial origin of wines is that they attempt to guarantee the quality of a wine through reference to the land upon which the vines are grown. By purporting to guarantee quality, however, such classifications also enable owners of such land to reap greater profits than would otherwise be realised from their vineyards in the form of a monopoly rent'.[19] This raises the spectre of unwarranted yet legally buttressed exclusive rights to a designation. Certain classificatory practices in Bordeaux and Burgundy grew out of the desire of entrenched interests to ensure continued profits.[20] Bordeaux benefitted from the rule that only wines from the proximate region were allowed entry into its port facilities.[21] Its wine

---

[14] Foulkes, *Larousse Encyclopedia of Wine*, 131.   [15] Maher, 'On Vino Veritas?', 1884.

[16] Duguid, 'Networks and Knowledge', 520–3.

[17] P. Duguid, 'Developing the Brand: The Case of Alcohol, 1800–1880' (2003) 4 *Enterprise and Society* 405, 425–6.

[18] Economists define rent as revenue higher than would be necessary to justify a given investment, i.e. pure profit. The expenditure of resources in an effort to capture these supra-normal revenues is described as rent-seeking. It is a common concern when property rights are sought. W. M. Landes and R. A. Posner, *The Economic Structure of Intellectual Property Law* (Harvard University Press, Cambridge MA 2003), 17–18.

[19] Unwin, *Wine and the Vine*, 312.

[20] Although the reference here is to the system of classifying vineyards into a hierarchy of *crus* within the appellation area. Ibid., 278.

[21] W. van Caenegem, 'Registered Geographical Indications: Between Rural Policy and Intellectual Property – Part II' (2003) 6 JWIP 861, 861–3.

producers and merchants also profited from the *privilège de la descente* (wines from other regions were not to be brought down the river to Bordeaux for sale before 11 November each year) and the *privilège de la barrique* (Bordeaux wines were exclusively entitled to the use of distinctive barrels that were larger and made of superior wood, thereby travelling better while also costing less as the freight was levied per barrel).[22] Consequently, Robert Ulin argues that the reputation for Bordeaux wines displays many of the characteristics of an invented tradition. 'Bordeaux's ascendancy to its current paramount position follows conjointly from its political and economic history and from a more general process of "invention" that disguises what is social and cultural in "natural" attire'.[23] In summation, it is well established that origin marking in the wine trade addressed a range of policy objectives, as well as occasionally enabling partisan agendas. What is noteworthy is that during the period under consideration here, *terroir* logic brought something new to these established practices.

3. A geology of *terroir*[24]

The French appellation system emerged in the context of urgent demands for state intervention as a direct response to the phylloxera crisis of the nineteenth century and premised on (a fluid notion of) *terroir*. Each of these constitutive influences does much to explain the manner in which it defines the circle of legitimate users of an appellation and why it excludes outsiders. *Terroir* is a key ingredient in differentiating between wines by indicating a distinct origin. It is a cipher operating as the explanation for why place of origin influences quality. According to Elizabeth Barham, this 'expression of place' refers 'to an area or terrain, usually rather small, whose soil and microclimate impart distinctive qualities to food products'. Here human agency is also acknowledged alongside terrain since the ideal pairing of people and place requires an act of 'interpreting or translating the local ecology, displaying its qualities to best advantage. A great deal of knowledge about the local terrain is needed for success, as well as respect for local natural conditions that can be expressed through the wine'.[25] Roger Bohmrich refers to the combination of soil, topography and climate with the human

---

[22] Ibid., 862.
[23] R. C. Ulin, 'Invention and Representation as Cultural Capital: Southwest French Winegrowing History' (1995) 97 *American Anthropologist* 519.
[24] My thanks to Alain Pottage for suggesting this title.
[25] Barham, 'Translating *Terroir*', 131.

84   The Appellation of Origin in France

contribution, where 'privileged' *terroir* is 'seen to reflect evolutionary adaptation to the natural environment [and] judged to be a complex interaction of factors, some still unknown'.[26] Others celebrate the palpable sense of 'somewhereness' expressed in the *goût de terroir* or taste of place, where it is considered important to let the wine evoke its region of provenance without too much fiddly authorial interference on the part of the winemaker.[27] Yet gauging a physical site's precise impact on the quality of the end product has been the subject of intense, unresolved debates.[28] Disambiguating the concept is an important task, because arguments mythologising or overemphasising the influence of place on quality can find traction with courts.

The two features of Champagne of prime importance for its uniqueness are the soil and climate in which the grapes are grown, and the method of manufacture by skilled personnel. *The first of those elements cannot be exactly duplicated anywhere in the world*, but the second can. It apparently is generally recognised among wine experts that the precise geographical location (i.e. soil and climate) for the growing of a vine is the *outstanding, unchanging factor which governs the final product*. Hence the predominance of place names for appellations (emphasis added).[29]

The region in which the Champagne vineyards are found is about one hundred miles east of Paris around Reims and Épernay, where there is a chalky, flinty soil and the climate is subject to extreme variations of heat and cold. *It appears that these factors give to the wine its particular qualities* (emphasis added).[30]

The words 'Great Western' as applied to wines whether still or sparkling are certainly a geographical term. *The natural characteristics of the locality give a special quality to the wine produced there* (emphasis added).[31]

Terroir therefore has legal significance and courts are often approached on the basis of geographically or biophysically deterministic arguments that account for this 'special quality'. In turn this forms the basis for claims to exclusive use of an appellation. The entire paradigm is also periodically contested. In the words of a League of Nations Report from 1922:

---

[26] R. Bohmrich, '*Terroir*: Competing Perspectives on the Roles of Soil, Climate and People' (1996) 7 *Journal of Wine Research* 33.

[27] M. Kramer, 'The Notion of *Terroir*', in F. Allhoff (ed.), *Wine & Philosophy: A Symposium on Thinking and Drinking* (Blackwell, Oxford 2008), 225.

[28] R. E. White, *Soils for Fine Wines* (Oxford University Press, New York 2003), 3 (*Terroir* 'evokes passion in any discussion'); J. Robinson (ed.), *The Oxford Companion to Wine*, 2nd edn (Oxford University Press, 1999), 700 (It is 'central to philosophical and commercial differences').

[29] *Comité Interprofessionnel du Vin de Champagne* v. *Wineworths Group Ltd* [1991] 2 NZLR 432, [10] (Wellington HC).

[30] *J. Bollinger* v. *Costa Brava Wine Co Ltd* [1961] 1 All ER 561, 563 (Ch D) (Danckwerts J).

[31] *Thomson* v. *B. Seppelt & Sons Ltd* [1925] 37 CLR 305, 313 (HCA) (Isaacs J).

A geology of *terroir*

[It is argued that] some products of the vine derive their special qualities from the peculiar characteristics of the soil or climate of one particular district, and are therefore inherently incapable of being produced of the same quality elsewhere. So far as this is really true, the particular district in which they are produced may be said to have an absolute natural monopoly of their production, and it would seem that any geographical appellation in their title can never be employed properly in a 'generic' sense as the result of use or custom. Unfortunately, there is not always general agreement either as to the fact of the regional monopoly or as to the limits of the area possessing such monopoly. There is a natural tendency to exaggerate the view that the special qualities of a wine are in reality a 'regional' monopoly, and in many cases there has been keen dispute as to the limits of the area (if it exists) which is alone capable of producing a speciality.[32]

The extent to which legal institutions have incorporated and legitimate *terroir*, as well as the particular iteration of *terroir* that is integrated, begins to matter a great deal. In this regard, it is helpful to identify at least three overlapping narratives which conceive of *terroir* as (1) a holistic or mythical anchor, associated with regional identity formation; (2) a deterministic influence, with the emphasis on physical geography and environmental conditions; or (3) a more contingent composite of natural and human factors, open to innovation. The first two assume static conceptions of place, while the third permits a more adaptive approach.

According to the first school of thought, *terroir* is a 'much discussed term for the total natural environment of any viticultural site. No precise English equivalent exists for this quintessentially French term and concept'.[33] The influential expert Hugh Johnson says that it 'means much more than what goes on beneath the surface. Properly understood, it means the whole ecology of the vineyard … not excluding the way the vineyard is tended, nor even the soul of the *vigneron*'.[34] Others believe that it extends beyond the chemical composition of the soil to indicate 'the coming together of the climate, the soil and the landscape'.[35] Considered by some as 'a mythic and holistic concept, terroir refers to the distinctive and inimitable environment of a specific vineyard'.[36] Thus conceived, *terroir* reaffirms

---

[32] Report on Unfair Competition, Particularly in Relation to False Marks and Indications [1922] *League of Nations Official Journal* 625, 630.

[33] Robinson, *Oxford Companion*, 700.

[34] See the Foreword to J. E. Wilson, *Terroir: The Role of Geology, Climate, and Culture in the Making of French Wines* (Mitchell Beazley, London 1998), 4.

[35] B. Prats, 'The Terroir is Important' (1983) 8 *Decanter* 16 cited in Unwin, *Wine and the Vine*, 45.

[36] W. Zhao, 'Understanding Classifications: Empirical Evidence from the American and French Wine Industries' (2005) 33 *Poetics* 179, 185.

86   The Appellation of Origin in France

the uniqueness of place by emphasising a spiritual bond. Such statements implicitly assume that place is both conveniently bounded and static. These perspectives appear to be a reworking of a previous, more complex version of the concept. Kolleen Guy has traced the term back to the late thirteenth century, where it initially refers to 'aptitudes of various soils for the production of grapes'. Yet by the eighteenth century, it 'had gone beyond linking soil and wine and was applied metaphorically to describe a host of qualities or defects not only in wine but also in people originating in certain *pays*'.[37] This transformation was in keeping with contemporary French medical practice, which studied the transfusion of the essence of place into physical as well as psychological conditions of its inhabitants, through the consumption of *terroir* products.

Some scholars situate this 'spiritual bond' within the broader project of environmental determinism, which produces 'a highly constructed, deeply essentialised and static conception of place'.[38] While this disciplinary perspective alludes to a particular legitimating function of *terroir*, an alternative and altogether more compelling account traces the conscious promotion of such mythical product–place relationships back to the formative politics after the collapse of the *Ancien Régime*, when a modern nation-building project was underway. Post-revolutionary France required symbols around which to coalesce and regional specialities became an important part of this process. These became 'closely associated with the creation of a national identity based upon the notion of regional and local diversity'.[39] The idea of a culinary heritage and the burgeoning aesthetics of gastronomy were positioned within the politics of preserving 'local customs, language and folklore against the centralising pressure of the Third Republic'.[40] The Industrial Revolution and improved transportation led to national markets, which in turn fuelled the sales of reputed regional speciality foods.[41] As a prominent part of

---

[37] K. M. Guy, *When Champagne Became French: Wine and the Making of a National Identity* (Johns Hopkins University Press, Baltimore 2003), 42.

[38] B. Parry, 'Geographical Indications: Not All Champagne and Roses', in L. Bently, J. C. Ginsburg and J. Davis (eds.), *Trade Marks and Brands: An Interdisciplinary Critique* (Cambridge University Press, 2008) 361, 364 (Environmental determinism theorises about the synergistic and mutually reinforcing relationship between a particular bounded territory and the activities of its inhabitants, such as the effect of climate and landscape on the local work ethic or artistic sensibilities. This in turn rests on a biologically informed model of nationhood).

[39] M. Demossier, 'Culinary Heritage and *Produits de Terroir* in France: Food for Thought', in S. Blowen, M. Demossier and J. Picard (eds.), *Recollections of France: Memories, Identities and Heritage in Contemporary France* (Berghahn Books, New York 2000), 141, 145.

[40] Ibid., 146.

[41] X. de Planhol, *An Historical Geography of France* (Cambridge University Press, 1994), 374.

A geology of *terroir* 87

this culinary heritage, 'wine consumption and *terroir* were fundamental references that the collective "France" elaborated for itself in the late nineteenth century'.[42] The authentic France was an organic entity constituted by the symbiotic relationship between landscape and those who lived in it. Conceived as a 'land of treasures' where the environment determined a way of life, France became unique as a nation, as opposed to others such as Germany that were premised upon an ethnic ideal.[43] Products of the vine were undeniably influenced by place and located between an art and a craft, making them exemplary symbols for this purpose. This socially constitutive role of *terroir* has been the subject of recent studies by ethnographers of folklore, who explore the formation of distinct regional identities. For instance, Philip Whalen demonstrates that aspects of the Burgundian identity are linked, via this more political notion of *terroir*, to the figure of the rustic vigneron. The techniques adopted to construct this link include festivals to celebrate regional produce, gastronomic fairs, parades and annual wine auctions.[44] Along with the belief that quality depended upon origin, this broader project of regional identity reinforcement provides the backdrop to late nineteenth century arguments that certain products were considered inimitable and tied to specific regions.

By contrast, the second iteration of *terroir* focuses on its physical and environmental elements. Once again, the inference is that the complex blend of natural conditions produces a unique place of origin. Under its influence, Italian wine denomination norms are perceived to 'codify ... and protect especially the environmental factor, which is the unique blend of climate and soil, the only element not reproducible and not transferable to another location'. While varietals and know-how can be transferred, the 'only fixed, non-reproducible factor is the territory, the climate–soil factor, the factor that influences exclusively and decisively the character, the quality and the typical attributes of a wine'.[45] According to this school of thought, *terroir* is found in:

---

[42] K. M. Guy, 'Rituals of Pleasure in the Land of Treasures: Wine Consumption and the Making of French Identity in the Late Nineteenth Century', in W. J. Belasco and P. Scranton (eds.), *Food Nations: Selling Taste in Consumer Societies* (Routledge, London 2002), 34, 43.

[43] Ibid., 43.

[44] P. Whalen, '"A Merciless Source of Happy Memories": Gaston Roupnel and the Folklore of Burgundian Terroir' (2007) 44 *Journal of Folklore Research* 21; P. Whalen, '"Insofar as the Ruby Wine Seduces Them": Cultural Strategies for Selling Wine in Inter-War Burgundy' (2009) 18 *Contemporary European History* 67.

[45] F. Castellucci, 'Geographical Indications: The Italian Scenario for the Wine Sector', 24 June 2003 (WIPO/GEO/SFO/03/10), [16], [18].

88   The Appellation of Origin in France

A plot of land or site, with its own individual fingerprint, made up of geological features, soil composition and structure, mineral content, exposure to general weather conditions, micro-climates, rainfall and drainage, sunshine, degree and variation in orientation, slope, all of which may vary in content and make-up throughout the site, and which has been so used for the growing of the vine through generations resulting in the land being composed of its natural constituents for that purpose.[46]

Or, as Bohmrich puts it:

The idea that the particular, sometimes unique characteristics of a given site, as opposed to another either in close proximity or contiguous, could lead to recognisable if subtle differences in the aroma and taste of wines produced from the same grapes and by the same methods is hardly of recent invention. The most celebrated wine of Roman times, Falernum, grown on Monte Massico in Campania, resulted from a classification of the locality into three subdistricts: Caucinian on the top of the hills, Faustian on the upper slopes and Falernian on the lower reaches. Here we have an early demonstration of a quality hierarchy within one wine type based on environmental factors.[47]

Amongst the various elements, geological formation is given great importance, as illustrated by the soil of Burgundy, formed by the gradual disintegration of mountain slopes. This is not only a crucial source of minerals and nutrients but also regulates the optimal drainage of rainwater.[48] Soil is said to have four prominent attributes – it holds up the vine, supplies moisture, warms up and cools down at a variable rate and supplies nutrients.[49] Apart from soil, other significant biophysical factors include topology (altitude and orientation to the sun) and climatic conditions.[50] Today these factors form a key component of the EU's wine labelling policy. Thus, for quality wines from specified regions, Recital 27 of Regulation No 479/2008 clarifies that the 'concept of quality wines in the Community is based, inter alia, on the specific characteristics attributable to the wine's geographical origin'.[51] In this, one sees glimpses of the '*conditions particulières de climat et de terroir*' argument encountered previously, which ties product to place. Both mythical and deterministic *terroir* advocate a unique product as the end result. In the past this has obscured a crucial dimension, which gives rise to a third account.

---

[46] A. Biss and O. Smith, *The Wines of Chablis* (Writers International, Bournemouth 2000), 49.

[47] Bohmrich, '*Terroir*: Competing Perspectives', 33–4.

[48] A. Hanson, *Burgundy* (Mitchell Beazley, London 2003), 58–9.

[49] Foulkes, *Larousse Encyclopedia*, 130.

[50] Bohmrich, '*Terroir*: Competing Perspectives', 35.

[51] Council Regulation (EC) No 479/2008 of 29 April 2008 on the Common Organisation of the Market in Wine [2008] OJ L148/1.

A geology of *terroir*

This third, more balanced notion of *terroir* encompasses a combination of the natural factors considered above with 'others that pertain to traditional winemaking processes'.[52] In terms of a semantic shift, *terroir's* 'recent path reflects the move from an almost exclusively naturalist usage to one that has gradually come to include the social and cultural dimensions of places and products'.[53] Acknowledgement of the human dimension is often traced back to Roger Dion's influential work on this history of French viticulture and viniculture.[54] Dion surmised that vines had been planted in France for over two millennia while several of the major vineyards had been growing grapes for over a millennium. Technical experience, arising from trial and error experimentation with viticultural practices, had accumulated over this period. Successful innovations would be adopted, disseminated and further adapted in time, as part of a process of adjustment to the surrounding environment. These included the practices of varietal and clonal selection, trellising systems for supporting vines, pruning and irrigation techniques. When successful, these techniques often attained the status of customs and would be broadly adopted within the area, but could also run the risk of becoming inflexible and hindering further innovation.

In addition to the human element in wine production, Dion's work also focuses on the consumption or demand aspect, detailing the important evolution of urban markets, the effects of national and international trade patterns and transportation costs. Contemporary research builds on this, acknowledging that:

> many factors are involved, including climate, soil, cultivar and human practices, and these factors interact. The best expression of terroir is achieved when the precocity of the grapevine variety is suited to the local climatic conditions in such a way that full ripeness is reached by the end of the growing season . . . However, great terroir emerges only when socio-economic conditions are favourable to the establishment of quality-orientated wine production.[55]

There is recognition that each winemaker 'builds on local traditions, legal requirements, and his or her own skills and experience to create

---

[52] E. Auriol, J. B. Le Sourd and S. Schilizzi, 'France', in K. Anderson (ed.), *The World's Wine Markets: Globalization at Work* (Edward Elgar, Cheltenham 2004), 64.

[53] M. Cegarra and F. Verdaux, 'Introduction', in L. Bérard, M. Cegarra, M. Djama and S. Louafi (eds.), *Biodiversity and Local Ecological Knowledge in France* (INRA-CIRAD, 2005), 19, 22.

[54] R. Dion, *Histoire de la Vigne et du Vin en France des Origines au XIXe Siècle* (Clavreuil, Paris 1959).

[55] C. van Leeuwen and G. Seguin, 'The Concept of *Terroir* in Viticulture' (2006) 17 *Journal of Wine Research* 1. See also J. van Niekerk, 'The Use of Geographical Indications in a Collective Marketing Strategy: The Example of the South African Wine Industry', 1 September 1999 (WIPO/GEO/CPT/99/8), 4.

90   The Appellation of Origin in France

a particular style of wine'.[56] Over time, producers have 'adapted their production practices to these particular conditions of their natural environment so as to bring out the specific characteristics of the produce of these unique locations to the best of their ability'.[57] These techniques and skills, such as selecting appropriate vine varieties suitable for local soil conditions, setting the permissible limits for sugar and alcoholic strength as well as best times for harvest subsequently found their way into the product specification decrees in French law.[58] 'A *terroir* links stakeholders, their history, their social organizations, activities – especially agricultural practices defined as specific and singular methods by which farmers implement techniques – and an area of land with its ecological characteristics, its configurations of shapes, expanses and surroundings, and its landscapes. These components of the *terroir* are in dynamic interaction'.[59] However, its supporters continue to claim that this interface between environmental conditions and production techniques results in unique products.[60]

Acknowledging this collective, inter-generational human investment over an extended period has three important consequences. First, it foregrounds the vital role of *savoir faire*, or particular techniques and know-how accumulated over time in response to the local environment.[61] This directly challenges the notion that a certain class of agricultural products are uniquely shaped by nature alone, having sprung forth unmediated. It also avoids the rhetorical temptation of celebrating fully formed, internalised origins for a product. Denis Vidal reminds us of the dangers of such myth making:

Plenty of myths, all over the world, assume the existence of some sort of exclusive relationship between a particular place and the people who are supposed to have originated from it. But this does not prevent us from realizing, whether we like it or not, that migration and displacement of all sorts are the stuff of history.

---

[56] Unwin, *Wine and the Vine*, 50. See also J. Halliday and H. Johnson, *The Art and Science of Wine* (Mitchell Beazley, London 1994), 19–20.

[57] J. Mesneir, 'Semantic Analysis and Draft Definition of the Word "Terroir"' (1997) 12 *AIDV Bulletin* 4.

[58] For the organisation of producer co-operatives and their role in this process, see G. G. Weigend, 'The Basis and Significance of Viticulture in Southwest France' (1954) 44 *Annals of the Association of American Geographers* 75, 84–93.

[59] J-P. Deffontaines, 'The *Terroir*, a Concept with Multiple Meanings', in L. Bérard, M. Cegarra, M. Djama and S. Louah (eds.), *Biodiversity and Local Ecological Knowledge in France* (INRA-CIRAD 2005) 38, 41.

[60] Moran, 'Rural Space as Intellectual Property', 264 ('Advocates argue that the unique qualities of certain products derive from a combination of features of the natural environment and traditional practices of the people living there. These combinations, it is claimed, cannot be replicated elsewhere').

[61] Barham, 'Translating *Terroir*', 135.

A geology of *terroir*

It would seem, however, that whenever it comes to the products of the soil, we seem to lose our sense of historicity. Instead we celebrate and rejoice in the exclusivity of the relationship between [the qualities of these products] and the places from which they come – places for which they supposedly become the expression and emblem.[62]

One finds within legal discourse precisely such allusions to mythical authenticity that need to be qualified or punctured.[63] The prominence given to know-how and experimentation acknowledges that influences may have come from many sources but the legislative objective was to preserve hard-earned regional reputations by setting down tried and tested methods resulting in products recognised for their quality, rather than appealing to changeless practices with internalised origins. In addition, since localised skills have for some time been recognised alongside geographical features, the parallels between GIs and Traditional Knowledge (TK) appear less forced and this synergy is explored in Part II. There is a further consequence. If AO status includes the recognition of collectively generated production techniques, instead of merely focusing on the brand recognition aspect, the AO can no longer be caricatured as the eccentric relative in the trade mark family photograph. It cannot be evaluated solely on the basis of criteria applicable to trade mark doctrine. Along with the end product, process also matters. Institutional recognition of this process helps resist the countervailing pressure to reduce regional products to purely physical commodities. The appreciation of place and process is situated within counter-narratives to a neoliberal projection of the frictionless, globalised and homogenised economy which marginalises the local.[64] Whilst alive to

---

[62] D. Vidal, 'In Search of "Basmatisthan"': Agro-nationalism and Globalisation', in J. Assayag and C. J. Fuller (eds.), *Globalising India: Perspectives from Below* (Anthem, London 2005), 47, 48–9.

[63] An apt illustration is provided by Advocate General Colomer during the *Feta* litigation. See *Canadane Cheese Trading* v. *Hellenic Republic* (C-317/95) [1997] ECR I-4681, [13] (AGO) ('This cultural context may to some degree be relevant to a case such as that now before the Court because, so far as cheeses are concerned, what matters is the natural element, *the rest being mystery and patience*: they have more to do with *immemorial custom* and traditional flavours than with recipes which, like the law, can be improvised' (emphasis added)).

[64] D. Aylward, 'Towards a Cultural Economy Paradigm for the Australian Wine Industry' (2008) 26 *Prometheus* 373, 374 ('The emergent message was that wine was being viewed less and less as a commodity and more as a process that delivered a range of experiences to the demanding consumer. Wine as a cultural asset was gaining traction'); Barham 'Translating *Terroir*', 129 (The 'presence of the GI on the label carries specific messages to the consumer about the process of production, as opposed to information on the inherent qualities of the product alone (ingredients, etc.) ... [These origin labels] hold the potential of re-linking production to the social, cultural and environmental aspects of particular places, further distinguishing them from anonymous mass produced goods, and opening the possibility of increased responsibility to place').

92   The Appellation of Origin in France

the politics associated with this form of resistance, there are those who recognise the potential for symbolic distinction in global markets and the associated 'de-fetishization' of the commodity:

> As Karl Marx observed, an important consequence of the emergence of industrial production was the elevation of the value of the commodity and the reduction of the value of workers' labour; hence the concept 'commodity fetishism'. Ascribing value to the means, location, or method of production would challenge this process of fetishization by urging consumers to purchase products that reflect the social lives of the producers; hence the term 'de-fetishization'.[65]

Second, as a corollary to the union of technique and topography, legal regimes acknowledge that regional products have histories. This includes a history of being consumed and being recognised as such.[66] The public awareness of a specific place of origin and associations of quality are forged over time. As opposed to any produce that satisfies a qualitative link, such as a newly discovered seam of marble, variety of plant or mineral in a region, these local products also have historic reputations. This is an expressly articulated requirement in the AO laws of certain countries.[67] Apart from consumer engagement and participation, it also implies that production techniques and boundaries could vary over time, avoiding the teleological sheen of perfection and finality sometimes ascribed to the registered product specification.

Third, producers have histories as well and once human input is recognised, the boundary drawing process becomes significantly more complicated. If internally homogenous parcels of place are no longer the sole or dispositive basis for defining authorised regions and historic contours of production also matter, a seductively objective basis for delimitation is lost. The rest of this chapter traces the process by which the institutions and actors within the French appellation regime were

---

[65] R. Coombe, S. Schnoor and M. Al Attar Ahmed, 'Bearing Cultural Distinction: Informational Capitalism and New Expectations for Intellectual Property' (2007) 40 *University of California–Davis Law Review* 891, 892–3, Fn 3.

[66] For the influential role of consumers, see D. Hancock, 'Commerce and Conversation in the Eighteenth-Century Atlantic: The Invention of Madeira Wine' (1998) 29 *Journal of Interdisciplinary History* 19, 197 ('The invention of Madeira wine was both an economic act—carried out in response to commercial motives—*and* a social act—not invented by a solitary "genius" but by an Atlantic network of producers, distributors, and consumers in intense conversation with one another').

[67] See, e.g., the discussion of Law No. 159/1973 Sb in J. Prošek and M. Vilimská, 'The Protection of Appellations of Origin in Czechoslovakia' [1975] *Industrial Property* 99, 100 ('[It] must have become generally known that a given geographical environment gives the product certain specific characteristics and that the appellation of origin is used precisely to emphasise that fact ... the objective existence of that fact does not suffice ... a link (must be) generally recognised by consumers and customers ... this result is attained after a certain period of intensive use').

compelled to reconsider *terroir* and ultimately recognise it as an amalgam of environmental and human factors, over a period of regulatory experimentation. If *terroir* helped provide conceptual resources, the more immediate prompt for regulation was phylloxera, the scourge which decimated French vineyards in the latter part of the nineteenth century. To better appreciate the magnitude of the problem let us first gaze into the unblinking compound eyes of the blight that prompted it.

4.   Phylloxera and fraud

The late nineteenth century was a sustained period of crisis for the French wine industry and the responses to this predicament would result in its systematic reorganisation. Phylloxera was not the only misfortune to beset French vineyards during this period. It was preceded by the onset of fungal diseases such as oidium or powdery mildew, which swept through European vineyards in the 1840s and 1850s, proving extremely difficult to control.[68] Whalen summarises the reasons for the gloom:

[The] challenges confronting French wine-producing regions during the late nineteenth and early twentieth centuries were collectively known as 'the wine crisis' (*la crise du vin*). Lasting nearly three quarters of a century, the wine crisis haunted the industry's biological, legal, sociological and economic vectors. Three biological blights of American provenance (imported with infected vines) – phylloxera (particularly between 1863 and 1900), mildew plasmopora viticola (1884), and blackrot uncinula necator (1898) – directly attacked the leaves, fruit and roots of French vines.[69]

Phylloxera is a tiny sap-sucking, aphid-like, root-louse[70] that feeds on the roots of grapevines. Native to the United States, it was accidentally introduced into Europe in the 1860s when infested vines from the East Coast of America were sent to France as museum specimens.[71] Ironically the steamers, otherwise feted for reducing the time of the journey, enabled the pest to survive it.[72] The consequences were devastating. As the roots of infected vines become distorted, the regeneration of new roots is inhibited thereby affecting the root system's ability to absorb water and minerals. The response to phylloxera was slow and co-ordinated at the regional level, in part because of

---

[68] Unwin, *Wine and the Vine*, 283–4.
[69] Whalen, '"Insofar as the Ruby Wine Seduces Them"', 68.
[70] Insert your favourite banker or lawyer joke here, gentle reader.
[71] M. G. Mullins, A. Bouquet and L. E. Williams, *The Biology of the Grapevine* (Cambridge University Press, 1992), 183.
[72] I. Stevenson, 'The Diffusion of Disaster: the Phylloxera Outbreak in the *Département* of the Hérault, 1862–80' (1980) 6 *Journal of Historical Geography* 47.

94   The Appellation of Origin in France

uncertainty as to whether the louse was the cause of infection or a symptom, being attracted to already weakened or infected vines. The infestation spread steadily and, by 1900, almost three quarters of French vineyards were affected. On the question of an appropriate response, a sharp division existed between those who favoured a largely chemical response[73] and those who advocated grafting vines on to resistant American rootstock. The latter ultimately proved successful, aided by experimental efforts in France alongside those of the redoubtable Texan plant scientist, Thomas V. Munson.[74] Once re-grafting was accepted as the best course of action, the remedy was straightforward in principle but required considerable further experimentation to find suitable vines that were not only resistant to the pest but also adapted to the soil and production conditions of each region. One important long-term consequence of this crisis was the emergence of a more scientific approach to viticulture and oenology.[75] However, in the short term, while the output from the traditional vineyards of Europe slumped during this period, demand did not. Ideal conditions were created not only for the fraudulent misrepresentation of origin but for cutting corners, adulteration and compromising on quality in general.

That there was manifest origin fraud during this period is recorded in a variety of sources. One wryly observes that the merchants of Burgundy were attempting to repeat the miracle at Cana. While not quite turning water into wine, they were certainly re-labelling Algerian reds as Burgundy originals.[76] Problems of wine adulteration and poor quality information for consumers created a 'market for lemons' situation with Sherry and Claret, leading to the collapse in the sales of genuine fine wines in the important British market.[77] During this period, both 'counterfeiting' (using a regional appellation in questionable or fraudulent circumstances) and adulteration (including the addition of water, sugar and artificial colouring) were not

---

[73] J. Simpson, 'Old World versus New World: The Origins of Organizational Diversity in the International Wine Industry, 1850–1914', Universidad Carlos III de Madrid, Working Papers in Economic History, (WP 09–01) (February 2009) 7, Fn 17 ('Injecting the vine's roots with liquid carbon bisulphide, spraying the vines with sulphocarbonate, or flooding the vineyard during the winter also temporarily halted phylloxera, but was too expensive as a solution for most growers').

[74] For an engaging account of the campaign to find a solution, see C. Campbell, *Phylloxera: How Wine was Saved for the World* (Harper Perennial, London 2004).

[75] H. W. Paul, *Science, Vine and Wine in Modern France* (Cambridge University Press, 1996).

[76] Foulkes, *Larousse Encyclopedia of Wine*, 131.

[77] J. Simpson, 'Selling to Reluctant Drinkers: the British Wine Market, 1860–1914' (2004) 57 *Economic History Review* 80.

uncommon.[78] Technological developments and organic chemistry in particular had opened up new possibilities to experiment with food and drink processing. While some of this experimentation was beneficial, Tim Unwin notes that other 'deleterious practices' which emerged in the wake of phylloxera included using hybrid vines producing unsuitable grapes, a general emphasis on quantity at the cost of quality and the addition of lead oxide to halt the acetification process.[79] Apart from the more extreme cases of adulteration, there was intense debate as to what constituted the authentic article. For instance, differences of opinion arose between *négociants* (merchant-manufacturers) and vignerons (vine growers) as to what genuine Champagne consisted of. Could merchants based in the *département* of Marne[80] source their grapes from outside the region and still label the end product as Champagne? What about Champagne houses based within the traditional region of production, who exported grapes to Germany for crushing and bottling? Guy asks: 'What *was* Champagne? Was it a blend of certain types of grapes? Was it a blend of grapes from an exclusive region? What were the boundaries of that region? Was there a relation between these boundaries and the manufacturing of the wine [and] what was the basis for these limits and boundaries?'[81]

The vine shortages caused by phylloxera had also forced merchants to search for new sources of supply, sometimes from other countries or through the production of artificial wines. This degree of greater flexibility was not surrendered without protest:

The subsequent recovery in domestic production was not accompanied by a marked reduction in these [alternative] supplies, and growers had to stand by and watch prices, and their profits, fall steeply from the turn of the twentieth century, leading to demands that the government intervene ... However, opinion was divided on the most appropriate forms of market intervention, and conflicts occurred not just between growers and merchants but also between large and small growers, producers of fine and ordinary wines, and growers in different geographic locations.[82]

---

[78] A. Stanziani, 'Information, Quality and Legal Rules: Wine Adulteration in Nineteenth Century France' (2009) 51 *Business History* 268 (exploring both innovation and adulteration as the consequences of advances in the artificial processing of foodstuff during this period).

[79] Unwin, *Wine and the Vine*, 313–14.

[80] France is presently divided into administrative units known as regions, which are further subdivided into *départements* (departments). At the lowest level of the administrative divisions, we find the *commune*, which is roughly equivalent to municipalities, parishes, towns or cities in other countries.

[81] Guy, *When Champagne Became French*, 121.

[82] J. Simpson, 'Cooperation and Conflicts: Institutional Innovation in France's Wine Markets, 1870–1911' (2005) 79 *Business History Review* 527, 528.

96   The Appellation of Origin in France

Along with a drop in quality, the epidemic resulted in an increase in quantity in its aftermath as well as successive price crashes for grape harvests. When overproduction was coupled with perceptions of widespread fraud, the relative value of wine to the French economy entered a decline and the government was forced to intervene. The task before it was therefore to address origin fraud while ensuring quality and also repressing overproduction.[83] Of great concern was the indiscriminate replanting of vines in well-known regions, since the adoption of high-yielding, lower quality vines pushed down prices and threatened the ability of vignerons to make a living. Charles Warner describes the result: 'The Government began to protect the winegrower from himself by protecting his product'.[84] This would ultimately lead to the controlled planting and cultivation of vines, and subsequent limitation of yields, as part of a regime designed to maintain standards of quality. Today European wine legislation continues to require the stipulation of quality related criteria, such as (1) the demarcation of the area of production; (2) the classification of vine varieties; (3) the specification of cultivation methods; (4) the minimum natural alcoholic strength by volume; (5) the yield per hectare etc.[85] However, the initial challenge was to identify the basis for delimiting the authentic product and its region of production.

5.   From the AO to the AOC

As a preface to what follows, two thematic trends are worth emphasising. The first concerns *terroir*. The French parliamentary response to this crisis reveals the extent to which *terroir*, in the geographically deterministic sense, was considered a necessary or sufficient condition to guarantee wine quality. The following episodes demonstrate that guaranteeing truthful origin labelling per se is an insufficient condition, as defining the region of origin is often a political, contentious act occasionally leading to large, geographically diverse regions being specified while the legal regime gradually recognised the importance of human agency in producing quality wine, by imposing stricter controls on production standards. Both these developments undermined the proposition that neat parcels of physical geography were dispositively responsible for the virtues of the end product.

---

[83] C. K. Warner, *The Winegrowers of France and the Government since 1875* (Columbia University Press, New York 1960), 26–9.

[84] Ibid., viii.

[85] J. Audier, 'Protection of Geographical Indications in France and Protection of French Geographical Indications in Other Countries', October 1997 (WIPO/GEO/EGR/97/8 Rev), 4.

From the AO to the AOC 97

The second trend relates to the continuity between IS protection and the emerging AO system. The ensuing legislative frameworks incorporated responses to perceived lacunae under the laws of 1824 and 1857, as well as the international treaties considered in Chapter 2. To begin with, an accurate delimitation at the national level was increasingly desirable as a precondition for effective international protection.[86] We have already encountered complaints that the boundaries for the region of origin in the home country were often too fluid to act as a helpful benchmark against which to measure all products bearing that designation. The second point arises out of extant French legislation addressing IS protection. Since these laws were focused on inaccurate labels of origin, there was no additional condition that the product must possess a reputation or certain qualities on the basis of its origin. In short, reputation and quality were not central to the enquiry.[87] Third, if generic use was established, then the place name was no longer reserved for producers or traders from the region in question. Such use was not considered objectionable on the basis of being misleading.[88] While certain representative associations such as those of Champagne could successfully resist genericide challenges within France,[89] others could not. There was also no uniform method for determining the boundaries of the production region. Finally, there was no mechanism for establishing minimum quality requirements, whereas the adulteration of wine had been a genuine concern in the latter half of the nineteenth century.[90] Thus concerns that initially arose out of experiences with the IS regulation system were incorporated and eventually addressed by the AO regime that followed.

---

[86] P. Roubier, *Le Droit de la Propriété Industrielle*, Vol. 2 (Editions du Recueil Sirey, Paris 1954), 754; Études Générales, 'La Question des Fausses Indications de Provenance et l'Arrangement de Madrid' [1920] *Propriété Industrielle* 40, 43.

[87] Roubier, *Le Droit de la Propriété Industrielle*, Vol. 2, 754.

[88] É. Calmels, *De la Propriété et de la Contrefaçon* (Cosse, Paris 1856), 267; L. Donzel, *Commentaire et Critique de la Convention Internationale du 20 Mars 1883* (Marchal & Billard, Paris 1891), 47–8.

[89] See, e.g., *Syndicat du Commerce des Vins de Champagne* v. *Ackerman Laurance* (Court of Appeal, Angers, 15 December 1891) reported in [1892] *Propriété Industrielle* 145 (The sale of wines from Saumur, using 'Champagne' on advertising materials and labels, was an act of unfair competition since Champagne had not become a generic term for sparkling wine); *Chapin et Cie* v. *le Syndicat du Commerce des Vins de Champagne* (Court of Appeal, Paris 1st chamber, 18 November 1892, reported in [1893] *Propriété Industrielle* 111 (Champagne refers to both a manufacturing process as well as a region of origin, so unlike eau de Cologne it cannot be used generically to describe the result of a manufacturing process).

[90] A. Stanziani, 'Wine Reputation and Quality Controls: The Origin of the AOCs in 19th Century France' (2004) 18 *European Journal of Law and Economics* 149, 157–9.

98   The Appellation of Origin in France

5.1   The Law of 1905

Previous attempts had been made to address particular fraudulent practices that affected wine quality,[91] but it is with the law of 1 August 1905 that a systematic response began to take shape.[92] Although its focus was on origin labelling, it is worth noting that there were other potential vectors for regulating the wine industry around this period and Whalen identifies 'estates (property) in Bordeaux, labels (manufacturer) in Champagne and varietals in Alsace' as possible targets for regulatory intervention.[93] The Law of 1905 was broadly targeted at the repression of fraud in the sale of merchandise as well as falsification of foodstuffs and agricultural products. In relevant part, Article 1 prescribed imprisonment or fines for anyone who deceived or attempted to mislead a contracting party (purchaser) as to the nature, substantial qualities, composition and content of the useful features of any goods, or mislead with regard to their variety or origin, where the false designation of variety or origin was considered the main cause for the sale.[94] This presupposed that benchmarks existed for genuine products, starting with a blueprint for the area of origin. Here the law proposed an important regulatory innovation. Under Article 11 it left the establishment of individual product specifications to administrative authorities by way of regulations (*règlements d'administration publique*). Regrettably, it did not identify criteria for delimiting boundaries around those places entitled to the use of a designation, which would lead to much ensuing conflict.

The first significant development was the Decree of 3 September 1907, which applied to wines, sparkling wines, brandies and spirits.[95] It confirmed the objective of protecting valuable wine appellations by restricting their use to owners, vignerons, *négociants* and traders within defined regions (Articles 10–12). The proscription would be activated by

---

[91] Such as the Loi Griffe of 14 August 1889, named after the Senator of Hérault, which legally defined wine as a beverage made by the fermentation of fresh grapes and thereby regulated practices such as the watering of wine. See Warner, *The Winegrowers of France*, 39–40.

[92] Loi du 1er Août 1905 sur les Fraudes et Falsifications en Matière de Produits ou de Services (5 August 1905) *Journal Officiel* 4813. Also reproduced in [1906] *Propriété Industrielle* 65.

[93] Whalen, 'Cultural Strategies for Selling Wine', Fn 46.

[94] Art. 1er – *Quiconque aura tenté de tromper le contractant*:
Soit sur la nature, les qualités substantielles, la composition et la teneur en principes utiles de toutes marchandises; Soit sur leur espèce ou leur origine lorsque, d'après la convention ou les usages, la désignation de l'espèce ou de l'origine, faussement attribuées aux marchandises, devra être considérée comme la cause principale de la vente ... Sera puni de l'emprisonnement pendant trois mois au moins, un an au plus, et d'une amende de cent francs (100 fr) au moins, de cinq mille francs (5000 fr) au plus, ou de l'une de ces deux peines seulement.

[95] See [1912] *Propriété Industrielle* 61.

the use on labels, containers, invoices and other documentation, of a geographical designation that would create confusion in the mind of the purchaser (Article 13). The demarcation process was also touched upon by the Law of 5 August 1908, which supplemented Article 11 of the Law of 1905.[96] It proposed that boundaries should be established on the basis of constant local usages of the appellation but did not provide any further guidance as to what this meant.[97] This framework may have been a well-intentioned response to fraud and an attempt to improve quality, but the myopic focus on origin proved disastrous. Joseph Capus, a prominent architect of the modern French AOC regime, steadily criticised the flawed assumption that by regulating the truthful use of geographical origin on labels, problems associated with product quality would fall into line.[98] Origin alone was simply insufficient to guarantee wine quality. He spent the better part of three decades arguing that recognising existing best practices and organising production along these lines was a crucial complement to geography. Under the 1905 Law, the problem of fraud as to quality remained unaddressed, while the competing lobbies associated with demarcating origin regions threatened to become unmanageable. Establishing boundary limits was not simply based on geological or geographical criteria but was a politically charged process. Interested parties scrambled to be on the right side of the line. This development severely undermined the proposition that the system was based on distinct geographical regions whose natural conditions deterministically influence and thereby guarantee quality.

A series of decrees were promulgated by the Conseil d'Etat between 1908 and 1912, based on the recommendations of local consultative commissions. These defined regions of production for well-known appellations including Champagne, Banyuls, Cognac and Armagnac,[99] but the boundaries proved to be divisive. Tensions emerged within the *département* of the Gironde, as a result of the delimitation exercise for Bordeaux. While growers in the Gironde were insistent that their grapes

---

[96] Loi du 5 Août 1908 Modification de l'Article 11 de la Loi du 1 Août 1905 et Completant Cette Loi par Un Article Additionnel (11 August 1908) *Journal Officiel* 5637.

[97] According to the Law of 1908, preventing misleading use required: '*la définition et la dénomination des boissons, denrées et produits conformément aux usages commerciaux ... [et] la délimitation des régions pouvant prétendre exclusivement aux appellations de provenance des produits. Cette délimitation sera faite en prenant pour base les usages locaux constants*'.

[98] See generally J. Capus, *L'Evolution de la Législation sur les Appellations d'Origine: Genèse des Appellations Contrôlées* (L. Larmat (impr. de Le Moil et Pascaly), Paris 1947). The text is available at www.inao.gouv.fr/public/home.php.

[99] A. Taillefer and C. Claro, *Traité des Marques de Fabrique et de la Concurrence Déloyale en Tous Genres, d'Eugène Pouillet*, 6th edn (Marchal et Godde, Paris 1912), 582–3.

were of superior quality and the appellation should have a local sourcing requirement, the opposition came from *négociants*. After a poor harvest, it would be harder to maintain both price and quality if grapes or wine from other regions could not be resorted to for blending purposes. The new regime also imposed additional administrative requirements and operational costs in its wake. Furthermore, restricting the use of Bordeaux to locally sourced wines from the Gironde could perversely incentivise low quality, high-yield vineyards within the region, creating a classic free rider problem.[100] Meanwhile the constitution of the commission itself had been a sensitive matter. While it initially consisted of a mix of administrators, local elected representatives (such as mayors), winemakers and *négociants*, as the number of growers' associations increased the commission finally resorted to an expedient bureaucratic solution. The Bordeaux production region was effectively mapped on to the contours of the administrative department of the Gironde, triggering protests by those who were excluded.[101] The opposition was partially based on the established practice of sending wine from outside the Gironde down the Garonne and Dordogne rivers to be sold in Bordeaux, while the commission had dismissed this practice as inconsequential. Attempts were subsequently made to redress this with revised delimitations by a new commission established after 1908. Here it was a group of technicians, archivists and professors of agriculture, but they broadly endorsed the previous commission's decision.[102] The Decree of 18 February 1911 ultimately restricted the use of the appellation to the Gironde, with several *communes* within it being identified for exclusion.[103]

By contrast, the demarcation of the Champagne production region was far more controversial. A number of conflicting interests pulled in different directions, impeding any consensus. First there were the established divisions between *négociants* and vignerons, who had been engaged in a longer term tussle over the 'soul of Champagne'.[104] The more successful Champagne houses had initially opted for individual branding as the preferred strategy, appeared to value production process rather than origin by mass producing Champagne, gained the ability to set prices for buying grapes and preferred to retain the flexibility to

---

[100] Simpson, 'Cooperation and Conflicts', 550–2 ('The establishment of the geographic appellation can be interpreted in two different ways: as an attempt to improve quality by excluding inferior wines from outside the region; or as an effort to restrict the number of growers who could use the Bordeaux name').

[101] Stanziani, 'Wine Reputation and Quality Controls', 160.

[102] Loubère, *The Wine Revolution in France*, 116.

[103] See [1912] *Propriété Industrielle* 64.

[104] See Guy, *When Champagne Became French*, Chapters 3 and 4.

source grapes from outside the Marne when required. On the other hand, the vignerons identified with the spiritual bond that *terroir* represented and their livelihood depended on regular purchases by the *négociants*. Given the fragmented pattern of landholding, the vignerons could muster large numbers and, over time, collectively organised to possess a powerful political voice. Subsequently a combination of phylloxera, ensuing fraud and the international misuse of Champagne seems to have gradually compelled these two broad groupings to work more closely together to define the authentic Champagne.

While this may have brought some harmony to the Marne, it was not sufficient to prevent matters reaching flash point as a result of the Decree of 17 December 1908, which restricted production to specified locations within the *départements* of Marne and Aisne.[105]

[The] modern department of the Marne contains Epernay and Reims, the two major centers of production, but the old province of Champagne was much more extensive, taking in also the modern departments of Aube, Haut-Marne and Ardennes. Growers in the Aube were particularly incensed at being excluded from the first boundary proposal, as they claimed they had replanted after the phylloxera crisis with low-yielding varieties to guarantee quality.[106]

What counted as customary local usage under the law of 1908 remained unclear and this decree resulted in the Aube's exclusion, despite claims that there was a history of production there, geographical conditions were also favourable and for centuries the Aube wines had been bought by the *négociants* of Reims and Epernay as true Champagne wines. This led to escalating protests and demonstrations. Another factor was the increase in Champagne exports, despite poor harvests in the traditional Champagne grape-growing regions, implying that winemakers within these regions were being less than scrupulous. Even stocks of reserves could not account for such healthy export figures and resentment against external sourcing of wine increased further. In one notorious incident, 5,000 protestors marched on Ay and then Epernay, which led to the dispatch of 15,000 troops to put down the violent protest.[107] Two subsequent interventions attempted to deal with this specific controversy, by (1) defining additional measures to ensure the provenance of the wine and keeping the activities of *négociants* in check, while also (2) expanding the Champagne appellation region to include a second

---

[105] See [1912] *Propriété Industrielle* 62.
[106] Simpson, 'Cooperation and Conflicts', 557.
[107] For details on the protests, see A. L. Simon, *The History of Champagne* (Ebury Press, London 1962), 106–10; Guy, *When Champagne Became French*, 158–85.

102   The Appellation of Origin in France

zone, which would have to be identified as such on bottles but included growers from the Aube, Haut-Marne and Seine-et-Marne.[108]

Even this synoptic appraisal suggests that appellation regions were often born out of compromises between contemporary administrative departments, geographically homogenous regions, previous incarnations of political boundaries as well as historic usage of the designation. Alessandro Stanziani observes that these early decrees were not even inspired by uniform delimitation principles.[109] These regions were therefore constructed rather than found. The political fallout of these difficult delimitations was so acute that a better fixation process was urgently sought. The Law of 1905 lacked an effective basis for defining regions of origin, while leaving substantive quality concerns unaddressed. Geographical origin as a proxy for authenticity was proving problematic, while the French regime had been premised on the idea that geographical origin would guarantee quality.[110] The contingency of this metric is thus exposed but the legislative response would have to wait until after the First World War to be put into effect.

5.2   The Law of 1919

The law of 1919[111] represents an attempt to respond to the shortcomings of the Law of 1905. It incorporated a more elaborate formula for determining the place of origin and shifted the power to make these determinations from administrative authorities to the judiciary, on a case-by-case basis. The law also formally moved beyond the IS and adopted Appellation of Origin terminology for the vector representing the link between product and place. The test for prohibited use is contained in Article 1 and applied where a person directly or indirectly indicated on a natural or manufactured product, in a prejudicial manner, a place of origin contrary to its actual origin, or contrary to the origin established by local, honest and constant usage.[112] There are a

---

[108] For the Law of 10 February 1911 and Decree of 7 June 1911, see [1912] *Propriété Industrielle* 62–3.

[109] Stanziani, 'Wine Reputation and Quality Controls', 161.

[110] See Auriol *et al.*, 'France', 64; Unwin, *Wine and the Vine*, 312; Zhao, 'Understanding Classifications', 184 ('In the French appellation system, a high-ranked appellation is officially recognized to be superior to a low-ranked appellation in producing wines with better quality').

[111] Loi du 6 Mai 1919 Relative à la Protection des Appellations d'Origine (8 May 1919) *Journal Officiel* 4726; [1919] *Propriété Industrielle* 61.

[112] *Toute personne qui prétendra qu'une appellation d'origine est appliquée à son préjudice direct ou indirect et contre son droit à un produit naturel ou fabriqué et contrairement à l'origine de ce produit, ou à des usages locaux, loyaux et constants, aura une action en justice pour faire interdire l'usage de cette appellation.*

number of additional interesting features that can only be mentioned in passing.[113] The attempt to replace administrative with judicial determination can be viewed as an experiment in testing relative institutional strengths and weaknesses. While administrative decrees within the framework law of 1905 had the advantage of being easy to update by tracking new technical developments and generated region-specific outcomes, the transition to judicial delimitation was an attempt to depoliticise the process and ground it in expert assessment. Stanziani also evaluates their comparative efficiencies by contrasting an administrative or 'rule' driven approach (*ex post* clarity, but also rigidity) with a judicial or 'standards' driven approach (*ex ante* ambiguity, but allowing for flexibility).[114] The new law of 1919 repealed the previously established decrees under the Law of 1905 (Article 24) but producers in these regions continued to have a presumptive right to use the appellation. On the other hand groups formerly excluded from an appellation could apply to be included, thereby modifying its established contours.

The necessary prompt for the determination was also curious. It occurred through the artifice of summary proceedings in a civil suit between a group claiming to represent the interests of the producers from the region and an individual who claimed an entitlement to use the appellation. This provides us with an instance of a systematic *sui generis* approach that is non-registration based. The suit was then advertised in local gazettes and opened up to other interested parties for intervention (Articles 2–4). Furthermore, the law operated on the basis that the courts would recognise existing rights rather than create them. The purpose of the suit was purely to define the conditions under which persons were entitled to use the appellation and the outcome was not just limited to the parties but applied *erga omnes* (Article 7). The legislation was clear that the right to protect an AO was also a collective right (Article 1, para. 2).[115] It refers to penal sanctions such as imprisonment and fines, arising out of state action (Articles 8 and 9) while leaving open the possibility for traders to initiate proceedings in *délict* under Article 1381 of the French Civil Code. Opting between penal or civil routes would be influenced by a comparison of the usual factors – the costs, evidentiary requirements

---

      La même action appartiendra aux syndicats et associations régulièrement constitués depuis six mois au moins, quant aux droits qu'ils ont pour objet de défendre.

[113] For a more detailed account of the factors leading to its enactment, see R. Guérillon, *Les Appellations d'Origine: Loi du 6 Mai 1919* (Journal l'Epicier, Paris 1919).

[114] See Stanziani, 'Wine Reputation and Quality Controls'.

[115] The right to bring an action was not restricted to individuals: '*La même action appartiendra aux syndicats et associations régulièrement constitués depuis six mois au moins, quant aux droits qu'ils ont pour objet de défendre*'.

104   The Appellation of Origin in France

and burden of proof to establish an infraction as well as the remedies available under each option. In addition there were detailed provisions to encourage truthfulness and monitor the production of wines, sparkling wines and brandies, such as the need for the harvester or distiller to make a declaration of origin and the need to maintain accurate production records (Articles 11–21). However, for our purposes, two features are of particular interest. The first was a specific rule for viticultural products, preventing the generic use of an appellation once it had been formally recognised,[116] which we have already seen debated in the context of the Madrid Agreement. The second concerns the possibility of inclusion within an appellation region on the basis of local, honest and long-standing usage (*usages locaux, loyaux et constants*) in Article 1. How precisely did these factors affect the boundary determination algorithm? Were they an *additional criterion* to truthful geographical origin labelling, referring to established production methods? Were they an *alternative* to being located in the named region of origin, whereby one could still access the appellation? Or were they an *optional supplement* to the origin requirement, brought into play only in certain cases?

While the legislative text is ambiguous, the drafting history makes it clear that these three factors were merely intended as an optional supplement in certain situations, thereby dashing the hopes of those who believed that the elusive quality controls had finally made an appearance. Widespread and customary production practices were seen to represent the distilled wisdom of experiments aimed at improving quality. While this was acknowledged in the formative legislative deliberations, when the Law of 1919 was finally enacted the infringement test was restricted to the truthful use of regions of origin alone. Where the contours of production based on historic regions extended beyond contemporary *départemental* boundaries, the local, loyal and constant use of the name by producers in the contiguous region could be the basis for lawfully using the appellation.[117] The focus was on legitimating the entitlement to use the appellation based on duration rather than on identifying long-standing production practices with an eye to improving quality. Capus draws on judgments parsing this provision to show that '*usages locaux, loyaux et constants*' was boldly interpreted by some as requiring the use of collectively established production methods while it was interpreted by others as the means for working out the contours of historical entitlement to use of the

---

[116] Art. 10 - *Les appellations d'origine des produits vinicoles ne pourront jamais être considérées comme présentant un caractère générique et tombées dans le domaine public.*
[117] Roubier, *Le Droit de la Propriété Industrielle*, 760–1.

name.[118] Two widely discussed judgments by the Court of Paris on 16 January 1923 concerning Champagne,[119] as well as decisions by the Cour de Cassation on 26 and 27 May 1925[120] confirmed that use of the appellation within the contours of the historic former province of Champagne would be permitted, since this was the sort of local, loyal and constant usage that the legislation catered for. On this basis, *communes* (municipalities) within the region of Bar-sur-Aube were included while those within the Bar-sur-Seine were not. These additional usage factors therefore assisted with the question of when to extend geographical coverage of an appellation region, but their foundation was open to criticism.

Paul Roubier identifies the vulnerability of this approach. The Law of 1919 continued to rely on origin as the touchstone for prohibiting objectionable uses. Yet ensuring truthful origin marking would only ensure the quality of the product for a handful of 'natural' products, such as mineral water or particular varieties of clay. By de-emphasising production conditions, vignerons located in a famous region or otherwise traditionally entitled to the use of the name would technically be able to use an appellation signifying a high-quality wine despite using inferior quality, high-yield vines or by attempting to grow vines in unsuitable soil within the region.[121] As one commentator suggests:

The courts of France elaborated [upon the geographic origin criterion] between 1919 and 1935. They emphasised through this period that *appellations d'origine* were protected primarily because conditions in particular regions produced certain beneficial results for goods such as wine. These natural conditions included soil, water, vegetation, fauna and climate unique to the area in question.[122]

The limitation of this approach was that while judges could define geographical boundaries, 'they were not competent to specify other production criteria for an appellation. All kinds of area could be, and were, declared to be appellations, the outcome being a host of appellations of origin throughout the wine industry'.[123]

---

[118] Capus, *L'Evolution de la Législation sur les Appellations d'Origine.*

[119] (December 1923) *Gazette du Palais* 615.

[120] *Syndicat Général des Vignerons de la Champagne Viticole Délimitée* v. *Syndicat Régional des Vignerons de Champagne; Syndicat Régional des Vignerons de Champagne* v. *Syndicat Général des Vignerons de la Champagne Viticole Délimitée* [1928] *Propriété Industrielle* 183–4.

[121] Roubier, *Le Droit de la Propriété Industrielle*, 780–5.

[122] L. C. Lenzen, 'Bacchus in the Hinterlands: A Study of Denominations of Origin in French and American Wine-Labeling Laws' (1968) 58 TMR 145, 178.

[123] OECD, Appellations of Origin and Geographical Indications in OECD Member Countries: Economic and Legal Implications (COM/AGR/APM/TD/WP(2000) 15/FINAL), 58.

106   The Appellation of Origin in France

A related concern under this approach was that such delimited regions might be geologically and environmentally indistinguishable from neighbouring regions. Commenting on Cassis, Daniel Gade observes that 'where the [appellation] follows political boundaries, the *terroir* notion is especially questionable'.[124] When Cassis is compared with neighbouring appellation regions such as Bandol, climate and soil types are much the same. He puts the difference between the two down to historical production choices such as the emphasis on red wines as opposed to whites.[125] This is a useful reminder that 'the manner in which assumptions about natural environmental influences are used to assert and justify political and territorial control' needs careful attention.[126] En route to a more justifiable and coherent system, an important milestone was achieved with the Law of 1927.[127] It responded to the persistent Champagne boundary controversy by moving closer to the ideal of directly ensuring minimum standards of quality. Here, in addition to production within the named geographical region, it introduced the requirements of stipulated vines and grape varieties while banning certain hybrids. It also contained requirements for site identification within the broader region, on the basis of geological conditions suited to those vines.[128] The law further specified that the traditional method of fermentation in the bottle was the only approved process. Cumulatively, these requirements were based on a more demanding interpretation of local, loyal and constant practices. This law reflects the progressive acknowledgement of the human contribution, which would be more fully recognised in the AOC regime that followed.

Before turning to the AOC, it is worth noting that conceptual ambiguity surrounding the link between product and place is not restricted to France alone. If a classification system expresses social values and embodies beliefs, any claims of purely deterministic influence based on geographical origin become contestable, despite the sheen of objectivity. Newer wine growing countries, such as the US and Australia, lack the centuries of experimentation where vine types were matched to particular regions and production practices, while they intentionally avoid being

---

[124] D. W. Gade, 'Tradition, Territory, and Terroir in French Viniculture: Cassis, France, and Appellation Contrôlée' (2004) 94 *Annals of the Association of American Geographers* 848, 864.

[125] Ibid., 864–5.

[126] W. Moran, 'The Wine Appellation as Territory in France and California' (1993) 83 *Annals of the Association of American Geographers* 694, 694.

[127] Loi du 22 Juillet 1927 Modifie La Loi Du 6 Mai 1919 (Protection Des Appellations D'origine) (27 July 1927) *Journal Officiel* 7762; [1927] *Propriété Industrielle* 146.

[128] N. Olszak, *Droit des Appellations d'Origine et Indications de Provenance* (TEC & DOC, Paris 2001), 43.

prescriptive and leave wine makers free to experiment.[129] However, the US and Australia have also chosen to delimit wine production regions by giving primacy to criteria based upon identifying geographically homogenous regions. Here physical geography is assumed to provide a seductively scientific and objective basis for drawing up regions, while also implicitly acting as a guarantor of consistent quality.

The recent Coonawarra dispute in Australia is a case in point and concerns the delimitation process for this reputed Australian wine region. The Geographical Indication Committee arrived at an initial determination based on both scientific and historical usage criteria. Predictably those from proximate vineyards who were excluded appealed this boundary. On appeal, the Administrative Appeals Tribunal (AAT) enlarged the boundary, giving importance to historical evidence.[130] Under the relevant rules, history includes factors such as the founding and development of the area, the history of the word/expression used to indicate the area, traditional divisions in that area and the history of grape and wine production there. Geography includes topographical features such as rivers and contour lines, natural formations, climate (temperature, atmospheric pressure, humidity, rainfall etc.), natural drainage basins, elevation etc.[131] The AAT found that proximity to the *terra rossa* strip was important. Nevertheless it held:

In establishing this particular region the criteria which relate to the history and traditional divisions within the area have been more useful as a means of determining the boundary of a reasonably homogenous tract of land. Further geographical features, consistent with this historical and traditional division have been used to establish a region reasonably discrete from its surrounding areas.[132]

On appeal it was held that the identification of the boundaries of a region, and the determination of a word or expression to be used to identify the region so determined, were separate matters under the relevant statute.[133] While history and human involvement could relate to the identification of the *name* of a GI, these factors should not influence the *contours of production*. For the latter, the aim was to identify a 'discrete and homogenous' tract of land based primarily on the physical

---

[129] This hands off approach is considered a crucial factor in the recent success of New World wines. See K. Anderson (ed.), *The World's Wine Markets: Globalization at Work* (Edward Elgar, Cheltenham 2004); R. Jordan, P. Zidda and L. Lockshin, 'Behind the Australian Wine Industry's Success: Does Environment Matter?' (2007) 19 *International Journal of Wine Business Research* 14.

[130] *Penola High School* v. *Geographical Indications Committee* [2001] AATA 844.

[131] Ibid., [20].   [132] Ibid., [146].

[133] *Beringer Blass Wine Estates* v. *GIC* 70 ALD 27 (2002) (FCA).

108   The Appellation of Origin in France

attributes of the area under consideration, despite an acknowledgement that 'climate, water, drainage and soil conditions did not provide discernible boundaries'.[134]

This kind of thinking has led to a renewed critical interest amongst geographers. Indicative of this interest, Glenn Banks and Scott Sharpe reassert the importance of human intervention. There 'is little that is solely natural in such productive economic geographies, parochial "myths" of local environments and wine quality notwithstanding'.[135] One implication is that metrics of quality can vary. In order to inform consumers about what to expect from the bottle, New World wines are classified primarily by grape varietals, while European wines are classified primarily on the basis of geographic origin. Thus Bordeaux, Chianti and Rioja wines sit alongside bottles of Chardonnay, Cabernet Sauvignon and Pinot Noir on shop shelves. While European regimes have spent decades gradually distancing themselves from a paradigm with physical geography given dispositive importance, New World regimes may be in danger of drifting towards it. The Law of 1919 therefore showcases the limits of an approach excessively reliant upon geographical boundaries alone.

5.3   The Laws of 1935 and 1947

There was an emerging consensus by this stage in France that guaranteeing geographical origin was insufficient and the Law of 1927 suggested the way forward. Since the judicial determination procedure generated uncertainty, a permanent official body was instead to be entrusted with recognising geographical boundaries as well as production specifications. In turn this would enable purchasers to rely on origin as a cue for specific, desirable product characteristics. The new regime was therefore conceived as a system for guaranteeing both origin and quality[136] and on 30 July 1935 the law creating the *Appellation d'Origine Contrôlée* (AOC) regime made its debut.[137] The change in nomenclature signals the transition towards greater product regulation and 'control'. The body which initially attempted to co-ordinate public and private interests in this field of regulation was the Comité National des Appellations d'Origine (CNAO). It began the monumental task of demarcating the vineyards

---

[134] Ibid., [72].

[135] G. Banks and S. Sharpe, 'Wine, Regions and the Geographic Imperative: The Coonawarra Example' (2006) 62 *New Zealand Geographer* 173, 174.

[136] Roubier, *Le Droit de la Propriété Industrielle*, 794.

[137] Décret-loi du 30 juillet 1935 Relatif à la Défense du Marché des Vins et au Régime Economique de l'Alcool (31 July 1935) *Journal Officiel* 8314.

From the AO to the AOC 109

and appellations, subsequently being renamed in 1947 as the Institut National des Appellations d'Origine (INAO),[138] which continues this work today.

The original purpose of INAO was twofold – the delimitation and definition of appellations, along with the repression of their fraudulent use. In the process of defining appropriate practices, it would also exercise broader regulatory functions such as controlling for overproduction. At present, the products which qualify under this regime are those that have a duly established 'notoriety' and whose production is subject to control and protection procedures[139] and include agricultural produce, forestry or food products as well as those from the sea, that meet the requirements of the AO in Article L115–1 of the Consumer Code.[140] Although usually a bottom-up process beginning with a voluntary submission from local producers, the registration procedure is elaborate and passes through several stages of scrutiny, whereupon the final product is specified in a decree.[141] At the time of writing, the initial request is submitted to the INAO regional office which in turn submits it to national committees, divided on the basis of product categories, for further scrutiny. A review commission is established which reports back to the national committee, advising acceptance, postponement or refusal. If accepted, an expert commission is then constituted to establish the geographical delimitation. The national committee then approves these boundaries and drafts a Decree, which is sent to the Ministry of Agriculture for approval and enactment.[142] At present, the application specifications usually contain the following: details of the applicant; the appellation name; product type; product description; delimitation of the area; method for obtaining the product; the elements justifying the link with geographical origin; references to control and inspection mechanisms; and, finally, details concerning labelling.[143] However, the

---

[138] Décret du 16 Juillet 1947 Fixant La Composition Du Comité National Des Appellations d'Origine (19 July 1947) *Journal Officiel* 6948.

[139] Art. L641–5 of the Code Rural et de la Pêche Maritime.

[140] Art. L115–1 defines the AO: *Constitue une appellation d'origine la dénomination d'un pays, d'une région ou d'une localité servant à désigner un produit qui en est originaire et dont la qualité ou les caractères sont dus au milieu géographique, comprenant des facteurs naturels et des facteurs humains.*

[141] The French registration procedure and relevant institutions involved are specified in some detail in EC 'Response to the Checklist of Questions: Review under Art 24.2', 26 March 1999 (IP/C/W/117/Add.10), 58–70.

[142] See F. Wenger, 'The Role of National Administrations in the protection of Geographical Indications: The Example of France', June 2001 (WIPO/GEO/CIS/01/3), 8–10; A. Paly, 'Organisation of the AOC Wine Industry in France' (2001) 26 *AIDV Bulletin* 2.

[143] For an overview of the registration process, see INAO, 'Guide du Demandeur d'une Appellation d'Origine (AOC/AOP)' (30 March 2009), available at www.inao.gouv.fr.

110   The Appellation of Origin in France

role of INAO was recalibrated in 2006–7, in what may be characterised as a gradual withdrawal of state supervision on the enforcement side.[144] Further changes to the system have been brought about as a result of the greater integration within the EU registration system for agricultural products and foodstuffs, considered in Part II of this book.

Once again, for the purposes of this chapter, our focus is on the re-conceptualisation of the link between product and place that was incorporated within the new regime. Since the aim was to guarantee quality, decisions under the Law of 1919 were superseded by product-specific decrees under the new law and a revised understanding of 'local, loyal and constant' was central to the transition. The goal was to identify established methods for obtaining the product, rather than recognition based on historic usage of the designation alone. One author interprets these criteria as follows: local is in contrast to individual, suggesting a collective interest; loyal is honest as opposed to questionable or fraudulent practices; and constant implies consistent, tried and tested techniques.[145] Stephen Ladas suggests that the 'basic condition for the recognition of such human factors ... is that they represent local usages lawfully and constantly practised for a sufficiently long period as to have become traditional in reflecting definite qualities and characteristics of the products concerned'.[146] French courts had already begun to incorporate such production practices into their decisions, even prior to the Law of 1935. According to one interpretation, long-standing but individual practices were not sufficient and the practice needed to have been collectively adopted in the region.[147] On the other hand, if the same conditions of production, including vines and soil types established by customary use, were satisfied, the use of the appellation could extend beyond the named area.[148] Particular modes of manufacture also

---

[144] D. Marie-Vivien, 'The Role of the State in the Protection of Geographical Indications: From Disengagement in France/Europe to Significant Involvement in India' (2010) 13 JWIP 121, 122 ('The French substantive reform of 2006 provided a step backward in state involvement and a transfer of activities from the state to the producer organizations. It reinforced the role of the producers in the building of the GI specification and it provided for the disengagement of INAO in the inspection and control activities').

[145] G. Lagarde, 'Place of Origin: France', in H. L. Pinner (ed.), *World Unfair Competition Law: An Encyclopedia*, Vol. II, (Sijthoff Leyden, Holland 1965), 636, 637.

[146] S. P. Ladas, *Patents, Trademarks and Related Rights: National and International Protection*, Vol. III, (Harvard University Press, Cambridge MA 1975), 1577.

[147] *Veuve Rodiès v. Société Civile d'Yquem et Autres* [1931] *Propriété Industrielle* 230 (Cour de Cassation, 4–6 June 1931); *Bravay et Autres v. Syndicat des Propriétaires Viticulteurs de Châteauneuf-du-Pape et Autres* [1935] *Propriété Industrielle* 76 (Cour de Cassation, 21 November 1933).

[148] *Syndicat Viticole de Sauternes et de Barsac v. Chaumel et Autres* [1935] *Propriété Industrielle* 76 (Bordeaux Court of Appeal, 19 February 1934).

From the AO to the AOC   111

formed the basis for identifying a practice, leading one court to recognise that it was customary to manufacture lace in the Haute-Loire region by hand, excluding mechanically made lace from the use of the appellation.[149] Jacques Audier concludes that, in light of the overall goal of promoting quality, the requirement could be summarised as 'stable customs voluntarily respected in a defined area'.[150]

Subsequent developments continued to undermine the ideology of deterministic physical geography. The regime opened up to products beyond wines and spirits, gradually encompassing a broad spectrum of agricultural products and foodstuffs.[151] Cheese was one of the first extensions to satisfy the natural *and* human factors amalgam. 'Roquefort' is a cylindrical, blue-veined cheese historically made from sheeps' milk.[152] It is specified that the milk of native sheep such as Lacaune and Manech is required, which graze on regional flora influenced by local soil and climatic conditions. The other famous local ingredient is the *Penicillium roqueforti* that is found in the deep limestone caves of the foothills of the Combalou,[153] encouraged to grow by the addition of rye bread placed there. This is part of 'the historic methods and usages of production, curing and development' that have evolved over time.[154] The Law of 2 July 1990[155] extends the AOC concept further beyond cheese, to include all unprocessed or processed agricultural or alimentary products

---

[149] *Chambre Syndicale des Fabricants de Dentelles et Passementeries de la Haute-Loire* v. *Gouteyron et Jérôme* [1931] *Propriété Industrielle* 188 (Le Puy-en-Velay Civil Court, 19 February 1931).

[150] J. Audier, 'Local, Honest and Constant Uses – Summary Contribution to a Definition' (1996) 6 *AIDV Bulletin* 5, 7.

[151] There were three National Committees, divided according to subject matter – Wines and Spirits; Dairy Products; and Other Agricultural Products. See Article L641–5 of the Code Rural. Before its incorporation into the broader European registration system, about thirty types of cheese, butter, milk-cream, poultry, walnut, etc. were protected. Audier, 'Protection of Geographical Indications, 5.

[152] Roquefort was amongst the first non-wine appellations to be recognised, while production criteria were also specified. Loi du 26 juillet 1925 Ayant pour but de Garantir l'Appellation d'Origine du Fromage de Roquefort (30 Juillet 1925) *Journal Officiel* 7190. It is presently registered as a PDO at the EU level. Details of the application by the Confédération Générale des Producteurs de lait de Brebis et des industriels de Roquefort can be found within the EU DOORS Database, available at ec.europa.eu/agriculture/quality/door/list.html.

[153] For further details on the traditional manufacturing process, see *Douglas et al.* v. *Newark Cheese Co* 274 NYS 406, 407 (1934).

[154] *Community of Roquefort* v. *William Faehndrich* 303 F2d 494, 495 (1962) (Kaufman J). The court held that Roquefort, which was protected as a certification trade mark, had not become a generic term in the US. Its use was prohibited on cheese imported from Hungary and Italy.

[155] See Art. 1 of Loi no 90–558 du 2 juillet 1990 relative aux appellations d'origine contrôlées des produits agricoles ou alimentaires, bruts ou transformés (6 July 1990) *Journal Officiel* 155.

112   The Appellation of Origin in France

that meet the AOC definition and satisfy the requirements set out in the governing decree. It has largely gone unnoticed in the legal literature on GIs that in France, the human factors were progressively more visible. Thus Laurence Bérard and Philippe Marchenay note:

Due to the intrinsic cultural content contained within any effort to determine the specificity of a product, anthropologists in particular have been called upon to analyse themes that are central to their discipline such as time, space, savoir-faire and tradition.[156]

This leads to a present day understanding of *Produits de Terroir* that embraces the human element. The focus is on collectively generated knowledge, its intergenerational transmission and relation to place:

[L]ocal and traditional food products or produce with a unique and identifiable character based upon specific historical, cultural or technical components. The definition includes the accumulation and transmission of savoir-fare;[157]

or

[L]ocal agricultural products and foodstuffs whose qualities cross time and space and are anchored in a specific place and history ... (and) depend on the shared savoir-faire of a given community and its culture.[158]

Accordingly when considering the effect of the place of origin, while many cultivated products rely to a greater extent on environmental conditions, for others it is 'human intervention, through technical knowledge and *savoir faire*, social organisation and representation, which makes sense of this *lien au lieu* (tie to a place), allowing these physical factors to express themselves'.[159] This could include the choice of fruit varieties or subsequent grafting, pruning and harvesting methods. As one moves across the spectrum from 'natural' agricultural products towards prepared foodstuffs such as *charcuterie*, local *savoir faire* is progressively accentuated. 'Animal breeds, plant varieties, landscapes, and microbial ecosystems correspond to an accumulation of knowledge, practices, and adjustments. These vary according to the nature of the products, which are themselves dependent upon local social and environmental conditions'.[160]

---

[156] L. Bérard and P. Marchenay, 'A Market Culture: *Produits de Terroir* or the Selling of Culture', in S. Blowen M. Demossier and J. Picard (ed.), *Recollections of France* (Berghahn Books, New York 2000), 154, 155.
[157] Demossier, *Culinary Heritage and Produits de Terroir in France*, 146.
[158] Bérard and Marchenay, 'Market Culture', 154.   [159] Ibid., 160.
[160] L. Bérard and P. Marchenay, 'Local Products and Geographical Knowledge: Taking Account of Local Knowledge and Biodiversity' (2006) 58 *International Social Science Journal* 109, 111.

From the AO to the AOC 113

Inevitably, such valorisation comes with its own baggage. The dangers of a romanticised past being recreated around the product, or dominant accounts overshadowing the marginal, are real. When it comes to pin-pointing local and constant practices (*des usages locaux et constants*), Roubier suggests that consensus was often difficult to reach and fixation ultimately depended on a variety of evidentiary sources – old advertise-ments, opinions from local Chambers of Commerce, old technical volumes, records of individual traders from the region, viticultural expert opinion, old invoices and records of local trade bodies' minutes etc. Decision makers would also require the production practices to be established as long-standing (often several decades) and sufficiently widespread across a group of producers in order to have stabilised.[161] These are supplemented by the recognition of oral history as valid evidence of production methods.[162] Amongst others, anthropologists have begun to explore how this technical culture evolved, is shared and also transmitted between generations, thereby creating spaces for inno-vation and improvement. Local producer groups need not legally claim internalised origins for all these innovations but they do put them to work. Authenticity is then seen as the by-product of collective experi-mentation over time but is still by no means an unproblematic concept. As part of this registration process, a number of actors including pro-ducers, consumers, local groups and political institutions come together to assemble the relevant tradition and reify the norms of good practice. The process is recursive, since the product specifications are usually contested and revised.

On occasion, tensions arise between traditional approaches and the need for innovation, such as disputes over raw materials or methods of production.[163] This is not restricted to the French AOC system and will occur wherever there are choices to be made in defining the authentic. Based on extensive fieldwork while researching the newly created GI for Feni in Goa, Dwijen Rangnekar writes of the 'politics in place' surroun-ding the drafting of its product specifications. Feni is distilled liquor, conventionally made from cashew or coconut.[164] Historically it was triple distilled, but in recent years double distillation has become the

---

[161] Roubier, *Le Droit de la Propriété Industrielle*, 761, Fn 1.

[162] L. Bérard and P. Marchenay, 'Localized Products in France: Definition, Protection and Value-Adding' (2007) *Anthropology of Food* S2, available at aof.revues.org/index415. html.

[163] Bérard and Marchenay, 'Market Culture', 163.

[164] D. Rangnekar 'Re-Making Place: The Social Construction of Geographical Indications' (2010) (Draft Manuscript, on file with the author); D. Rangnekar *Geographical Indications and Localisation: A Case Study of Feni* (ESRC Report 2009).

114   The Appellation of Origin in France

norm. This is less time consuming, while the end result is less alcoholic and therefore more palatable to a wider market – this is the published norm in the final specification. The GI specification has also edited out the coconut variety and claimed the Feni GI for cashew liquor alone. Other new materials and techniques include the mechanised crushing of the cashew apples, which has largely replaced the more traditional foot crushing method and developments in cooling methods, to prevent the distillation vessel from cracking. The specification is also silent with regard to the provenance of the cashew apples, since a significant quantity is imported from the states adjacent to Goa, i.e. outside the designated region. Many of these changes give producers desirable flexibility and the ability to scale up production, but they also favour certain (capital intensive) production techniques. The extent to which local hierarchies and entrenched interests are reinforced in the construction of the 'authentic process' calls for a reflective engagement with such processes. As Chapter 6 points out, recent research emphasises the role of institutional design when responding to these concerns. This also broaches the topic of change and subsequent innovation. While experimentation leading up to the original product specification is acknowledged, why should we presume that at the time of fixation this was the last word? Therefore it is possible, yet complicated in practice, to modify an AOC specification, in recognition of the tension between permitting innovations while retaining the cachet of historically enduring production methods.[165]

In recent years, the categories of tradition and authenticity have been subjected to scrutiny that is as critical as it is insightful.[166] They have also been critiqued in the context of the appellation system.[167] Yet when *'usages locaux, loyaux et constants'* is unpacked, it is not as simplistic or flat-footed as it is made out to be. Human skill and know how associated with traditional products is neither timeless, nor self-contained. Instead

[165] E.g. Gade, 'Tradition, Territory, and Terroir in French Viniculture', 853 (He records the evolution of the Cassis AOC specifications, noting that '(a)ppellation rules are not inflexible').

[166] The standard reference point is E. Hobsbawm and T. Ranger (eds.), *The Invention of Tradition* (Cambridge University Press, 1983), 1 ('"Invented tradition" is taken to mean a set of practices, normally governed by overtly or tacitly accepted rules and of a ritual or symbolic nature, which seek to inculcate certain values and norms of behaviour by repetition, which automatically implies continuity with the past').

[167] B. Beebe, 'Intellectual Property and the Sumptuary Code' (2010) 123 *Harvard Law Review* 809, 869 ('Through the commodification of what are essentially forms of pre- or anti-modernity, traditional producers seek to sell the distinction of *terroir*, history, and legend to a world that has otherwise been deterritorialized, dehistoricized, and disenchanted'). See also Parry, 'Not All Champagne and Roses'; T. Broude, 'Taking "Trade and Culture" Seriously: Geographical Indications and Cultural Protection in WTO Law' (2005) 26 *University of Pennsylvania Journal of International Economic Law* 623.

this *savoir faire* was the result of collective effort, based on much experimentation with empirically tested methods and tied to local geographical and socio-economic conditions. Place thus becomes the catchment area for production techniques and not necessarily the fount. If 'local, loyal and constant' alludes to a tradition, it is a tradition or continuity of localised experimentation. However, this collective innovation dimension seems to have been largely edited out of GI discourse, eclipsed by the authorship ascribed to physical geography.[168]

Remembering this history of collective innovation has important repercussions for the characterisation of IGO protection in international negotiations. In opposing GI extension at the TRIPS Council, Australia has argued that:

IP rights were normally granted to those who had discovered or created something. Protection was given to creators, scientists, inventors, authors and researchers in order to reward them for having come up with new products, new processes and new works of art. At the same time, they, and their investors, were given an incentive to continue doing so. By protecting these IPRs, governments were in effect rewarding them with a monopoly for their creative work. But the important question worth asking was whether governments should grant similar monopoly rights *based on an accident of history where there would be a geographical connection to a product* (emphasis added).[169]

A historical perspective therefore allows us to appreciate the French AOC regime's eventual rejection of '*conditions particulières de climat et de terroir*' as the sole or sufficient basis for protection, while also hinting at an alternative foundation which recognises collectively generated and intergenerational *savoir faire*.

6.   Doing things differently: Germany and the UK

Before concluding the chapter, this section outlines alternative approaches to identifying a regional product, determining its region of production and legally recognising those producers or traders entitled

---

[168] See, e.g., S. Wagle, 'Protection of Geographical Indications and Human Development: Economic and Social Benefits to Developing Countries', November 2003 (WIPO/GEO/DEL/03/7), 3 ('Importantly, geographical indications differ from other forms of IP like patents which are essentially rewards for new creations. GIs, in contrast are not *created*, but only *recognized*').

[169] TRIPS Council, 'Minutes of the Meeting on 25–27 and 29 November, and 20 December 2002', 5 February 2003 (IP/C/M/38), [72]. This line of argumentation makes another flawed assumption. By focusing on the creative/inventive species of IP, it ignores the existence of trade marks as well as the protection of the intangible value associated with signs as an important part of the IP canon. It also ignores the legal protection of effort/investment type intangibles such as databases, also protected under IP regimes.

116   The Appellation of Origin in France

to use the geographical name on their products. France was engaged in *formally pinning down the qualities of the product and its production process*, while its neighbouring jurisdictions continued to rely on unfair competition law to regulate the manner in which the *sign represented the product*. The distinction is important. In France, those legitimately using an AOC had to jump through a number of hoops to ensure that their product lived up to the specification. Those who bypassed this while using the AOC on similar products were undermining the guarantees as well as policy goals of this regulatory framework and threatening its viability. From a broader regulatory perspective, the preference for strong or enhanced protection for AOCs is therefore easier to comprehend. By comparison, Germany and the UK had continued to rely on unfair competition doctrine, where protection hinges on the narrower set of policies associated with trade and consumer perception of the sign in question. The constitutive influences of the wine trade, which are central to the French experience, are absent in these national regimes. Given the differences in regulatory goals and the absence of conceptual resources associated with *terroir*, similar issues have played out in different ways. Recognition and protection is tied to the communicative content of the geographical sign. Within territorial confines, each system performs adequately in protecting geographical signs against use by (safely) external trade rivals, but does not concern itself with the definitional or regulatory aspects central to the appellation system.

As an alternative to adopting France's intricate legislative framework for appellations, Germany has considerable experience with accommodating signs used for regional products under its unfair competition statute of 1909.[170] The use of misleading or confusing statements in the course of trade, including those concerning geographical origin, was prohibited under s. 3. This was later supplemented by protection against non-confusing yet proscribed associations (dilution and misappropriation) under the general provision in s. 1.[171] Under the UWG, determining whether an indication is misleading depends upon the understanding of the relevant public. As a regime which is 'essentially a creation of

---

[170] Gesetz gegen den unlauteren Wettbewerb (UWG) of 7 June 1909 [1909] RGBl 499, (hereafter, UWG 1909). The law was substantially amended and upgraded in 2004, for which see F. Henning-Bodewig, 'A New Act against Unfair Competition in Germany' [2005] IIC 421. It must be noted that a more systematic approach to origin marking did exist for wines, while subject specific legislation also existed for a few products such as hops.

[171] See generally W. Tilmann, *Die Geographische Herkunftsangabe* (CH Beck-Verlag, Munich 1976); A. C. Streber, *Die Internationalen Abkommen der Bundesrepublik Deutschland zum Schutz Geographischer Herkunftsangaben* (Max Planck Institute, Cologne 1994).

Doing things differently: Germany and the UK 117

judge-made law',[172] this provision was interpreted to permit an action to prevent consumer deception while also recognising that a valuable collective reputation may be protected as industrial property. Whoever wants specific merchandise need not tolerate misleading substitutions.[173] A court would first test for whether the term was geographically descriptive, i.e. it had geographical significance to consumers and was not considered generic or fanciful. Then it would see if the defendant's use was misleading (the product did not originate from the place indicated) and could influence the purchase decision. To determine this, courts would assess consumer and trade perceptions, often through the use of surveys.[174]

German law therefore followed a trajectory distinct from the specification-based AOC model. To begin with, German doctrine has traditionally been more generous concerning admissible subject matter and includes reputed handcrafted or even industrially produced items.[175] The 'natural versus manufactured' distinction was therefore irrelevant, since the protected interest – a regional product's valuable reputation – may or may not depend on *terroir* factors. Reputed but 'quality-neutral' indications of source were thus protected and this category included Solingen steel, Brussels lace or Swiss clocks.[176] Legal tests were designed to estimate the sign's impact on the relevant public and the mental response it would trigger, as opposed to a registration procedure designed to identify specific product characteristics. This approach partially explains Germany's conspicuous absence from the Lisbon Agreement. There was concern that the Lisbon AO definition was so *terroir*-infused that it potentially excluded several important German indications,[177] many of which were reputed crafted, manufactured or recipe-based products, such as Lübecker Marzipan.[178]

---

[172] G. Schricker, 'Protection of Indications of Source, Appellations of Origin and other Geographic Designations in the Federal Republic of Germany' [1983] IIC 307, 308.

[173] A proposition established by *Rügenwalder Teewurst* [1956] GRUR 270 (BGH).

[174] A. Conrad 'The Protection of Geographical Indications in the TRIPS Agreement' (1996) 86 TMR 11, 15–16.

[175] E. Ulmer, 'The Law of Unfair Competition and the Common Market' (1963) 53 TMR 625, 643–4.

[176] F-K. Beier and R. Knaak, 'The Protection of Direct and Indirect Geographical Indications of Source in Germany and the European Community' [1994] IIC 1, 2.

[177] A. Krieger, 'Revision of the Lisbon Agreement for the Protection of Appellations of Origin' [1974] *Industrial Property* 387, 390; R. Plaisant, 'The Revision of the International Treaty Provisions Dealing with Appellations of Origin and Indications of Source' [1980] *Industrial Property* 182, 187.

[178] H. Harte-Bavendamm, 'Ende der geographischen Herkunftsbezeichnungen? "Brüsseler Spitzen" gegen den ergänzenden nationalen Rechtsschutz' [1996] *GRUR* 717, 717. However, when it is unpacked in Chapter 4, the definition of an AO proves to be more accommodating. The real obstacle for Germany may instead have been the absence of an *ex ante* recognition system at the national level.

118   The Appellation of Origin in France

This rejection of a systematic geographical delineation and quality fixation regime in favour of a case-by-case approach created the need for alternative doctrinal mechanisms when confronting similar issues. For instance, how is origin to be determined when the final product incorporates raw material from diverse sources, or stages of production are spread across different locations? Courts attempted to uncover the region 'which, in the view of the market place, is essential for the evaluation of the merchandise'.[179] From the consumer's perspective human skills or processing may be just as important as the raw materials. It would therefore be misleading to use 'Dutch liqueur' on liqueur from distillates of Dutch origin but ultimately processed in Germany.[180] At the next stage, once the general place of production is identified, how are its precise contours determined? As Gerhard Schricker puts it:

> How, though, is the 'correct' area of origin to be delimited? In the [German] law on wines there are special regulations covering the area of source; in the context of Sec. 3 [of the UWG 1909] there is lacking a legislative or administrative mechanism for setting limits.[181]

Once again, the view of the trade – a broad term including both producers and consumers – is crucial, regardless of formal administrative boundaries or geological factors.[182] As Schricker puts it, the 'finally determinative opinion of the public will normally consider as "origin" that place which is perceived as giving the goods in question their characteristic imprint'.[183]

Finally, despite bypassing a registration procedure or formal product specification, German unfair competition law nevertheless incorporated the notion of specific quality standards in certain situations. In response to the free rider threat, it was considered abusive for a producer within the designated region to market merchandise of inferior quality under that sign.[184] As for consumer expectations of quality, this was recognised

---

[179] F-K. Beier, 'The Protection of Indications of Geographical Origin in the Federal Republic of Germany', in H. C. Jehoram (ed.), *Protection of Geographic Denominations of Goods and Services* (Sijthoff & Noordhoff, Netherlands 1980), 11, 30.

[180] Ibid., 30–2.

[181] Schricker, 'Protection of Indications of Source in the Federal Republic of Germany', 320.

[182] See H. J. Ohde, 'Zur demoskopischen Ermittlung der Verkehrsauffassung von geographischen Herkunftsangaben' [1989] *GRUR* 98 (concerning the measurement of trade perceptions); W. Tilmann, 'Zur Bestimmung des Kreises der an einer geographischen Herkunftsangabe Berechtigten' [1980] *GRUR* 487 (concerning the drawing of a boundary around legitimate producers and regions of productions). I am grateful to Bahne Seivers for assistance with translations.

[183] Schricker, 'Protection of Indications of Source in the Federal Republic of Germany', 321.

[184] Beier, 'Protection of Indications in the Federal Republic of Germany', 32.

Doing things differently: Germany and the UK

by the BGH in a case involving Scotch whisky in 1969.[185] Responding to a claim of misleading use, the district court prohibited an importer from using 'Scotch Whisky' on whisky manufactured in Scotland but not aged for three years, as was required under Scottish law at the time. On appeal the importer argued there was no finding of fact that consumers were aware of specific requirements such as the three-year aging period, thereby questioning whether they were misled on this point. The BGH's response was as follows:

> The decision in the instant case, therefore, does not depend upon whether prospective consumers have a definite idea of the statutory provisions in Great Britain concerning the use of the designation Scotch Whisky and, in particular, whether they know that a three year aging period is required. The public would view a particular product at least with reservations if it became known that it does not correspond to the marking requirements in the country of origin, since it is assumed that these requirements are designed to ensure a certain standard quality and are not merely formal requirements having nothing to do with product quality. Therefore, using such designations for products not corresponding to these requirements, here the aging period requirement, violates not only the interests of the consumer, but also those of competitors who use the same designation but only after fulfilment of the normally costly requirements. Such conceptions, even if they lack the definitive content deemed necessary by the defendant, are protectable...[186]

So long as consumers were aware that Scotch whisky followed certain production standards in the country of origin and the impugned product did not, this was misleading conduct which ought to be prohibited. In conclusion, it can be seen that the entire regime is built up around an estimation of the communicative content of the geographical sign.

In the UK, broadly similar outcomes were reached by relying on the tort of passing off, which seeks to prevent those marketplace misrepresentations that are injurious to a trader's goodwill. Lord Oliver's depiction of goodwill, misrepresentation and damage sets out the key requirements:

> The law of passing off can be summarised in one short general proposition – no man may pass off his goods as those of another ... First, [the claimant] must establish a goodwill or reputation attached to the goods or services which he supplies in the mind of the purchasing public by association with the identifying 'get-up' (whether it consists simply of a brand name or a trade description ...) such that the get-up is recognised by the public as distinctive specifically of the plaintiff's goods or services. Second, he must demonstrate a misrepresentation by the defendant to the public (whether or not intentional) leading or likely to lead the public to believe that goods or services offered by him are the goods or

---

[185] *Scotch Whisky* [1970] IIC 402 (BGH).   [186] Ibid., 405.

120   The Appellation of Origin in France

services of the plaintiff ... Third, he must demonstrate that he suffers or, in a *quia timet* action, that he is likely to suffer damage by reason of the erroneous belief engendered by the defendant's misrepresentation that the source of the defendant's goods or services is the same as the source of those offered by the plaintiff.[187]

This is a more detailed elaboration of the archetypical wrongful conduct in passing off: 'A man is not to sell his goods under the pretence that they are the goods of another man'.[188]

However, thus far, passing off has not been extended beyond misrepresentation to include pure free riding or misappropriation.[189] The legally protected interest is also clearly identified. Passing off protects the invasion of a property interest by misrepresentation. As opposed to the sign or designation itself, it is the 'property in the business or goodwill likely to be injured by the misrepresentation'[190] that is protected. This has traditionally belonged to a single commercial entity, which generates the goodwill through sales or marketplace presence. The trade name or sign is then the peg to which this attractive reputation attaches. In consequence, the goodwill is preserved by protecting the sign. A person 'who engages in commercial activities may acquire a valuable reputation in respect of the goods in which he deals ... The law regards such a reputation as an incorporeal piece of property, the integrity of which the owner is entitled to protect'.[191] Unlike the more wide-ranging UWG, not every commercial misrepresentation entitles a claimant to a remedy; only where this potentially damages goodwill will it be actionable.

A significant preliminary hurdle when commencing an action for passing off related to the formal recognition of the collective interest in geographical terms. If the badge or symbol of goodwill had conventionally indicated a single trade source, how was group or collective goodwill to be identified and accommodated? The doctrinal expansion into 'extended passing off'[192] began in response to the *Spanish Champagne* decision[193] Prior to this:

---

[187] *Reckitt & Colman Products Ltd* v. *Borden Inc* [1990] RPC 341, 406 (HL).
[188] *Perry* v. *Truefitt* (1842) 6 Beav 66, 73 (Lord Langdale, MR).
[189] The expansion was most recently rejected in *L'Oréal SA* v. *Bellure NV* [2007] EWCA Civ 968.
[190] *A. G. Spalding & Brothers* v. *AW Gamage Ltd* (1915) 32 RPC 273, 284 (HL) (Parker LJ).
[191] *H. P. Bulmer Ltd and Showerings Ltd* v. *J. Bollinger and Champagne Lanson Père et Fils* (1977) 2 CMLR 625, 629 (Buckley LJ) (Champagne cides and Champagne Perry).
[192] The authorities for extended passing off have been admirably summarised by Arnold J, in *Diageo* v. *Intercontinental Brands* [2010] EWHC 17 (Ch); [2010] ETMR 17 (Vodka).
[193] *J. Bollinger* v. *Costa Brava Wine Co Ltd* [1960] Ch 262 (Spanish Champagne).

Doing things differently: Germany and the UK

[T]here was considerable doubt whether any one or more persons could sue, either individually or jointly, alleging passing-off by the use of the word Champagne notwithstanding its great reputation, since it did not represent the wine of any one producer exclusively, and it was not wholly, and in some cases not at all, part of a reputation and goodwill which any particular producer or his predecessors had built up. Any person may set up business as a producer of Champagne provided he does so in the Champagne district of France and complies with the stringent regulations...[194]

In *Spanish Champagne*, a dozen Champagne producers sought an injunction to prevent the importation and sale in the UK of sparkling wine from Spain, under the labels 'Champagne' and 'Spanish Champagne'. It was held that 'it ought not to matter that the persons truly entitled to describe their goods by the name and description are a class producing goods in a certain locality, and not merely one individual. The description is part of their goodwill and a right of property'.[195] Here consumers would still be misled into thinking the goods were the goods of or associated with someone else. The fact that this 'someone else' was a group rather than an individual should not matter provided the group could be identified. Collective goodwill was further elaborated in another dispute over Champagne: 'The ability of any one Champagne House to describe its product as Champagne is of value to it not in relation to the Champagne market but in relation to the wider wine market [in] distinguishing their products from other wines'.[196] What was distinguished here was a type of product instead of a single trade source. Thus each individual producer had a stake in the collective goodwill apart from their own brand names.

Four important clarifications have arisen out of subsequent decisions, which are relevant for the purposes of our comparison. First, the protection under extended passing off is not restricted to products whose qualities are linked to the geography of a particular region. Those producing goods of a particular description can restrain rival traders from using that term, or a confusingly similar term, in relation to goods which do not correspond to that description. Extended passing off thus protects classes of products where a shared geographic origin may be the defining feature of the class but alternative methods of defining the class are equally acceptable.[197]

---

[194] *H. P. Bulmer Ltd and Showerings Ltd* v. *J. Bollinger SA and Champagne Lanson Père et Fils* (1977) 2 CMLR 625, 660 (CA) (Goff LJ).

[195] *Spanish Champagne* [1960] Ch 262, 284.

[196] *H. P. Bulmer Ltd and Showerings Ltd* v. *J. Bollinger SA*, 636 (Buckley LJ).

[197] *Erven Warnink B. V. v. J. Townend & Sons (Hull) Ltd* [1979] FSR 397 (HL) (Advocaat defined on the basis of its ingredients).

122   The Appellation of Origin in France

Second, the focus was on identifying the product with reasonable precision – this would be used in turn to define the circle of legitimate users of the term:

[It] is the reputation that that type of product itself has gained in the market by reason of its recognisable and distinctive qualities that has generated the relevant goodwill. So if one can define with reasonable precision the type of product that has acquired the reputation, one can identify the members of the class entitled to share in the goodwill as being all those traders who have supplied [such] a product which possesses those recognisable and distinctive qualities ... It cannot make any difference in principle whether the recognisable and distinctive qualities by which the reputation of the type of product has been gained are the result of its having been made in, or from ingredients produced in, a particular locality or are the result of its having been made from particular ingredients regardless of their provenance; though a geographical limitation may make it easier [to define the type of product, establish its recognizable qualities and consequent harm to goodwill].[198]

Third, unlike the French requirement for time-tested production standards that ensure desirable quality, under passing off there was no need to establish that the class of products possessed actual distinctive or superior quality. In *Chocosuisse*, Laddie J held that extended passing off was applicable even in cases where 'a reasonably identifiable group of products ... have a *perceived* distinctive quality. If there is no difference or discernible difference in quality and ingredients between goods sold under or by reference to the term and competing goods, that should not prevent a successful passing off action from being brought'.[199] In reasoning which strikes a chord with the BGH's whisky decision seen above, Laddie J was clear that consumers need not be aware of specific details. The reputation for quality established by trade and consumer evidence was for chocolate produced in Switzerland, according to Swiss food regulations[200] and he did not wish to define the class of products more narrowly.[201] Fourth, while the damage or injury requirement in extended passing off may flow from actual or potential lost sales, the erosion of distinctiveness is also a recognised category of harm. The relevant type of harm in these cases 'is mainly reduction of the distinctiveness of the [collectively used] term which is relied on as relevant

---

[198] Ibid., 410 (Diplock LJ).

[199] *Chocosuisse Union des Fabricants Suisse de Chocolat* v. *Cadbury Ltd* [1998] RPC 117, 128 (Ch D).

[200] Ibid., 135.

[201] Nevertheless Chocosuisse chose to define the class of products more narrowly before the Court of Appeal by emphasising the absence of added vegetable fat, which gave Swiss chocolate a creamier taste. See *Chocosuisse Union des Fabricants Suisses de Chocolat* v. *Cadbury Ltd* [1999] RPC 826, 840 (CA).

Doing things differently: Germany and the UK   123

damage'.[202] Recognition of this category of harm responds to the long-standing concern that such regional products are otherwise vulnerable to generic use, where external rivals may use the term without necessarily following authentic production techniques.

When it comes to protecting these geographical signs, all three regimes achieve functionally similar outcomes at the national level, despite variations in scope. Misrepresentation is prohibited under French, German and UK law, while the first two regimes also prohibit misappropriation or free riding via the use of the designation on similar or even dissimilar goods.[203] Yet Germany and the UK do not seriously engage with the definitional aspect. Whilst they are open-ended in their acceptance of subject matter on a case-by-case basis, these systems assume that a stable production region, group of producers as well as product specification can be identified at the time of litigation. Neither of them overtly relies on *terroir* linkages as the basis for protection.[204] Furthermore, legal recognition and protection rests upon the consumer understanding of the designation. Will the relevant public be misled by the defendant's use of the sign on similar products produced outside the named region? Will suitably qualified use on a product label avoid liability? Do consumers and the trade consider the sign to be generic for a class of products? Revisiting the emergence of French appellation law is particularly edifying because it reminds us that for the better part of a century, until the 1905 regime, French law was broadly similar in approach to these neighbouring jurisdictions. Here too consumer and trade understanding of the designations laid the groundwork for the right to use the sign as well as bring an action to prevent its use by others. The particular contingencies of the wine industry during this period, as well as the need to develop more effective international

---

[202] *Chocosuisse Union des Fabricants Suisse de Chocolat* v. *Cadbury Ltd* [1998] RPC 117, 128 (ChD), 127.

[203] See for example *Institut National des Appellations d'Origine* v. *Yves Saint Laurent* [1994] EIPR D74 (Court of Appeal, Paris 1993) (Champagne used to launch a luxury perfume); *Tea Board of India* v. *Jean-Luc Dusong* (Court of Appeal, Paris, 4th Chamber, Reg No. 05/20050, 22 November 2006) (Darjeeling used on books and stationery); '*A Champagne among Mineral Waters*' [1988] IIC 682 (BGH) (Champagne used to advertise mineral water).

[204] However, this logic may subtly influence certain doctrinal aspects of each system. For instance, under German law, courts will be reluctant to make a finding of generic status for products perceived to 'owe their essential qualities to particular natural characteristics of the place of origin'. See Beier, 'Protection of Direct and Indirect Geographical Indications', 23. Within these systems that are apparently subject matter neutral, courts may adopt techniques to favour such products including raising or lowering evidentiary thresholds, reversing burdens of proof, setting up rebuttable presumptions or resorting to the use of legal fictions.

124   The Appellation of Origin in France

protection, would redirect French law onto a different path, with an increasing emphasis on the referent product.

7.   Conclusion

By the end of Chapter 2, it was evident that *terroir* logic had begun to influence international industrial property negotiations. A particular version of it also informs the Lisbon Agreement, while supporting more expansive claims concerning the scope of IGO protection. AO regimes are portrayed as having distinct aims when compared with trade mark or general unfair competition legislation and thus entitled to differential treatment. The conceptual underpinnings of this influential legal category were developed in the context of the legal regulation of the wine industry in France. The relevant history of this period in Chapter 3 is therefore helpful for three reasons. First, it provides us with the necessary context to better appreciate the influence, as well as limitations, of wine as the subject-matter kernel for GIs in general. Second, it reveals a series of transformations in the legal recognition and legitimation of the link between product and place, through the interplay between different versions of *terroir*. These conceptual shifts are carried forward into the Lisbon Agreement, considered in the following chapter. Third, it delineates the two overlapping yet distinct epistemic frameworks which begin to operate in this area. If the initial framework had been based on truth telling or communicative logic and realised by unfair competition rules, the emerging AO regime prioritised the historic and qualitative dimensions of the link between people, products and places. What an audience would understand by the use of the sign in a given context was no longer dispositive in determining which uses were unjustified. The enquiry turned to whether the imitator's product actually lived up to the original specifications and the valorisation of production techniques. While the second and third insights – the link between product and place as well as diverging epistemologies – are considered at greater length in Chapter 4, the first insight requires further elaboration.

This chapter has proposed that the French wine appellation model forms the basis for contemporary *sui generis* GI law. To begin with, an awareness of this history helps account for key descriptive claims in contemporary IGO debates. It is worth noting that each of the following claims is made at a level of generality in IGO discourse, as if universally applicable to all subject matter, but they can be traced to specific episodes concerning French wine regulation. It is worth asking whether the story of wine should become the story for all GIs. Meanwhile an awareness of wine as the subject matter archetype allows for a more

Conclusion 125

reflexive engagement with these descriptive claims. First is the core claim that the quality of certain types of regional products can be causally related to distinct places. While this could be true of many agricultural products, geographical origin has long been considered an important proxy for quality in the wine industry. An unsettled question is the algorithm for identifying the larger category for which wines are the exemplar. Second, the associated attribute of uniqueness – such regional products are irreproducible elsewhere – appears to have been sustained by at least three different developments:

(1) The initial emphasis on physical geography in wine regulation systems was the basis for arguing that, artificial ski slopes or beaches notwithstanding, places cannot be identically reproduced. To the extent that physical geography was treated as a dispositive influence, the corollary was that products from such places could not be duplicated elsewhere.

(2) It may also be related to politics of distinct French regional identities which *terroir* products were supposed to symbolise as well as sustain.

(3) It has been further supported as well as undermined by the gradual recognition of human factors. Regional products are associated with unique histories specific to the region – techniques of production are tailored to specific local environments – and the historic dimension is important to purchasers, representing a desirable cachet of authenticity. According to this version, process matters alongside the end product so historic ties serve as an anchor. However, the emphasis on human intervention and methods of production implies that tools and techniques can migrate, perhaps with perfect fidelity. Taken to one extreme, if we consider regional wine or cheese as a physical commodity, then, as far as organoleptic qualities are concerned it may be possible to successfully replicate them elsewhere.

Third, the assertion that GI regimes are also concerned with the regulation of quality is better understood in light of the experiences of the French wine industry. Following on from the supply slump in quality wines in post-phylloxera France, 'traditional' or 'local, loyal and constant' production methods were eventually interpreted as empirically verified and distilled best practices over time. Preserving standards of quality was an important aspect of the ensuing regulatory response. Fourth, the notion that GIs are not just a part of IP law but part of broader agricultural policy regulatory mechanisms stems from the regulation of overproduction, the need to preserve rural livelihoods in a time of crisis as well as to encourage excellence in the wine industry. Finally, arguments that traditional regional products have cultural salience, in

126   The Appellation of Origin in France

the sense that they enable the formation of collective identities, have been a strand of the AO narrative for some time. Regional products and localised labour/producer identities had been mobilised to buttress regional identities and resist centripetal pressure from Paris. This would go on to inform the rhetoric of *terroir*. These are just a selection of insights and no doubt other general claims can be traced back to this product, place and timeframe. This yield makes it well worth the dalliance with the history of wine regulation in France, as well as with the contrasting approaches in Germany and the UK that remain situated within the communicative paradigm. In the next chapter, we return to the level of international negotiations, to see how the AO is received and reconstituted at the multilateral level.

4 The Appellation of Origin in the Lisbon Agreement

1. Introduction

The Lisbon Agreement of 1958[1] represents the high water mark in the international protection of IGOs. The Agreement creates another Special Union, permitted under Article 19 of the Paris Convention. It continues the story of the AO and was the consolation arising from the failure to strengthen rules under the Paris Convention and Madrid Agreement. This chapter revisits the process by which the link between certain types of products and places is broadened out, evaluating the concomitant expansion of subject matter in the process. If wine was the archetype, on what basis was the circle of AO products expanded? It is also illuminating to contrast the more richly textured and nuanced tale of the French AOC with the formalistic discourse that sustains the Lisbon AO. A certain degree of abstraction and compromise is inevitable in international negotiations, but at what cost? According to the explanatory memorandum, the objective was to establish more 'effective international protection' for narrowly defined subject matter. The Madrid Agreement, including the special treatment for products of the vine in Article 4, was endorsed as a step in the right direction but did not go far enough. Prohibiting the use of false or misleading indications and preventing the ensuing detriment to consumers was a worthy goal, but this was only one aspect of unfair competition law.[2]

Moving beyond this consumer-centric agenda, the proposal introduced the Appellation of Origin (AO) and recognised the need to protect economic benefits associated with valuable reputations. This gave the proposed agreement a distinct theoretical basis when compared with its

---

[1] Lisbon Agreement for the Protection of Appellations of Origin and their International Registration, 31 October 1958, 923 UNTS 205 (1974), (hereafter, the Lisbon Agreement). It entered into force on 25 September 1966.

[2] Actes de la Conférence de Lisbonne (Bureau de l'Union, Geneva 1963), 813, (hereafter, Actes de Lisbonne). An unofficial yet expedient British Government translation is found in Revision at Lisbon: Preparatory Work on the Agenda (BT 209/785).

127

128   The Appellation of Origin in Lisbon

predecessors.[3] The key features of this agreement are (1) recognition of the AO as distinct subject matter; (2) international registration based on prior recognition at the national level; and (3) desirable consequences flowing from this registration, including the prohibition of a range of (mis)uses beyond misleading ones and the prevention of subsequent generic use after registration. Having reviewed the history of the Madrid Agreement in Chapter 2, it is evident that many of these features had been on the wish list for several decades. Despite this, the Lisbon Agreement is labelled a 'radical departure'[4] from its predecessors and perceived as signalling that 'the protection of geographical indications should be as strict as it was for trade marks'.[5] Each of these observations is only partially accurate but helps to explain its limited membership,[6] with only twenty-seven parties having joined to date.[7]

In the following paragraphs, the attempt is to clarify concepts, arguments and implicit assumptions without necessarily subscribing to them. My interest in the Lisbon Agreement is threefold in this chapter. First, the AO is developed as a separate conceptual category in this agreement. The IS had languished in the shadows of unfair competition law and customs rules, while trade mark registration systems could not satisfactorily integrate these signs. An independent place at the IP table was now being demanded for the AO. Reputation protection was clearly one motivating factor, but this was shared with trade mark and trade name protection systems. The case for independent recognition rested on the identification of a link between an appropriately qualified product and its region of origin. Since much depends upon this link, how has it been characterised in the Lisbon AO definition? It is therefore instructive to juxtapose the analysis of the Lisbon AO with developments in France, considered in Chapter 3.

---

[3] Actes de Lisbonne, 813 (*'Cependant, le développement de l'usage des dénominations géographiques renommées afin de désigner des produits déterminés a conféré une grande importance économique et juridique aux appellations d'origine. La pratique industrielle et commerciale a donc posé la base d'une théorie juridique des appellations d'origine distincte de celle des indications de provenance'*).

[4] J. T. McCarthy and V. Colby Devitt, 'Protection of Geographical Denominations: Domestic and International' (1979) 69 TMR 199, 207–8.

[5] S. D. Goldberg, 'Who Will Raise the White Flag? The Battle between the United States and the European Union over the Protection of Geographical Indications' (2001) 22 *University of Pennsylvania Journal of International Economic Law* 107, 114.

[6] Other disincentives include the threshold requirement for recognition as an appellation 'as such' in the country of origin and the freeze preventing subsequent generic usage. See A. Conrad, 'The Protection of Geographical Indications in the TRIPS Agreement' (1996) 86 TMR 11, 26.

[7] For membership particulars, see www.wipo.int/treaties/en/registration/lisbon/index.html. All those who have joined do not seem to have submitted instruments of ratification.

Introduction 129

Second, I wish to pursue a more pragmatic line of enquiry. When it comes to the functioning of the registration system, how effectively is it working? Addressing this question has contemporary relevance. There is a renewed interest in the Lisbon Agreement as a potential blueprint for the international registration system currently being debated at the TRIPS Council.[8] According to Daniel Gervais, the Agreement 'which led a mostly uneventful life until recently, now has a possible new role to play as the multilateral register' being negotiated under Article 23.4 of TRIPS.[9] Gervais goes on to propose that the Lisbon Agreement might be reinvented to meet the needs of a TRIPS mandated registration system, through the adoption of protocols.[10] In a recent speech, the Director General of WIPO identified additional factors relating to the Lisbon Agreement's appeal. He referred to the growing number of countries which have already established *sui generis* GI protection systems. Many of these countries are concerned about products other than wines or spirits, while the enhanced protection provisions in Article 23 of TRIPS are reserved solely for this category. The Lisbon Agreement is therefore attractive since it offers comparable enhanced protection to all products, while remaining flexible enough to accommodate a number of different national approaches to recognition and protection.[11] Given this potential, WIPO has concluded a survey of both Lisbon members and non-members, with a view to clarifying existing provisions and possibly expanding membership.[12] Much of this renewed interest is sustained by the apparent strength of international protection under the Lisbon Agreement. Since it manages to break through the misrepresentation barrier, it is perceived to come 'close to establishing a system of absolute protection for registered geographic denominations'.[13] Yet when it comes to the operation of its provisions, there is a surprising degree of dissent and interpretative uncertainty (perhaps flexibility is kinder) within its membership. Ascertaining sites of disagreement and their

---

[8] See Chapter 6.
[9] D. Gervais, 'The Lisbon Agreement's Misunderstood Potential' (2009) 1 *WIPO Journal* 87, 101.
[10] D. Gervais, 'Reinventing Lisbon: The Case for a Protocol to the Lisbon Agreement (Geographical Indications)' (2010) 11 *Chicago Journal of International Law* 67.
[11] F. Gurry, *Commemoration Speech*, Ceremony to Mark the 50th Anniversary of the Adoption of the Lisbon Agreement, 31 October 2008 available at www.wipo.int/about-wipo/en/dgo/speeches/gurry_lisbon_08.
[12] WIPO, 'Results of the Survey on the Lisbon System', 18 June 2010 (LI/WG/DEV/2/2), (hereafter, Lisbon Survey).
[13] McCarthy and Devitt, 'Protection of Geographical Denominations', 228; L. Baeumer, 'Protection of Geographical Indications under WIPO Treaties and Questions Concerning the Relationship between Those Treaties and the TRIPS Agreement', October 1997 (WIPO/GEO/EGR/97/1 Rev), [32] (referring to 'strong protection' for AOs).

130   The Appellation of Origin in Lisbon

underlying foundations is the second goal of this chapter. One key finding is that the attempt to give dispositive importance to home country status has met with considerable resistance and there are useful lessons here for TRIPS.

The third reason for my interest in the Lisbon Agreement is epistemic. How effectively do justifications supporting protection at the national level scale up to the international arena? The Lisbon Agreement is correspondingly intriguing because it provokes the question of scalability. To what extent can normative guidance found within unfair competition doctrine provide the basis for the Lisbon Agreement rules? When determining the scope of protection under national law, this usually turns on the requirement that consumers are aware of the AO product, within the context of unfair competition prevention or IP regimes. By contrast, if the AO is protected regardless of consumer perception at the multilateral level, why should this be the case? Having set out these three broad avenues of enquiry, the introduction concludes by raising a toast of appreciation to the deep pockets and litigious instincts of the two Budweisers.[14] Matters have frequently come frothing to a head and their incessant skirmishes[15] have included reliance by the Czech beer producer on the Lisbon-registered AO Budweiser, followed by the inevitable challenge to this status by its American opponent. Their repeated clashes in courtrooms have contributed to the precious few judicial decisions that consider at least some of these questions.

2.   The Appellation of Origin: Article 2

Reviewing the process by which the AO was realised in the Lisbon Agreement is instructive. It is the most influential multilateral attempt at crystallising a definition derived from different national traditions.[16] The negotiations were influenced by the sometimes conflicting goals

---

[14] Academic gratitude is added to that of IP practitioners, with illumination replacing remuneration. For the latter, see Lord Justice Jacob's astute observation in *Budějovický Budvar Národni Podnik* v. *Anheuser Busch* [2009] EWCA Civ 1022, [6] ('It would be an interesting but very substantial exercise to collect all the decisions of all the courts and all the trade mark registries of all the countries where the battles have taken place. Many lawyers and their families in many places must be grateful that these two parties apparently cannot produce a once and for all world-wide settlement').

[15] An excellent survey is found in C. Heath, 'The Budweiser Cases – A Brewing Conflict', in C. Heath and A. Kamperman Saunders (eds.), *Landmark Intellectual Property Cases and their Legacy* (Kluwer Law International, Alphen aan den Rijn 2011), 181.

[16] It is not the first. That honour arguably belongs to the Stresa International Convention for the Use of Appellations of Origin and Denominations of Cheeses, 1 June 1951, (hereafter, Stresa Agreement), reproduced in WIPO, 'Texts of International Instruments

The Appellation of Origin: Article 2

of clearly identifying suitable subject matter on the one hand and appealing to a broad constituency on the other. The endeavour to find common ground would require reaching out beyond wines and spirits to include other products, while also running the risk of incoherence through compromise. Chapter 2 has documented previous compromise proposals along these lines, during attempts to revise the Madrid Agreement. The contours of this expansion would once again depend on the link between product and place. If the rationale for the Lisbon Agreement was that a certain category of products merited special treatment within an independent treaty framework, the basis for identifying this category is worth studying. For instance, given the discussion of *terroir* as an anchor within the Paris Convention and Madrid Agreement frameworks, would the Lisbon Agreement favour 'natural' over 'manufactured' products? In addressing these issues, let us begin with the definition of an AO in Article 2:

(1) In this Agreement, 'appellation of origin' means the geographical denomination of a country, region, or locality, which serves to designate a product originating therein, the quality or characteristics[17] of which are due exclusively or essentially to the geographical environment, including natural and human factors.

(2) The country of origin is the country whose name, or the country in which is situated the region or locality whose name, constitutes the appellation of origin which has given the product its reputation.

The definition of the AO is presumed to have influenced the GI definition in Article 22.1 of TRIPS[18] and continues to operate as an international reference point. It is presently being reconsidered in light of suggestions to amalgamate the AO with the definition of a GI, or include the GI as an alternative entry point into the Lisbon registration system, in an attempt to boost membership.[19] Sifting through its constituent elements serves as a useful prelude to TRIPS.

Concerning the Protection of Appellations of Origin and Other Indications of Source', 28 June 1974 (TAO/I/3). For a summary, see WIPO, 'Present Situation and Possible New Solutions', 28 June 1974 (TAO/I/2), [31]–[36]; G. Trotta, 'The Stresa Convention on the Uses of Names of Cheeses and the WIPO Draft Treaty on the Protection of Geographical Indications' (1977) *Industrial Property* 113.

[17] There was some ambiguity as to whether the provision required 'quality and characteristics', found in previous English translations, or 'quality or characteristics' which is the translation suggested by the official French text as finally adopted. The latter is preferred. See Actes de Lisbonne, 1006. WIPO has recently amended the definition to reflect this in the reprint to WIPO Publication No. 264 (E).

[18] WIPO, 'The Definition of Geographical Indications', 1 October 2002 (SCT/9/4), [7].

[19] Lisbon Survey (Responses to Q1 and Q2).

132   The Appellation of Origin in Lisbon

To begin with, where were these elements sourced from? The French model and related national experiences were clearly influential. Prior to the Lisbon Conference, the International Bureau had invited a committee of experts to comment upon a draft agreement to establish a registration system for AOs. Artin Develetian of France's INAO was the Rapporteur for this committee, which also included representatives from Portugal, Spain, Italy and Switzerland. The report of this group supplemented the International Bureau's own *exposé des motifs* and was accompanied by a detailed survey of national legislation regulating the use of both the IS and the AO.[20] Furthermore, transnational attempts at defining an AO existed within resolutions passed by trade and professional bodies, while proposing amendments to the Paris Convention and Madrid Agreement. One of the earliest is that of the International Chamber of Commerce, in its Berlin resolution of 1937. It acknowledged that the AO was a distinct category of sign that was legally defined as well as regulated under national legislation.[21] Given its strictly controlled usage and tightly defined referent in the home country, it was therefore entitled to 'absolute' protection and should never be considered generic for a type or category of product. When considered in light of the transition to the French AOC, this reference to regulation in the home country is unsurprising.

In 1950, the AIPPI Congress expressed the wish that all AOs should be protected against any kind of misleading use. Here, by contrast, AOs were defined as a broad category, regardless of whether they were applied to products which derive their qualities from soil or climate, or applied to industrial products, and regardless of whether they enjoyed notoriety.[22] Meanwhile, Article 3 of the Stresa Agreement of 1951

---

[20] Copies of these documents are available in the Board of Trade files at the UK National Archives: Meeting of a Committee of Experts on 3 December 1956 to Discuss System of Registration of Appellations of Origin (BT 209/1131); Proposed System of Registration of Appellations of Origin (BT 209/1132). An English translation of the experts' report is available as BIRPI 'The Protection and International Registration of Appellations of Origin' [1957] *Industrial Property Quarterly* 49. Develetian also wrote extensively on the topic during this period. For an abridged version in English, see: A. Develetian, 'The Protection of Appellations and Indications of Origin' [1957] *Industrial Property Quarterly* 6 (referencing a more detailed study in French).

[21] Actes de Lisbonne, 963 (*'Ces appellations d'origine, dès qu'elles sont légalement définies et contrôlées dans les pays respectifs, ne doivent jamais être considérées comme désignant des « types génériques » et ne doivent être admises en aucune façon dans la désignation, la réclame, les étiquettes, les cartes, les documentations, etc., relatives à des produits qui ne sont pas exactement ceux provenant réellement des régions limitées qui ont droit légal à ces appellations'*).

[22] Ibid., 964 (*'Le Congrès émet le vœu que toutes les appellations d'origine, qu'elles soient appliquées aux produits tirant leurs qualités du sol ou du climat, ou à des produits industriels, qu'elles jouissent ou non d'une notoriété, soient protégées'*).

The Appellation of Origin: Article 2

stipulated that the AOs of cheeses specified in an Annex were 'exclusively reserved to these cheeses whether they are used alone or accompanied by a qualifying or even corrective term such as "type", "kind", "imitation", or other term'.[23] Prominent cheese AOs under Stresa included 'Roquefort', 'Gorgonzola' and 'Parmigiano Reggiano'. These AOs were described as being 'the object of internal legislation reserving their use, within the territorial confines of one of the Contracting Parties, to cheese manufactured or matured in traditional regions, by virtue of local, loyal and uninterrupted usages'.[24] Once again, the mention of widespread, tried and tested production techniques is better understood in light of Chapter 3. Stresa also refers to different stages of production (manufacturing or maturing) being sufficient contact points with an appellation region.

The AIPPI Congress, at its Stockholm session in 1958, finally adopted a formal definition in a Resolution responding to Q7.[25] The relationship between the IS and AO was clarified, while setting out the necessary elements for an AO in a manner which evidently drew on the French national experience.

The appellations of origin constitute a particular category of the indications of source. The appellation of origin of a product is the geographic name of the place (country, region, locality, etc.) where that product is cultivated, manufactured or produced in any other manner, providing that it derives its qualities or its reputation from the soil, the climate, the traditional usages or the techniques of the place in question.

It is apparent that prior to the Lisbon conference, several key features were in circulation as part of the international conversation on AOs. These included the idea of a referent product which the geographical sign evokes; the causal connection between that product's quality and its place of origin; 'natural' influences on quality, such as soil and climate; 'human' influences, such as local, loyal and constant production techniques; the presence (or irrelevance) of a reputation for quality based on origin; and identification as well as regulation in the home country, presumably to preserve levels of quality. Taken together, these would form the building blocks for the Lisbon Agreement definition of the AO. Before that, however, the AO had to be sufficiently differentiated from the IS, in order to justify a separate agreement.

---

[23] Art. 1 also mentions the repression of unauthorised uses of AOs in translated form.

[24] WIPO, 'Texts of International Instruments', 11.

[25] AIPPI, Resolution on Appellations of Origin at the 23rd Congress of Stockholm, 26–31 May 1958, [1958] *Annuaire* 44.

134   The Appellation of Origin in Lisbon

During the Lisbon negotiations, the AO as a distinct category is initially fleshed out during discussions on a proposed amendment to the content of 'Industrial Property' in Article 1(2) of the Paris Convention. The description in Article 1(2) included 'indications of source *or* appellations of origin' (emphasis added). The concern was this suggested the two are conceptually equivalent, while the experiences of Union members at the national level suggested otherwise. Although the clarification proved unsuccessful, it generated an account of the differences between these two categories of signs.[26] The IS was described in familiar language. Depending upon the product, it merely indicated the place of production, manufacturing, extraction or collection. It could therefore be applied to any product. It was usually integrated into the broader framework of civil and criminal sanctions which existed to prevent misleading uses under the general rules of unfair competition law. Here the relationship between producers and consumers was the relevant axis of analysis. By contrast, the AO was a geographical denomination corresponding to a country or place within it, serving as the name for products originating there and displaying, according to regulations established for that purpose or local, loyal and constant uses, typical (i.e. characteristic) and reputed qualities due exclusively or essentially to the place as well as method of production, extraction etc.[27] Appellations therefore could only be applied to suitably qualified products. This was supported using the illustrations of Bordeaux and Burgundy, provided by The Director of the International Office of Vine and Wine.[28] AOs were the object of rights to which all legitimate producers from the eponymous region were entitled. The relevant axis of enquiry here was the competitive relationship between producers and trade rivals. Additional points of difference were also highlighted. The pertinent geographical region was usually renowned for producing the products in relation to which the AO was used, while there was no such requirement for the use of the IS. This introduces the requirement for an existing reputation. In terms of instrumental goals, the IS was projected as a policy instrument for protecting the national interest, by enabling discrimination between national and foreign goods or to facilitate

---

[26] Actes de Lisbonne, 771–2.

[27] Ibid., 771 (*'L'appellation d'origine désigne toute dénomination géographique correspondant à un pays, une région, une contrée ou un autre lieu quelconque servant d'appellation à des produits qui en sont originaires et qui présentent, selon les règlements établis a cet effet ou les usages locaux, loyaux et constants, des qualités typiques et renommées, dues exclusivement ou essentiellement au lieu et à la méthode de production et de fabrication, d'extraction ou de groupement de ces produits'*).

[28] Ibid., 773.

The Appellation of Origin: Article 2   135

selective tariff regimes. On the contrary, the object of the AO was the protection of private (albeit collective) interests. This emphasis on private interests, as opposed to regulation primarily in the public interest, is subsequently reiterated by the International Bureau.[29] Moreover, the use of the IS was usually compulsory, especially for exports, while the AO was optional. Finally, while general rules regulating false indications, trade names and trade marks were designed to prevent the use of misleading geographical names, when it came to the AO, the subject matter itself was always a geographical designation.[30] In terms of their relationship *inter se*, there was broad agreement with the German delegate's classification of the AO as a specialised sub-category of the IS.[31] Overall, the thrust of these arguments was directed towards unequivocally situating the AO within the domain of IP. They drew attention to the positive recognition of rights to control a valuable reputation, rather than relying on a blend of rules designed to achieve diverse policy goals and largely limited to ensuring truth-telling on labels.

It may therefore come as a surprise that – despite the identification of the key features of the AO, the desire to treat it separately from the IS and the move to recognise it as a legitimate member of the IP family – the draft text did not contain an official definition.[32] Instead, the country of origin was defined, accompanied by a description of the AO as part of the explanatory memorandum. This description can be analytically parsed as follows: an AO was (1) any geographical denomination (whether of a country or place within it); (2) used as a distinctive sign on products from that place; and (3) representing, according to established rules or custom, certain typical and well known qualities of the product; (4) where these qualities are exclusively or essentially attributable to the place of origin *and* method of production, extraction

---

[29] Ibid.

[30] This point is not entirely clear from the *travaux*, but may have alluded to the difference between 'negative' protection (stopping others from using the sign in certain contingent circumstances) and 'positive' protection (granting rights to the use of the sign to a defined group).

[31] Ibid., 774–5.

[32] While considering the draft agreement, even the committee of experts acknowledged that, while the concept of the AO was sufficiently widespread, national laws differed on significant details. They adopted the following description: the AO 'consists of any geographical name corresponding to a country, a region, a locality or any other place, used as a distinctive sign on the products of those places and presenting, according to the rules established for their use, or to be established, and unvarying local customs, typical and well-known qualities arising exclusively or essentially from the place of production, manufacture, extraction or assembly of these products'. See BIRPI, 'The Protection and International Registration of Appellations of Origin', 51.

136   The Appellation of Origin in Lisbon

etc.[33] Right from the start, the intention was to appeal to a broad constituency by recognising the importance of the human contribution in establishing a product's reputation. An AO could apply equally to products deriving their qualities from soil or climate and to industrial products. Products of industry or craft (*'activité industrielle ou artisanale'*) could enjoy a special reputation connected with the place of origin, by virtue of the distinctive skills or qualifications of the workers in a certain place, or due to the existence of certain raw materials available there, or sometimes in relation to climate or other peculiarities of the environment.[34] It must be noted that the introduction of the human dimension potentially loosens the connections to physical place since people and know-how frequently cross borders,[35] a point to which we return. This openness to a range of subject matter was maintained in subsequent registration practice and remains underappreciated. International registrations cover not only the usual suspects such as 'Champagne' for wine, 'Cuba' for leaf or manufactured tobacco and 'Tequila' for spirit drinks[36] but also 'Olinalá' for wooden handcrafted objects, 'Jablonec' (or 'Gablonz') for utility and decorative glassware, and 'Kraslické Krajky' for embroidery and lace goods.[37] While the majority of registrations fall within the expected categories (wines, spirits, agricultural products, cheese)[38] the presence of cultural artefacts suggests

---

[33] Actes de Lisbonne, 813 (*'l'appellation d'origine ... constituée par toute dénomination géographique correspondant à un pays, une région, une contrée ou un autre lieu quelconque, utilisée comme signe distinctif des produits originaires de ces derniers et présentant, selon les règlements établis pour leur emploi ou les usages locaux, loyaux et constants, des qualités' typiques et renommées dues exclusivement ou essentiellement au lieu et a la méthode de production, fabrication, extraction ou groupement de ces produits'*).

[34] Ibid., 813–14.

[35] K. Raustalia and S. R. Munzer, 'The Global Struggle Over Geographical Indications' (2007) 18 *European Journal of International Law* 337, 353 (asserting that 'the more human factors – which are moveable – matter, the weaker is the rationale for protecting a GI only in a specified region').

[36] Respectively Registration Nos. 231, 477 and 669 in the Lisbon Express Registry database, available at www.wipo.int/ipdl/en/search/lisbon/search-struct.jsp. See also WIPO, 'Questions to be Examined With a View to the Modification of the Regulations under the Lisbon Agreement', 10 May 2000 (LI/GT/1/2), [7] ('Wines and spirits are the products most frequently covered by international registrations made under the Lisbon Agreement').

[37] Respectively Registration Nos. 732, 66 and 22. Others include Hungarian crafts such as lace from Kiskunhalas and the porcelain of Herend (Nos. 495 and 737).

[38] An empirical study of Lisbon statistics put these four categories cumulatively at 84.1 per cent of the registrations in 2001. See S. Escudero, 'International Protection of Geographical Indications and Developing Countries' (Working Paper No. 10, South Centre, July 2001), 18. For current descriptions of product categories, divided into (1) Beverages and Related Products, (2) Food and Related Products and (3) Non-Food products, see the Lisbon Agreement's official publication, the WIPO *Appellations of Origin Bulletin.*

The Appellation of Origin: Article 2   137

that the possibilities are greater than is supposed. Subsequent international AO laws have followed suit by expressly incorporating craft products.[39]

Returning to the initial resistance to defining an AO, the proposal was clear that there was no need for a formal definition. This would be left to the national legislation of members, which would identify the AO (the sign), product to which it refers, zone of production, conditions of production etc.[40] During the course of the negotiations, a definition was finally incorporated in Article 2, on Israel's prompting and despite the objection that this might limit membership.[41] There is an overt reference to the need for a standard against which to measure applications. While this would not prejudice national definitions, it could operate as a reference point for national courts when testing the legitimacy of an internationally registered appellation. It would also prevent subjective or arbitrary determinations by Members as to whether a given application satisfied the Lisbon Agreement subject matter requirements. It was therefore intended to act as a benchmark and, as we will see, it has been applied as such by national courts but on the basis of highly questionable interpretations. Given its function as a standard, certain prominent features of the definition are worth unpacking: (1) the nature of the link between product and place; (2) the requisite influences of place, both natural and human; (3) the requirement for a 'geographical name'; and (4) the criterion of reputation.

2.1   *The link between product and place*

The link between product and place is identified in Article 2(1), where the 'quality or characteristics of [the AO product] are due exclusively or essentially to the geographical environment'. Therefore either quality or (qualitatively evaluated) distinctive features[42] are 'exclusively or

---

[39] S. 1(c) of WIPO Model Law for Developing Countries on Appellations of Origin and Indications of Source (Geneva 1975) ('"product" means any natural or agricultural product or any product of handicraft or industry'). Cf. Art. 212 of Decision 486 of the Cartagena Agreement by the Andean Community (14 September 2000) (Crafts have been expressly mentioned while defining the users of AOs).

[40] Actes de Lisbonne, 815.   [41] Ibid., 831–2.

[42] See s. 1(a) of WIPO Model Law 18 (replacing 'quality or characteristics' with 'characteristic qualities' for greater clarity). In the context of deciding whether 'characteristic qualities' would be substantively examined as part of an international registration system, its possible meanings were explored by a committee of experts. They considered whether there was a need to 'establish the criteria for the minimum quality' which the AO product should possess. WIPO, 'Draft of the Model Law for Developing Countries on Appellations of Origin and Indications of Source', 30 October 1974 (TAO/I/ INF.l), 30–40.

138 The Appellation of Origin in Lisbon

essentially' attributable to the influence of place. But when is this link satisfied? Clues may be found in the various iterations preceding this final definition. Israel initially proposed a definition whereby an AO (1) indicated the origin of the product as well as (2) indicating that the quality or nature of the product was especially attributable to that origin.[43] This focuses on the causal relationship between place and its effect on quality. It suggests that, as opposed to rare ingredients or cutting-edge technology, it was the influence of place that was responsible for distinctive quality. France then suggested the addition of existing and collective practices (*'les usages existants et collectifs'*) or the human facets of place. The definition cycled through one more draft, which suggested that the particular or special nature of the product was due exclusively to the place of origin and method of production or extraction.[44] Consensus was reached and it then settled into its present form.

Based on insights from the French AO experience discussed in the preceding chapter and drawing on the Lisbon Agreement's drafting history, the link is better understood when unpacked along the following lines:

(1) Certain products possessed distinctive, typical or characteristic features relating to their quality, which would make them stand out from broadly similar products (e.g. other blue cheeses).
(2) When looking for an explanation for this distinctive quality, place – including both physical and cultural geography components – essentially answered this. Place, broadly construed, was the response to the question of what makes these products qualitatively stand apart.
(3) There was a simple causal nexus between place and distinctive quality, where place had a verifiable impact on quality.

In summary, we can infer the following core requirement – the product's distinctive quality should be causally attributable to place, which explained this relative or differential distinctiveness whereby the wines, cheese or other products from a particular place could be set apart.[45]

---

[43] Actes de Lisbonne, 832 (*'Appellation d'origine signifie une dénomination géographique indiquant le pays, la région ou la localité d'où le produit considéré provient et impliquant en outre la notion de qualité ou de nature du produit particulière à ce pays, cette région ou cette localité'*).

[44] Ibid., 833 (*'On entend par appellation d'origine au sens du présent Arrangement la dénomination géographique d'un pays, d'une région ou d'une localité servant à designer ou à qualifier un produit qui en est originaire et dont l'emploi correspond à des qualités ou à une nature particulière de ce produit, dues exclusivement au lieu et a la méthode de production, de fabrication ou d'extraction de ces produits'*).

[45] This interpretation is offered with the caveat that the boundary between descriptive and normative claims is particularly porous here. However, it is supported by the drafting history of the definition.

The Appellation of Origin: Article 2   139

Given the specific references to artisanal products and their subsequent registration, the distinguishing link for such products is the human skill and local environmental conditions which have *demonstrably shaped* the product. If anything, there may be a latent claim that the history of the product is singular and that it is produced according to defined quality standards, rather than the product itself being inimitable. While this conceptualisation may give rise to other complications, the use of 'exclusively or essentially' here does not suggest that the applicant must prove the product is exclusive, i.e. unique to the region in a manner that can be established by the natural sciences.

Unfortunately, this is precisely the approach adopted by at least three national courts when interpreting the AO under the Lisbon Agreement. The Italian Supreme Court has interpreted 'exclusively or essentially' to require a product solely available in the designated place alone. It held that Article 2 requires the product to be unique, i.e. it cannot be reproduced anywhere else with the same fidelity.[46] In adopting this interpretation, the court followed its own precedent established in a case concerning 'Pilsener' lager.[47] The dispute arose as one of a series of international contestations over the exclusive rights to the terms 'Budweiser' and 'Bud' for lager, between the prominent US brewery Anheuser-Busch (AB) and the Czech state-owned Budějovický Budvar corporation (BB). BB had challenged AB's use of the unregistered but well known marks 'Budweiser' and 'Bud', on the basis of its Lisbon registrations. The Supreme Court endorsed the factual finding of the District Court that the *'milieu géographique'* requirement was not satisfied by the appellants who had a registration for, *inter alia*, 'Budweiser' under the Lisbon Agreement.[48] The court reasoned that even admitting that the water, hops, barley and malt of Bohemia used by the appellants for the production of its beer are of an excellent quality and have specific characteristics, this did not mean that:

---

[46] *'Budweiser'* [2003] IIC 676 (Corte Suprema di Cassazione, 2002).

[47] *Pilsen Urquell v. Industrie Poretti SpA* [1998] ETMR 168 (Corte Suprema di Cassazione 1996). At issue was whether the use of 'Pilsener' in the defendants' trade mark infringed the claimants' registered designation of origin. The defence was that it was generic use and therefore non-infringing. The trial judge seems to have inexplicably reasoned that because the expression was de facto *used* generically (depending on what people understand), it lacked the 'exclusive or essential' causal link (depending on verifiable product quality) to the region of origin. This showcases the clashing epistemologies in this area.

[48] *'Budweiser'* [2003] IIC 676 (Corte Suprema di Cassazione, 2002), 678.

140   The Appellation of Origin in Lisbon

[The] said taste, colour and look of Bohemian beer derive exclusively and exactly from complex environmental conditions (climate, soil, etc.), *unrepeatable in another place and considered a decisive factor,* nor from complex manufacturing and production techniques that are not (or not especially) feasible in different environments; this does not mean that the natural and human factors are so closely associated to the environment that they are necessary influences on the product to *render it absolutely unique and unrepeatable elsewhere* (emphasis added).[49]

The court further implied that AO products ought to possess *superior* quality whereas in this case 'the American product [did] not have characteristics that are inferior to the genuine Bohemian one'.[50]

This understanding of AO products as literally unique and of a superior quality is both inconsistent with the negotiating history and an impossibly high hurdle for the majority of existing registrations under the Lisbon Agreement. One needs to only step back for a moment and consider the evidence it would take to prove uniqueness. Analogous reasoning was evident in a dispute between the same parties, before the Civil Court of Lisbon in 1995.[51] Here the court concluded that:

Neither the beer manufactured by the defendant nor any other beer have characteristics or qualities that are exclusively or essentially connected to natural factors (soil, climate etc.) or to human factors existing only in the locality where they are manufactured ... Neither the raw materials, nor the manufacturing method are influenced by *natural or human factors existing only in a determined place or exclusively or essentially related with that place or area.* Therefore it is perfectly *possible to manufacture beer with the same qualities and characteristics in different geographical places* and areas (emphasis added).[52]

Once again the dial for the link between product and place is set to inimitability. A third instance of this reading is found in a French decision by a Strasbourg court,[53] under appeal at the time of writing. Predictably, the party successfully attacking AO status was AB, via a local representative. The court's reasoning further implies that since beer per se was an industrially produced commodity and its sensory or

---

[49] Ibid., 678–9.   [50] Ibid., 679.

[51] *Budweiser*, Civil Court of Lisbon, 13th Chamber, 3rd section, case 7906 (Unreported, 8 March 1995) considered in detail by A. Corte-Real, 'The Conflict Between Trade Marks and Geographical Indications – The Budweiser Case in Portugal', in C. Heath and A. Kamperman Sanders (eds.), *New Frontiers of Intellectual Property Law: IP and Cultural Heritage, Geographical Indicators, Enforcement, Overprotection,* IIC Studies Vol. 25 (Hart, Oxford 2005), 149, 156–7.

[52] Ibid., 157.

[53] *Kronenbourg Breweries v. Budějovický Budvar Národní Podnik* (RG 2002/04572), Tribunal de Grande Instance of Strasbourg, 30 June 2004 (Unreported).

The Appellation of Origin: Article 2

analytic properties could be faithfully replicated in different locations around the world, no beer could qualify as an AO.[54]

In conclusion, this notion of the AO representing uniqueness or inimitability is not confined to these three judgments and appears elsewhere in the literature.[55] This reading is understandable in light of the broader discursive context. Generic use was countered under the Paris Convention and Madrid Agreement frameworks with the '*conditions particulières de climat et de terroir*' reasoning being deployed to suggest there can be no substitutes. However, this was not the formulation chosen by those signing up to the Lisbon Agreement. By drawing on the Lisbon Agreement's drafting history and subsequent operation, I suggest that 'exclusive or essential' was never intended to require that the physical commodity was uniquely available in the designated place. Instead this phrase refers to a *demonstrable connection* between the human and natural geography, which essentially accounts for the product's characteristic or distinctive qualities. This view is all the more compelling in light of French experiences with defining the AO at the national level, the difficulties in circumscribing the region of production and the reasons for the transition to the AOC. The requirement is that the physical and human geography must leave distinctive traces upon product quality. The alternative adopted by the Italian and Portuguese courts would place most registered AOs under a cloud.

2.2   Natural and human influences

The text of Article 2 is clear that both natural *and* human influences are required for AO recognition. This is explicable in light of Chapter 3, where wine was identified as the archetype for IGOs. The recognition of technique *alongside* soil and climate was firmly established by the time of the AOC. Despite the recognition of human factors, under the French model the necessary influence of land results in it being considered a co-author of the regional product by some. Land acts as an anchor.

---

[54] Ibid. ('*Le produit concerné en l'espèce, à savoir la bière, est obtenu par un procédé industriel ... ses propriétés analytiques et sensorielles sont déterminées par les matières premières, notamment la variété de levure, et par les procédés de fabrication, ... paramètres qui ne sont pas influencés par la situation géographique d'une brasserie ou par le climat, comme en témoigne le fait que de nombreux brasseurs fabriquent de la bière identique dans différents endroits du monde*').

[55] See, e.g., M. Geuze, 'Let's Have Another Look at the Lisbon Agreement', 18 June 2007 (WIPO/GEO/BEI/07/10), [6] (Under Art. 2(1), the AO product 'has specific geographically-determined qualifications – in accordance with that definition – *which make the product unique* (i.e. in the sense that other products, originating outside the geographical area of which the denomination constitutes the appellation of origin, cannot have these qualifications)' (emphasis added).

142   The Appellation of Origin in Lisbon

It also explains certain formal legal features of the appellation regime, including the extended duration, collective nature and inalienability.[56] Having identified a core model of subject matter, it becomes easier to see traces of its influences on these requirements. This dual requirement is therefore unambiguous but sits awkwardly alongside the welcome given to 'industrial' appellations – an abstruse category – which may solely depend on manufacturing techniques historically associated with the region of production. If it's primarily about human rather than natural influences, should such AOs be registered? There may be independent and normatively compelling arguments to protect such signs, but what then is the understanding of the G in IGOs?

The question is relevant since people and production techniques tend to migrate. If producers can circulate with these skills, the role of physical place as an anchor is negated. Knock-on effects include question marks over the process of defining the region of origin, identifying the circle of producers and justifying the scope of protection. For the wine appellation model, physical geography had played an important role in all these enquiries. This unresolved issue was papered over during subsequent discussions concerning the drafting of a WIPO Model Law on Appellations of Origin. Here the suggested definition of an AO replaced 'natural and human' with 'natural factors, human factors, or both natural and human factors'.[57] Unless the human skills can be verifiably related to the physical environment, it is difficult to square this with the history of the discourse in this area. While presenting these as alternative influences affords greater flexibility in accepting subject matter, it simultaneously undermines the historic foundations of IGO protection. The dilemma is neatly captured in the following example: Dharamshala, situated in Northern India, is home to members of the Tibetan community in exile. Would traditional crafts produced by a highly skilled craftsperson of Tibetan origin but presently resident in India qualify as an appropriately designated AO under the Lisbon Agreement ('Tibetan Crafts')? If human input is prioritised over the natural environment and skilled producers being historically situated in a region is sufficient for the link, then why disallow Tibetan crafts-persons an AO registration when they move elsewhere with the same

---

[56] M-A. Hermitte, 'Les appellations d'origine dans la genèse des droits de la propriété intellectuelle', in P. Moity-Maïzi, C. de Sainte Marie, P. Geslin, J. Muchnik and D. Sautier (eds.), 'Systèmes Agroalimentaires Localisés: Terroirs, Savoir-faire, Innovations' (2001) 32 *Etudes et Recherches sur les Systèmes Agraires et le Développement* 195, 202–3.

[57] See s. 1(a) of WIPO Model Law 18.

The Appellation of Origin: Article 2   143

expertise? By contrast, the Lisbon register at present contains numerous examples where crafts reflecting human skill also have demonstrable connections to place. One such connection would be where certain raw materials have been historically sourced locally.[58] Any reconsideration of the AO definition along these lines will need to address this issue.

2.3 Geographical denomination

Matters are relatively more straightforward for this element of the AO definition. The wording of Article 2 suggests that only 'geographical denominations' are recognised. There has been some debate over whether this is limited to place names per se or whether it also includes designations which indirectly indicate geographical origin. There is compelling evidence to suggest it is not limited to place names. The problem may have arisen in part due to WIPO's previous practice of translating '*dénomination*' in the authoritative French text[59] as 'name'. Thus the recent Lisbon Survey included a proposal that '"geographical name" might be replaced by "indication used to identify a product as originating in . . .", in order to encompass also traditional denominations with a geographical connotation'.[60] When comparing the Lisbon AO's ability to accommodate signs with the TRIPS GI, the argument goes that 'Article 2 of the Lisbon Agreement does not cover appellations which are constituted by a sign other than a geographical name, for example, a non-geographical name or a figurative element, although such signs would fall under the definition of [GIs in] the TRIPS Agreement'.[61]

The records of the Lisbon Assembly suggest otherwise. The matter was first raised by Members of the Lisbon Council as far back as 1970, in an early survey to assess the working of the Agreement, which had

---

[58] One such example is 'Olinalá' from Mexico (Lisbon Registration No. 732) for wood crafted lacquer ware such as boxes, trays and folding screens. The lacquer pigments consist of a mixture of the oil of a local seed, ash, earth and powdered colorants to form a thick paste. Cf. E. R. Cisneros, 'The Protection of Geographical Indications in Mexico', September 2001 (WIPO/GEO/MVD/01/7); R. A. Lopez, *Crafting Mexico: Intellectuals, Artisans, and the State After the Revolution* (Duke University Press, Durham NC 2010).

[59] Actes de Lisbonne, 1006.   [60] Lisbon Survey Annex, [21]–[22].

[61] M. Ficsor, 'Challenges to the Lisbon System', 31 October 2008 (WIPO/GEO/LIS/08/4), [10]; F. Gevers, 'Topical Issues in the Protection of Geographical Indications', October 1997 (WIPO/GEO/EGR/97/5), 5 (The TRIPS Agreement 'speaks of a "geographical indication". This is obviously wider than the terminology used in the Lisbon Agreement, where one speaks of a "geographical name"').

144   The Appellation of Origin in Lisbon

only come into effect in 1966. An overarching concern was potential divergences in the interpretation of the new agreement. To clarify this issue, the 'Portuguese Administration declared itself to be in favour of an interpretation of the concept of the appellation of origin which would extend protection to names corresponding to geographical areas, even if the names themselves are not, properly speaking, geographical names, but serve to designate products originating [in those geographical areas]'.[62] Subsequently the 'Council was unanimous in the view that it was not contrary to the spirit of the Agreement to interpret Article 2(1) in such a way as to permit the registration and protection of names which, while not, properly speaking, "geographical" names, correspond to specific geographical areas and fulfil all the other conditions laid down by the Agreement'.[63] Therefore while TRIPS may be broader in that it envisages 'indications', i.e. not just words but images, symbols or perhaps even shapes, the Lisbon Agreement was clearly intended to apply to both direct as well as indirect geographical denominations. The question of whether Lisbon permits indirect indications of geographical origin, such as 'Bud' in the Budweiser disputes, has been the subject of recent litigation in Europe.[64] In one of the disputes, Advocate General Ruiz-Jarabo Colomer obligingly described indirect geographical designations as follows:

Geographical indications and even designations of origin do not always consist of geographical names. They are called 'direct' when they do and 'indirect' when they do not, provided the indication or designation at least informs consumers that the [product] to which it relates comes from a specific place, region or country ... In the same way that the words 'Cava' or 'Grappa' call to mind the Spanish and Italian birthplaces of a sparkling wine and of a liqueur respectively and that 'Feta' identifies a Greek cheese, were it to be found that 'Bud' represents a geographical indication, Czech consumers would have to associate the expression with a precise place and with the brewing of beer.[65]

Clarity on the matter would help set this controversy to rest. The Lisbon Agreement was evidently intended to apply to indirect indications and the reference to 'denominations' could even include figurative elements or other signs as well.

---

[62] Lisbon Council, 'Problems Arising from the Practical Application of the Lisbon Agreement', July 1970 (AO/V/5), [4].

[63] Lisbon Council, 'Report of the Fifth Session', September 1970 (AO/V/8), [19].

[64] *Budějovický Budvar, Národní Podnik* v. *OHIM* (Joined cases T-225/06, T-255/06, T-257/06 & T-309/06) [2008] ECR II-3555 (CFI); *Budějovický Budvar Národní Podnik* v. *Rudolf Ammersin GmbH* (C-478/07) [2009] ECR I-7721 (ECJ Grand Chamber).

[65] Ibid., [68], [72] (internal citations omitted).

The Appellation of Origin: Article 2

2.4   Reputation

Under this element of the AO definition, there are two related enquiries to consider. Must an application for an AO demonstrate that it possesses a reputation? And what extent of reputation will suffice? The drafting history as well as current provisions of Lisbon clearly indicates that, *in addition* to satisfying the link discussed above, reputation in the country of origin is a separate requirement. First, according to the text of Article 2(2), when identifying the country of origin, we have to look for the country containing the place 'which has given the product its reputation'. Second, Article 1(2) specifies that Members of the Lisbon Union have an obligation to protect AOs 'recognised and protected as such in the country of origin'. During the Lisbon negotiations, it becomes apparent that 'recognised' reflected an AO's existing reputation. The Commission was unanimous when it emphasised the principle that, unlike the IS, AOs represented products enjoying a certain notoriety.[66] Third, a related point is that in Article 1(2), the AO is a sign that not only indicates a place but also 'serves to designate a product originating therein' (e.g. Champagne standing for both region and product). This ability to indicate a specific product from the place is only acquired over time, as the product gains a reputation. According to Devletian, 'there must be a constant and genuine local usage of the geographical name to designate a product and ... [it] must enjoy a certain reputation'.[67] Therefore in addition to the qualitative link, reputation in the home country is a further requirement.

This makes sense at a very fundamental level. The valuable intangible that is being protected is the reputation that a regional product has accrued over time, so establishing that it exists in the home country is a reasonable condition. This is in contrast to the TRIPS definition in Article 22.1, where the link requirement states that 'a given *quality, reputation or other characteristic* of the good [has to be] essentially attributable to its geographical origin' (emphasis added).[68] Here three

---

[66] Actes de Lisbonne, 831 ('*Ensuite, la Commission a estimé à l'unanimité que le mot « reconnues » était plus approprié soit pour souligner le principe général de droit que l'appellation d'origine concerne toujours un produit jouissant d'une certaine notoriété, soit pour marquer sa différence avec l'indication de provenance*').

[67] A. Devletian, 'The Lisbon Agreement' [1973] *Industrial Property* 308, 310.

[68] WIPO, 'International Protection of Geographical Indications: The Present Situation and Prospects for Future Developments', 1 September 1999 (WIPO/GEO/CPT/99/1), [6] ('Arguably, goods which have "merely" a certain reputation, but not a specific quality being due to their place of origin are not covered by the definition of appellation of origin as provided by the Lisbon Agreement'); Cf. WIPO, 'Protection of Geographical Indications: General Introduction, International Protection and Recent Developments', June 2001 (WIPO/GEO/CIS/01/1,) [5].

146   The Appellation of Origin in Lisbon

alternate means of satisfying the link are presented with reputation as one of them. The importance of reputation as a free-standing option and its role in fostering compromise during the TRIPS negotiations will be considered in Part II. Thus while otherwise agreeing with much of Gervais' analysis of the 'reputation' factor in Lisbon, one cannot agree with his conclusion that 'the definitional gaps, if any, between TRIPS and Lisbon are such that most if not all of those differences can be considered functionally irrelevant'.[69]

Before concluding, it is worth noting that, as regards the extent of the reputation, this only needs to be established in the country of origin. Given the mechanics of the Lisbon Agreement, the AO is then protected in all Members without needing to prove that it is reputed or even known in any given Member. We return to this point when considering the scope of protection below, but in this regard the Lisbon Agreement provides registrants with enhanced protection that spreads beyond the semantic footprint of the sign. This is an unusual development. Conventionally, the recognition and protection of signs in intellectual property law has been restricted to specific national jurisdictions by the principle of territoriality.[70] Famous or Well Known Marks are one category which transcend territoriality and international discussions have considered the possibility of protecting such a mark in a country where it may have an extant reputation but where it lacks valid registration or perhaps even an official channel of distribution.[71] Here the reputation of the famous mark has spilled over into the territory of dispute, despite these other requirements being absent. Unlike this scenario, the Lisbon Agreement merely requires that reputation be established in the country of origin, after which it is protected in all Members. We consider the reasons for this divergence below.

3.   International registration and its effects

The Lisbon Agreement is notable for establishing a register of AOs and represents a functioning multilateral registration system.[72] At the heart

---

[69] Gervais, 'Misunderstood Potential', 91–4, 100.

[70] G. Dinwoodie, 'Trade Marks and Territory: Detaching Trade Mark Law from the Nation-State' (2004) 41 *Houston Law Review* 885.

[71] See Art. *6bis* of the Paris Convention; Art. 16 of TRIPS Agreement; WIPO Joint Recommendation concerning Provisions on the Protection of Well-Known Marks (1999); F. W. Mostert, *Famous and Well-Known Marks: An International Analysis*, 2nd edn (INTA, New York 2004).

[72] A convenient overview is found in Annex II of WIPO, 'Possible Improvements of the Procedures under the Lisbon Agreement', 10 February 2009 (LI/WG/DEV/1/2 Rev), (hereafter, Lisbon Overview).

International registration and its effects 147

of the system is the desire to magnify the effects of national recognition by projecting this across its Membership. A closer examination of its operational mechanics reveals that the system does work. However, it does so with caveats, qualifications and curbs not otherwise apparent from its text. Considering that it was established as a haven for those in favour of enhanced IGO protection, the degree of dissent is remarkable. The analysis below is broadly divided into (1) the process of registration and (2) the consequences of registration.

3.1   Process of registration

A prerequisite for international registration is that Members protect appellations of origin 'as such' at the national level (Article 1(2)), which could be via domestic registration, administrative decree or judicial determination.[73] Therefore the Lisbon Agreement is relatively neutral as to the form of recognition and protection. Mihály Ficsor notes that it 'does not necessarily have to be based on a Lisbon-like domestic registration system'.[74] Despite this flexibility, the 'as such' requirement was perceived as a hindrance to expanding its membership. Prominent among its critics, Germany had complained that this was one of the principal obstacles to its involvement with the Lisbon system, despite otherwise supporting greater international protection for IGOs.[75] 'As such' has also been reconsidered in the recent survey on the Agreement.[76] There are two relevant aspects to this requirement. The German objections were based on the understanding that 'recognised and protected as such in the country of origin' mandates *prior state recognition of the AO through an official act*, even though this may take many different forms. For countries such as Germany, which had previously protected

---

[73] Rule 5(2)(vi) of the Regulations under the Lisbon Agreement for the Protection of Appellations of Origin and their International Registration (as in force 1 January 2010) requires that the application must include 'the title and date of the legislative or administrative provisions, the judicial decisions or the date and number of the registration by virtue of which the [AO] is protected in the country of origin'. The French case study in Chapter 3 outlines three of these options – administrative decrees, judicial decisions and registration – being experimented with in a single jurisdiction over time.

[74] Ficsor, 'Challenges to the Lisbon System', [27]; Cf. Lisbon Overview, [8].

[75] See, e.g., Lisbon Council, 'Report of the Second Session', December 1967 (AO/II/5), [17]; Lisbon Council, 'Territorial Extension of the Lisbon Union', June 1971 (AO/VI/4), (letter from the Federal Republic of Germany reproduced in the Annex); WIPO, 'Report Adopted by the Committee of Experts', 15 November 1974 (TAO/I/ 8), 13–30 (several delegates stating that their countries did not join Lisbon because of the 'as such' requirement).

[76] Lisbon Survey (Responses to Q1).

148   The Appellation of Origin in Lisbon

IGOs under unfair competition law, recognition and protection arose on a case-by-case basis, as and when a dispute arose. Given the doctrinal approach,[77] the concern was that several important German regional products could not be recognised, since they were neither governed by specific legislation, nor had they been defined by the judicial resolution of a dispute.[78] With the pan-European registered IGO regime now in operation, this is no longer a concern for EU Members as well as those belonging to other regional appellation protection systems[79] but it continues to be an obstacle for others. Since prior formal recognition is required in the home country, one possible alternative is for regional producers to file for a certification or collective trade mark. As we have seen in Chapter 2, the vast majority of states have provisions for at least the latter. Here the second aspect of 'as such' operates as an additional hurdle. The AO must not only be recognised in the country of origin, it must also be 'protected as such', i.e. afforded the high levels of protection to be found in Article 3.[80] Few registered trade mark systems afford such high levels of protection and it is presently doubtful whether even anti-dilution provisions available in many trade mark regimes will practically benefit collective or certification marks.[81] Therefore 'as such' requires that the national regime of a Member (1) maps its subject matter on to the Lisbon AO definition, (2) enables prior official recognition of the AO, while remaining flexible about the form of recognition and (3) affords levels of protection comparable to Article 3.

---

[77] See Chapter 3, Section 7.

[78] A related concern was that German unfair competition law focused on defining the territorial limits for a reputed regional appellation, whereas the Lisbon Agreement also required the user group of the appellation to be identified when applying for international registration. In response, it was clarified that the Lisbon Agreement does not require an exhaustive list of producers but merely requires an algorithm for clearly defining the circle of those with the right to use the appellation. Defining those entitled to the appellation indirectly, by defining the territory and production conditions, was possible. Lisbon Council, 'Territorial Extension', [5]–[7].

[79] WIPO is therefore studying the possibility of such regional registration systems joining the Lisbon framework. See the self-explanatory WIPO, 'Study on the Relationship between Regional Systems for the Protection of Geographical Indications and the Lisbon System and the Conditions For, and Possibility Of, Future Accession to the Lisbon Agreement by Competent Intergovernmental Organizations', 6 August 2010, (LI/WG/DEV/2/3).

[80] Lisbon Survey Annex, [5] ('The various contributions received ... would appear to confirm that the condition that an [AO] must be recognized and protected as such in the country of origin means that the [AO must satisfy the definition in Art. 2] and that is protected against unauthorized use (in accordance with Article 3 of the Lisbon Agreement')).

[81] D. Gangjee, 'The Business End of Collective and Certification Marks', in I. Simon Fhima (ed.), *Trade Mark Law and Sharing Names: Exploring Use of the Same Mark by Multiple Undertakings* (Edward Elgar, Cheltenham 2009), 79.

International registration and its effects 149

For Members who satisfy this threshold requirement, the national office,[82] usually on behalf of the producer collective or those otherwise entitled to use the appellation, then applies for an international registration. The application can be in the name of any 'natural persons or legal entities, public or private, having, according to their national legislation, a right to use such appellations' (Article 5(1)). Two issues arise here. While Article 5(1) refers to the 'right to use', a previous version of the Lisbon Regulations mentioned 'the owner or owners of the appellation of origin'.[83] The language of ownership suggests an accompanying property framework.[84] Whether AOs can be generally assumed to be the objects of property rights and, if so, the nature of the property interest (individual or some form of collective or communal property) is a notoriously difficult area and there are differences in the various national approaches. We return to this issue when considering whether GIs are private rights under TRIPS in the following chapter. As far as the Lisbon Assembly was concerned, the intention was merely to conveniently identify the group that could legitimately use the appellation in the home country and was associated with the AO. Therefore the present version of the Regulations (2010) bypasses this minefield and refers instead to the 'holder or holders of the right to use'.[85] The second issue concerns the most convenient as well as accurate way of describing this group. The question arose as to whether the name of each individual entitled to the use of the appellation is required to be placed on the register. Where an appellation such as Bordeaux covers a large number of producers, perhaps running into the thousands, such a requirement would prove impracticable. In response, the Lisbon working group has confirmed that the agreement merely requires a clearly specified circle of owners,[86] who can be designated collectively.[87] Apart from specified rights holders, other requirements for the application include the country of origin, the specific AO (sign) which is to be protected, the

---

[82] It is for the contracting country to decide who this authority shall be. See WIPO, 'Questions to be Examined', [15]–[17].

[83] For discussions of the inconsistency between the Article and the Rule, see Lisbon Working Group, 'Report Adopted by the Working Group', 12 July 2000 (LI/GT/1/3), [27]–[33]; Cf. WIPO, 'Questions to be Examined', [18]–[24].

[84] At some points during the Lisbon negotiations, the language of property was used to describe the AO, usually in contrast to the IS. See Actes de Lisbonne, 796, 813–14, 861–3.

[85] E.g. Rules 1(xi); 5(2)(ii); 5(2)(vi)(b).

[86] WIPO, 'Questions to be Examined', [22]–[23].

[87] Rule 5(2)(ii) requires that the application mentions 'the holder or holders of the right to use the appellation of origin, designated collectively or, where collective designation is not possible, by name'.

150   The Appellation of Origin in Lisbon

associated product, the area of production and details on the formal national recognition of the AO.[88]

WIPO then notifies Members of this registration request[89] and within one year of the receipt of this notification, a national office can declare that it cannot ensure the protection of an AO in its territory, while providing grounds for its decision.[90] This possibility for refusal cannot prejudicially alter the pre-existing status quo for protected terms under international agreements, national legislation or court decisions.[91] In effect, the refusal option should not be an opportunity to backslide and lower protection for tactical reasons. Furthermore, the national office does not act on its own motion and issues a declaration under Article 5(3) on the basis of submissions by interested parties. Refusal is also not the end of the story. The intention was to open up a space for negotiation between the home country and the country opposing the AO. According to the Lisbon conference records, the grounds for refusal constitute a possible basis for discussion between the two Members, for the purpose of reaching an understanding. The understanding may form the basis for withdrawing the refusal.[92] This intention seems to have been translated into practice and countries do occasionally withdraw refusals.[93] Under Rule 11 of the Regulations, a procedure is available for the notification of such withdrawals and their being recorded in the International Register. Finally, there is the possibility of a partial refusal, which could relate to a part of the goods applied for, or a part of the AO which may be considered generic, such as 'Beurre des Charentes' where no protection would be given to the 'butter' component.[94] Otherwise, following receipt of a declaration of refusal from a competent authority, within the prescribed period, WIPO notifies the competent authority of the home country, enters the refusal in the International Register and publishes it in the Bulletin.

Since the refusal must be accompanied by grounds, a list of such reasons has been collated in the half century of Lisbon's operation.[95]

---

[88] Art. 5 and Rule 5.   [89] Art. 5(2).

[90] Art. 5(3). Upon receiving notice of this refusal, the competent authority of the country of origin communicates it in turn to the parties concerned, who may avail themselves of the same administrative and legal remedies against the refusal as nationals of the country which gave notice of refusal, under Art. 5(5).

[91] Art. 4.   [92] Actes de Lisbonne, 817.

[93] See, e.g., Lisbon Council, 'Report on the Activities of the Lisbon Union and Financial Questions', June 1972 (AO/VII/3), [7] ('As can be seen ... declarations of refusal to grant protection have been made, since the entry into force of the Lisbon Agreement ... in respect of 84 appellations of origin out of 550 recorded in the international register. Of those refusals, 24 were subsequently withdrawn').

[94] WIPO, 'Questions to be Examined', [45]–[47].

[95] A summary of reasons for refusal are contained in the official WIPO publication for the Lisbon Agreement. I have relied on (2009) 38 Appellations of Origin 75–8. Condensed

International registration and its effects 151

These can relate to any situation of fact or law and there are three main headings, each of which includes sub-categories. This compilation makes for interesting reading, because the breadth of sub-categories is far greater than the narrow grounds envisaged at the original negotiations.[96]

(1) Refusal based on Article 2, i.e. *the definition of an AO*. This includes the following reasons:
   (i)   the proposed AO is a generic indication for a type of product;
   (ii) it is merely an indication of the origin of products (IS-like), without satisfying the other requirements of the definition;
   (iii) it is an homonymous denomination that does not meet the definition, by presumably not indicating a specific country of origin;
   (iv) the denomination is not geographical, which highlights the importance of resolving the issue of indirect appellations;
   (v)   the denomination is insufficiently precise to be able to meet the definition; or
   (vi) the competent authority is not convinced that the denomination meets the definition, a ground which is again questionable, since the authority is not supposed to act on its own volition.
(2) Then there are refusals based on *an earlier right*. Protection of the AO is
   (i)   prevented by an earlier homonymous appellation of origin;[97]
   (ii) refused to the extent only that it cannot be used to prevent the use of a specified homonymous appellation of origin (i.e. aiming for co-existence of AOs);
   (iii) refused conditionally, unless a specified homonymous denomination can co-exist;
   (iv) prevented by an earlier trade mark, which is one of the most frequently cited reasons for refusal;[98] and
   (v)   disallowed because an opposition or request for cancellation has been filed against the AO.

---

summaries are also available in Gueze, 'Another Look at Lisbon', [20]; Gervais, 'Misunderstood Potential', 101.

[96] Actes de Lisbonne, 817, 835–7, 861 (where limited grounds for refusal were contemplated).

[97] The grape liquor 'Pisco' provides a helpful illustration of the tussle over homonyms, where both Peru and Chile claim the appellation. While Chile is not a Member, the Lisbon record for the Peruvian AO 'Pisco' (No. 865) displays refusals by countries which have entered into agreements with Chile. These agreements refer to the protection of Chilean Pisco. See the Lisbon Express database, available at www.wipo. int/ipdl/en/lisbon/.

[98] WIPO, 'Notes Concerning the Proposals for Modification of the Regulations under the Lisbon Agreement', 19 January 2001 (LI/GT/2/3), 10 (The 'ground for refusal most frequently cited by the authorities of contracting countries is the fact that the [AO] conflicts with a prior mark (in about half of all cases)').

152   The Appellation of Origin in Lisbon

(3) Lastly, there is the *'other grounds'* category for refusals. These include situations where
   (i)   the use of an AO is likely to generate confusion;
   (ii) the registration of the AO has not taken place in respect of all producers in the region; and
   (iii) the AO is against religious values, ethics or public order.

This final category helps to explain why the Islamic Republic of Iran has rejected an enormous number of AOs relating to wines, spirits and beers. According to its declarations of refusal, the Islamic Penal Code prohibits the production, distribution and consumption of alcoholic beverages. Presumably, on the same basis, large scale infringement of such AOs in Iran may not be a concern. This surfeit of reasons has led to proposals to consolidate grounds for refusal and include them in the text of the Agreement, while one respondent remained concerned about systematic and loosely substantiated refusals based on political reasons.[99]

3.2   Consequences of registration

Once the appellation is registered, there are some important consequences, representing attempts to depart from general principles of registered trade mark or unfair competition law. One is that the AO continues to be protected as long as it remains protected in the country of origin, without the need for periodic refresher registrations.[100] Another is that those traders who have been using the appellation within the territory of a contracting party (e.g., as part of a trade mark) prior to its registration can avail themselves of a two-year phase out period within which to cease such use, provided WIPO is notified.[101] This implies a qualified trumping by the AO over a prior trade mark, where a formal notification of refusal on the basis of that prior mark has not been made.[102] Perhaps most significantly, Article 6 establishes that a registered appellation 'cannot . . . be deemed to have become generic, as long as it is protected as an appellation of origin in the country of origin'. This suggests that the communicative function of the registered sign is not the basis for protection and underlines the apparently proprietary nature of the interest. The emphasis is on preserving the designation for a defined group of producers in the country of origin and the international

---

[99] Lisbon Survey Annex, [68]–[71].   [100] Art. 7(1).   [101] Art. 5(6).
[102] As we will see below, even if the refusal has not been declared at this stage, the prior trade mark owner retains the option of revoking the AO in court.

International registration and its effects 153

registration fails only when this group can no longer be demarcated with clarity in the home country.

There are two ways to make sense of this *de jure* freezing of meaning. One would be to read this provision as an affirmation of the logic that '*conditions particulières de climat et de terroir*' will ensure that no competitor's product from outside the region would ever be a truthful substitute for such unique products. Precisely this argument surfaced during the negotiations at Lisbon in 1958, during the unsuccessful attempts to expand the scope of exception in Article 4 of the Madrid Agreement.[103] However, this interpretation was not suggested during the discussion of the draft Lisbon Agreement and does not sit comfortably with the concession in Article 6 that genericide may occur in the home country. Article 6 therefore represents a pragmatic rather than principled accord to prohibit the use of generic terms beyond the limited reach of territorial sovereignty. It is yet another indicator that the Lisbon Agreement seeks to export the home country protected status to all signatories. This negotiating triumph must be appreciated against the backdrop of several ineffectual attempts to amend Article 4 of the Madrid Agreement, which allows national courts to make a determination of generic status at any point, with the exception of products of the vine. Therefore care was taken to make this 'freezing of AO status' explicit in the draft of Article 6, as Members might otherwise be tempted to find exceptions.[104]

Despite this express intention, the Italian Supreme Court held that Article 6 only amounted to a presumption, which remained open to a genericide challenge. In a dispute concerning the status of the Czech appellation 'Plzeň' and, *inter alia*, its translation 'Pilsener', the court reasoned that Article 6 would allow the appellation users to merely rely 'on a presumption of legitimacy in its use',[105] which then shifted the burden of proof onto the party alleging generic use. This interpretation is irreconcilable with the express provisions of the agreement but highlights the judicial discomfort generated by a provision depriving national courts of the ability to track meaning in the marketplace. A recent study queries whether 'cannot ... be deemed to have become generic' operates as a bright line rule at all, while asking whether related defences such as acquiescence – based on sufficiently long-standing and uninterrupted use by external traders – would continue to operate.[106] This is further

---

[103] Actes de Lisbonne, 796–7.   [104] Ibid., 838.
[105] *Pilsen Urquell* v. *Industrie Poretti SpA* [1998] ETMR 168, 176.
[106] Ficsor, 'Challenges to the Lisbon System', [30] ('Firstly, does it only prevent an appellation from having been deemed generic but not from in fact becoming generic, or, does it also exclude the latter? Secondly, does that Article prevent the operation of other, but similar, legal principles such as that of acquiescence?').

154   The Appellation of Origin in Lisbon

evidence of the clash between an approach built around the ascertainment of a sign's meaning and one which seeks to protect the reified signifier as a valuable 'thing' for other reasons.

The question of subsequent generic use leads to an overarching issue that has attracted remarkably little attention.[107] To what extent can registered appellations be subject to judicial review? Can an internationally registered AO be revoked or otherwise invalidated in a Member (besides the home country)? This is most likely to occur in situations where the AO is challenged on the grounds of genericide, where a prior trade mark right exists or because it does not satisfy the definitional link requirements, as was argued in the *Budweiser* cases above. Christopher Heath makes out a convincing case that while the Agreement does not expressly address this issue, from a combined reading of the text, the revised Rules, the accompanying *travaux* for these and the historical transition from the perceived inadequacies of the Madrid Agreement to the standards of the Lisbon Agreement, there are very limited grounds for judicial discretion outside of the home country.[108] These include Article 7, which implies that courts can check the status of the appellation in the country of origin at any point, and the determination of whether an AO has been infringed under Article 3. Despite this, as seen above, the Italian and Portuguese courts applied their own standards when deciding whether 'Pilsener' and 'Budweiser' satisfied the conditions for an AO.

An interpretation more closely aligned with the text and the drafters' intentions is found in a series of decisions by the Israeli Supreme Court that once again concerned 'Budweiser'. Based on the Lisbon registration BB had registered the AO for 'Budweiser Bier' in 1969, in accordance with the domestic law of Israel.[109] When AB's licensee began to produce American 'Budweiser' in Israel, BB objected. AB responded by, *inter alia*, challenging the validity of the AO registrations, arguing that the quality and characteristics are not dependent upon origin and that the former German names Budweiss and Budweiser are no longer geographical denominations for the town of Ceske Budejovice, as it is presently named.[110] BB responded with the argument that registrations could not be challenged once they had been accepted by a national office, after

---

[107] A notable exception is C. Heath, 'Geographical Indications: International, Bilateral and Regional Agreements', in C. Heath and A. Kamperman Sanders (eds.), *New Frontiers of Intelléctual Property Law: IP and Cultural Heritage, Geographical Indicators, Enforcement, Overprotection*, IIC Studies Vol. 25 (Hart, Oxford 2005), 97, 112–19.

[108] Ibid., 112. Cf. C. Heath, 'A Hungarian Chapter to the Budweiser Saga' [2009] IIC 328, 331–5.

[109] Israel Appellation of Origin Law 5725 of 1965.

[110] *Budweiser I* [1991] IIC 255, 256–7 (Israel SC, 1990).

International registration and its effects 155

the one-year period for declarations of refusal had expired. The district court rejected this contention, primarily on the following basis:

The district court ... has jurisdiction to test the validity of the appellation of origin. The court based this decision on its general jurisdiction and upon the interpretative approach which does not approve of the removal of this jurisdiction. In the opinion of the court, it should not be supposed that the Registrar's investigation of the appellation of origin is the final word as to its validity. A person should not be given an appellation of origin to which he is not entitled at law. In the opinion of the court, this approach does not conflict with Israel's international obligations pursuant to the Lisbon Convention ... Israel agreed to protect an appellation of origin within the meaning of the Convention and not a quasi appellation of origin.[111]

On appeal, Justice Barak revisited the policy underpinnings for the Lisbon Agreement: 'This policy was the giving of comprehensive protection to a foreign appellation of origin and giving it the status in the foreign state which it enjoyed in the original state ... Only if in the original state the appellation is no longer protected will it cease to be protected in the foreign state.'[112] Having identified what is arguably the only basis for objecting to an appellation registration – a collapse in the home country – he reasoned that an 'indirect ground' for objection should not be encouraged, namely 'whether it is sufficient that, in the opinion of the foreign state, (here Israel) there is a ground on the strength of which the appellation of origin may be deleted in the country of origin'.[113] While national courts certainly retained the *jurisdiction* to consider the validity of an AO registration, the *grounds* for invalidation were severely limited.[114] The result was that BB's registration was valid.

This interpretation was confirmed by a five-member Supreme Court panel. AB once again raised the concern that, if the initial registration in the country of origin was 'effected unduly' or questionable, such an interpretation would deny external courts the ability to scrutinise this.[115] The court's response was that since Israel had an interest in protecting 'Jaffa' oranges, it:

[A]ssumed international obligations to the agreement's member states, and it would not be correct to evade them. Accordingly, one must assume that the legislature ... sought to give validity to such international obligations as were agreed upon in the Lisbon Agreement ... What is conspicuous as the fundamental principle of the agreement is the wish to spread an international screen of wide protection over a commercial appellation which a certain state ... considers an appellation of origin which is exclusive to and characterises the state

---

[111] Ibid., 257.   [112] Ibid., 261.   [113] Ibid., 262.   [114] Ibid., 262–3.
[115] *Budweiser II* [1994] IIC 589, 598, 592–3 (Israel SC, 1992).

156   The Appellation of Origin in Lisbon

or its people, and also that other members of the agreement shall honour the property rights reserved to it or to a commercial body acting within it, provided that such a property right has been recognised by such state and duly registered. [The Court then refers to futile attempts at stronger IGO protection under previous international IP instruments.] Against this background, one can understand the very wide and almost absolute protection afforded by the Lisbon Agreement ... to the appellation of origin of a foreign country which has been recognised as such in the international framework and which was properly registered in the agreement's member state.

Undeterred, AB raised new grounds of objection, primarily on the formality that ownership of the AO had changed and this was not reflected on the international register. This third attempt also failed,[116] although this did not signal the end of the litigation.[117] These decisions cumulatively represent a thorough examination of the commitment that Lisbon entails, but subsequent developments have undermined their importance. A new provision in Israel's Appellation Law[118] allows for challenging the definition at any stage. In light of the Italian and Portuguese decisions, the Lisbon Regulations have been modified to incorporate situations where a national court has invalidated an AO registration as it applies to that Member. In 2002, Rule 16 was added:

Where the effects of an international registration are invalidated in a contracting country and the invalidation is no longer subject to appeal, the invalidation shall be notified to the International Bureau by the competent authority of that contracting country.

WIPO's International Bureau acknowledged that it could not determine the correctness of these national decisions and that the issue was contro-versial.[119] The damage is now done and it appears that other Members will follow suit, as suggested by recent Hungarian decisions.[120] On the

---

[116] Noted in *Budweiser III* [1997] IIC 596 (Israel SC, 1997).
[117] For subsequent developments, see P. Zylberg, 'Geographical Indications v. Trade Marks: The Lisbon Agreement: A Violation of TRIPS?' (2002–3) 11 *University of Baltimore Intellectual Property Law Journal* 1, 53–4.
[118] Under Chapter 5.1, 'Rights in Respect of Trade Marks', Art. 33B has been added: 'In any proceedings before the Registrar or the Court in which a party raises a claim that he is proprietor of a geographical indication, the opposing party may claim that the geographical indication is not a geographical indication'. Full text available at www. wipo.int/clea/docs_new/en/il/il010en.
[119] Lisbon Working Group, 'Report Adopted', [70], [83].
[120] *Anheuser Busch Inc* v. *Budějovický Budvar Národní Podnik* [2009] IIC 353 (Hungary SC, 21 March 2007) ('*Bud*')(The Supreme Court implicitly accepted the Court of Appeal's approach which allowed third parties to request invalidation of the AO after the expiry of one year refusal period mentioned in the Lisbon Agreement); *Anheuser Busch Inc* v. *Budějovický Budvar Národní Podnik* [2009] IIC 357 (Hungary SC, 28 March 2007) ('*Budweis Beer*') (The court reasoned that the Lisbon registration is effectively

The scope of protection: Article 3

contrary, the original perception was that '[o]nce protected, the debate as to each term is ended'.[121] The controlling status of protection in the country of origin is evident from a reading of Article 1 (appellations recognised and protected as such in the country of origin), Article 2 (which defines the country of origin) and Article 6 (where post-registration genericide is fatal only in the country of origin).[122] By undermining this, the very foundations of the agreement are weakened. Bearing in mind the possibility of invalidation, there is an urgent need to clarify the link between product and place, which becomes the litmus test for the validity of the AO. If the Italian Supreme Court's standards of unique product or unique human/natural environment are applied, this threatens the validity of a large number of registered appellations. These tensions within Lisbon are invisible both within the legal literature and at TRIPS Council debates, where a multilateral register is under consideration.

In conclusion, the registration system established under this Agreement is revealed to be surprisingly flexible (to the extent of incoherence in places), in large part because of divergent interpretations by Members,[123] with WIPO's International Bureau having a non-prescriptive and limited facilitative role. If the attempt was to settle the matters of definitional validity and protected status in the home country, then export this status to the entire Lisbon Membership, this has only partially succeeded.

4. The scope of protection: Article 3

The Lisbon Agreement is thought to provide 'absolute' protection for AOs.[124] But what does this mean? Relatively speaking, compared to the emphasis on misleading uses in the Paris Convention and the Madrid Agreement, this treaty established a significantly expanded zone of protection by proscribing several additional uses that are also classified

---

translated into a national AO right and subject to the same vulnerabilities, including the possibility of revocation).

[121] R.W. Benson, 'Toward a New Treaty for the Protection of Geographical Indications' [1978] *Industrial Property* 127, 132.

[122] The Lisbon Agreement was finalised within an international consensus that included the Stresa Convention and bilateral agreements. These were premised on protection in the country of origin being dispositive. See R. Plaisant, 'The Revision of the International Treaty Provisions Dealing with Appellations of Origin and Indications of Source' [1980] *Industrial Property* 182, 189.

[123] A concern identified as early as 1969, three years after the agreement came into effect. Lisbon Council, 'Report of the Fourth Session', September 1969 (AO/IV/5), [12]–[15].

[124] Actes de Lisbonne, at 791–2, 794, 809 (in the context of amendments to The Madrid Agreement), 826.

158   The Appellation of Origin in Lisbon

as unfair competition in several national jurisdictions. However, the qualitative differences are worth teasing out, because they reveal a more fundamental departure contained in this agreement. The following paragraphs attempt to (1) identify the various categories of prohibited conduct; (2) show how this yet again represents an awkward amalgamation of justificatory frameworks; and (3) suggest that the Lisbon Agreement drew its inspiration from a model owing more to contract law than to IP or unfair competition law, which explains why there are gaps and puzzles when approaching it from either of these perspectives.

Once more, it is useful to begin with the text of the Lisbon Agreement along with the unofficial headings provided by WIPO:

Article 3 [Content of Protection]
Protection shall be ensured against any usurpation or imitation, even if the true origin of the product is indicated or if the appellation is used in translated form or accompanied by terms such as 'kind', 'type', 'make', 'imitation', or the like.

Article 4 [Protection by virtue of Other Texts]
The provisions of this Agreement shall in no way exclude the protection already granted to appellations of origin in each of the countries of the Special Union by virtue of other international instruments, such as the Paris Convention [as revised], and the Madrid Agreement [as revised], or by virtue of national legislation or court decisions.

From a reading of Article 3, it is evident that 'any usurpation or imitation' is the general proscribed category and three illustrations of prohibited conduct (qualified use indicating true origin, translations, qualified use suggesting equivalence) are provided. In the concluding paragraphs of this chapter, I demonstrate that these Lisbon Agreement standards deserve the 'absolute' label, because they transcend the conventional domestic understanding of misrepresentation, dilution or misappropriation prevention. In a nutshell, Lisbon standards cannot be fully explained by drawing parallels with even generous national unfair competition regimes. Norms against these kinds of referential activities assume that the relevant audience would understand the protected sign to have certain attributes and carry certain meanings. The Lisbon standards are not concerned with this line of enquiry and were designed to protect the sign as a reified, potentially valuable thing in itself, by reserving the sign for home country producers.

4.1   Nominate categories of prohibited uses

Let us begin with the illustrative categories of forbidden conduct and work towards the general prohibition. The situations of qualified use can

The scope of protection: Article 3 159

be conveniently addressed together: (1) It is considered to be 'usurpation or imitation' even if the true origin of the product is mentioned, so the use of 'Portuguese Roquefort'[125] or 'Spanish Champagne' is no longer an option; (2) The use of 'Roquefort-style' and 'Imitation Roquefort' would also be prohibited. According to the original proposal, there were dual dangers associated with such uses.[126] They would actively encourage the use of 'Roquefort' as a generic expression, by suggesting that the same product, or a close substitute, was available from outside the region of origin. Such uses might not also succeed in warding off confusion, since much would depend on the actual deployment of qualifiers on the packaging. This may be referred to as the 'fine print' concern.[127] We have already encountered opposition to qualified uses of this sort during unsuccessful attempts to amend Article 4 of the Madrid Agreement along similar lines.[128] These concerns were also reiterated as the basis for a similar provision in subsequent WIPO Model Law discussions.[129] Additional arguments against such qualified use are to be found in the literature. Such usage would suggest an exact equivalence, thereby misleading consumers as to quality.[130] There is occasional reliance on *terroir* logic to suggest that such products simply cannot be produced elsewhere, underscoring the misrepresentation.[131] In its form as either an argument contingent upon misrepresentation,

---

[125] 'Roquefort' was registered as AO No. 459 in 1967.

[126] Actes de Lisbonne, 797.

[127] For an illustration of this, see 'Saunders Whisky' [1989] IIC 543 (Oberster Gerichtshof, Austria, 1987) ('whisky' prominently used on the label but stating in small letters, at the edge of the label, 'Made in Austria').

[128] See Chapter 2, text accompanying fns 252–4.

[129] WIPO, 'Draft of the Model Law', 52 ('If an [AO] could be used where the only common factor is that the products concerned were manufactured using the same methods, the registered [AO] might well become a generic term in a very short time. For this reason the model law prohibits such a practice – in line with the provisions of the Lisbon Agreement').

[130] E.g. Plaisant, 'Revision of the International Treaty Provisions', 188 (The consumer 'is quite probably misled as to a taste, style, quality or other characteristics which he expects to be somehow similar'). Cf. *In re Salem China Co* 157 USPQ 600 (TTAB 1968) (The use of the trade mark 'American Limoges' on porcelain would mislead as to 'grade or quality'); *S. M. W. Winzersekt GmbH v. Land Rheinland-Pfalz* (C-306/93) [1995] 2 CMLR 718, [20]–[21] ('designations which include delocalising terms such as "style", "type", "brand" and "method" … are intended to take advantage of the prestige [of an IGO and] liable to create the impression that the inherent qualities of the product are on a par' with authentic products').

[131] In the context of a similar provision under EU law, Brouwer considers this argument while being critical of the underlying assumption of irreproducibility elsewhere. O. Brouwer, 'Community Protection of Geographical Indications and Specific Character as a Means of Enhancing Foodstuff Quality' (1991) 28 *Common Market Law Review* 615, 629.

160   The Appellation of Origin in Lisbon

or as pure free riding, qualified use would take advantage of the hard-earned reputation of the original producers in the home country, who are otherwise helpless to prevent this.[132] This presents a mixed bag of arguments mobilising consumer interests (preventing misrepresentation as to quality, or in the 'small print' situations, perhaps even origin) and home country producer interests (preventing genericide and free riding).

Finally Article 3 prohibits the use of translations as well, to satisfy a long-standing demand at previous international negotiations. This was clarified when addressing Czechoslovakian concerns that the protection guaranteed to 'Pils' should extend to 'Pilsner' or 'Pilsen' as well.[133] Despite clear acknowledgment of this penumbral protection, in subsequent practice Members would play it safe and often filed separate registrations for clusters of translated version.[134] Possibly an unnecessary precaution, it defines the registered subject matter with greater clarity.[135] Therefore translated and transliterated names are now optional additions during an application.[136]

An important issue that arises here is what qualifies as a translation? This is significant as the scope of the right may be extended by the inclusion of transliterations or other forms of referring to the same place. In a non-Lisbon context, a narrow approach was adopted in New Zealand in yet another Budweiser dispute. Here AB claimed that BB was infringing its 'Budweiser' mark. BB unsuccessfully argued that as 'Budweiser' was a translation of the geographical name Budějovický, which in turn was part of its trading name, it should be entitled to an 'own name' defence.[137] The Court of Appeal reasoned that:

The term 'Budějovický' is the adjective formed from the name 'Budějovice'. Similarly, the word 'Budweiser' is the adjective formed in German from the name Budweis. Contrary to claims throughout the evidence that 'Budweiser' is a translation of Budějovický, it is not. It is another name for the same place used by people who speak a different language. It is no more a translation than Aotearoa is a translation of New Zealand.[138]

---

[132] See, e.g., Actes de Lisbonne, 813–14.   [133] Ibid., 834.

[134] E.g. Registrations 1 and 2 on the Lisbon Register, which covered Plzeňské Pivo/ Pilsner Bier Pilsener/Bière de Pilsen (Plzeň) Pilsner/Pilsen Beer Pils and Plzeň/Pilsen Pils/ Pilsener/Pilsner.

[135] WIPO, 'Questions to be Examined', [29]–[31].

[136] Rule 5(3)(ii) of the Lisbon Regulations 2010.

[137] Under s. 12(a) of the Trade Marks Act 1953, in response to a claim of trade mark infringement, a company had a defence based on the bona fide use of its own name.

[138] *Anheuser-Busch Inc* v. *Budějovický Budvar Národní Podnik* [2003] 1 NZLR 472 (CA), [16].

The scope of protection: Article 3   161

This raises the issue of alternative names for the same place, even though they are not direct translations. A more liberal approach was adopted by the Portuguese Supreme Court:

> [In AB's opinion] the expression 'Budweis' or 'Budweiss' is not the German translation of the Czech city Ceské Budéjovice. Nevertheless, this does not hinder the people of German or of Austrian origin or nationality, especially within the border zone between those three countries, from calling that city located near the border by the name 'Budweis', not least since that city has been called 'Budweis' at least until 1918 ... It is generally accepted that any location may have more than one name without the names being necessarily synonymous (e.g. 'Islas Malvinas or Falkland Islands'). One geographical name may indeed be the translation of another name for the same region, although it may also be a synonymous expression. The meaning to be taken into consideration must simply designate the same region.[139]

This approach – to determine as a matter of fact the denotative effect of a linguistic variation – has also been adopted by a Swedish court, albeit once again in a non-Lisbon context. The court was attempting to determine whether 'Budweiser' would have geographical significance for Swedish consumers, despite not being the present formal name of the city (Ceské Budéjovice).[140] The Portuguese Supreme Court, in *Budweiser* litigation based on protection under a bilateral agreement, has noted that unless protection against translated uses is provided in an era of global communication, the original producers would be deprived of hard earned goodwill.[141] Heath favours this interpretation, while arguing that the key point is that all variants should refer to the same geographical location, in order to enjoy the protection of Article 3.[142] A similar approach was recently adopted by the Advocate General, when deciding whether protection for Italian 'Parmigiano Reggiano' under the European regime would prohibit the use of 'Parmesan' in Germany.[143] Presumably the

---

[139] *Budějovický Budvar Národní Podnik* v. *Anheuser Busch Inc* [2002] ETMR 96, 1182, 1187 (Supremo Tribunal De Justiça, 2001).

[140] *Anheuser-Busch Inc* v. *Budějovický Budvar Národní Podnik and Ors* [2006] ETMR 77 at 1089, 1095–7 (Swedish SC) (held that Swedish consumers would be unlikely to consider 'Budweiser' as having geographical significance).

[141] The issue here was whether translated versions included those in other languages apart from those of the signatories to the bilateral agreement. *Budějovický Budvar Národní Podnik* v. *Anheuser Busch Inc* [2002] ETMR 96, [34].

[142] Heath, 'International, Bilateral and Regional Agreements', 121.

[143] *Commission of the European Communities* v. *Federal Republic of Germany* (C-132/05) [2008] ECR I-957 (AG), [49] (The 'two terms must generally be regarded by consumers as equivalent'). The ECJ finally considered 'Parmesan' to be an impermissible evocation or a case of 'bringing to mind'. This is a broader test and bypassed the translation issue. *Commission of the European Communities* v. *Federal Republic of Germany* (C-132/05) [2008] ECR I-957 (ECJ), [48]–[50].

162   The Appellation of Origin in Lisbon

basis for the prohibition against translations is that it suggests the equivalence of the products and therefore the same arguments against qualified use would apply here.

A final point remains to be made. If one reads these three examples of prohibited uses *eiusdem generis*, it is arguable that the Lisbon Agreement was only intended to provide for Article 3 levels of protection on identical or similar goods. The Consorzio which had applied via the national authority to register Parmigiano Reggiano as an AO could prevent its use on other cheese but not on surfboards or mouse mats. However, this interpretation remains open to question and was a live issue during the recent survey on the agreement.[144]

4.2   The general prohibition against usurpation or imitation

Having considered the categories of qualified uses and translations, what are we to make of the general prohibition against 'any usurpation or imitation' ('*toute usurpation ou imitation*') in Article 3? Here the conference proceedings provide limited guidance and the language seems to have been adopted based on French domestic legislation.[145] The first reference to the scope of protection in the proposed agreement mentions preventing usurpation and counterfeiting ('*contrefaçon*') in any form, while referring to existing national legislation, bilateral and multilateral agreements which already provide for this.[146] The draft Article 3 also makes a reference to *contrefaçon*. Usurping or counterfeiting uses are identified as significant threats to the reputation of well-known regional products.[147] Apart from the inclusion of the prohibition against translations, not much else is revealed in the subsequent discussion on the draft Article 3.[148] The original draft Article 4 also contained a reference to the unfair competition provisions in Article 10*bis* of the Paris Convention, which would include a whole range of commercial uses beyond just misleading ones.[149] While the draft Article 4 was ultimately dropped, the present Article 4 does refer to the fact that Lisbon in no way reduces the protection available under Article 10*bis* of the Paris Convention. One is left with the impression that once the AO has been defined in the country of origin, its use is reserved exclusively for those in the home country identified by this process. The intention was that any use by 'external' traders would be deemed usurping or misleading, in keeping

---

[144] See the responses to Q3 and Q4 in the Lisbon Survey.
[145] J. Hughes, 'Champagne, Feta, and Bourbon – The Spirited Debate about Geographical Indications' (2006) 58 *Hastings Law Journal* 299, 319, 349.
[146] Actes de Lisbonne, 814.   [147] Ibid., 815.   [148] Ibid., 834.   [149] Ibid., 816.

The scope of protection: Article 3   163

with national legislation in this area.[150] In light of these references to misleading or usurping uses and the specific reference to unfair competition in the draft Article 4, we can therefore assume that at least three categories of uses by external traders will be caught by the prohibition in Articles 3 and 4. These are misrepresentation, dilution (including blurring and tarnishment) and misappropriation.[151]

Misrepresentation is the most universally prohibited use and the least problematic. The prevention of misrepresentation, initially as to origin and with the subsequent assimilation of quality, is a familiar trope. As we have seen in Chapter 2, averting origin fraud was the stated basis for including the IS within the Paris Convention, while Madrid negotiations reveal concerns about misleading indications relating to quality. The historical record describes French legislation emerging as a reaction to fraudulent wine labelling, while there is a similar fraud-related prompt for British Merchandise Marks legislation. The national unfair competition regimes explored in Chapter 3 all sanction this category of wrongful conduct, with passing off operating squarely within its confines. Given the price differential between prestigious appellation products and lower priced substitutes, fraudulent activity continues to date. In early 2007, a Belgian court found a wine importer to be guilty of criminal offences relating to fraud, for supplying repackaged and relabelled Spanish sparkling wine as Champagne to a major Belgian retail chain.[152] Darjeeling tea producers are stewing with indignation over statistics which indicate that misleading labelling is rampant. 'According to a rough estimation, around 40 million kg of orthodox tea is being sold worldwide as "Darjeeling" tea every year, which is four times the production of authentic "Darjeeling" tea'.[153] There are complaints about the proliferation of fake Colombian Coffee,[154] as well as Antiguan Coffee.[155]

---

[150] Ibid. ('*La protection doit être assurée contre toute atteinte portée aux droits exclusifs des titulaires des appellations d'origine, soit par l'adoption illicite de ces dernières — ce qui, dans certaines législations, est appelé usurpation ou contrefaçon — soit contre l'imitation frauduleuse des appellations d'origine. L'interdiction de l'adoption illicite n'a pas besoin d'être mentionnée dans l'Arrangement, car elle est évidemment comprise dans l'engagement à prendre par les pays de protéger les appellations d'origine enregistrées*').

[151] These are also the categories identified in the Lisbon Survey, [39]–[45].

[152] *Comité Interprofessionnel du Vin de Champagne* v. *Simon*, CFI Namur, Belgium (Criminal Division), 24 January 2007 (Unreported).

[153] K. Das, 'International Protection of India's Geographical Indications with Special Reference to "Darjeeling" Tea' (2006) 9 JWIP 459, 480.

[154] M. Vittori, 'The International Debate on Geographical Indications (GIs): The Point of View of the Global Coalition of GI Producers—oriGIn' (2010) 13 JWIP 304, 309.

[155] D. Giovannucci, T. Josling, W. Kerr, B. O'Connor and M. Yeung, *Guide to Geographical Indications: Linking Products and their Origins* (International Trade Centre, Geneva 2009), 149 ('It has been estimated that between 100–125% more coffee bags are

164   The Appellation of Origin in Lisbon

Within an IP framework, the justification for a norm prohibiting the misleading use of signs has been worked out in the trade mark context. Protecting the communicative integrity of trade marks serves a dual purpose. Granting exclusive rights to the sign prevents consumer deception or confusion as to origin. It simultaneously shields legitimate producers against this particular type of unfair competition.[156] An instrumentalist account is the predominant theoretical justification for this exclusivity, in a marketplace characterised by information asymmetries.[157] In the case of experience goods such as wines or foodstuffs, asymmetric information exists between buyers and sellers, which causes the problem of 'adverse selection' where low-quality products drive high-quality products out of the market.[158] This represents a common type of market failure, which often requires government intervention of some sort. In response, granting (contingent) proprietary rights over trade marks enhances efficiency. These signs reduce consumer search costs by making

labelled and exported as 'Antigua' than those truly produced within the limits of the origin. These include counterfeits from nearby regions and Antigua coffee mixed with other coffee').

[156] *Two Pesos, Inc* v. *Taco Cabana, Inc* 505 US 763, 782 (1992), fn15 (The US Supreme Court referred to the Senate Report on the Lanham Act: 'The purpose underlying any trade mark statute is twofold. One is to protect the public so it may be confident that, in purchasing a product bearing a particular trade mark which it favorably knows, it will get the product which it asks for and wants to get. Secondly, where the owner of a trade mark has spent energy, time, and money in presenting to the public the product, he is protected in his investment from its misappropriation by pirates and cheats. This is the well-established rule of law protecting both the public and the trade mark owner'). *S. A. Cnl-Sucal NV* v. *Hag GF AG* (C-10/89) (1990) 3 CMLR 571, 582–3 ('*HAG II*') (Jacobs AG) (Trade marks 'reward the manufacturer who consistently produces high-quality goods and they thus stimulate economic progress. Without trade mark protection there would be little incentive for manufacturers to develop new products or to maintain the quality of existing ones. Trade marks are able to achieve that effect because they act as a guarantee, to the consumer, that all goods bearing a particular mark have been produced by, or under the control of, the same manufacturer and are therefore likely to be of similar quality ... A trade mark can only fulfil that role if it is exclusive. Once the proprietor is forced to share the mark with a competitor, he loses control over the goodwill associated with the mark. The reputation of his own goods will be harmed if the competitor sells inferior goods. From the consumer's point of view, equally undesirable consequences will ensue, because the clarity of the signal transmitted by the trade mark will be impaired. The consumer will be confused and misled').

[157] W. M. Landes and R. A. Posner, 'Trade Mark Law: An Economic Perspective' (1987) 30 *Journal of Law and Economics* 265; N. Economides, 'The Economics of Trade Marks' (1988) 78 TMR 523. For a compelling alternative account, see B. Beebe, 'The Semiotic Analysis of Trade Mark Law' (2004) 51 *University of California Los Angeles Law Review* 621.

[158] G. A. Akerlof, 'The Market for "Lemons": Quality Uncertainty and the Market Mechanism' (1970) 84 *Quarterly Journal of Economics* 488.

The scope of protection: Article 3 165

products easier to identify in the marketplace – prospective purchasers can trust the sign – while encouraging producers to invest in maintaining or improving levels of quality. Rights to prevent misleading uses ensure that proprietors, and not their rivals, reap the reputational rewards of that investment. In order to preserve the communicative integrity of such signs, unauthorised use by third parties should therefore be prohibited.

The IGO literature on this topic suggests a similar economic rationale,[159] along with an added dimension. These geographical signs exhibit features of club goods, whereby the right to exclude is enjoyed by all members of the club.[160] Where a collective reputation is at stake, institutional mechanisms are required in response to collective action problems. There is a need to set up and police common standards of production, ensuring that competing members will co-operate to the extent necessary to maintain quality. Otherwise in light of their functional similarity, instrumentalist theory accounts for the right to exclude in a congruent manner for trade marks and GIs. In Europe, the ECJ justified the basis for protection in broadly similar terms in *Sekt*. The legitimacy of these national regimes was assured provided they could 'satisfy the objectives of such protection, in particular the need to ensure not only that the interests of the producers concerned are safeguarded against unfair competition, but also that consumers are protected against information which may mislead them'.[161] The benefit in preserving the sign's message was again reiterated by the Court in *Exportur*: 'Such names may nevertheless enjoy a high reputation amongst consumers and constitute for producers established in the

---

[159] See OECD, 'Appellations of Origin and Geographical Indications in OECD Member Countries: Economic and Legal Implications', December 2000 (COM/AGR/APM/TD/WP(2000)15/FINAL), 7–8, 31–4; D. Rangnekar, 'The Socio-Economics of Geographical Indications: A Review of the Empirical Evidence from Europe', UNCTA/ICTSD Issue Paper No. 4 (May 2004), 13–16; W. van Caenegem, 'Registered Geographical Indications: Between Rural Policy and Intellectual Property – Part I' (2003) 6 JWIP 699, 709–10; F. Thiedig and B. Sylvander, 'Welcome to the Club? An Economical Approach to Geographical Indications in the European Union' (2000) 49 *Agrarwirtschaft* 428; C. Bramley and J. F. Kirsten, 'Exploring the Economic Rationale for Protecting Geographical Indicators in Agriculture' (2007) 46 *Agrekon* 69; D. Benavente, 'The Economics of Geographical Indications: GIs modelled as Club Assets', Graduate Institute of International and Development Studies Working Paper No.: 10/2010.

[160] Club goods are impure public goods characterised by partial excludability, no or partial rivalry of benefits, and congestion phenomena. J. M. Buchanan, 'An Economic Theory of Clubs' (1965) 32 *Economica* 1.

[161] *Commission of the European Communities* v. *Federal Republic of Germany* (C-12/74) [1975] ECR 181, [7] (ECJ) (Sekt/Weinbrand).

166   The Appellation of Origin in Lisbon

places to which they refer an essential means of attracting custom. They are therefore entitled to protection'.[162]

While the prohibition against misrepresentation or confusion is well established, there are other forms of allusive use which are prohibited under the umbrella of unfair competition. Dilution is one such prominent category and it is far more controversial. Like misrepresentation, it also relates to alleged harm to the sign and comes in two flavours.[163] Here we can usefully draw parallels with trade mark law, in order to summarise the principles. Tarnishment or detriment to repute is more intuitively accessible but relatively under-theorised. It is defined in US law as the 'association arising from the similarity between a mark or trade name and a famous mark that harms the reputation of the famous mark'.[164] The ECJ recently described it as occurring when 'the [reputed] trade mark's power of attraction is reduced. The likelihood of such detriment may arise in particular from the fact that the goods or services offered by the third party possess a characteristic or a quality which is liable to have a negative impact on the image of the mark'.[165] In the case of AOs, one can easily imagine certain objectionable uses on dissimilar goods, such as the use of 'Champagne' to sell toilet paper or drain cleaners. However, beyond these core cases, (1) the ease with which a use may be considered to be incompatible with the image of the reputed sign and (2) whether there actually would be a negative effect in the minds of consumers are issues deserving further consideration.[166]

The second limb of dilution is blurring.[167] Dilution itself was historically synonymous with the harm known as blurring, involving detriment to the uniqueness[168] or distinctiveness[169] of a trade mark. In the

---

[162] *Exportur SA* v. *LOR SA and Confiserie du Tech SA* (C-3/91) [1992] ECR I-5529, [28] (ECJ).

[163] The extent to which these two flavours – blurring and tarnishment – share any common ground under the 'dilution' label is not yet clear.

[164] 15 USC § 1125(c)(2)(C).

[165] *L'Oréal SA and others* v. *Bellure NV and others* (C-487/07) [2009] ECR I-5185; [2009] ETMR 55, [40].

[166] See, e.g., *'Get Champagne, Pay for Sparkling Wine'* [2002] IIC 990 (BGH) (The defendant sold computers, peripherals and software and used this slogan to advertise their business. The court considered tarnishment to Champagne's image merely on the basis that the aura of exclusivity is vitiated).

[167] For blurring, I have drawn on Part 2 of R. Burrell and D. Gangjee, 'Trade Marks and Freedom of Expression: A Call for Caution' [2010] IIC 544.

[168] F. Schechter, 'The Rational Basis of Trade Mark Protection' (1926–27) 40 *Harvard Law Review* 813, 831 ('[The] preservation of the uniqueness of a trade mark should constitute the only rational basis for its protection').

[169] Unlike uniqueness, distinctiveness is a term of art and relates to the origin indicating function of a trade mark. Apex courts seem to prefer this iteration of blurring: *Moseley* v. *Victoria's Secret Catalogue Inc* 123 S Ct 1115 (2003); *Intel*

The scope of protection: Article 3

paradigmatic case, it affords owners of legally protected signs that enjoy a significant reputation with a means of preventing use of an identical or similar sign on goods or services that are dissimilar to those for which the mark has been registered. As Frank Schechter suggested in 1932, 'if you allow Rolls Royce restaurants and Rolls Royce cafeterias, and Rolls Royce pants, and Rolls Royce candy, in 10 years you will not have the Rolls Royce mark any more'.[170] However, blurring was controversial because of the lack of a common vocabulary describing the quality or relationship being harmed: Uniqueness? Distinctiveness? Exclusivity? Image? Attractiveness or 'pulling power'?[171] It now appears that a consensus has emerged around distinctiveness (i.e. the ability to indicate a distinct origin for goods) being the quality detrimentally affected, but how do we measure this detriment? A recent review of empirical attempts to measure this impairment suggests that – in the absence of any consumer confusion – any mental slowdown in the mind of the consumer as they sort through the claimant and defendant's uses may be too minimal to affect a purchasing decision.[172] In the Rolls Royce example above, on being prompted with the sign, a potential customer will not be sufficiently inhibited from recalling the luxury car, because direct measurements of consumer response slowdown suggest insignificant levels of harm. Should we then resort to proxy criteria, or legal presumptions, to favour a finding of blurring? To draw on a decided case, if a pet accessory manufacturer sells chew-toy handbags under the 'Chewy Vuitton' label, is this likely to negatively affect the ability of the 'Louis Vuitton' sign to connote luxury hand bags and related products?[173] Should we presume it will, merely on the basis that consumers will make a connection between the two signs?

While problematic variations of the dilution argument such as the 'diversion or weakening of fame' are adopted by those seeking greater international AO or GI protection,[174] aspects of both tarnishment and

---

Corp Inc v. *C. P. M. United Kingdom Ltd* (C-252/07) [2008] ECR I-8823; [2009] ETMR 13 (ECJ).

[170] In his statement at the Trade Marks: Hearings before the House Committee on Patents, 72d Cong., 1st Sess. 15 (1932).

[171] For attempts to unpack these issues, see I. Simon Fhima, 'Dilution by Blurring: a Conceptual Roadmap' [2010] IPQ 44; M. Senftleben, 'The Trade Mark Tower of Babel – Dilution Concepts in International, US and EC Trade Mark Law' [2009] IIC 45.

[172] R. Tushnet, 'Gone in 60 Milliseconds: Trade Mark Law and Cognitive Science' (2008) 86 *Texas Law Review* 507.

[173] The answer was no in *Louis Vuitton Malletier* v. *Haute Diggity Dog* 507 F 3d 252 (4th Cir, 2007).

[174] Baeumer, 'Protection of Geographical Indications under WIPO Treaties and Questions Concerning the Relationship between Those Treaties and the TRIPS Agreement', [18];

168   The Appellation of Origin in Lisbon

blurring remain deeply controversial.[175] Nevertheless in one particular situation, blurring may be a genuine concern. This arises where the geographical sign is used on similar goods such that there is the subsequent threat of generic use. Blurring refers to the erosion or weakening of the ability of a sign to indicate goods from a specific (trade or geographical) origin and this ability is not just weakened but destroyed by generic use.[176] In several jurisdictions, hoover, aspirin or champagne are generic descriptors for vacuum cleaners, acetylsalicylic acid and sparkling wine respectively, suggesting that this is a plausible threat to the IGO's ability to communicate more specific information.

While both the general categories considered so far – misrepresentation and dilution – refer to harm to the communicative ability of a sign, misappropriation may or may not do so. As it is conventionally understood, the 'mis' in misappropriation might refer to a situation where (1) a third party benefits from the use of a reputed sign while simultaneously harming the reputed sign, also sometimes referred to as parasitic use (e.g. with blurring as an injurious side effect of misappropriation); or (2) that the third party simply free rides on the investment to create the reputed sign and does not make suitable efforts on its own, without any harm as a necessary consequence.

Let us first consider allegedly harmful parasitic use. This holds that misappropriation and dilution-type harm are two sides of the same coin and one inevitably entails the other. Two illustrations will suffice here. In *Darjeeling*, where the complaint concerned the use of 'Darjeeling' on advertising and communication services[177] the Paris Court of Appeal held that:

[It] is of little significance that the products referred to in the registration are different since, by adopting this name associated with a drawing of a teapot, [the respondent] has attempted to benefit from the renown associated with this geographical indication which identifies the tea originating in this region in the mind of the public as being synonymous with excellence and sophistication and the know-how of the Tea Board in promoting this product *whilst using*

F. Wenger, 'The Role of National Administrations in the protection of Geographical Indications: The Example of France', June 2001 (WIPO/GEO/CIS/01/3).

[175] Apart from Tushnet, 'Gone in 60 Milliseconds' and Burrell and Gangjee, 'Trade Marks and Freedom of Expression', see also C. Haight Farley, 'Why We Are Confused About the Trade Mark Dilution Law' (2006) 16 *Fordham Intellectual Property Media & Entertainment Law Journal* 1175; C. Long, 'Dilution' (2006) 106 *Columbia Law Review* 1029.

[176] WIPO, 'The Need for a New Treaty and its Possible Contents', 9 April 1990 (GEO/CE/I/2), [77]. On dilution as genericide, see Chapter 9 of T. Martino, *Trade Mark Dilution* (Oxford University Press, 1996).

[177] Along with the inspired slogan: 'Communication is our cup of tea'.

The scope of protection: Article 3

its reputation free of charge; this use for products other than tea infringes ... by making it appear ordinary *and undermining its distinctive nature* (emphasis added).[178]

Similarly, in the *Havana* case, the Paris Court of Appeal reasoned:

> That the company Aramis' choice for the term 'Havana' to promote a luxury perfume for men is not born of coincidence but indicates a deliberate will to convey through its especially strong evocative power, an image of prestige, sensuality and of good taste attached to the Havana cigar and the appearance of the smoke when exhaled;
>
> That the risk of misappropriation of the appellation of origin Havana is real and is found to have its own identity;
>
> Whereas it must moreover be noted that ... *the misappropriation of this brand awareness as evocative and prestigious as this, runs necessarily the risk of weakening it* when it is utilised by a company owning establishments all over the world and ... *necessarily destroys the unity and the distinctiveness of the cigar*, notably in France (emphasis added).[179]

This approach suggests that misappropriation will inexorably result in the attrition of distinctiveness or some other desirable quality of the sign. Perhaps the metaphor of parasitism encourages this belief that one's benefit is always at another's cost. The advantage of this conceptualisation, *if it is valid*, is that the unjustness of the benefit obtained is explained by the harm caused. Yet there are convincing arguments ranged against this. The dilution of exclusiveness or uniqueness is a self-serving and circular argument. You may very well demand rights to preserve uniqueness or exclusivity, but if the conditions for uniqueness or exclusivity in turn depend on being given rights in the first place, then this is a circular argument. All sign owners would like the (semiotic) room to stretch and a big stick with which to enforce this, but why should they be given this room in the first place? If the response is that distinctiveness is harmed by allusive uses on dissimilar goods, why shouldn't the use of 'Darjeeling' on stationery act as free advertising and reinforce the denotation of the tea from specific Indian tea gardens so as to strengthen distinctiveness? Alternatively, will the context in which we encounter signs enable us to make disambiguations and prevent detriment to distinctiveness? For reasons elaborated in the literature

---

[178] *Tea Board of India* v. *Jean-Luc Dusong*, Paris Court of Appeals, 4th Chamber, Reg. No. 05/20050 (22 November 2006) 4 (Unreported) (I am grateful to Latha Nair for a copy of the judgment).

[179] *Societe Empresa del Tabaco Cubatabaco* v. *Aramis Inc & Ors*, Paris Court of Appeal, 4th Chamber Reg. No. 1998/10814 (17 May 2000) 13 (Unreported).

170   The Appellation of Origin in Lisbon

cited on blurring above, it is very difficult to assume that impairment will necessarily follow such imitative uses, because the construction and reconstruction of meaning is a dynamic process. Since proving blurring is notoriously difficult, some have argued that this limb of dilution is nothing but a thinly disguised substitute for pure misappropriation. Dilution prevention masquerades as a more acceptable norm since it apparently concerns harm to the claimant, but the hidden agenda is to stop those who free ride on the investment of others.[180]

This is a convenient juncture at which to consider the pure misappropriation or free riding argument. Once again returning to the parallel context of trade mark law, the 'deceptively simple' logic of misappropriation is summed up by Robert Bone:

[A] defendant who attracts consumers by using the plaintiff's mark improperly benefits from the plaintiff's goodwill. It does not matter whether consumers are confused or even whether the defendant's use diverts business from the plaintiff. Nor does it matter whether plaintiff's goodwill is impaired or diminished in any way. It is enough that ... the defendant 'reap[s] where it has not sown.' In other words, the wrong, both moral and legal, consists in free riding, that is, benefiting from something of value that another has invested in creating.[181]

There are numerous examples of this complaint in the AO literature.[182] Norbert Olszak vividly depicts the outrage of the French wine grower of Chablis, who trembles each year during the freezing spring and invests heavily to protect vines from the frost, only to see a mass-produced

---

[180] D. S. Welkowitz, 'Re-examining Trade Mark Dilution' (1994) 44 *Vanderbilt Law Review* 531, 579–80 ('The best explanation for pure dilution cases appears to be that some courts view it as a way of granting protection when the evidence of confusion is weak, but the court believes the defendant's use of the mark to be unfair'); H. Carty, 'Dilution and Passing Off: Cause for Concern' (1996) *Law Quarterly Review* 632, 650 (The 'concept of "pure dilution" is in effect misappropriation in disguise. What is being protected is the mark's effectiveness as an advertising tool in itself'); D. J. Franklyn, 'Debunking Dilution Doctrine: Toward A Coherent Theory of the Anti-Free-Rider Principle in American Trademark Law' (2004–5) 56 *Hastings Law Journal* 117 (While 'American dilution law purports to be about preventing dilutive harm, it really is about preventing free-riding on famous marks. Because of this mismatch between dilution's stated purpose and hidden goal, it is a clumsy and largely incoherent doctrinal device').

[181] R. Bone, 'Hunting Goodwill: A History of the Concept of Goodwill in Trade Mark Law' (2006) 86 *Boston University Law Review* 547, 550.

[182] E.g. A. Devletian, 'The Protection of Appellations and Indications of Origin' [1957] *Industrial Property Quarterly* 6, 11 ('Whatever may be the reasons given by persons who infringe (that is to say, improperly use) an appellation of origin and wish to justify their act, fundamentally their principal motive is the desire to profit from the already existing reputation and market for the particular product which is rightly entitled to use that appellation'); Wenger, 'The Role of National Administrations', 13; N. Ozanam, 'Protection of Geographical Indications – Food Products – The Example of Champagne Industry, France', November 2003 (WIPO/GEO/DEL/03/11.rev).

The scope of protection: Article 3   171

wine sold in a carton under the same name.[183] This sense of injustice is an oft repeated motif:

Regional names, whether they be for cigars, cheeses, or wines, do indeed have significance beyond mere identification of source. They are not simply coined advertising slogans, but instead represent names that through decades or even centuries of craftsmanship have earned the respect of consumers and merchants around the world, well beyond the white clay hillsides of the town of Chablis. In order to protect both those who labour and those who enjoy the fruits of their labour, a crafty latecomer should not be able to reap where the first has sown.[184]

The free riding or reaping without sowing metaphor often characterises this category of wrong. It is a feature of unfair competition law in several civil law jurisdictions.[185] It also formed the basis for the US Supreme Court's controversial *International News Service (INS)* decision in 1918.[186] However, that precedent was subsequently restricted to similar 'hot news' fact patterns in the US and although it was considered by appellate courts in other common law jurisdictions, it was ultimately rejected.[187] The resistance is broadly organised around the understanding that not everything which involves investment and has economic value should be propertised. It is simply not possible to summarise the protracted legal debate around misappropriation, and my intention is merely to show that this is a controversial basis for granting rights over signs.[188] In the context of 'reaping without sowing', Richard Posner reminds us that analogies with theft or piracy are false because it obscures the difference between the consequences of such activities for

---

[183] N. Olszak, *Droit des Appellations d'Origine et Indications de Provenance* (TEC & DOC, Paris 2001), 32–3.

[184] K. H. Josel, 'New Wine in Old Bottles: The Protection of France's Wine Classification System beyond Its Borders' (1994) 12 *Boston University International Law Journal* 471, 495–6.

[185] See, generally, F. Henning-Bodewig, *Unfair Competition Law: European Union and Member States* (Kluwer Law International, The Hague 2006); R. W. De Vrey, *Towards a European Unfair Competition Law: A Clash between Legal Families* (Martinus Nijhoff, The Hague 2006).

[186] *International News Service* v. *Associated Press* 248 US 215, 239 (1918). The leading case which confined *INS* to its facts is *Cheney Bros* v. *Doris Silk Corp.* 35 F 2d 279 (2d Cir 1929) (Justice Learned Hand).

[187] Summarised by C. Wadlow, 'Unfair Competition by Misappropriation: The Reception of *International News* in the Common Law World', in C.W. Ng, L. Bently and G. D'Agostino (eds.), *The Common Law of Intellectual Property: Essays in Honour of Professor David Vaver* (Hart, Oxford 2010), 307.

[188] We have considered the arguments against a broad free riding prohibition norm in greater detail in D. Gangjee and R. Burrell, 'Because You're Worth It: L'Oréal and the Prohibition on Free Riding' (2010) 73 *Modern Law Review* 282.

172 The Appellation of Origin in Lisbon

tangibles and intangibles.[189] The copying of intangibles is often greatly beneficial from an expressive or pro-competitive point of view, without denying the proprietor the use of the intangible.[190] The whole point of having limited legal monopolies in patent or copyright subject matter is to ensure that these are available in the public domain and can be freely copied after the expiry of the protection period. In the case of signs, allowing access to signal competitive substitutability or perhaps to criticise the product is important. 'Once it is acknowledged that free riding on intellectual property is not always a bad thing, it becomes difficult to give a simple meaning to "misappropriation" that will enable it to serve as the organizing principle of intellectual property law'.[191] It helps to remember that the original plant varietals for Darjeeling tea were sourced from China and Assam, while certain technological innovations associated with Champagne were introduced to the region from elsewhere.[192] We all get by with a little help from our friends, or even strangers for that matter. A general prohibition against borrowing or free riding is overbroad and specific forms of wrongful copying therefore need to be identified and justified.

4.3   Absolute protection

Even this synoptic survey of the possible contents of 'usurpation or imitation' in Article 3 demonstrates that while misrepresentation prevention is an acceptable component, dilution and misappropriation prevention are viewed with greater circumspection. It is useful to differentiate analytically between these norms at this juncture, because we will return to them in the context of TRIPS standards in Part II. However, the Lisbon Agreement has one final surprise in store. Each of these three broad categories – misrepresentation, dilution and misappropriation – may have counterparts in the domestic legislation or doctrine of Lisbon Member states. Under domestic law, each of these proscriptions takes as

---

[189] R. A. Posner, 'Misappropriation: A Dirge' (2003) 40 *Houston Law Review* 621, 622–3. Others also question the applicability of concepts initially developed in response to tangible property. See M. A. Lemley, 'Property, Intellectual Property, and Free Riding' (2005) 83 *Texas Law Review* 1031.

[190] A point emphasised recently by Jacob LJ in *L'Oréal SA & Ors* v. *Bellure NV & Ors* [2010] EWCA Civ 535.

[191] Posner, 'Misappropriation', 625.

[192] See respectively M. L. Heiss and R. J. Heiss, *The Story of Tea: A Cultural History and Drinking Guide* (10 Speed Press, Berkeley CA 2007), 198; B. Parry, 'Geographical Indications: Not All Champagne and Roses', in L. Bently, Jane C. Ginsburg and Jennifer Davis (eds.), *Trade Marks and Brands: An Interdisciplinary Critique* (Cambridge University Press, 2008), 361.

The scope of protection: Article 3

their starting point the (consumer) audience reaction to the defendant's use of an identical or similar sign. Having established that *the relevant public or audience know of the claimant's sign* and often requiring in addition that the claimant's sign has a reputation, the adjudicator will then apply the rules to decide (1) whether the public will be misled, (2) whether the use of the defendant's sign will result in dilution of the claimant's sign in the minds of the audience, or (3) whether the defendant's use is free riding off the claimant's sign. In stark contrast, the goal here was to move beyond this contingency and protect the registered AO regardless of whether the relevant public in the country of the dispute had even heard of it. Once registered, under Article 3 the AO is protected against 'any usurpation or imitation' in all twenty-seven signatories. At the time of writing, there are over 800 recorded registrations on the Lisbon register. It stretches the limits of credibility to suggest that all these products are familiar names in every one of the twenty-seven member countries. To take up just one illustration, 'Maíz Blanco Gigante Cusco' or Giant White Maize was registered by Peru in 2007.[193] From the registration record, in the home country of Peru it appears to have been granted official protection as recently as 26 September 2005. Yet it is protected against usurpation or imitation *inter alia* in Burkina Faso, Bulgaria, France, Iran and Serbia. It is highly unlikely that the maize has an extant reputation in all of these countries which can then be demonstrably or even presumptively blurred or misappropriated. If the product is unknown in these countries, there can be no dilution or free riding. The only conceivable manner in which an unauthorised or external producer would be committing a wrong would be by the very act of adopting a sign similar or identical to the Giant White Maize AO.

The Lisbon Agreement does not provide for modulating devices such as acquired distinctiveness or reputation; all appellations are protected equally, regardless of these requirements and, for several hundred products, Lisbon is a register *to preserve their potential ability to communicate in the future.*[194] None of the conventional justifications for

---

[193] Registration No. 868; Publication No. 36 (01/2007).

[194] In all fairness, it must be pointed out that modern trade mark registers also work on this assumption to some extent, especially in vast commercial territories such as the US or EU. See, e.g., S. Wilf, 'The Making of the Post-War Paradigm in American Intellectual Property Law' (2008) 31 *Columbia Journal of Law and the Arts* 139, 143 ('Registration of a trade mark under the Lanham Act established constructive notice for trade marks throughout the United States, even in those places where a product had not yet been used in commerce or even advertised'). However, the principle of revocation for non-use ensures that the sign must be used in the territory where the rights are obtained.

174   The Appellation of Origin in Lisbon

misrepresentation, dilution or misappropriation, individually or in combination, will fully account for Article 3 obligations. If protecting the existing communicative ability of a sign is not the basis for protection, and thus far it had been the basis under unfair competition law, alternative explanations are needed. Under the Lisbon Agreement we seem to be protecting AOs as 'things', rather than protected status depending upon the message these signs communicate at any given point of time. This needs to be first acknowledged and then justified. We return to this point in Chapter 6, to explore some of the emerging rationales for GI protection. Otherwise arguments tend to run together and the language of misrepresentation is deployed to buttress provisions targeting misappropriation, while the free riding idiom masks protection better characterised as absolute. These discrepancies are then obscured amidst multilateral compromises. For the sake of coherence, we need to ensure that the means adopted match the ends selected. Being attentive to these different tiers of protection is necessary if we are to appreciate the different meta-epistemic frameworks operating in this area that compete with the communicative paradigm, i.e. protection based on the actual ability of the sign to communicate specific messages to a given audience.

Disentangling the strands of protection into norms against (1) misrepresentation, (2) dilution, and (3) misappropriation as well as (4) in favour of 'absolute' protection also has immediate practical consequences. The contents of Article 3 ultimately depend on the domestic rules of Members to be given effect (Article 8). These national rules on unfair competition or specific statutes for the recognition of AOs will need to specifically incorporate this 'absolute' standard. The normal application of domestic rules will not otherwise satisfy the Article 3 obligation, because these rules depend on evaluating how the AO is understood by the relevant public. The recognition of such 'absolute' protection as a separate tier is evident in a dispute which involves familiar antagonists. According to the decision in *Budějovický Budvar Narodní Podnik* v. *OHIM*,[195] unlike national unfair competition regimes Lisbon Agreement protection is considered 'absolute' for identical or similar goods. In effect, once an AO is registered, no reputation needs to be established in each Lisbon Member and no evidence of a wrong (diminution of the sign's distinctiveness or misappropriation) needs to be adduced. Here AB applied for registration of the word and figurative

---

[195] *Budějovický Budvar Národní Podnik* v. *OHIM* (Joined Cases T-53/04 to T-56/04, T-58/04 and T-59/04) [2007] ECR II-57 (CFI).

The scope of protection: Article 3 175

marks relating to 'BUDWEISER' and 'BUD' as Community Trade Marks (CTMs). BB objected *inter alia* based on its prior Lisbon AO registrations for variations on 'Budweiser',[196] claiming that these appellations were protected in France, a Lisbon signatory. In working through this claim, the court drew an important distinction between French domestic unfair competition law and protection under the Lisbon Agreement. BB objected to AB's application, which also related to a variety of products dissimilar to beer, such as stationery, articles for cleaning purposes, clothing, pastry and confectionery. The court reasoned that that protection under the Lisbon Agreement was 'absolute' for a narrow field; usurpation or imitation was prohibited for similar or identical products,[197] without the need to demonstrate that an AO's reputation would be likely to be misappropriated or weakened by another's use of an identical or similar signs.[198] On the other hand, French unfair competition law did extend to preventing the use of a sign on dissimilar products, provided a reputation was established and there was the likelihood of the third party's uses weakening or misappropriating the AO's reputation. In other words, the opponent would have to work harder to claim this more expansive protection under French law, based on the AO's connotations in that jurisdiction. The court also endorsed the OHIM Board of Appeal's finding that it could not 'be presumed that foreign appellations of origin which are protected in France under the Lisbon Agreement possess a reputation in France'. Since (1) 'absolute' protection under Lisbon did not extend to dissimilar products, (2) mere registration with WIPO did not necessarily generate discrete national reputations as a by-product, and (3) French law required a national reputation to be established before broad unfair competition protection was available for dissimilar products, BB had fallen into this gap. It failed to 'adduce any evidence that the appellations of origin possess a reputation in France' as well as failed 'to show how the reputation of the appellations of origin, even if it is assumed

---

[196] Registration Nos. 49 to 52.
[197] *Budějovický Budvar* v. *OHIM* [2007] ECR II-57 (CFI), [173] ('Article 3 of the Lisbon Agreement provides that protection is to be ensured "even if the true origin of the product is indicated" or if the appellation is used in translated form or accompanied by terms such as "kind", "type", "make", "imitation", or the like. Given the terms employed, those specific terms make sense only when the products in question are identical or, at the very least, similar').
[198] Ibid., [181]–[182] (Under Lisbon, AOs are protected 'without its being necessary to demonstrate that those appellations possess a reputation in France, nor a fortiori that that reputation is liable to be misappropriated or weakened').

176 The Appellation of Origin in Lisbon

to exist, would be likely to be misappropriated or weakened' if AB were allowed to register their signs.[199]

A further question to consider is this: if the infringement rules in national legislation and unfair competition law are designed around what consumers think and what consumers think is no longer relevant for Article 3 levels of protection, do we need new infringement tests? In the context of 'absolute' protection, do we need to instead look to copyright law to gauge whether a sign infringes an AO (is it identical or similar enough to suggest it was copied from the original AO), instead of the default tests, which begin by considering whether consumers will make a mental connection to the original AO upon seeing the defendant's sign? Or do we rely on strained legal fictions and presumptions about consumer responses?

Having established that 'absolute' protection marks a departure from conventional rules in this area, one closing question remains. What is the inspiration for such extensive protection in Lisbon? It is unconvincing to assert that all Lisbon Members share a common understanding of some form of property grounding for AOs. The Lisbon system also clearly goes beyond national unfair competition rules or the scope of protection found in trade mark legislation, so how did this model emerge? There are hints to suggest that the stimulus may have been contractual, or more accurately, based on the bilateral treaty model.[200] In one particular model of bilateral treaty which arose during this period, each of the two parties would append a list of protected geographical designations to the agreement, whereupon these would then be considered protected expressions.[201] Consent and the expectation of mutual benefits was the basis for such accepting the obligation to protect the signs of others. Under these agreements, the nature and degree of protection would vary – some would ensure that the home country's substantive standards of protection were applied extra-territorially, while the procedural and remedial aspects would

---

[199] Ibid., [165].   [200] Actes de Lisbonne, 814, 836.

[201] The Lisbon Agreement came into force in 1966, by which point several important bilateral agreements had been negotiated. This was even considered as the basis for the European model. G. Schricker, 'The Efforts towards Harmonization of the Law of Unfair Competition in the European Economic Community' [1973] IIC 201, 208 ('For a uniform protection of designations of geographical origin, the bilateral agreements concluded recently between France, Germany and Italy (French–German Agreement of 1960, German–Italian Agreement of 1965, and French–Italian Agreement of 1964) might serve as models. The regulation of protection provided for in these agreements is particularly suited to take account of the request for an increased protection of designations of geographical origin, as well as of the differing interests and legal approaches of the Member States'); E. Ulmer, 'Unfair Competition Law in the European Economic Community' [1973] IIC 188, 200.

Conclusion 177

depend on the country of dispute; others would acknowledge that the substantive rules of the country of dispute would apply; some would specify that the use of the designations in the lists was exclusively reserved for legitimate producers in the home country and any other use was prohibited.[202]

The Lisbon register may therefore have been envisaged as a list of lists, with an emphasis on identifying the AO and circle of users alongside the further assumption that any such use outside this defined circle was prohibited. However, the prohibition was given effect under domestic rules which usually set out to discover the audience understanding of the sign, unless the specific features of the Lisbon compact were taken on board by national courts. This contractual approach to GI protection, with national interest-based bargains setting out protected status via legislative or executive fiat, remains underexplored in the literature, with the notable exception of Antony Taubman's work, but may provide the most realistic explanation for this approach to IGO protection.[203]

5. Conclusion

The Lisbon Agreement embodies the formal transition from the IS to the AO, which emerges as a distinct category of subject matter. In exploring this shift, each of the three lines of enquiry identified at the start of this chapter has generated useful results. First, the Lisbon Agreement attempts to define the type of subject matter suitable for favoured treatment. In formulating the AO, the Lisbon signatories seem to implicitly acknowledge the transition from the AO to the AOC in French law. Human factors are recognised alongside natural ones, leading to an expansive subject matter category. However, a system which was

---

[202] See WIPO, 'Introduction to Geographical Indications and Recent Developments in the World Intellectual Property Organization', 12 June 2003 (WIPO/GEO/SFO/03/1), [31]–[32]; WIPO, 'Present Situation and Possible New Solutions', [59]–[80]; Schricker, 'The Efforts towards Harmonization of the Law'; Plaisant, 'Revision of the International Treaty Provisions', 187; Several such bilateral agreements are reproduced in [1974] *Industrial Property* 371–86.

[203] A. Taubman, 'Thinking Locally, Acting Globally: How Trade Negotiations over Geographical Indications Improvise "Fair Trade" Rules' [2008] IPQ 231, 233 (Taubman suggests that despite their questionable theoretical legitimacy, these pragmatic bargains may work on the ground. The 'logic of trade negotiations means that "new world" producers are reluctant to give up this linguistic flexibility without buying other forms of access to "old world" markets – for instance, in gaining secure regulatory approval for new production techniques as a trade-off for relinquishing the generic connotation of commercially valuable terms ... Trade negotiating dynamics can opt for such pragmatic trade-offs between disparate regulatory issues, in favour of objective rulemaking that would ostensibly craft optimal rules that are objectively defensible in their own terms as regulatory interventions').

178 The Appellation of Origin in Lisbon

originally designed with agricultural goods in mind – products of the vine, rooted to place – cannot be satisfactorily extended to products that have only a loose link to physical geography, without running the risk of incoherence. If AOs represent the socio-economic and cultural dimensions of the interaction between people and a specific place, this requires an anchor to physical geography. Otherwise geographical indications may be transformed into historic ones or cultural-geographic indications, requiring an altogether distinct foundational basis. Yet, at the same time, the Lisbon model did not require that such products need to be unique or inimitable. Notwithstanding the interpretations of some courts, it is suggested that Article 2 requires that a causal relationship be established between product and place, not a matchless one.

Turning to the consideration of the system in operation, it does seem to be working but the degree of flexibility as well as dissent is surprising. Thanks largely to the ceaseless striving of the two Budweisers, judicial interpretations have developed along diverging paths. The detailed analysis of the agreement in operation should therefore be of use to those who are presently Members, those considering joining it and those who would look to it when considering a multilateral register under the TRIPS Agreement. Finally, it is imperative to acknowledge the full effect of 'absolute' protection, which suggests that unlike the previous international treaties or national unfair competition regimes, what the sign means to a particular audience is no longer the basis for protection. If we are deviating from a familiar cluster of justifications, then what are their replacements? One potential candidate proved unsatisfactory. We have considered the movement away from '*conditions particulières de climat et de terroir*' logic as the predominant justification for anchoring a product in a place. This is for a variety of reasons: places of origin are difficult to demarcate according to consensual criteria, innovation means that products change over time, and – as opposed to deterministic approaches to physical geography alone – human skill is increasingly acknowledged in the history of regional products. If we can no longer confidently claim that clearly defined places produce (empirically verifiable) unique products, then why should we grant expansive or 'absolute' rights to prohibit the use elsewhere of identical or similar signs? Implicit in the Lisbon Agreement is the second possible explanation – accepting multilateral obligations on the basis of mutual convenience and benefit. You protect ours and we'll protect yours. This requires a certain amount of pragmatic calculus from each state, when considering whether to join. Bearing in mind the potential domestic AOs from that country, will it be worthwhile? In Part II, we explore other possible explanations for protecting these signs in the absence of familiar unfair competition preconditions.

Conclusion

We therefore conclude Part I with a reminder of three key insights:

(1) Modern GI law has its origins in the primordial soup of unfair competition prevention, whereby national legal systems adopted various norms to prevent third parties from misusing signs in the course of trade. A collectively generated reputation was the valuable intangible that these rules were applied to protect. While a number of regimes had previously existed to regulate the use of geographical signs on products, the IS was situated within the field of international IP when it was identified as the vessel for this collective reputation. On this basis, it entered into the Paris framework and has much in common with the subject matter of contemporaneous trade mark and unfair competition law.

(2) However, justifications for protection based on communicative content, which work well at the national level, are considered inadequate at the international level. They don't scale up satisfactorily. Given the semantic vulnerabilities of signs when used in international trade, an alternative basis is proposed to justify special treatment for these signs, which incorporates *terroir*. These conceptual developments are in turn greatly influenced by the French national experience. The archetypal subject matter of wine does much to explain many of the implicit assumptions, overt claims and institutional arrangements that we encounter when considering GIs as a distinct category within IP law. The extent to which this is appropriate is an enquiry that needs to be developed further.

(3) The initial international framework drew sustenance from the near-universal norm against misleading or confusing uses. Yet proponents of IGO protection wished to protect geographical signs as reified objects, closed things of actual or potential value, regardless of the contingencies of meaning before any given audience. These developments were driven by *terroir* influenced conceptualisations of the link between product and place.

Without being expressly articulated, competing epistemic frameworks have been operating in this area. Those who conceive of the regulation of *geographical signs* within the broader framework of unfair competition law (itself an unsettled category) continue to ask why proponents of greater protection desire rules which deviate from communicative logic. Meanwhile proponents of greater protection for *regional products* are beginning to explore alternative justifications. These are considered in Part II and may provide the arguments of principle or policy otherwise lacking. Having identified the actors and props, sub-plots and set pieces, dialogue and asides that characterise this long running drama, let us now turn to the contemporary stage of TRIPS.

Part II

5 TRIPS today

1. Introduction

The GI provisions in TRIPS attest to the continuing relevance of the local, in the face of the global. Improved transportation, migration flows, better standards of living and cosmopolitan appetites have raised the profile of regionally specific foodstuffs, beverages and crafts. This trend is evident both within domestic markets and at the level of international trade. While by no means a new phenomenon, it is one which is gathering momentum. As these products gain in commercial significance, GIs can no longer afford to remain as exotic footnotes in the IP story. There is substantial evidence of consumer demand for locally sourced, traditionally produced goods. Even if we set aside wines and spirits, an EU estimate puts this value at €14.2 billion for agricultural products and foodstuffs.[1] As a result, GIs are no longer solely conceived of as signs which must *actually* provide useful information to consumers in an established market, as the baseline for protection. It is their *potential* to do so which has captured the imagination. It is argued that they could help generate improved incomes and tangible benefits for groups of rural or marginalised producers. Supporting regional products is therefore desirable in order to achieve a variety of policy outcomes and legal protection is subsumed within these broader agendas. Riding this aspirational wave, GI protection regimes are viewed as vectors to improve agricultural product quality (and therefore competitiveness), increase incomes in rural regions (to help counter a rural exodus), identify and sustain traditional methods of production as well as recognise regional or national cultural heritage.[2] These are the interests and expectations being brought to bear on international GI protection today.

---

[1] Proposal for a Regulation of the European Parliament and of the Council on Agricultural Product Quality Schemes COM (2010) 733 final (10 December 2010), 6 ('The overall value of agricultural products and foodstuffs sold under PDOs and PGIs is 14.2 € billion (1997) at wholesale prices, and estimated at 21 € billion at consumer prices').

[2] These policy initiatives and associated arguments are evaluated in Chapter 6.

184   TRIPS today

The TRIPS Agreement contains the current framework for the international protection of GIs and Part II of this book tries to make sense of its provisions. More specifically, it accounts for the shape and form of contemporary rules. Following this, it considers the extent to which prescriptive attempts to relocate or reinvent the basis for GI protection can build upon historic foundations, informed by unfair competition logic and dependent upon the meaning of the sign. The present and future rest on the past, which remains poorly understood. Although TRIPS has been hailed as a landmark in this area and frames contemporary international debates, the final two chapters argue that it creaks ominously, burdened with unstable compromises. The regime in Articles 22 to 24 attempts to paper over the century long disagreements we have already considered. These compromises are not restricted to penumbral aspects and key features of this regime remain difficult to explain, such as the equivocal definition of a GI or the existence of two levels of protection.

By establishing continuities, this chapter identifies and unpacks the unfinished business that distorts the TRIPS architecture. As it stands, it cannot provide a coherent blueprint for international protection, while on-going negotiations for extension are conducted upon these uneven foundations. Its status as a template and extensive membership ensures that the incoherence hard-wired into its provisions is then amplified worldwide. On a more promising note, the indeterminacy of its provisions makes possible the reconceptualisation of GI protection within the existing framework. The unpacking in this chapter identifies menus of options and alternative possibilities, as resources for those with rehabilitative agendas in the future. It also serves as a cautionary tale for those who presume the GI to be a conceptually stable and coherent legal category. Assuming that Article 22.1 refers to a clearly defined category of subject matter, with an associated or preferred form of protection, is a serious mistake.[3] This point cannot be overemphasised. The TRIPS Agreement focuses on outcomes. The qualifying sign must be protected in accordance with its standards, regardless of the mode of protection. The concomitant institutional apparatus to operationalise these standards

---

[3] After a century of ambiguity, the yearning for clarity is understandable. Unfortunately some suggest that TRIPS delivers on this. See, e.g., S. Strauch and K. Arend, 'Section 3: Geographical Indications', in P-T. Stoll, J. Busche and K. Arend (eds.), *WTO – Trade-Related Aspects of Intellectual Property Rights* (Martinus Nijhoff, Leiden and Boston 2009), 351, 382 (The TRIPS definition's 'language, content and purpose are precisely and explicitly determined'); J. Audier, *TRIPS Agreement – Geographical Indications* (EC Office for Official Publications, Luxembourg 2000), 15 ('Art 22.1 of TRIPS carefully defines protected geographical indications').

An outline of Articles 22 to 24 185

remains unspecified – registration based or case-by-case recognition within a tort law regime? A *sui generis* protection system, increasingly read as a cipher for the EU model, or the Certification Trade Mark route? Often the arguments made in support of enhanced GI protection, which emphasise GIs as vectors of sustainable development, income redistribution or heritage preservation, assume an accompanying institutional form. For instance, much of the disagreement often relates to the extent to which the state is engaged in GI formation and subsequent protection. When it comes to the preferred embodiment of the GI, the game is still in play, although frontrunners have emerged. To that extent, the following sections disrupt the narrative of progress which suggests that TRIPS is a conceptually tidier improvement over its predecessors.[4] They also trace the gravitational influences of the two competing epistemic frameworks – communicative logic which emphasises the sign and *terroir* logic which emphasises the product – that continue to shape this regime.

2. An outline of Articles 22 to 24

The TRIPS GI regime can be thematically summarised along the following lines: (1) the definition of a GI; (2) general protection for all GIs; (3) enhanced protection for wines and spirits; and (4) exceptions as well as unresolved issues for future negotiations. Before delving deeper, the scope of the enquiry needs to be set out. This chapter focuses on specific puzzles indicative of the underlying conceptual dissonances. The reader interested in a descriptive account of Articles 22 to 24 is directed to more general reference works on TRIPS.[5] The overview here is streamlined, with in-depth coverage reserved for the awkward and the unexplained features of TRIPS – the ambiguous definition of the GI, the existence of two distinct levels of protection, the vexed issue of genericide as well as conflicts between GIs and trade marks. Cumulatively, these issues illustrate the divergences in the conception of GIs as distinct

---

[4] Cf. A. P. Cotton, '123 Years at the Negotiating Table and Still No Dessert? The Case in Support of TRIPS Geographical Indication Protections' (2007) 82 *Chicago–Kent Law Review* 1295, 1312 ('The TRIPS definition reflects a logical evolution from the earliest indication-of-source discussions in Paris and Madrid Agreement negotiations').

[5] P-T. Stoll, J. Busche and K. Arend (eds.), *WTO – Trade-Related Aspects of Intellectual Property Rights* (Martinus Nijhoff, Leiden and Boston 2009), 351–431; D. Gervais, *The TRIPS Agreement. Drafting History and Analysis*, 3rd edn (Sweet & Maxwell, London 2008), 290–324; C. M. Correa, *Trade Related Aspects of Intellectual Property Rights: A Commentary on the TRIPS Agreement* (Oxford University Press, 2007), 209–56; *UNCTAD-ICTSD Resource Book on TRIPS and Development* (Cambridge University Press, Cambridge/New York 2005), 267–321; M. Blakeney, *Trade Related Aspects of Intellectual Property Rights: A Concise Guide to the TRIPS Agreement* (Sweet & Maxwell, London 1996).

186   TRIPS today

objects of property rights, the nature of the interests they serve and the manner in which they have been problematised.

Since we will explore the definition of a GI in the following pages, it is worth restating. Article 22.1 of the Trade Related Agreement on Intellectual Property Rights (TRIPS) identifies the object of protection as follows:

> Geographical indications are, for the purposes of this Agreement, *indications which identify* a good as originating in the territory of a Member, or a region or locality in that territory, where a given *quality, reputation or other characteristic* of the good is *essentially attributable to its geographical origin* (emphasis added).

Features of interest are the requirement that a GI is an 'indication' (a sign communicating specific meaning) associated with a product; the product is connected to an identifiable place on the basis of its quality, reputation or other characteristics (read disjunctively); and that these alternative linkages are essentially attributable to the place of origin. In the next two sections, we review the components of this definition and its peculiar blend of objective and subjective factors. We also consider the implications for registration systems premised upon this definition.

The second problematic feature is the two different levels of protection. Under Article 22 the scope of protection for all GIs consists of the following three components:

- Protection against uses of indications that mislead the public as to the origin of the goods[6] or are false despite being literally accurate (such as perfume made in Paris, Texas);[7]
- Protection against uses of indications where this amounts to an act of unfair competition within the meaning of Article 10*bis* of the Paris Convention;[8] and
- Refusal or invalidation of trade marks that contain or consist of indications, where they may mislead the public as to the origin of the goods.[9]

This clutch of substantive rules seeks to preserve the integrity of consumer information by preventing misleading use, while also protecting producer goodwill and thereby enabling product differentiation in the marketplace. However, to prove misleading conduct, the rights holder has the burden of establishing the sign's reputation acquired through prior use in that jurisdiction, as well as public recognition of the associated product. Similarly, in order to establish unfair competition under Article

---

[6] Art. 22.2(a).   [7] Art. 22.4.

[8] Art. 22.2(b). The limited potential of Art. 10*bis* has been considered in detail in Section 2.3 of Chapter 2.

[9] Art. 22.3.

10*bis*, there must be a proven element of confusion, falsehood or an act misleading the public.[10]

By contrast protection for wines and spirits is significantly stronger and is often referred to as 'absolute' protection.[11] There are three commitments involved here:

- Members shall provide the legal means for interested parties to prevent the use of GIs for wines and spirits on such products when they do not originate in the designated place, 'even where the true origin of the goods is indicated or the [GI] is used in translation or accompanied by expressions such as "kind", "type", "style", "imitation" or the like'.[12] This is familiar language and, in Chapter 4, we have seen an equivalent provision in the Lisbon Agreement.
- Trade marks for wines and spirits which contain or consist of such GIs shall be refused or invalidated, where the trade marked goods are not from the region which the GI relates to.[13] There is no need to establish that use of the trade mark will be misleading.
- Coexistence in the case of homonymous GIs for wines and spirits, provided misleading uses are minimised as far as practicable by differentiating between the two uses.[14] Homonymous indications have been described as those 'which are spelled and pronounced alike, but which designate the geographical origin of products stemming from different countries', such as Rioja designating wine from both Spain and Argentina.[15] Another potential beneficiary is 'Pisco', caught up in a spirited dispute between Chile and Peru.[16] It must be

---

[10] L. R. Nair and R. Kumar, *Geographical Indications: A Search for Identity* (Lexis Nexis, New Delhi 2005), 105.

[11] See, e.g., M. Geuze, 'Protection of Geographical Indications under the TRIPS Agreement and Related Work of the World Trade Organisation', October 1997 (WIPO/GEO/EGR/97/2), [9] ('[Art 23] provides for a more absolute form of protection for GIs for wines and spirits ... This applies even where the public is not being misled, there is no unfair competition and the true origin of the good is indicated or the geographical indication is accompanied by expressions such as "kind", "style", "type", "imitation" or the like'); T-L. Tran Wasescha, 'Recent Developments in the Council for TRIPS (WTO)', September 1999 (WIPO/GEO/CPT/99/2), [12]; WIPO, 'Protection of Geographical Indications: General Introduction, International Protection and Recent Developments', June 2001 (WIPO/GEO/CIS/01/1), [19].

[12] Art. 23.1.   [13] Art. 23.2.   [14] Art. 23.3.

[15] F. Addor and A. Grazioli, 'Geographical Indications beyond Wines and Spirits: A Roadmap for a Better Protection for Geographical Indications in the WTO/TRIPS Agreement' (2002) 5 JWIP 865, 879; D. De Sousa, 'Protection of Geographical Indications under the TRIPS Agreement and Related Work of the World Trade Organization (WTO)', October 2001 (WIPO/GEO/MVD/01/2), Annex 1, 2.

[16] F. Mekis, 'Appellations of Origin, Position of Chile's Vineyards in the Concert of the New World, and in Relation to the Negotiations with the European Union', October 2001 (WIPO/GEO/MVD/01/4), 2.

188   TRIPS today

noted that beyond the wine and spirits category there are other GIs which would benefit from coexistence, such as the heated disagreement over 'Gruyère' between the Swiss and French, or 'Basmati' between India and Pakistan, which has been on the boil for some time.

The scope of protection for all GIs in Article 22 is relatively unproblematic so our focus shifts to Article 23. Here we pursue two unresolved issues. The reasons for selecting the restricted categories of wines and spirits and the manner in which this exceptional protection is justified remain unclear.

The provisions relating to the definition and scope of protection are followed by a patchwork of exceptions and commitments to further negotiations. Here two key themes are the relationship between GIs and third party entitlements to use similar signs such as trade marks where they conflict and the preservation of generic use. These inbuilt provisions for further negotiations were crucial safety valves to prevent the draft agreement from imploding during the Uruguay Round. They form the basis for the on-going negotiations at the TRIPS Council, considered in Chapter 6, while serving as a reminder of the 'work in progress' nature of the GI regime. Looking at the individual components of this patchwork, first there is the commitment to further negotiations at the TRIPS Council to establish a multilateral system of notification and registration for wine GIs, eligible for protection in those Members participating in the system.[17] Spirits were subsequently included in the negotiations for this register, despite not being mentioned in the text of the agreement.[18] Second, Members have agreed to enter into negotiations aimed at increasing the protection of individual GIs for wines and spirits under Article 23.[19] One sees evidence of this in a series of bilateral wine agreements which the EU has pursued, which establish or improve protection for its wine appellations.[20] Third, an

---

[17] Art. 23.4.

[18] This was added around the time of the Ministerial Conference of Singapore of 1996. See WTO, 'Report (1996) of Council for TRIPS', 6 November1996 (IP/C/8), [34]. It was subsequently addressed at Doha, as part of the implementation related issues and concerns. See WTO, 'Doha Ministerial Declaration', November 2001 (WT/MIN(01)/ DEC/1), [18] (Members 'agree to negotiate the establishment of a multilateral system of notification and registration of geographical indications for wines and spirits').

[19] Art. 24.1.

[20] See, e.g., Agreement between the European Community and Australia on Trade in Wine [1994] OJ L 86/94, superseded by the Agreement between the European Community and Australia on Trade in Wine [2009] OJ L 28/3; Agreement between the European Community and the Republic of South Africa on Trade in Wines [2002] OJ L 28/4; Agreement between the European Community and the Republic of South Africa on Trade in Spirits [2002] OJ L 28/113; Agreement Between the European Community and Canada on Trade in Wines and Spirit Drinks [2004] OJ L 35/3; Agreement between the European Community and the United States of America on Trade in Wine [2006] OJ L 87/2. For commentary, see H. Rademeyer, 'The Protection

An outline of Articles 22 to 24

inbuilt monitoring and periodic assessment process is established, whereby the Council for TRIPS reviews the implementation of the GI provisions and facilitates the compliance process.[21] Fourth, Members should not tactically backslide or diminish protection of GIs that existed immediately prior to the date on which TRIPS entered into force (i.e. 1 January 1995 for developed countries).[22] The resort to strategically designating certain terms as generic, often through legislation, to the advantage of external producers is a long-standing concern in this area. A controversy arose as to whether the US had violated this obligation via its Taxpayer Relief Act of 1997, which codified administrative regulations permitting the use of semi-generic designations where the designation is accompanied by the true place of origin (e.g., Californian Chablis).[23] Another potential dispute concerned an amendment to Canadian Trade Marks legislation adopted in 1994, which incorporated a list of generic names including 'Bordeaux' and 'Médoc' while there was evidence to suggest they retained origin indicating ability in the Canadian market.[24] These illustrate the anxieties behind this provision.

These rules are complemented by a series of grandfathering or insulating provisions – those that exempt someone already involved in a certain activity from the effect of new rules regulating that activity. For wine and spirit GIs, there is the option to grandfather the use of those designations by third parties[25] on any goods or services, provided they have used them in a continuous manner (1) for at least 10 years preceding 15 April 1994, or (2) in good faith preceding that date.[26] For all GIs, a grandfathering intention is again evident when it comes to prior trade marks. Nothing in TRIPS shall affect the registration of a trade mark or the right to its use where these have been acquired in good faith,

---

of Geographical Indications in South Africa', September 1999 (WIPO/GEO/CPT/99/3b), 2; F. Vital, 'Protection of Geographical Indications: The Approach of the European Union', September 1999 (WIPO/GEO/CPT/99/5), 10; B. Rose, 'No More Whining about Geographical Indications: Assessing the 2005 Agreement between the United States and the European Community on the Trade in Wine (2007) 29 *Houston Journal of International Law* 731.

[21] Art. 24.2.   [22] Art. 24.3.

[23] See L. A. Lindquist, 'Champagne or Champagne? An Examination of U.S. Failure to Comply with the Geographical Provisions of the TRIPS Agreement' (1999) 27 *Georgia Journal of International and Comparative Law* 309. The prospective use of semi-generics has finally been ended, although existing uses are grandfathered. See Agreement between the European Community and the United States of America on Trade in Wine [2006] OJ L 87/2.

[24] Report on the Lack of Protection of the Wines with Geographical Indication 'Bordeaux' and 'Médoc' (EU Trade Barrier Regulations Committee, 2003). Once more the matter was approached under the bilateral wine agreement framework.

[25] Referring here to those who are not amongst the circle of home country GI producers or commercial operators authorised to use it.

[26] Art. 24.4.

190   TRIPS today

via registration or use, either before the application of the TRIPS GI provisions in the Member in question or before the GI is protected in the country of origin.[27] There are two areas of ambiguity here. The first relates to the fundamental purpose of this provision. Does it permit prior trade marks not only to continue to exist but also to *trump* subsequent GIs? Or does it instead mandate the *co-existence* of prior trade marks with subsequent GIs? In the only WTO Panel Report which has considered GIs to date,[28] the issue arose but, frustratingly, it was left unresolved. The US argument before the adjudicators can be parsed as follows:[29] (1) Article 24.5 protects grandfathered trade marks and is an exception to GI protection; (2) registration and use of a trade mark, in order to be meaningful, relies on the right to the exclusive use (recognised in Article 16.1 of TRIPS) so that the mark can communicate effectively in the marketplace;[30] (3) unless a prior trade mark could trump a subsequent GI, this right to exclusive use would be compromised; (4) therefore exclusivity should not be prejudiced by co-existence. The EU responded along the following lines:[31] (1) the 'boundary between GIs and trade marks is defined by Article 24.5 which provides for coexistence with earlier trade marks'; (2) co-existence was a negotiated compromise; (3) the compromise is reflected in the wording – while the registration or use of the trade mark should not be prejudiced, this did not imply that *exclusive* use should not be prejudiced; (4) co-existence did not affect the former, merely the latter.

When addressing the issue, the Panel sat on the fence to the point of discomfort. Its 'preliminary conclusion [was] that it is inappropriate to imply in Article 24.5 *either* the right to prevent confusing uses *or* a limitation on the right to prevent confusing uses'.[32] However, it did consider that the provision was not a sufficient basis for supporting co-existence because it would be prejudicial to express rights under Article 16.1. We are left with the mere suggestion that Article 24.5 does not support co-existence between these two species of signs.[33] This is a questionable interpretation, for its effect is to make the provision practically meaningless. The second area of ambiguity relates to the scope of

---

[27] Art. 24.5.

[28] WTO Panel Report, *European Communities – Protection of Trademarks and Geographical Indications for Agricultural Products and Foodstuffs*, 15 March 2005 (WT/DS174/R), (hereafter, (DS174)).

[29] Ibid., [7.579]–[7.582].

[30] The economic rationale for granting exclusivity over commercial signs has been discussed in Chapter 4, section 4.

[31] (DS174), [7.583]–[7.590].   [32] Ibid., [7.619].

[33] Co-existence was finally achieved in the WTO dispute and is considered in section 7 below.

good faith. Standards vary under national law and several jurisdictions presume good faith in every trade mark application, subject to its rebuttal by actual evidence of bad faith.[34]

One also sees the rights of trade mark holders preserved in an estoppel or laches type rule. For a trade mark which conflicts with a GI, the opposition must be within five years of either coming to know of its adverse use or the date of publication, whichever is earlier, and provided the GI itself has not been registered in bad faith. After this period the trade mark registration cannot be affected by this conflict.[35] Provision is made for an 'own name' defence, where a third party's name or that of their predecessor in business might otherwise conflict with a GI.[36] There is also encouragement for home country protection as the basis for international protection under TRIPS. Without this, there 'shall be no obligation ... to protect [GIs] which are not or cease to be protected in their country of origin, or which have fallen into disuse in that country'.[37] Finally perhaps the most important exception in Article 24.6 relates to generic use and is developed in Section 6 below. For all products, generic status occurs where the 'relevant indication is identical with the term customary in common language as the common name for such goods or services in the territory of that Member' where the question has arisen. For products of the vine, this occurs as of the date of entry into force of the WTO Agreement where 'the relevant indication is identical with the customary name of a grape variety existing in the territory'. In such situations there is no obligation to apply the GI provisions of TRIPS and such signs are effectively unprotected. While this provides a snapshot of the TRIPS provisions today, negotiations are presently underway – proceeding with all the dynamism of a snail on holiday – to extend Article 23 levels of protection to all products and establish an international registration system for GIs. Both these developments are considered in Chapter 6.

3.   Pathways to TRIPS

In this section and the next, it is argued that the GI concept in Article 22.1 was born out of strategic concessions and retains the birthmarks to prove it. To begin with, it is uncontroversial that drafting TRIPS was controversial. Today's agreement is a register of intensely political negotiations, of wins and losses. Its story is told in terms of victories for particular industrial or commercial lobbies in the developed world,

---

[34] Gervais, *TRIPS Agreement*, 316–17.   [35] Art. 24.7.   [36] Art. 24.8.
[37] Art. 24.9.

192   TRIPS today

with corresponding adverse outcomes for developing countries.[38] It is therefore unsurprising to discover that the GI provisions were also the result of negotiated settlement, as opposed to principled accord. However, I wish to go further than this and explore why the settlement took the particular configuration that it did. What were the models and conceptual resources the parties drew upon during the negotiations? This leads us out of the Uruguay Round and back to developments at WIPO as well as within the European Community (EC) between the 1970s and early 1990s. It is here that we discover important clues which assist in decoding TRIPS.

3.1   TRIPS as compromise(d)

Let us begin by setting out the argument that although TRIPS represents certain advances, its conceptual importance is overstated. The TRIPS Agreement has clearly raised the international profile of IGOs.[39] Daniel Gervais observes that TRIPS is 'groundbreaking' as the first multilateral instrument to address GIs and 'may rightly be considered an important step in this difficult field'.[40] It is perceived as 'a fundamental step forward' and a 'true milestone' in this area.[41] Reasons for this include its broad membership and therefore 'wide effect',[42] as well as the binding nature of its substantive obligations which ensures compliance.[43] Additionally, TRIPS provides for the periodic review of its standards and locks in further negotiations for GIs. When compared

---

[38]   See, e.g., P. Drahos and J. Braithwaite, *Information Feudalism: Who Owns the Knowledge Economy* (Earthscan, London 2002), 108–49; S. K. Sell, *Private Power, Public Law: The Globalization of Intellectual Property* (Cambridge University Press, New York 2003).

[39]   T. Cottier, 'The Agreement on Trade-Related Aspects of Intellectual Property Rights', in P. F. J. Macrory, A. E. Appleton and M. G. Plummer (eds.), *The World Trade Organization: Legal, Economic and Political Analysis*, Vol. I (Springer, New York 2005), 1041, 1045.

[40]   Gervais, *TRIPS Agreement*, 293. See also M. Agdomar, 'Removing the Greek from Feta and Adding Korbel to Champagne: The Paradox of Geographical Indications in International Law' (2008) 18 *Fordham IP Media and Entertainment Law Journal* 541, 543.

[41]   I. Calboli, 'Expanding the Protection of Geographical Indications of Origin under TRIPS: "Old" Debate or "New" Opportunity?' (2006) 10 *Marquette Intellectual Property Law Rev* 181, 189–90.

[42]   S. D. Goldberg, 'Who Will Raise the White Flag? The Battle between the United States and the European Union over the Protection of Geographical Indications' (2001) 22 *University of Pennsylvania Journal of International Economic Law* 107, 116.

[43]   J. M. Cortes Martin, 'TRIPS Agreement: Towards a Better Protection for Geographical Indications?' (2004) 30 *Brooklyn Journal of International Law* 117, 125. Geuze, 'Protection of Geographical Indications under the TRIPS Agreement and Related Work of the World Trade Organisation', [3], [4].

Pathways to TRIPS

with the multilateral instruments analysed in Part I, the combination of binding substantive obligations, broad membership and enforcement options clearly represents an improvement. Yet the substantive content of these obligations does not live up to these buoyant expectations.

The Uruguay Round negotiating records indicate that the GI provisions were especially controversial.[44] An initial catalyst for negotiations was Article IX:6 of GATT, which prohibited the use of trade names that 'misrepresent the true origin of the product, to the detriment of such distinctive regional or geographical names of products'. Although the provision itself had been interpreted narrowly by a Panel in a dispute between the EC and Japan,[45] it formed the basis for a bid in 1987 to include GIs within the new Agreement then being negotiated.[46] By 1988, GIs had been discussed sufficiently for a catalogue of concerns to emerge.[47] The question of generic use remained unresolved; despite figuring in the negotiations, 'a participant noted that the concepts of unfair competition and misleading use had not been fully defined'; the use of 'style', 'type' etc. remained controversial as did suggestions to export home country levels of protection to other countries; a registration system appeared problematic to administer; finally the EC's 'specific reference to products of the vine demonstrated that the Community proposal was more based on expediency than principle'. The EC's response was that given 'the importance

---

[44] For a more detailed treatment, see S. Fusco, 'Geographical Indications: A Discussion of the TRIPS Regulation after the Ministerial Conference of Hong Kong' (2008) 12 *Marquette Intellectual Property Law Review* 197, 216–22.

[45] GATT Panel Report, *Japan – Customs Duties, Taxes and Labelling Practices on Imported Wines and Alcoholic Beverages*, 10 November 1987 (BISD 34S/83). Here Japanese manufacturers were using European wine appellations to designate categories of locally made products, where the categories were relevant for liquor tax laws. The Panel examined the EC's complaint that the use of French names, those of other European languages and European label styles or symbols by Japanese manufacturers misled Japanese consumers as to the origin of the liquors, and that the indication of a Japanese manufacturer did not clarify these activities. It was unable to find that the use by Japanese manufacturers of labels written partly in English (in the case of whisky and brandy) or in French (in the case of wine), the use of the names of varieties of grapes (such as 'Riesling' or 'Semillon'), or the use of foreign terms to describe Japanese spirits ('whisky', 'brandy') or Japanese wines ('chateau', 'reserve', 'vin rose') had actually been to the detriment of EC GIs. Japan was a signatory to the Madrid Agreement and had provisions in national laws to prohibit misleading labelling, thereby satisfying the (limited) obligation in Art. IX:6.

[46] GATT, 'Meeting of the Negotiating Group of 10 June 1987', 23 June 1987 (MTN.GNG/ NG11/2), [5]. See also GATT, (MTN.GNG/NG11/9) at [18], [32]; GATT, 'Compilation of Written Submissions and Oral Statements', 5 February 1988 (MTN.GNG/NG11/W/ 12/Rev.1), [19]. All documents are available at docsonline.wto.org/.

[47] GATT, 'Meeting of the Negotiating Group of 5–8 July 1988', 29 August 1988 (MTN. GNG/NG11/8), [42].

194   TRIPS today

attached to [GIs] by the Community; it would continue to figure prominently in Community proposals'.[48]

Apart from concerns regarding the re-appropriation of generic terms, the European proposals were viewed as an attempt to amplify the Madrid and Lisbon Agreement standards as a means of overcoming their modest membership.[49] In response, the EC resorted to the tropes of 'misuse' and 'unfairness' in 1989, renewing efforts at increasing the international protection of GIs. The EC delegation suggested this was an issue of interest to developing countries, who also had a stake in appellation products.[50] The US and Australian delegations remained opposed to these proposals primarily on the issue of generic usage.[51] By contrast, the US position was premised on the minimalist platform of preventing consumer confusion and preferred trade marks as the means of achieving this. Once again there is concern expressed at 'the suggestion in the Community paper that protection should be accorded to appellations of origin to the extent that it was accorded in the country of origin'.[52] Although not explicitly stated in the final text, certain provisions make sense when viewed from this perspective, having been crafted with an eye to exporting home country protection as far as possible.[53]

As we have seen in Chapter 4, a similar agenda prevailed in the context of the Lisbon Agreement but it would remain divisive. GI provisions were therefore subject to the competing forces of 'international trade and global economics',[54] motivated by 'pricing concerns',[55] which involved a perceived disparity in benefits to parties such as the US.[56] A Japanese official who participated in the negotiations observes that

---

[48] Ibid., [46].

[49] GATT, 'Meeting of the Negotiating Group of 12–14 September 1988', 13 October 1988 (MTN.GNG/NG11/9), [9].

[50] GATT, 'Meeting of the Negotiating Group of 12–14 July 1989', 12 September 1989 (MTN.GNG/NG11/14), [53].

[51] Ibid., [56].   [52] Ibid., [59].

[53] From the mid-twentieth century onwards, several bilateral treaties between European countries adopt this principle whereby each agrees to grant 'home country' equivalent protection to the GIs of the other. See G. Schricker, 'The Efforts towards Harmonization of the Law of Unfair Competition in the European Economic Community' [1973] IIC 201, 208 (discussing the trend setting Franco-German Agreement); R. Plaisant, 'The Revision of the International Treaty Provisions Dealing with Appellations of Origin and Indications of Source' [1980] *Industrial Property* 182 (discussing the general structure of such agreements).

[54] Goldberg, 'Who Will Raise the White Flag?', 151.

[55] H. Kazmi, 'Does it Make a Difference where that Chablis Comes From? Geographic Indications in TRIPS and NAFTA' (2001) 12 *Journal of Contemporary Legal Issues* 470, 472.

[56] C. Haight Farley, 'Conflicts between U.S. Law and International Treaties Concerning Geographical Indications' (2000) 22 *Whittier Law Review* 73, 74.

Pathways to TRIPS

progress on the GI provisions involved a trade-off for concessions made by the EU in the accompanying agricultural negotiations.[57] Commentators recognise the provisions reflect this give and take, noting that unlike many other contentious intellectual property issues this involved a North–North divide, with the cleavage being roughly along Old World – New World lines, where the continued use of designations by emigrant populations was the trigger.[58] In light of these inauspicious beginnings, 'the incoherence of the final, compromised form ... is testament to the deep divisions over how GIs ought to be protected'.[59]

3.2   The WIPO negotiations

Amidst all these competing agendas, certain underlying themes are visible. We see glimpses of the strategy evident in Lisbon – the extent to which the protected status in the home country could be exported, to avoid the vagaries of protection contingent upon the meaning of the sign. Yet influential background developments have remained unexplored, which archival research brings to light. Other desirable (or tolerable) features of an international regime had also been considered in the period between Lisbon and the conclusion of TRIPS. Two developments are of particular interest – the incremental progress towards a broad definition of a GI and the appropriateness of two levels of protection.

In the mid-1970s, WIPO established a committee of experts to consider four potential avenues of progress for the improved international protection of IGOs: (1) revising the Lisbon Agreement to make it more attractive to prospective members; (2) merging the Madrid and Lisbon Agreements; (3) drafting an entirely new treaty for GI protection; and (4) analysing the teachings from existing bilateral agreements.[60]

---

[57] A. Ojima, *Detailed Analysis of TRIPS* (Japan Machinery Center for Trade and Investment, Tokyo 1999), 87–8 (Translation kindly provided by the IIP Tokyo). See also Wasescha, 'Recent Developments in the Council for TRIPS (WTO)', [4].

[58] P. Zylberg, 'Geographical Indications v. Trade marks: The Lisbon Agreement: A Violation of TRIPS?' (2002–2003) 11 *University of Baltimore Intellectual Property Law Journal* 1, 25–6; J. R. Renaud, 'Can't Get There from Here: How NAFTA and GATT Have Reduced Protection for Geographical Trade Marks' (2001) 26 *Brooklyn Journal of International Law* 1097, 1115; J. Watal, *Intellectual Property Rights in the WTO and Developing Countries* (Kluwer, The Hague 2001) 263; Cortes Martin, 'TRIPS Agreement: Towards a Better Protection for Geographical Indications?', 127–8; Addor and A. Grazzioli, 'Geographical Indications Beyond Wines and Spirits', 883.

[59] M. Handler, 'Case Comment: The WTO Geographical Indications Dispute' (2006) 69 *Modern Law Review* 70, 71.

[60] WIPO, 'Present Situation and Possible New Solutions', 28 June 1974 (TAO/I/2), [1]–[5]. See also WIPO, 'Revision of the Lisbon Agreement or Conclusion of a New Treaty', 25 August 1975 (TAO/II/3).

During these deliberations, the concept of a Geographical Indication was first introduced as an umbrella term, to gather up the existing terminology. It appeared in Article 2(i) of the draft treaty: 'the expression "geographical indications" covers indications of source and appellations of origin as defined ... below'. As a more efficient collective reference, its use would also avoid 'the necessity of deciding on a possible hierarchy' between the IS and AO.[61] This usage would surface again in proposals for the revision of the Paris Convention, with the proposed addition of Article 10*quater*.[62] This amendment was aimed at strengthening the protection of the IS and AO vis-à-vis the use of these geographical terms as trade marks. In addition, it contained a special provision in favour of developing countries, which would allow them to pre-emptively reserve a certain number of GIs for the future, even if they were not widely known to be GIs at the time. Such recognition would block their use as trade marks or generic terms by third parties.

Since the Diplomatic Conference for these proposed revisions was never concluded, the umbrella term usage could not be formally adopted. Related to this wide definition was the consensus that a mandatory form of protection was undesirable. The GI incorporated the IS and Chapter 2 has established that a variety of overlapping regimes and sanctions – penal, administrative and those offering civil remedies – were all understood to satisfy IS protection obligations. Participants at the WIPO deliberations therefore agreed that while protection in the country of origin was a necessary first stage for international protection, the form of protection should not be prescribed.[63] In order to accommodate as many different national regimes as possible, this approach continued right up to the early 1990s: 'it would be sufficient if the geographical indication benefited from some protection in the territory of the Contracting Party of origin, be it under general legislation or general principles of law (for example, on the repression of unfair competition or consumer protection) or resulting from registration as a collective mark or a certification mark'.[64]

While the GI = IS + AO formulation initially held sway, towards the end of this period it was gradually being edged out by a more substantive definition, closer to the one eventually found in TRIPS.

---

[61] WIPO, 'Draft Treaty on the Protection of Geographical Indications', 25 August 1975 (TAO/II/2), 8. See also WIPO, (TAO/I/ 8), [32].

[62] WIPO Director General's Memorandum, 'Basic Proposals – Supplement to PR/DC/3', 30 August 1979 (PR/DC/4).

[63] WIPO, (TAO/I/ 8), at [34].

[64] WIPO, 'Report Adopted by the Committee of Experts', 1 June 1990 (GEO/CE/I/3), [56].

Pathways to TRIPS

The problem was simply this – the IS was already broad enough to accommodate the AO. All signs which indicated the geographical origin of a product could qualify as an IS. Those which also indicated an appropriate qualitative link would qualify as AOs. Therefore the 'GI as umbrella' added very little if the IS could do that job. The need to differentiate the GI seems to have been driven by the desire to avoid the fate of the IS.

> The term 'geographical indication' has the same coverage as the expression 'indication of source.' The term 'geographical indication' seems to be preferable to the expression 'indication of source' because the latter expression frequently is understood to imply a lower level of protection, in comparison with the strong protection of appellations of origin. The use of the term 'geographical indication' is intended to underline that both appellations of origin and indications of source are covered and that the protection to be established is not limited to the protection which at present exists with respect to indications of source.[65]

Since the GI being discussed here was positioned as somehow different from the IS, this created an explanatory gap. Some additional criterion seemed necessary to fill out the GI.

At this juncture, the EC representative introduced the requirement of a link between product and place in 1990. The link was pitched at the level of being more than the IS (mere origin connection) and less than the AO (a verifiable qualitative connection).

> [The EC Representative suggested that] in order for a geographical indication to be 'protectable', some kind of link must exist between the geographical area to which the indication refers and the goods which originate from that area. [The EC further suggested that] protectable geographical indications should be those which 'designate a product as originating from a country, region, or locality where a given quality, reputation or other characteristic of the product is attributable to its geographical origin, including natural and human factors'. It was explained that this 'quality link' was broader than the restrictive definition of 'appellation of origin' under the Lisbon Agreement. Whereas Article 2 of the Lisbon Agreement speaks of (i) 'quality and characteristics' which are due, (ii) 'exclusively or essentially' to the geographical environment, under the definition proposed by the services of the Commission of the European Communities, the link need not consist of a given quality but may consist of a given 'reputation or other characteristic' and such characteristic need not be 'exclusively or essentially' attributable to its geographical origin.[66]

Two important ingredients of the TRIPS definition – the stand-alone reputation option to satisfy the link and the relative loosening of this

---

[65] WIPO, 'The Need for a New Treaty and its Possible Contents', 9 April 1990 (GEO/CE/I/2), [6].

[66] WIPO, (GEO/CE/I/3), [49].

198   TRIPS today

link – are introduced at this stage. While this proposed definition demanded more than the IS, the previous lowest common denominator, it would not exclude those who preferred collective or certification trade marks as an adequate means of GI protection. It could include non-European regimes regulating the use of wine designations, such as those of the US.[67] Some agreed that IS-plus protection required IS-plus standards for subject matter, while others were concerned that this new definition would narrow the scope of protected subject matter and the link 'would be difficult to determine and prove through objective means'.[68] We have almost arrived at the dénouement and in Section 3.4 below, it is submitted that today's TRIPS definition is directly influenced by internal compromises within Europe in the late 1980s and early 1990s, which arose during the drafting of the EU's registration system for agricultural products and foodstuffs.

Alongside these efforts to establish a definition simultaneously broad enough to sustain consensus, yet with more substantive content than the IS, the possibility of two distinct levels of protection was also explored. Since the GI was initially conceived of as an umbrella term in 1974, the treaty would provide for two levels of protection – essentially Madrid levels preventing misleading use for all simple geographical indications of origin and Lisbon levels for those signs which would satisfy the requirements for the international registration system being discussed under the draft treaty.

The new system should provide for protection on two levels: in general, all geographical indications should be the subject of a provision, such as that contained in the Madrid Agreement, prohibiting deceptive practices in relation to the geographical origin of a product; in addition, a special system of protection, based on a formal procedure ... should be set up for specific geographical indications (namely, for appellations of origin and for those kinds of indications of source specially defined as being included in the special system).[69]

By contrast, once a new substantive definition for the GI was under consideration in 1990, these two levels merged into a one. The scope of

---

[67] The regulations of the Alcohol and Tobacco Tax and Trade Bureau (formerly Bureau of Alcohol, Tobacco, Firearms and Explosives) indirectly protect geographical indications through its power to regulate the labelling of alcoholic beverages and determine American Viticultural Areas. For an overview, see M. Torsen, 'Apples and Oranges (and Wine): Why the International Conversation Regarding Geographical Indications is at a Standstill' (2005) 87 *Journal of the Patent and Trade Mark Office Society* 31, 45–8. The relevant wine labelling laws are available at www.ttb.gov/labeling/index.shtml.
[68] WIPO, (GEO/CE/I/3), [50]–[52].
[69] WIPO, (TAO/I/8), [33]. See also WIPO, (TAO/II/2), 2.

protection for any GI related to the prohibition of its use 'for goods not originating in the geographical area to which the [GI] refers, or a generic name of a product or as a trade mark'.[70] The important point here is that differential treatment has historically been justified on the basis that AOs deserve this broader scope of protection, due to the nature of the link between product and place. The proposal to grant AO-type products enhanced protection had already been debated in the context of Article 4 of the Madrid Agreement.[71] The notion of two levels of protection was therefore not an unfamiliar one. These negotiations spanning the three decades between Lisbon and TRIPS set out a menu of choices for those involved in the Uruguay Round negotiations.

3.3   *Compromise and its consequences*

Three important and interlinked consequences flow from this quest for a stable consensus, which unfolds through a series of compromises. The first relates to the absence of any prescribed form of protection. Unlike national patent, copyright or trade mark systems around the world, which look recognisably similar at a certain level of abstraction, GI regimes vary considerably. Thus speaking of the GI definition in TRIPS as if it were derived from comparable national definitions is both inaccurate and unhelpful. Reminiscent of the IS, the breadth and ambiguity of Article 22.1 provides ideal breeding grounds for a swarming diversity of legal configurations, which could satisfy the substantive criteria of Articles 22 to 24.[72] Two surveys by WIPO[73] and the WTO[74] showcase the assortment of legal responses to GI protection commitments. The WIPO survey divides these existing regimes into (1) Unfair Competition including Passing Off; (2) Appellations of Origin and Registered Geographical Indications; (3) Collective and Certification Trade Marks (referred to subsequently as group marks); and (4) Administrative schemes, such as those regulating wine labelling. The WTO Summary of Responses from its Members analytically separates the available means of protection into (a) Laws

---

[70] WIPO, (GEO/CE/I/2), [7].   [71] See Chapter 2, section 3.2.

[72] Art. 1.1 of TRIPS preserves the freedom of Members to 'determine the appropriate method of implementing the provisions of this Agreement within their own legal system and practice'.

[73] WIPO, 'Document SCT/6/3 Rev. on Geographical Indications: Historical Background, Nature of Rights, Existing Systems for Protection and Obtaining Protection in Other Countries', 2 April 2002 (SCT/8/4).

[74] WTO, 'Review under Article 24.2 of the Application of the Provisions of the Section of the TRIPS Agreement on Geographical Indications', 24 November 2003 (IP/C/W/253/ Rev.1).

200   TRIPS today

focusing on Business Practices (which incidentally prevent the misuse of GIs, such as food safety labelling); (b) Trade Mark Law (both preventing the registration of geographically misleading trade marks and enabling the registration of group marks); and (c) Special Protection (including dedicated *sui generis* regimes). Despite the analytic value of these divisions, in practice many of these regimes overlap. For example, the UK simultaneously offers protection by way of the tort of passing off, administrative regulations governing truthful marking and trading standards, registration as a certification trade mark with the Intellectual Property Office, or recognition as an EU Protected Designation of Origin (PDO) or Protected Geographical Indication (PGI)[75] via the Department for Environment, Food and Rural Affairs.

At the risk of repetition, many of these regimes have evolved with discrete policy underpinnings, catering to diverse constituencies and responding to a miscellany of proscribed uses, categories of harm and protected interests. An archetypal registration-based regime such as that of France (categories (2) and (c) above) would ensure production not only in the region of origin, but also according to collectively developed and defined criteria which had evolved over time. It would therefore include minimum quality standards over which a dedicated administrative agency of the state had oversight. By contrast, under food safety, customs or fraudulent labelling prevention rules (categories (4) and (a) above), the sign might only need to accurately indicate the place of origin, without any further verification of quality.[76] This suggests that the very nature of the guarantee offered by the sign can vary considerably. These systems also diverge as regards the requirement for prior registration or official recognition. Then there is the related question of who monitors the use of the sign – an inter-professional syndicate supported by the state, which carries out inspections on its own members and brings actions against third parties; *ex officio* by customs authorities; the private entity which owns the collective mark; one or more individual traders under a tort or unfair competition regime?

---

[75] For a more detailed discussion of the PDO and PGI, see Section 4.4 below.

[76] Japan provides several examples of the range of laws providing such supplemental protection. See M-C. Wang, 'The Asian Consciousness and Interests in Geographical Indications' (2006) 96 TMR 906, 925–6 ('The Law to Prevent Unjustifiable Premiums and Misleading Representations, a special law supplementing the Unfair Competition Prevention Law, prohibits "improper representations" (including false or misleading representations) of the place of origin. The Customs Tax Act prohibits importation of foreign products bearing false or misleading geographical indications. The Law Regarding the Standardization and Quality Indication of Agricultural and Forest Products imposes labelling requirements for vegetables and fruits, requiring labelling of the product's name as well as the place of origin').

Pathways to TRIPS 201

To this we can add the disparities in remedies or penalties across these systems – revocation of membership from the group, fines, imprisonment, compensatory or exemplary damages, injunctions to prohibit future infringement and so on. It is unhelpful to speak of the GI in TRIPS as if it references something uniform and stable across the WTO membership. Even the policy arguments considered in the next chapter are contingent upon the specific regimes available in any individual WTO Member.

While international GI protection discourse has swirled around these options, in recent years it appears to have settled upon two favoured forms.[77] The first of these is the group mark – collective or certification marks[78] – within national or regional trade mark registration systems. This system is strongly favoured by the US.[79] All members of the Paris Convention are obliged to accommodate collective marks (Article 7*bis*) and many also do so for certification marks.[80] The second is the *sui generis* model of registration-based protection, exemplified by the EU regime for agricultural products and foodstuff set out in Regulation 510/2006.[81] This is confirmed by a recent survey:

> Of the 167 countries that protect GIs as a form of intellectual property, 111 (including the EU 27) have specific or *sui generis* systems of GI laws in place. There are 56 countries using a trade mark system, rather than or in addition to specific GI protection laws. These countries utilize certification marks, collective marks or trade marks to protect GIs.[82]

The US and EU have spent significant political and economic capital in advocating their preferred models.[83] Although the current focus is on these

---

[77] The emergence of these two models as frontrunners is being recognised in the literature. See Wang, 'The Asian Consciousness', 914; M. Echols, *Geographical Indications for Food Products: International Legal and Regulatory Perspectives* (Kluwer, Alphen aan den Rijn 2008), 3; G. E. Evans, 'The Comparative Advantages of Geographical Indications and Community Trade Marks for the Marketing of Agricultural Products in the European Union' [2010] IIC 645.

[78] See Chapter 2, section 2.3.2.

[79] See USPTO, 'Geographical Indication Protection in the United States' available at www.uspto.gov/ip/global/geographical/index.jsp.

[80] WIPO, 'Technical and Procedural Aspects Relating to the Registration of Certification and Collective Marks', 15 February 2010 (SCT/23/3).

[81] Council Regulation (EC) No 510/2006 of 20 March 2006 on the Protection of Geographical Indications and Designations of Origin for Agricultural Products and Foodstuffs [2006] OJ L 93/12. This has replaced its similarly titled predecessor, Council Regulation (EC) No 2081/92 of 14 July 1992 [1992] OJ L 208/1.

[82] D. Giovannucci, T. Josling, W. Kerr, B. O'Connor and M. Yeung, *Guide to Geographical Indications: Linking Products and their Origins* (International Trade Centre, Geneva 2009), 14.

[83] See generally, EU–Asean Project on the Protection of Intellectual Property Rights (ECAP III), available at www.ecap-project.org/; Organisation for International Geographical Indications Network, available at www.origin-gi.com/; US Patent and

202   TRIPS today

two models, the expansive coverage of the TRIPS definition encourages diversity and several regimes overlap. As we will see in the next chapter, even these two preferred avenues have significant differences *inter se*, so it remains unhelpful to assume the TRIPS GI has a settled referent.

The second consequence follows on from the first. It relates to the assessment of GIs as 'private rights'. If there is no prescribed legal form for GI protection, then it is nonsensical to generalise here as well. The Preamble to TRIPS contains the following language: '*Recognizing* that intellectual property rights are private rights'.[84] This implicit taxonomic status as private property has important repercussions in at least two situations. The first concerns a 'takings' or expropriation situation, where deprivation of the right to use a GI by state action could lead to demands for compensation for the loss of a proprietary interest. This argument is unsuccessfully rehearsed in the ECJ's *Tocai* decision.[85] As a result of an agreement between the EU and Hungary, the use of the Italian grape variety 'Tocai friulano' would have to give way to the Hungarian appellation 'Tokaj'. In the challenge to the Italian law which gave effect to this, one issue was whether it was inconsistent with the right of ownership protected by multilateral human rights instruments. While deciding that a grape varietal designation is not the same as a GI, the court nevertheless did consider this within the broader category of 'incorporeal goods of economic value'. It held that the deprivation was reasonable and not disproportionate. Italian wine could continue to be marketed using regional appellations and alternative names for the grape varietal.[86]

Trade Mark Office (USPTO) Video, *Protecting Geographical Indications*, available at www.uspto.gov/video/index.htm; USPTO, 'Program in China Underscores Importance of Protecting Geographical Indications and Trade Marks', 02 June 2006. At the time of writing, China has both AO-type and certification mark regimes co-existing and occasionally conflicting, under three systems. It is the target of much wooing. B. M. Bashaw, 'Geographical Indications in China: Why Protect GIs with Both Trade Mark Law and AOC-Type Legislation?' (2008) 17 *Pacific Rim Law and Policy Journal* 73; Wang, 'Asian Consciousness'; W. Xiaobing and I. Kireeva, 'GI protection in China: New Measures for Administration of Geographical Indications of Agricultural Products' (2010) 5 *Journal of Intellectual Property Law & Practice* 778.

[84] Reasons offered for its presence include (1) clearly identifying private party interests as the focus of TRIPS, as opposed to governmental measures in the rest of the WTO Agreements; (2) ensuring that Members were not obliged to take *ex officio* action and rights holders would protect their own interests; (3) more tentatively, characterising IPRs as investments in intangible assets, thereby prohibiting expropriation without compensation. See Correa, *Commentary on TRIPS*, 10–11.

[85] *Regione autonoma Friuli-Venezia Giulia* v. *Ministero delle Politiche Agricole e Forestali* (C-347/03) [2005] ECR I-3785.

[86] For another perspective on the takings argument, where it was alleged that recognition of the Czech appellation for Budweiser in Portugal deprived Anheuser Busch of their 'Budweiser' trade mark application in Portugal, considered to be a possession, see *Anheuser-Busch Inc* v. *Portugal* [2007] ETMR 24 (ECHR Grand Chamber).

Apart from expropriation by state action, the second situation where a private property tag is relevant relates to conflicts between trade marks and GIs. It is argued that if both regimes regulate comparable proprietary interests in signs which serve to distinguish products in the marketplace and prevent unfair competition, this is all the more reason for equal treatment. Since GIs under TRIPS are deemed to be private rights and also intellectual property, this is tantamount to treating them like other forms of private (intellectual) property.[87] In particular, they should be treated akin to trade marks, as a corrective to the European tendency to treat GIs as somehow superior in situations where they conflict with trade marks. Unfortunately the loosely conceived assertion that GI laws generally recognise these signs as the objects of private property rights is self-evidently erroneous. To begin with, there is the matter of the form of protection. National unfair competition regimes or consumer protection regulations may not require any proprietary rights to be established as a precondition for intervening. Attention will be directed towards the nature of the defendant's conduct and effect of the use of the sign on the relevant public. These systems are very clearly included within the mixed bag of GI laws, so sweeping generalisations depicting GI protection as resting on the foundation of property are inaccurate. Only certain forms of GI protection correlate with proprietary interests.

Here too, there is considerable debate as to the nature of the property. It is by no means clear whether even GIs at the AO end of the spectrum are the objects of conventional private property rights at all. Based upon their link to territory, one opinion holds that the state is the primary rights holder for such signs.[88] Others suggest that

---

[87] L. Beresford, 'Geographical Indications: The Current Landscape' (2007) 17 *Fordham Intellectual Property Media & Entertainment Law Journal* 979 ('The TRIPS Agreement tells us that GIs are [IP] rights and because TRIPS deals only with private rights, GIs are private property rights'). See also B. Goebel, 'Geographical Indications and Trade Marks – The Road from Doha' (2003) 93 TMR 964; Cotton, '123 Years at the Negotiating Table and Still No Dessert?', 1295.

[88] WIPO, (GEO/CE/I/2), [4] ('Compared with other objects of industrial property ... appellations of origin and indications of source present a particular feature, namely a relationship with an existing factual situation, since they refer to the particular geographical origin of a product. Thus, each [AO and IS] necessarily "belongs" to a country (the country where the geographical area to which the indication refers is located), even if its good will and reputation may have been developed through the efforts of certain individuals or entities'). Cf. L. A. García Muñoz-Nájar, 'Some Notes on the Protection of Appellations of Origin in Countries with Emerging Economies: the Adean Community', November 2001 (WIPO/GEO/MVD/01/6), 6 ('Experts on the subject and also various laws state that " ... the appellation is a public good, it belongs inalienably and imprescriptibly to the national or regional community, as the case may be, and its protection is usually the responsibility of the public authorities or

204   TRIPS today

AOs are the objects of some form of joint or communal property rights.[89] Those who contrast GI law with trade mark law suggest that GIs lack key indicia of private property since they cannot be bought, sold or licensed to producers outside of the region.[90] This is further developed in a debate between Professors Jim Chen and Louis Lorvellec when considering the French AOC regime. While the former focuses on the powerful property-like rights of producers to exclude outsiders in situations of misrepresentation or misappropriation under French appellation laws,[91] the latter argues that it is 'legally inaccurate to characterize this as a perpetual property right' since the AOC 'can never be privately owned, and this is where AOC law differs from intellectual property law'.[92] This approach is reiterated in France's official response to a WTO survey, where appellations are categorically not associated with private ownership but instead with a right to use.[93] With the conventional economic justifications for intellectual property depending upon the subject matter being freely transferable, with minimum transaction costs,[94] several types of GIs are a poor fit. The mismatch is also stressed in a survey of national laws undertaken by the AIPPI in its response to Q.191, where the majority of respondents were clear that under their national systems,

---

the State. The appellation of origin is considered part of the national heritage, and ultimately under State control'").

[89] One author suggests parallels with the German law concept of Gemeinschaft zur gesamten Hand. A. F. R. de Almeida, 'Key Differences between Trade Marks and Geographical Indications' [2008] EIPR 406, 410.

[90] L. Baeumer, 'Protection of Geographical Indications under WIPO Treaties and Questions Concerning the Relationship between those Treaties and the TRIPS Agreement', October 1997 (WIPO/GEO/EGR/97/1 Rev), [19]; Y. Bénard, 'Geographical Indication around the World', 22 July 2003 (WIPO/GEO/SFO/03/20/ Rev.), 2.

[91] J. Chen, 'A Sober Second Look at Appellations of Origin: How the United States Will Crash France's Wine and Cheese Party' (1996) 5 *Minnesota Journal of Global Trade* 29, 37–8 ('The power to exclude is the power of property, and the AOC system gives that power to French farmers in abundance').

[92] L. Lorvellec, 'You've Got to Fight for Your Right to Party: A Response to Professor Jim Chen' (1996) 5 *Minnesota Journal of Global Trade* 65, 68–9.

[93] See Q.17 in EC 'Response to the Checklist of Questions: Review under Art 24.2', 26 March 1999 (IP/C/W/117/Add.10), 61. See also N. Ozanam, 'Protection of Geographical Indications – Food Products – The Example of Champagne Industry, France', November 2003 (WIPO/GEO/DEL/03/11.rev), 4 ('In that respect, growers and Houses have a right to use the name Champagne, but they do not own the name'); WIPO, 'Draft of the Model Law for Developing Countries on Appellations of Origin and Indications of Source', 30 October 1974 (TAO/I/ INF.l), 16, 32, 50.

[94] See W. M. Landes and R. A. Posner, *The Economic Structure of Intellectual Property Law* (Harvard University Press, Cambridge MA 2003), Chapter 1.

Pathways to TRIPS 205

GI designations are not the object of private property rights.[95] Somewhat ironically, this appears to be the US view as well, at least as far as domestic appellations of origin for wine, known as American Viticultural Areas (AVAs), are concerned. The California Court of Appeal held that for the purposes of determining whether the state has expropriated property without compensation, American wine GIs in the form of certificates of label approval (COLAs)[96] for the brand names 'Napa Ridge', 'Rutherford Vintners' and 'Napa Creek Winery' were not private property.[97] The court held that such labels were highly regulated by the state and possessed only a part of the bundle of rights that conventionally make up property.[98] This resonates with the regulatory underpinnings of the French AOC system, as summed up by Antoine Vialard:

[The French AOC] is a legal governmental institution consisting of a distinctive, recognized symbol, controlled and protected by laws in the public interest. *This distinctive symbol is inalienable and indefeasible from the land.* It defines precise geographic areas for production as well as quality factors tied to those areas, which are under state control (emphasis added).[99]

Thus while IGOs are located within intellectual property doctrine as distinctive signs capable of generating a commercially valuable intangible reputation, this is in a very different sense from conventional trade

---

[95] See AIPPI Working Committee, Resolution on Question Q191: Relationship between Trademarks and Geographical Indications (2006), 3 available at www.aippi.org/reports/resolutions/q191_E.pdf. (Question 2 specifically asked whether the registration of a GI confers a property right. According to the summary of responses, 'the majority of Group Reports (Australia, Belgium, Brazil, Estonia, Germany, Latvia, Luxembourg, Malaysia, Peru, Portugal, Republic of Korea, Singapore, Switzerland, and UK) note that the registration of a GI does not confer a property right. Similarly, there is generally no individual "proprietor" or "right holder" in these countries. A number of Group Reports (Belgium, Brazil, France, Latvia, Luxembourg, Portugal, Russia, Slovenia, Spain, Thailand) state that a GI is best seen as a public good or a collective right').

[96] The regulations establishing COLAs are part of a regulatory scheme designed to protect consumers from false, misleading or inaccurate labels and to protect competitors from unfair business practices and administered by the Alcohol and Tobacco Tax and Trade Bureau (TTB). Wine may not be sold or shipped in interstate commerce unless it is in conformity with COLA requirements. See generally 27 CFR §§ 4 and 13 (2006). Appellations of origin for wine are specifically regulated as one of these requirements. See 27 CFR §§ 4.25 (2006).

[97] *Bronco Wine Co* v. *Jolly* 129 Cal App 4th 988 (2005); [Cert. denied 126 S Ct 1169 (Mem) (2006)] (The appellant Bronco Wine possessed COLAs and challenged a California state law which denied its use of these labels based on a stricter standard, i.e. the wine must contain 85 per cent of its grapes from the eponymous region instead of 75 per cent as required by federal law. One of the arguments was that this stricter standard deprived it of a proprietary interest without compensation).

[98] Ibid., 1030–3.

[99] A. Vialard, 'Regulating Quality Wines in European and French Law' (1999) 19 *Northern Illinois University Law Review* 235, 243.

206   TRIPS today

mark law. When it comes to regimes within the AO family, these signs are tethered to place,[100] have restrictions on transferability, are often closely regulated by the state and conceived as rights to use. Additionally many regimes regulating IGOs do not require prior recognition as private property. It makes little sense to consider this taxonomical issue at the abstract level of TRIPS, or assume that TRIPS settles the issue.

Apart from the variety of forms of protection and the associated difficulty of classifying all GIs as private rights, there is the third and related issue of the message and guarantee associated with a GI. There is general consensus that GIs need to be protected to preserve the coherence of the message they communicate. But what is the content of the message? Let us take Anette Kur's diagnosis as an illustration:

> The indication of geographical origin of a product can furnish important and valuable information for consumers. This concerns in particular those goods where such indications imply a message about the specific taste or quality derived from the geographical source, as may typically be the case with foodstuff and other agricultural products. There is no doubt at all that it is in the interest of consumers as well as of producers that such information is correct and complete, and that efficient means exist to prevent the misleading use of such designations.[101]

The scope of protection is subsequently modulated depending upon the message communicated by the sign. While an IGO communicates a product's geographical origin, to what extent is it also a guarantee of quality based on regulated production techniques? Can it provide assurances of tradition or authenticity? GI proponents often argue that such signs communicate these additional messages and index these to related policy arguments.[102] It is worth reminding ourselves that these assertions depend upon the specific mode of GI identification and protection under consideration. The point being made is that Article 22.1 provides limited intrinsic guidance.

---

[100] This has been recognised by courts; e.g., by the Swiss Federal Court of Justice, in the context of the narrower category of Appellations of Origin. See *Anheuser-Busch Inc* v. *Budějovický Budvar Národní Podnik* [2001] ETMR 77, 82 ('The function both of trade mark protection and of protection for appellations of origin is to ensure the distinguishing function of the designation and to prevent mistaken attributions – whether regarding the manufacturer or the place of origin. But unlike trade marks, appellations of origin attribute the goods for which they are used not to a certain undertaking but to a country, a region or a place'). See also C. Bramley and J. F. Kirsten, 'Exploring the Economic Rationale for Protecting Geographical Indicators in Agriculture' (2007) 46 *Agrekon* 69, 87.

[101] A. Kur, 'Quibbling Siblings – Comments to Dev Gangjee's Presentation' (2007) 82 *Chicago–Kent Law Review* 1317.

[102] See Chapter 6.

Regimes towards the AOC end of the spectrum will require explicit production and quality standards to be documented. As we have seen in Chapter 3, the product specification is built around historically established techniques, with an eye to achieving desirable characteristics in the end product. Acknowledging that GIs could communicate specific quality standards suggests that we should prevent misleading uses related to quality, not just those implicating origin. This aspect has been recognised by wine appellation regimes for some time.[103] Similarly in *Feta*, Greek producers complained that cheese described as 'Feta' was made in Denmark, Germany and the Netherlands using cows' milk and an industrial ultra-filtration process, which is more economical than the traditional method of natural straining using ewe's milk. The result was an industrially produced and palpably dissimilar product, sold under the same name.[104] By the same token, Cognac producers opposed Brazilian legislation which 'gathers under the general name of *conhaque* several types of spirits which have different technical specifications, are produced from different raw materials and follow different production processes'.[105] Layered upon the geographical origin and quality message is an associated reputation. While bringing GIs within the fold of IP, this also highlights affinities with the conventional logic of trade mark protection. As Laddie J observed while deciding a claim of passing off, it is Champagne's 'cachet which made products sold under that word attractive to the customer is the hallmark of a particularly valuable mark'.[106]

So does Article 22.1 prescribe a particular sequence for fitting these elements of origin, quality and reputation together? One approach is to ask whether all GIs satisfying the TRIPS definition possess this objectively verifiable quality dimension, which then acts as the basis for reputation. Here there is equivocation on whether the reputation is contingent on the product's empirically verifiable qualities linked to the region of origin (e.g., sulphur based compounds in the soil, which

---

[103] See, e.g., F. Castellucci, 'Geographical Indications: The Italian Scenario for the Wine Sector', 24 June 2003 (WIPO/GEO/SFO/03/10), [8] (When 'talking about Italian wines under Denomination of Origin, "quality" is an intrinsic characteristic, rigorously controlled by the specialised Laboratories and by the pools of wine tasting experts of each Chamber of Commerce'). He goes on to mention the regulation of grape types, climate and soil regions and human factors, including the cultivation techniques, production, preservation and ageing methods.

[104] *Canadane Cheese Trading AMBA* v. *Hellenic Republic* (C-317/95) [1997] ECR I-4681, [17], [60]–[62] (AGO).

[105] See the Report on Proceedings Concerning Brazilian Practices Affecting Trade in Cognac (EU Trade Barrier Regulations Committee, 1997), 9.

[106] *Chocosuisse Union des Fabricants Suisse de Chocolat* v. *Cadbury Limited* [1998] RPC 117, 128 (ChD).

208 TRIPS today

are drawn up by vines, in turn enhancing the flavour of the wine) or whether reputation is an independently sufficient criterion. It could exist by happenstance, possibly because producers in the region were the first to come up with the product. On the one hand, this broadly reputational link to a place seems to satisfy the TRIPS definition.[107] For both general unfair competition regimes and collective mark protection systems,[108] the adjudicator would not necessarily enquire as to the efforts made by the club to define product standards, so long as the club could be defined and establish that it had a reputation to protect. Yet if a purely 'reputational' link to origin is sufficient for TRIPS, WIPO conceives of the GI slightly differently:

A [GI] points to a specific place or region of production that determines the characteristic qualities of the product that originates therein. It is important that the product *derives its qualities and reputation* from that place. Since those qualities depend on the place of production, a specific 'link' exists between the products and their original place of production (emphasis added).[109]

As the objects of IP protection, all GIs should have a local, national or occasionally international reputation. This is the valuable intangible being protected.

However, the extent to which any given system verifies the basis for this reputation remains ambiguous. Chapter 3 has established that the French AOC system emerged in response to concerns that the quality guarantee was eroding, which was damaging to the reputation of well-known wines. By contrast, we cannot claim that all GIs under the TRIPS definition represent guarantees of quality, for which there is oversight by an independent body. By and large, the trade mark regime is indifferent to *terroir* factors. A certification mark applicant may wish to include collective and experimentally derived methods of production and details about local geographical conditions, but the system is not designed around the verification of these requirements. In fact, this flexibility is advertised as a virtue of the

---

[107] O'Connor & Co, 'Geographical indications and TRIPS: 10 Years Later . . . A Roadmap for EU GI Holders to Gain Protection in Other WTO Members – Part I' (Report for European Commission (DG Trade) 2007) 6 ('This definition expands the [Lisbon AO concept] to protect goods which merely derive a reputation from their place of origin without possessing a given quality or other characteristics which are due to that place').

[108] An example of a dedicated regional collective mark system, which is light touch as regards product specifications, while emphasising proof of reputation acquired through use, is found in Japan. See J. Tessensohn and S. Yamamoto, 'Japan: Trade Marks - Japan's New Regional Collective Trade Mark System will Protect Famous Goods and Services from Regional Communities' [2006] EIPR N145.

[109] WIPO FAQ: 'What does a geographical indication do?', available at www.wipo.int/geo_indications/en/about.html#whatdoes.

Pathways to TRIPS 209

certification mark regime.[110] When it comes to *sui generis* GI protection, the product's reputation appears to rest on its qualities derived from geographical source.[111] As the Italian Supreme Court describes it:

> The reason for affording protection [for designations of origin] lies in the fact that the product draws a particular character from its place of origin. This character is objectively discernable through a complex of the natural and human elements making up its environment of production ... [It] is aimed at reassuring the consumer of the place of origin, itself also an assurance of quality.[112]

Terroir linkages recognise that origin influences quality and this quality goes on to sustain a product's reputation. This chain of reasoning has been endorsed by the ECJ on several occasions. In its *Rioja II* decision, the court held that:

> The reputation of designations of origin depends on their image in the minds of consumers. That image in turn depends essentially on particular characteristics and more generally on the quality of the product. It is on the latter, ultimately, that the product's reputation is based.[113]

Building further on this, the current position is more nuanced. GIs rest on historically derived specifications which guarantee quality.[114] This is what provides the initial reputational nub and, further downstream, maintaining this reputation 'will depend significantly on factors which are extraneous to the product itself ... inter alia the amount of investment in promoting the appellation of origin, how intensive use of the appellation of origin has been and the market share held by the product'.[115] While resting on a foundation of intrinsic product quality, the necessity for effective marketing to sustain and develop this reputation is also recognised.[116]

---

[110] See generally J. Hughes, 'Champagne, Feta, and Bourbon – The Spirited Debate about Geographical Indications' (2006) 58 *Hastings Law Journal* 299.

[111] It must also be noted that a porous barrier exists between the two categories of 'reputational link' and 'reputation stemming from *terroir* link'. Once a local product gains a reputation, it is sometimes convenient to discover or invent a *terroir* link, depending upon the evidence national authorities are willing to accept.

[112] *Pilsen Urquell* v. *Industrie Poretti SpA* [1998] ETMR 168, 172 (Corte Suprema di Cassazione 1996).

[113] *Belgium* v. *Spain* (C-388/95) [2000] ECR I-3123; [2000] ETMR 999, [56] (ECJ). This was reiterated in *Consorzio del Prosciutto di Parma* v. *Asda Stores Ltd and Hygrade Foods Ltd* (C-108/01) [2003] ECR I-5121; [2004] ETMR 23, [64] (ECJ), (hereafter *Prosciutto di Parma*); *Ravil SARL* v. *Bellon Import SARL* (C-469/00) [2003] ECR I-5053; [2004] ETMR 22, [49] (ECJ).

[114] See the contrasting points of view in Advocate General Saggio's opinion, in *Belgium* v. *Spain* (C-388/95) [2000] ECR I-3123, [33]–[39] (AGO).

[115] As argued by OHIM in *Budějovický Budvar Národní Podnik* v. *OHIM* (Joined Cases T 53/04 to T 56/04, T 58/04 and T 59/04) 12 June 2007, [134] (CFI).

[116] J-M. Girardeau, 'The Use of Geographical Indications in a Collective Marketing Strategy: The Example of Cognac', September 1999 (WIPO/GEO/CPT/99/7);

210   TRIPS today

Regimes developed around the AO concept also incorporate a guarantee in this sequence connecting origin, quality and reputation. While defending European GI regimes against the challenge that they created obstructions to the free movement of goods, the European Commission has justified their existence by arguing that a PDO 'guarantees that a product comes from a defined area. In addition it guarantees that the product displays certain characteristics'.[117] The ECJ subsequently endorsed this position, identifying the 'essential function'[118] of a designation of origin as the ability 'to *guarantee* that the product bearing it comes from a specified geographical area and displays certain particular characteristics' (emphasis added).[119] There are some who go further and suggest that such appellation regimes also guarantee 'authenticity'[120] and that such symbols 'transmit and guarantee to the consumer the values concentrated therein, which may include up to hundreds of years of traditional artisan craftsmanship and the region's particular natural and environmental characteristics, which are embedded into the specific product'.[121] This aspect has also been recognised by courts: 'For consumers, the link between the reputation of the producers and the quality of the products also depends on his being assured that products sold under the designation are authentic'.[122] Authenticity – an undefined term which presumably relates to historically stabilised and collectively generated methods of production – comes at a price since traditional ingredients and techniques often increase production costs.[123] As one study illustrates, 'traditional Balsamic Vinegar from

---

J. van Niekerk, 'The Use of Geographical Indications in a Collective Marketing Strategy: The Example of the South African Wine Industry', September 1999 (WIPO/GEO/CPT/99/8), 12–13 (referring to the development of regional food and wine festivals; sports event sponsorship; the distribution of brochures; liaising with tourism organisations etc.); K. Das, 'Prospects and Challenges of Geographical Indications in India' (2010) 13 JWIP 148, 163.

[117] See, e.g., *Ravil SARL* v. *Bellon Import SARL* (C-469/00) [2003] ECR I-505 [38] (AGO).

[118] A key concept in European IP law, intellectual property is viewed as a limited legal monopoly which is only justified so far as the extent of protection is necessary to enable the essential and socially desirable functioning of that particular IP regime. The concept serves as a focusing lens, albeit at an abstract and a-historical level, to identify the essence of protection for the various IP regimes in Europe.

[119] See the first 'Rioja' case of *Etablissements Delhaize Frères et Compagnie Le Lion SA* v. *Promalvin SA* (C-47/90) [1992] ECR I-3669, [17].

[120] van Niekerk, 'The Use of Geographical Indications in a Collective Marketing Strategy', 5 ('To be part of a successful collective marketing strategy, the authenticity of geographical indications needs to be guaranteed, controlled and protected').

[121] Zylberg, 'The Lisbon Agreement', 3.

[122] *Ravil SARL* v. *Bellon Import SARL* (C-469/00), [49] (ECJ).

[123] OECD, Food Safety and Quality Issues: Trade Considerations (COM/AGR/CA/TD/TC (98)151/FINAL), 12–13.

Modena is barrel-aged for 12 years, whereas imitations are made with an addition of caramel'.[124] Research also suggests that PDO Brie is 40 per cent more expensive to produce than generic substitutes, due largely to artisanal/manual techniques.[125]

Yet even within established *sui generis* regimes, these guarantees of quality and authenticity can sometimes ring hollow. The EU's Regulation 510/2006 for agricultural products and foodstuffs grants both PDOs and PGIs the same scope of protection. Here PGIs are permitted a greater degree of flexibility in the sourcing of their materials, as well as the strength of the link with the designated region.[126] The European Commission has itself been rethinking this aspect of the PGI.

> It is essential that registrations meet consumer expectations for quality products in order to maintain confidence in the geographical indications system ... For some names for processed foods, the link between the place and the production rests on the processing rather than the farming of the ingredients and on the reputation attached to the product. The raw materials may therefore come from outside the area, and this might not be what the consumer is expecting. For many products the quality and reputation does not rest exclusively on factors linked to origin and/or the *savoir faire* of local producers.[127]

The Commission goes on to ask whether the criteria for PGIs should 'be made stricter to emphasise the link between the product and the geographical area'.[128]

In some cases, the link may be attenuated to the point of insubstantiality. Consider the frankly bizarre outcome in the case of the appellation Jaffa for oranges. This AO is understood to be the primary motivation for Israel signing up to the Lisbon Agreement. It is protected both within Israel and under the Lisbon Agreement.[129] The registrant had decided to take advantage of the seasonal inversions in the southern hemisphere and licensed South African growers to use the AO for oranges cultivated in South Africa and marketed in England under the name 'Jaffa'. The fruit were derived from saplings and know-how imported from Israel.

---

[124] Dominique Barjolle and Erik Thévenod-Mottet, Final Report: Work Programme 6 – Policies Evaluation (DOLPHINS Concerted Action, Contract QLK5–2000–0593, European Commission, June 2003), 13.

[125] Z. Bouamra-Mechemache and J. Chaaban, 'Determinants of Adoption of Protected Designation of Origin Label: Evidence from the French Brie Cheese Industry' (2010) 61 *Journal of Agricultural Economics* 225.

[126] Art. 2 only requires that 'the production and/or processing and/or preparation [must] take place in the defined geographical area'. This implies that raw material can be sourced from elsewhere.

[127] European Commission, Green Paper on Agricultural Product Quality COM(2008) 641 final (Brussels, 15 October 2008), 13.

[128] Ibid.   [129] Lisbon Registration No. 512.

212   TRIPS today

When the registrant applied to renew the AO in Israel, the registrar refused this on the basis that the *applicant's own use of the appellation* was suggesting that the quality and characteristics of the oranges grown in two non-contiguous countries was identical. In short, it made a mockery of the very notion of an AO. Before the Board of Appeal, the appeal was allowed and registration was permitted, essentially on the basis that such use did not constitute an admission that Jaffa was not an AO is Israel, where the appellation continued to satisfy the requisite link.[130] The Board's decision seems to prioritise licensing revenue over the potentially misleading effect of Jaffa on UK consumers, unless they paid attention to the qualifier which indicated South African origin.

As a result, one cannot identify the components of the GI message or guarantee without first identifying the substratum of the particular national legal regime. To this is added a further complication. Consumers are certainly interested in origin-labelled products and we return to this phenomenon in the next chapter. Yet some evidence from Europe suggests that their understanding is 'rather diverse and confused' so that they 'rely on a range of other factors other than official designations'. While the awareness of particular producer groups such as the Consorzio of Parmigiano Reggiano is high, the awareness is lower for official quality symbols, including the precise meaning of the PGI or PDO symbol.[131] A Eurobarometer survey published in 2004 concluded that '61% of people had never seen or heard of "*Appellation d'Origine Contrôlée*/Registered Designation of Origin"; 80% of those polled said they had never seen or heard of "Protected Designation of Origin"; The level of awareness of "Protected Geographical Indication" was even lower (86% had never seen or heard of it)'.[132] More recent research suggests that recognition remains low, at around 8 per cent of consumers surveyed, although recognition is much higher in certain EU Members such as Greece and Italy.[133] This has resulted in attempts to clarify the message by raising the profile of the symbols which signify PGI and

---

[130] N. Wilkof and S. Uzrad, 'In the Matter of the Appellation of Origin for "Jaffa"' (2008) 3 *Journal of Intellectual Property Law & Practice* 17 (commenting on *The Citrus Division of the Plant Production and Marketing Board* v. *Israel Commissioner of Patents and Trade Marks* [2007] 1011/05, Appeal Board (Jerusalem), 12 July 2007).

[131] Concerted Action DOLPHINS, WP4: Final Report – Link between Origin Labelled Products and Consumers and Citizens (Key Action No. 5, July 2002), 8.

[132] However, recognition was significantly higher in individual countries such as France and Spain. See EC Special Eurobarometer, European Union Citizens and Agriculture from 1995 to 2003 (September 2004), 51.

[133] London Economics, et al. Evaluation of the CAP Policy on Protected Designations of Origin (PDO) and Protected Geographical Indications (PGI) – (Final Report for the European Commission, November 2008), 154.

The definition of a GI: Article 22.1   213

PDO status, much in the same way that ® and TM are expected to communicate information.[134] From 2009 onwards, it became compulsory to use the PDO and PGI symbols, or their figurative devices or abbreviations, where the associated products are marketed under the registered name (e.g., Prosciutto di Parma).[135]

Finally, a swarm of associations cluster around designations for traditional regional products, such as superior quality, healthiness, safety, artisanal production, the heritage dimension, environmental friendliness, nostalgia and rustic imagery as well as encouraging rural development.[136] Research also suggests that for certain markets, origin by itself is insufficient as a guarantee, where the appeal of regional foods for consumers is based on broader notions of enhanced freshness, taste, nostalgia and naturalness.[137] By way of a reality-check, to what extent can or should GI regimes legally guarantee this penumbra of associations? Therefore the third consequence that flows from the compromised nature of the GI in TRIPS is that, whilst it accommodates a large number of regimes, the message communicated and guarantees offered vary considerably. It is unwise to generalise about the GI in TRIPS.

4.   The definition of a GI: Article 22.1

Law is both constitutive as well as reflective. It is evident that TRIPS does not merely reflect an established consensus on the appropriate subject matter to be protected. The definition arose out of incremental and cautiously manoeuvred compromises, as an intermediate option between the IS and AO. The GI was fabricated specifically for TRIPS and its distinguishing feature is the three alternative routes – quality, characteristic or reputation – to establish the link between product and place. To what extent does it incorporate unresolved tensions from trying to expand beyond wine as the paradigm subject matter? And is this definition viable? It needs to be, because it functions as a filter for

---

[134] See, e.g., Opinion of the European Economic and Social Committee on Geographical Indications and Designations, [2008] OJ C 204/57, [1.1.6] (emphasising that 'greater backing must be given to initiatives to promote Community marks so as to provide operators with more information and make GI products more recognisable to consumers, especially in those countries where they are less common').

[135] See Art. 8.2 of Regulation 510/2006. For further details on these symbols, including examples of the new colour schemes, see Commission Regulation (EC) No. 628/2008 of 2 July 2008 amending Regulation (EC) No. 1898/2006 laying down detailed rules of implementation of Council Regulation (EC) No. 510/2006, [2008] OJ L 173/3.

[136] DOLPHINS, WP4: Final Report, 9–10.

[137] A. Tregear, S. Kuznesof and A. Moxey, 'Policy Initiatives for Regional Foods: Some Insights from Consumer Research' (1998) 23 *Food Policy* 383.

214   TRIPS today

identifying the subject matter to which TRIPS applies. In order to 'have a workable international system, the first logical step would be to define "geographical indication" more explicitly so that all countries are referring to the same idea when debating the GI issue on an international scale'.[138] Clarity is all the more desirable in light of the proposed multilateral register for wines and spirits, where the definition is the entry point into the registration system.[139]

There is also no denying the ascendancy of the TRIPS definition. According to a WIPO study in 2002, 'a number of countries now use the TRIPS definition as the basis for their national legislation on geographical indications, thus establishing it as a common denominator in this field of law'.[140] Recent discussions at the meetings of WIPO's Standing Committee on the Law of Trademarks, Industrial Designs and Geographical Indications (SCT) have adopted the TRIPS definition.[141] The EU has resorted to the TRIPS criteria in defining 'geographical indications' in bilateral wine agreements with Australia,[142] Chile[143] and South Africa[144] while the US first subsumes GIs within the general rubric of trade mark law, then defines them in TRIPS language in free trade agreements (FTAs) with Jordan,[145] Singapore[146] and Australia.[147] In general, commentators recognise the advantage of a single definition replacing the IS, AO and other concepts which preceded it.[148] Therefore it is worth asking to what extent TRIPS lives up to these expectations. While certain elements of the definition are clear,

---

[138] Torsen, 'Apples and Oranges (and Wine)', 60.

[139] See the extensive scrutiny of Art. 22.1 in WTO, 'Discussions on the Establishment of a Multilateral System of Notification and Registration of Geographical Indications for Wines and Spirits: Compilation of Issues and Points', 23 May 2003 (TN/IP/W/7/Rev.1), 5–13. The definition was also reconsidered when debating the extension of Art. 23 to all products. See WTO, 'Issues Related to the Extension of the Protection of Geographical Indications Provided for in Article 23 of the TRIPS Agreement to Products Other Than Wines and Spirits', 18 May 2005 (TN/C/W/25), [20]–[32].

[140] WIPO, The Definition of Geographical Indications', 1 October 2002 (SCT/9/4), [4].

[141] WIPO, (SCT/7/4), 4; WIPO, (SCT/8/7), [280].

[142] See Art. 2(1)(a) of the Agreement between the European Community and Australia on Trade in Wine 94/184/EC [1994] OJ L 086/1.

[143] See Art. 3(b) of the Agreement on Trade in Wines in Annex V of the EC–Chile Association Agreement [2002] OJ L 353/3.

[144] See Art. 3(b) of the Agreement between the European Community and the Republic of South Africa on Trade in Wine [2002] OJ L 028/4.

[145] Art. IV.6 of the US–Jordan FTA. For the text of these agreements, see www.ustr.gov/trade-agreements/free-trade-agreements.

[146] Art. 16.2 of the US–Singapore FTA.   [147] Art. 17.2 of the US–Australia FTA.

[148] See, e.g., S. Escudero, 'International Protection of Geographical Indications and Developing Countries', (Working Paper No. 10, South Centre, July 2001), 10; *UNCTAD-ICTSD Resource Book on TRIPS*, 270 (The 'use of the term "geographical indication" in TRIPS was intended to help bring coherence to an unsettled area').

The definition of a GI: Article 22.1   215

there is significant equivocation in others. The following key features of the definition all reflect the underlying compromises and invite closer consideration: (1) the sign; (2) the goods; (3) region of origin; and (4) the link between product and place.

4.1   The sign

An indication is a sign, which is the object of protection under TRIPS. Its communicative purpose is twofold. A signifier such as 'Darjeeling' must not only refer to the product, but also the place of origin.[149] During the WIPO negotiations preceding TRIPS, it was suggested that for the 'purposes of a treaty for the international protection of geographical indications, this reference should be precise and specific. The geographical indication should refer to an identifiable place or region, with precise boundaries, so as to leave no doubt as to the geographical origin of the goods in connection with which the indication is or may be used'.[150] Unlike the notion of an appellation, which relates to geographical names,[151] the indication is considered more accommodating.

[It] is generally agreed to mean the 'name' of, or a denomination referring to, a geographical area (e.g. 'St. Emilion'). The question arises whether other signs or expressions which refer to a specific geographical area should also be encompassed by [a GI ...] such as signs (e.g. a national flower), expressions (e.g. 'Tequila'), unofficial names of States, in the form of a noun or an adjective (e.g. 'Holland' or 'Dutch' as referring to the Netherlands), symbols (e.g., the Empire State building as referring to New York City) and other indirect indications which in themselves do not specifically refer, but are nonetheless understood or known to refer, to a particular geographical area.[152]

This question is usually answered in the affirmative and includes indirect indications such as Cava (sparkling wine from Spain) and Mortadella (sausages from Bologna, Italy).[153] It could also encompass three-dimensional

---

[149] Audier, *TRIPS Agreement*, 15 ('A [GI] identifies a product as originating in the territory of a member or a region or locality there').

[150] WIPO, (GEO/CE/I/2), [72].

[151] A. Kamperman Sanders, 'Incentives for Protection of Cultural Expression: Art, Trade and Geographical Indications' (2010) 13 JWIP 81, 83; I. Kireeva and B. O'Connor, 'Geographical Indications and the TRIPS Agreement: What Protection is Provided to Geographical Indications in WTO Members?' (2010) 13 JWIP 275, 279 ('Some countries only allow registration of direct geographical names – indications of geographical places, administrative districts, regions or, in exceptional cases, whole countries').

[152] WIPO, (GEO/CE/I/2), [73].

[153] For several examples, see S. Strauch and K. Arend, 'Before Articles 22–24', in P-T. Stoll, J. Busche and K. Arend (eds.), *WTO – Trade-Related Aspects of Intellectual Property Rights* (Boston 2009), 351, 354–5.

216   TRIPS today

shapes or packaging, such as the infamous 'goat's pouch' shape of the *Bocksbeutel*.[154] A broad range of signs fit within the indication category, provided they *actually function as indications* which connote products from specific places. This makes sense, since indirect GIs are only effective if the audience understands them as such. Antony Taubman reminds us of the dichotomy in international discourse, where GIs are alternatively treated as slippery signs or static, protected objects:

> [A] word that qualifies as a GI in one social or legal context may not in other contexts. Any claim for GI protection hinges, naturally, first of all on whether the term does actually meet the definition of Article 22.1, does it *indicate* at all, and if so, does it identify a good as coming from some specific location? This will depend, to large extent, on whether a universalist or objective (even 'positivist') approach is taken to the application of this interpretation, or whether greater weight is given to the subjective, and the diverse functions of language.[155]

While TRIPS suggests that a GI must signal or indicate a specific product and place in its home country, there is disagreement as to whether this requirement should be maintained as we scale up to international protection. Since the various elements of the definition and the rationale for protection are interrelated, this has consequences for the scope of protection. As we will see, Article 22 levels of protection continue to conform to the communicative paradigm, where the GI must function as an actual indication conveying meaning. With Article 23, there is pressure to abandon this paradigm and treat fluid signs like reified, fixed entities.

4.2   The goods

TRIPS is clear that the indication should 'identify a good', so the definition seems restricted to tangible articles of commerce. Part I established that there is a conventional core of agricultural products associated with GIs but this has expanded over time.

> Traditionally, the use of GIs is linked to agricultural products due to specific geographical climatic and geological conditions ... However, GIs may also highlight the specific qualities of a product due to human factors that can only be found in the place of origin of the products such as specific manufacturing

---

[154] *Criminal Proceedings against Karl Prantl* (C-16/83) [1984] ECR 1299; *Bocksbeutelflasche* [1971] GRUR 313 (BGH).

[155] A. Taubman, 'The Way Ahead: Developing International Protection for Geographical Indications: Thinking Locally, Acting Globally', November 2001 (WIPO/GEO/MVD/01/9), 7.

The definition of a GI: Article 22.1 217

skills and traditions. Therefore, inclusion of handicraft and industrial products within the scope of protection of geographical names is also justified and can be found in the legislation of a number of countries.[156]

Within the broad field of agricultural products, the majority of IGOs are associated with wines, spirits and foodstuffs. In 2001 Sergio Escudero calculated that '84.1 per cent of the 766 registrations currently in force [under the Lisbon Agreement] correspond to only four different categories of products: wines, spirits, cheese, tobacco and cigarettes. Appellations of origin for wines and spirits account for 70.9 per cent of all the international registrations in force'.[157] While the Lisbon Register is open-ended, provided the AO definition is satisfied, in light of its legislative basis, the EU register under Regulation 510/2006 is presently restricted to only certain agricultural products and foodstuffs.[158] Agricultural products include beers, flowers, essential oils, cork and wool. The EU also has a separate registration system for wines and spirits. All registered GIs in the EU can now be conveniently searched for within electronic databases.[159] Then again, for countries such as India, crafts and textiles are important and constitute around 62 per cent of applications at the time of writing.[160] TRIPS is non-prescriptive and encompasses all these goods, provided the link requirement in Article 22.1 is established.

By specifying that GIs relate to goods, the provision of services has clearly been excluded despite its presence in some of the early TRIPS draft submissions.[161] In practice this omission amounts to very little, since TRIPS merely provides a baseline and members are free to recognise and protect geographically specific services under their national

---

[156] Kireeva and O'Connor, 'Protection in WTO Members', 281.

[157] Escudero, 'International Protection and Developing Countries', 26.

[158] Art. 1(1) of Regulation 510/2006. The product classifications are found in Annex II of Commission Regulation (EC) No. 1898/2006 of 14 December 2006 Laying Down Detailed Rules of Implementation of Council Regulation (EC) No. 510/2006 [2006] OJ L 369/1.

[159] The DOORS database for agricultural products and foodstuffs contains details on product specifications and can be searched at: ec.europa.eu/agriculture/quality/index_en.htm. For wines, the E-BACCHUS database is found at: ec.europa.eu/agriculture/markets/wine/index_en.htm.

[160] These constitute 142 of the 230 applications listed in the *Indian Geographical Indications Journal*, Vol. 37, (4 January 2011). Cf. D. Marie-Vivien, 'The Role of the State in the Protection of Geographical Indications: From Disengagement in France/Europe to Significant Involvement in India' (2010) 13 JWIP 121.

[161] Communication from Switzerland, 'Standards and Principles Concerning the Availability, Scope and Use of Trade Related Intellectual Property Rights', 11 July 1989 (MTN.GNG/NG11/W/38), 5; The consolidated Anell Draft of 23 July 1990, (MTN.GNG/NG11/W/76), 14.

218   TRIPS today

regimes. Jurisdictions such as Switzerland, Estonia, Uruguay, Peru, Korea and Morocco recognise GIs for services in the hospitality, banking, financial or health and traditional healing sectors.[162] Service provision also fits within the collective trade mark rubric. The inclusion of services within national GI systems is on the one hand unsurprising, as Swiss Banking and Kerala Ayurvedic Massages have international reputations. Reputation appears to be an independent basis for satisfying the link to origin under TRIPS and today human factors are acknowledged alongside those of physical geography. Yet in previous discussions on international GI protection, the inclusion of services has proved to be contentious.[163] While a particular service may have a historic association with a place, if it depends primarily on human skills then what is to prevent skilled service providers from moving elsewhere and offering the same service? Since there is a relatively weak anchor to place – one wonders what the threshold for 'essentially attributable' to geographical origin will be in these cases – then the only basis for including services within GI protection regimes is based on the communicative rationale found in unfair competition law. Any group with a collective reputation may wish to protect it on this basis and there is little to set apart the GI from the collective mark. As opposed to professional qualifications (are the group members highly qualified bankers or highly skilled traditional healers), geography seems to be a problematic basis for defining a group of service providers, unless the link between the services and the region is clearly established. The category of services exposes fractures in the compromise between reputation based and *terroir* approaches.

4.3   Region of origin

Article 22.1 stipulates that the product must originate within the territory of a member, or a region or locality within that territory. Here there is further evidence of the different operational assumptions underpinning the reputational basis for protection, illustrated by the German and UK experiences within the unfair competition paradigm and the *terroir* approach. A question which precipitates the issue is whether the name of an entire country should qualify as a GI. At the TRIPS Council, a Jamaican delegate proposed an affirmative answer, giving the example

---

[162] Kireeva and O'Connor, 'Protection in WTO Members', 282; WTO 'Review under Article 24.2', 11.

[163] WIPO, (TAO/II/2), 8; AIPPI, 'Resolution on Q62: International Protection of Appellations of Origin and Indications of Source' [1975] *Annuaire* 137 (Report on the 29th Congress of San Francisco, 3–10 May 1975); WIPO, (GEO/CE/I/3), [47].

The definition of a GI: Article 22.1   219

of 'Swiss' for watches.[164] The Australian delegate supplemented this with 'Kenyan coffee' and 'Jamaican rum' but flagged up the paradox that the EU's Regulation 2081/92 permitted a country name to be registered as a PDO or PGI only in 'exceptional cases'.[165] This was confirmed by the delegate from New Zealand, who had been informed that 'New Zealand Chardonnay' would not qualify under EU wine appellation regulations since the area was too large.[166] Participants in these deliberations conclude that since reputation is an independent criterion, there is no reason why a country name cannot form part of a reputed GI.[167]

The question of whether an entire country name can be protected has also resurfaced in the context of GI extension debates at the TRIPS Council.[168] These exchanges are revealing since they hint at the deterministic *terroir* hangover in international GI law, based on the wine appellation protection model. Within the EU, the stipulation that country names qualify for registration only in 'exceptional cases' has been considered in the *Feta* decision. The answer suggested was that only territorially modest EU Members would qualify for this, since they might possess sufficiently homogenous geomorphology and environmental conditions as well as evenly distributed human factors.[169] For Feta itself, the production area did not extend to the whole of Greece, but was sufficiently large to be in dispute. The court was eventually convinced since domestic legislation required Feta to be produced from the milk from breeds of ewes and goats raised using traditional methods and adapted to the region of manufacture, where the flora of that region must be the basis of their feed. The features distinguishing this (otherwise expansive) region of origin were the mountainous nature of the terrain, the climate and the vegetation which the excluded areas

---

[164] TRIPS Council, 'Minutes of the Meeting on 17–19 September 2002', 8 November 2002 (IP/C/M/37/Add.1), [136].

[165] Ibid., [152].

[166] Ibid., [163]. The EU has subsequently modified its regime to allow for country names as wine appellations 'in exceptional cases'. See Art. 34 of Council Regulation (EC) No. 479/2008 of 29 April 2008 on the Common Organisation of the Market in Wine [2008] OJ L 148/1.

[167] TRIPS Council, (IP/C/M/37/Add.1), [147]. See also TRIPS Council, (IP/C/M/38), [139]; Communication from Bulgaria et al. 'The Extension of the Additional Protection for Geographical Indications to Products other than Wines and Spirits', 24 June 2002 (IP/C/W/353), [7].

[168] WTO, 'Issues Related to Extension', (TN/C/W/25), [24]–[26].

[169] See *Federal Republic of Germany and Kingdom of Denmark v. Commission of the European Communities* (C-465/02 and C-466/02) [2005] ECR I-9115; [2006] ETMR 16, [AG32]-[AG35] (AGO).

220   TRIPS today

lacked.[170] In effect, the product specification seems to have been read cumulatively with the specified geographical region to suggest discrete 'islands' of production within the larger territory, which were sufficiently homogenous.

This reluctance to embrace a national GI option is related to the suspicion that large national territories cannot share internally homogenous geographical attributes which can also be demarcated from neighbouring regions. It stems from the old *terroir* thinking associated with wine production but – as we have seen in the German and UK approaches described in Chapter 3 – it is irrelevant for the reputational basis for protection. So long as a group can be identified that should benefit from the goodwill or reputation associated with a particular product, the interest of the collective in protecting that reputation is recognised. Under unfair competition regimes, the basis for that collective goodwill or reputation need not be founded upon physical and human geography factors specific to a region. The clearest evidence for this is found in recent UK passing off decisions, confirming that all producers of vodka, defined according to production parameters such as alcohol by volume (ABV) content and not geographical origin, are entitled to protect the goodwill associated with the product. Here the proprietors of SMIRNOFF vodka could successfully prevent the manufacturer of a vodka-and-citrus based drink from marketing it as VODKAT, on the basis that it would mislead customers.[171] Where geography is a factor under unfair competition approaches, its function is to define the circle of those who can initiate proceedings under unfair competition law. Place is relevant to the extent that consumers consider it to be relevant and entire countries can unquestionably qualify.[172] Thus the reputation and *terroir* approaches to the region of origin diverge in this respect.

Having considered the size or scale of the region of origin, the other controversial issue concerns the basis for delimitation, which TRIPS leaves to national legislation to resolve. This is particularly problematic where the region in question straddles two countries. Applicants based

---

[170] *Federal Republic of Germany and Kingdom of Denmark* v. *Commission of the European Communities* (C-465/02 and C-466/02), [51]–[69] (ECJ).

[171] *Diageo North America* v. *Intercontinental Brands* [2010] EWHC 17 (Ch); Confirmed on appeal: *Diageo North America* v. *Intercontinental Brands* [2010] EWCA Civ 920 (VODKAT had an overall ABV of 22 per cent compared with the minimum 37.5 per cent required for vodka by European Regulations, which helped to establish the damaging misrepresentation).

[172] *Chocosuisse Union des Fabricants Suisses de Chocolat* v. *Cadbury Ltd* [1998] RPC 117 (Ch D); Cf. *Chocosuisse Union des Fabricants Suisses de Chocolat* v. *Cadbury Ltd* [1999] RPC 826 (CA).

The definition of a GI: Article 22.1

in both India and Pakistan have faced considerable difficulty in trying to draw up the specifications for Basmati rice.[173] Apart from these trans-border GIs, in national legislation referring to defined geographical units the 'terms employed often involve political and administrative boundaries, but also non-political geographical areas'. The latter category is associated with products of the vine and frequently refers to vineyard sites or viticultural zones.[174] Once again wine is the standard point of reference. 'The criteria for delimiting non-political geographic areas, a practice most frequently conducted in the context of wine production, was found to aim at establishing the homogeneity of a production area and its distinctiveness as compared to other such areas'.[175] A WIPO study states that standard criteria include natural features (rivers, contour lines); geographical characteristics (soil drainage, climate, elevation); human influences (choice of plant variety, method of production); historical associations and economic considerations (equivalence of yield).[176] Consequently for agricultural products which fit the parameters of the wine appellation model, the understanding is that 'the place or region ... must be defined as a geographical environment with specific natural and human factors and which is capable of giving an agricultural product or foodstuff its specific characteristics. The area of origin referred to must, therefore, present homogenous natural factors which distinguish it from the areas adjoining it'.[177]

However, this algorithm is of limited assistance when it comes to products with a more fluid or socio-economic link with the region of origin. Here certain textiles, crafts and recipe-based products come to mind. What are the benchmarks for demarcation in such cases? Some systems such as the Indian GI Registry bypass the problem for crafts by adopting contemporary administrative boundaries for the entire state (federal unit) or administrative sub-unit within which production is located, without any further attempt to narrow down the region.[178] The obvious downside is that this large administrative region bears little correlation with historic patterns of production and an associated place. An alternative is to rely on consumer perception – where do customers expect the product to come from? Quite understandably, this approach

---

[173] H. V. Chandola, 'Basmati Rice: Geographical Indication or Mis-Indication' (2006) 9 JWIP 166, 173–4; D. Marie-Vivien, 'From Plant Variety Definition to Geographical Indication Protection: A Search for the Link Between Basmati Rice and India/Pakistan' (2008) 11 JWIP 321.

[174] WIPO, (SCT/9/4), [16].   [175] Ibid., [19].   [176] Ibid., [20].

[177] *Federal Republic of Germany and Kingdom of Denmark v. Commission of the European Community* (C-465/02 and C-466/02), [50].

[178] I am grateful to Delphine Marie-Vivien for this point.

222   TRIPS today

rarely generates a sufficiently high resolution map of the region, while leading to further complications. For craft or recipe based products, the degree of public perception and associated reputation will have fluctuated over the history of production. The difficulty is compounded by the strategic positioning associated with drawing boundaries. A perception based approach can help when gauging whether customers expect Swiss chocolate to come from Switzerland, but cannot aid us where one producer located 5 km away from another falls outside the boundary. At this stage, certain producers may seek to exclude competitors and draft boundary demarcations to achieve this.[179]

In such disputes, without soil or micro-climatic homogeneity to resort to, what kinds of evidence ought to suffice? Can history help to draw boundaries in the place of geography? In the EU system for PGI registration, one finds references to historical sources relating not only to the establishment of a product's reputation over time but also the boundaries of production, where techniques develop in response to prevalent climatic or socio-economic conditions. The following sources have been considered relevant in associating products with defined regions: (1) customs and revenue records; (2) literary references; (3) local histories; (4) newspaper archives and advertisements; (5) trade publications and journals; (6) sales invoices; (7) records of festivals which celebrate a local product; and (8) established channels of transport to markets, such as railways, highways and rivers.[180] A recent guide endorses this approach:

The history of the product is important to consider when defining the production area, as it can evolve over time (it can expand and shrink), according to economic cycles and trade conditions. It can be useful to define the 'minimum' area of production where production has always been maintained, as it possesses the optimal conditions that will serve to select the criteria for the GI area's delimitation. Indeed, the delimitation could partly

---

[179] Two disputes where this issue has arisen are: (1) *Northern Foods Plc* v. *DEFRA, Melton Mowbray Pork Pie Association* [2005] EWHC 2971 (Admin); On appeal: *R (on the application of Northern Foods Plc)* v. *Secretary of State for the Environment, Food and Rural Affairs* [2006] EWCA Civ 337 (Melton Mowbray Pork Pie); (2) *Molkerei Grossbraunshain & Ors* v. *Commission of the European Communities* (C-447/98 P) [2002] ETMR 55 (Altenberger cheese). For more detailed analysis of the historical factors considered relevant in drawing up boundaries, see D. Gangjee, '*Melton Mowbray* and the GI Pie in the Sky: Exploring Cartographies of Protection' (2006) 3 IPQ 291.

[180] These categories of evidence inform the following product specifications, all of which can be retrieved via the DOORS database: Chouriço de Abóbora de Barroso – Montalegre sausages; Mantequilla de Soria butter; Limone Femminello del Gargano; Melton Mowbray pork pies; Geraardsbergen Matten tarts.

The definition of a GI: Article 22.1   223

differ from the present location of production, depending on how the potential for production is taken into consideration.[181]

A final point concerns the nature of inputs from this geographical region. The text of Article 22.1 does not refer to natural and/or human factors, although it had appeared in early drafts.[182] It is left to the discretion of Members to recognise human factors and most do so, although this does not seem to be an essential requirement.[183] The significance of human intervention and innovation was emphasised in Chapter 3, in the context of the French appellation system. Laurence Bérard and Philippe Marchenay remind us that certain regional products are closely linked to socio-economic practices:

French cheeses such as *Comté* and *Abondance*, for example, bring to mind specific cheese-making practices and a particular agro-pastoral system built on livestock farming and the social organization required by a given natural environment. *Charolais* beef defines the landscape and economy of an entire region. Much appreciated for its flavour, the meat relies on a form of animal husbandry that combines subtle grazing management with skilful selection, fattening and growth-monitoring.[184]

As a result, there is a case to be made for requiring as a necessary precondition *that all GIs must demonstrate at least some degree of human intervention and collective know-how,* which in turn supports certain emerging justifications for protection.

4.4   The link between product and place

A GI is a sign which indicates that 'a given quality, reputation or other characteristic of the good is essentially attributable to its geographical origin'. Why are there three alternative criteria to link product to place? What does each consist of? And when is each of these 'essentially attributable' to geographical origin? An obvious starting point is the drafting history of Article 22.1, where a helpful resource is the

---

[181] FAO and SINER-GI, *Linking People, Places and Products: A Guide for Promoting Quality Linked to Geographical Origin and Sustainable Geographical Indications*, 2nd edn (FAO, Rome 2009–10), 61.

[182] E.g., GATT, 'Guidelines and Objectives Proposed by the EC', 7 July 1988 (MTN. GNG/NG11/W/26).

[183] WTO, 'Review under Article 24.2', [44] ('Some ... have highlighted the relevance of human factors to matters such as quality, traditional methods of production, vinicultural practices and methods of production, preparation and cultivation. Some, however, have also indicated that no specific level of human creativity is called for and the contribution of human factors is not essential').

[184] L. Bérard and P. Marchenay, *From Localized Products to Geographical Indications: Awareness and Action* (CNRS, Bourg-en-Bresse 2008), 9.

224   TRIPS today

Secretariat's synoptic table of proposals accumulated by early 1990.[185] The European Community's proposed definition closely resembles the final TRIPS version, with the addition of 'geographical origin, including natural and human factors'. It is worth noting that, unlike the Lisbon AO, TRIPS contains the additional 'reputation' option and the less onerous form of linkage ('essentially attributable to its geographical origin'). The only other proposed definition is the broader Swiss one, where GIs are classified as simple geographical origin indicating signs, along the lines of the IS. We have already witnessed the emergence of the EC definition during the contemporaneous WIPO negotiations, but to what does it owe its inspiration? Much hinges on this question. With this more flexible definition, certain Southern European countries have deviated from a trajectory with considerable momentum behind it, fuelled by the argument that certain products deserve special treatment on the basis that their qualities are distinctively or even uniquely derived from identifiable regions. Article 22.1 gives equal recognition to products which merely have a reputation for being produced in a certain place. Does this development have the potential to displace wine as the archetype for GIs? One might assume that this was a concession designed to ameliorate the concerns of GI sceptics such as the US and Australia. This establishes common ground by including certification and collective marks within the GI definition. These were, after all, established categories of marks and potential vectors for the protection of a collectively sustained reputation. However, a more compelling answer is proposed here. Instead of being crafted to bridge a trans-Atlantic divide, the origins of this European proposal can be traced to an internecine dispute between European neighbours. There is evidence to suggest that it was designed to reconcile differences between the French and German approaches to IGO protection, previously reviewed in Chapter 3. The traces of this compromise are found within the drafting history of Regulation 2081/92.[186]

Regulation 2081/92, along with its successor Regulation 510/2006,

---

[185] See GATT, 'Synoptic Tables Setting Out Existing International Standards and Proposed Standards and Principles', 2 February 1990 (MTN.GNG/NG11/W/32/Rev.2), 68–9.

[186] Council Regulation 2081/92 of 14 July 1992 on the Protection of Geographical Indications and Designations of Origin for Agricultural Products and Foodstuffs [1992] OJ L 208/1 (Regulation 2081/92). In light of a recent WTO Panel Ruling, several amendments have been carried out and it has arisen, phoenix-like, as the similarly titled Council Regulation 510/2006 of 20 March 2006 [2006] OJ L 93/12 (Regulation 510/2006).

The definition of a GI: Article 22.1 225

seeks to establish a framework of Community rules for the protection of registered designations of origin and geographical indications relating to certain agricultural products and foodstuffs in cases where there is a link between the characteristics of the product or foodstuff and its geographical origin. That regulation provides for a system of registration at Community level of geographical indications and designations of origin which will confer protection in every Member State.[187]

It is directed towards the improvement of the agricultural product quality, as well as the protection of consumer and producer interests by preventing unfair competition.[188] This registration system was finalised by 1992, around the time TRIPS was also assuming its present form. Intriguingly, it contained two alternative definitions of subject matter. Protected Designations of Origin (PDOs) and Protected Geographical Indications (PGIs) were defined in Article 2 as follows:

(a) designation of origin: means the name of a region, a specific place or, in exceptional cases, a country, used to describe an agricultural product or a foodstuff:
  – originating in that region, specific place or country, and
  – the *quality or characteristics* of which are *essentially or exclusively due* to a particular geographical environment with its inherent natural and human factors, and the *production, processing and preparation* of which take place in the defined geographical area (emphasis added).
(b) geographical indication: means the name of a region, a specific place or, in exceptional cases, a country, used to describe an agricultural product or a foodstuff:
  – originating in that region, specific place or country, and
  – which possesses a specific *quality, reputation or other characteristics attributable to* that geographical origin and the *production and/or processing and/or preparation* of which take place in the defined geographical area (emphasis added).

While a PGI link may be based on a reputation attributable to its region of origin, a PDO requires the qualities or characteristics of the product to be essentially or exclusively attributable to its place of origin. Additionally, for the PDO, the production, processing and preparation all have to take place in the defined region, whereas any one of them will

---

[187] *Bayerischer Brauerbund eV* v. *Bavaria NV* (C-120/08) [2011] ETMR 11, [AG6] (AG Mazák).
[188] See Recitals 1–6 of each Regulation.

226   TRIPS today

satisfy the PGI requirement. Effectively, the link between a product and its place of origin is stronger in the case of a PDO.[189] As Lord Hoffmann puts it, for a PGI 'the causal link between the place of origin and the quality of the product may be a matter of reputation rather than verifiable fact'.[190] However, both species of GIs enjoy the same expansive scope of protection under Regulation 2081/92.[191] An explanation for this puzzle of two entry points into the same system emerges from the Regulation's drafting history. Recent accounts of international GI protection depict Europe as its champion, exhorting in a unified voice for improved standards, as the 'protection of geographical indications constitutes an area of intellectual property rights, which is, both for historical and economic reasons, of particular importance for the European Community and its Member states'.[192] Yet a shared vision was not always the case. Amidst current TRIPS controversies, the European divide that was bridged relatively recently, appears to have faded from memory.

The PDO is better appreciated as a marginally refracted version of the French AOC,[193] while the reputation option within the PGI seems to be a nod towards the qualified indication of source, recognised by German unfair competition law. Through the 1970s and 1980s, it appears that only the former was recognised as a legitimate category by the ECJ.

---

[189] As confirmed by the European Commission, in its First Written Submission before a WTO Dispute Settlement Panel. See Annex B, Report of the WTO Panel: European Communities – Protection of Trademarks and Geographical Indications for Agricultural Products and Foodstuffs, 15 March 2005 (WT/DS174/R/Add.2), B-34, [46].

[190] *Consorzio del Prosciutto di Parma* v. *Asda Stores Limited and Others* [2001] UKHL 7; [2002] FSR 3 at [8].

[191] Described in Article 13(1) as:
  (a) any direct or indirect commercial use of a name registered in respect of products not covered by the registration in so far as those products are comparable to the products registered under that name or insofar as using the name exploits the reputation of the protected name;
  (b) any misuse, imitation or evocation, even if the true origin of the product is indicated or if the protected name is translated or accompanied by an expression such as 'style', 'type', 'method', 'as produced in', 'imitation' or similar;
  (c) any other false or misleading indication as to the provenance, origin, nature or essential qualities of the product, on the inner or outer packaging, advertising material or documents relating to the product concerned, and the packing of the product in a container liable to convey a false impression as to its origin;
  (d) any other practice liable to mislead the public as to the true origin of the product.

[192] Audier, *TRIPS Agreement*, 2. See also the summary of the EU's position in current WTO debates available at www.wto.int/english/tratop_e/trips_e/gi_background_e.htm.

[193] J. Audier, 'Protection of Geographical Indications in France and Protection of French Geographical Indications in Other Countries', October 1997 (WIPO/GEO/EGR/97/8 Rev), 2.

The definition of a GI: Article 22.1

During this period, the case law reveals traces of a suspicion of labelling regimes protecting simple indications of source, which could have operated as disguised restrictions on the free movement of goods within the common market.[194] The AOC, with its purportedly objective link between origin and quality, provided an acceptable basis for prohibiting the use of appellations by those outside the designated regions. It would take several years before the Court acknowledged the protection of a valuable reputation, alongside the prevention of unfair competition, as an alternative basis for restricting the use of geographical designations. Two prominent decisions of the ECJ bracket this transition. In the *Sekt/Weinbrand* decision,[195] the validity of German legislation which restricted the use of certain wine designations was challenged. It reserved the designations 'Sekt' and 'Weinbrand' to domestic products and the appellation 'Praedikatssekt' to wines produced in Germany from a fixed minimum proportion of German grapes. The law further prescribed that imported sparkling wine and wine brandy not in compliance with the requisite conditions for the protected appellations had to use different terminology ('Schaumwein' and 'Branntwein aus Wein'). The European Commission queried the law's compatibility with the former Article 28 (now Article 34 of the Treaty on the Functioning of the European Union (TFEU)) claiming that the legislation, by reclassifying generic terms as indirect IGOs, favoured domestic production and operated as a measure equivalent to a quantitative restriction on imports. Germany responded with the argument that these restrictions were justified on the basis of protecting consumers and legitimate producers against unfair competition, as a permissible exception to Article 28 contained in Article 30 (now Article 36 TFEU). While dismissing the German argument, the Court made the following observation:

These [wine] appellations only fulfil their specific purpose [i.e. to safeguard producers against unfair competition and prevent consumers being misled] if the product which they describe does in fact possess qualities and characteristics which are due to the fact that it originated in a specific geographical area.

---

[194] IGOs indicating national territories, but without any objectively verifiable basis for selecting such a large territory, may be masquerading as campaigns to appeal to patriotic buying. The ECJ has in the past given such legal regimes short shrift where they encourage consumers to buy solely on the basis of national origin and classified them as unacceptable restrictions upon the free movement of goods. See, e.g., *Commission of the European Communities* v. *Ireland* (C-249/81) [1982] ECR 4005 ('Buy Irish'); *Apple and Pear Development Council* v. *KJ Lewis Ltd* (C-222/82) [1983] ECR 4083 (English apples and pears).

[195] *Commission of the European Communities* v. *Federal Republic of Germany* (C-12/74) [1975] ECR 181.

228   TRIPS today

As regards indications of origin in particular, *the geographical area of origin* of a product *must confer on it a specific quality and specific characteristics* of such a nature as to *distinguish it from all other products* (emphasis added).[196]

Since this qualitative link was not invoked, restrictions on these terms were found to violate Germany's obligations under the EEC Treaty and prevailing Community provisions on wine labelling. The outcome of the decision was not considered objectionable. Such expressions were arguably generic at the time, so in trying to artificially impose a specific geographical meaning the contested legislation was vulnerable on this ground alone.

However, the reasoning applied in reaching this decision proved divisive. The controversy stemmed from the ECJ's suggestion that reputation-based indications of source did not fall within the limited exceptions to the free movement of goods principle. The AO appeared to be the only legitimate species of IGO worthy of shelter under the exceptions, prompting forceful critiques of the decision.[197] A measure of their potency is the outcome in the ECJ's subsequent *Exportur* decision.[198] Here, the question was whether the Spanish geographical designations 'Touron Alicante' and 'Touron Jijona' could be used on nougat confectionery produced in France. These were reserved IGOs under a Franco-Spanish Treaty, notwithstanding the absence of an objective or *terroir*-based link. The court held that, despite this, indications of provenance 'may nevertheless enjoy a high reputation amongst consumers and constitute for producers established in the places to which they refer an essential means of attracting custom. They are therefore entitled to protection'.[199] Celebrating this vindication of the reputational basis for GI protection, Professor Beier argued that a version of Regulation 2081/92, then only recently implemented, which represented the AO ideal alone would have been a 'monstrosity'.[200]

While this eventual judicial recognition of both *terroir* and reputation approaches provides the backdrop, there is ample evidence that Regulation 2081/92 institutionalises this compromise. It fuses together these distinct approaches within a common framework, premised upon registration-based legal recognition. The text begins with the concession

---

[196] Ibid., [7].

[197] See, for e.g., D. Wyatt, 'Free Movement of Goods and Indications of Origin' (1975) 38 *Modern Law Review* 679; F-K Beier, 'The Need for Protection of Indications of Source and Appellations of Origin in the Common Market: The Sekt/Weinbrand Decision of the ECJ' [1977] *Industrial Property* 152.

[198] *Exportur SA v. LOR SA and Confiserie du Tech SA* (C-3/91) [1992] ECR I-5529.

[199] Ibid., [28].

[200] F-K Beier, 'Case Comment: Court of Justice - Case No. C-3/91 "Turron"' [1994] IIC 73, 81.

The definition of a GI: Article 22.1 229

that 'existing practices make it appropriate to define two different types of geographical description, namely protected geographical indications and protected designations of origin'.[201] The existence of two different types of GIs attests to the underlying fissures and factionalism in the run up to the Regulation. Writing at the time of its enactment, one commentator noted that on '14 July 1992, contrary to common belief and indeed much to general amazement, the EC Regulations on the "protection of designations of geographical origin" ... were passed by the European Council despite the number of disputed issues which remained unresolved until the last moment'.[202] The initial French memorandum submitted in 1988 was restricted to designations of origin, along the lines of the AO, which was subsequently supported by Italy and Spain.[203] However, the draft text of the Commission's proposed Regulation contained references to both PGIs and PDOs.[204] The influence of the AO model remains visible in the Opinion of the Economic and Social Committee, which reveals *terroir* glimpses at crucial junctures. Thus, while acknowledging the importance of protecting a product's reputation, the Committee noted that the 'special characteristics of the food involved derive from their origin, soil conditions, geographical and climatic environment, the varieties and species used, and the way they are prepared or produced. It is these factors which give the product its name and reputation in the marketplace'.[205]

During this phase, the drafting process involved negotiations between two competing Northern and Southern groups. Marina Kolia observes that when the proposals reached the European parliament in September 1991, GI protection was again restricted to PDOs and 'the applicants were required to produce convincing evidence that the product's characteristics were essentially due to the geographical origin'.[206]

---

[201] Recital 10.

[202] M. Kolia, 'Monopolizing Names of Foodstuffs: The New Legislation' (1992) EIPR 333.

[203] Vital, 'Protection of Geographical Indications: The Approach of the European Union,' 2. For an excellent general background, see O. Brouwer, 'Community Protection of Geographical Indications and Specific Character as a Means of Enhancing Foodstuff Quality' (1991) 28 *Common Market Law Review* 615.

[204] Proposal for a Council Regulation (EEC) on the Protection of Geographical Indications and Designations of Origin for Agricultural Products and Foodstuffs (SEC (90) 2415 final; 6 February1991) [1991] OJ C30/9; as amended by (COM (92) 32 final; 18 March1992) [1992] OJ C69/15.

[205] Opinion on the proposal for a Council Regulation (EEC) on the Protection of Geographical Indications and Designations of Origin for Agricultural Products and Foodstuffs [1991] OJ C269/62, [1.2].

[206] M. Kolia, 'Monopolising Names: EEC Proposals on the Protection of Trade Descriptions of Foodstuffs' [1992] EIPR 233, 235.

230 TRIPS today

The European Parliament did not accept the proposal in this form and the draft Regulation returned to the Commission, where it was further debated. At this stage, Germany began 'to promote the idea of a very broad category under which all geographical names would be mutually recognised'.[207] When faced with this option of a single broad definition, negotiators revived the alternative option of the PGI. An acceptable compromise was arrived at in the form of two distinct pathways into registration and the crisis was averted. Yet vestigial unease lingered around the formal requirements of the new registration system, with one scholar noting that 'the specification features appeared to be the greatest obstacle to the protection of German geographical indications'.[208] Rules governing product specifications are usually designed around wine appellation models. Fitting reputational GIs within these parameters could prove awkward. Roland Knaak goes on to note that 'German geographical indications of source, such as "Lübeck marzipan", "Aachener Printen" or "Munich beer", which are considered as so-called simple geographical indications of source under German law, have in the meantime been registered pursuant to the Regulation. This practice on the part of the Commission has defused many conflicts'.[209] This alternative route is now well established, with the ECJ recently confirming that a purely reputational link is a satisfactory basis for PGI recognition.[210]

The delicate state of equilibrium that resolved these intra-European disagreements would prove influential in shaping the TRIPS definition. The Commission's draft for Regulation 2081, containing both the PDO and PGI, specifically notes that:

[It] also broadly reflects the position which the Community has defended in the international negotiations on intellectual property in GATT.

In the Uruguay Round negotiating group on intellectual property, the Community proposed a definition of, and appropriate protection for, geographical indications, including designations of origin, which the Commission has taken into account.[211]

---

[207] Ibid., 235–6.
[208] R. Knaak, 'Case Law of the European Court of Justice on the Protection of Geographical Indications and Designations of Origin Pursuant to EC Regulation No.2081/92' [2001] IIC 375, 378.
[209] Ibid.
[210] *Bavaria NV, Bavaria Italia Srl* v. *Bayerischer Brauerbund eV* (C-343/07) [2009] ECR I-5491; [2009] ETMR 61, [95]–[98].
[211] Proposal for a Council Regulation on the Protection of Geographical Indications, [9]–[10].

This provides us with the final piece of the puzzle and accounts for the twin strands within the TRIPS definition. The internal compromise between the German (communicative logic premised on the reputation link) and French (*terroir* logic premised on a qualitative link) approaches went on to inform the Community position during the Uruguay Round, while the EC was the driving force behind the GI provisions in TRIPS. This 'fusion' definition was also acceptable to countries that recognised a shared interest in reputation within trade mark law, via certification or collective marks. The consequences of this compromise have not yet been fully appreciated. The hasty amalgamation of two different logics of GI protection has repercussions at a number of levels. On the one hand, reputation protection per se has always been a part of the international IGO protection discourse. Part I of this book reveals that from the inception of international regimes in this area it was the motivation for developing IS rules. On the other hand, AOs have conventionally been set apart by the notion of a causal connection between the quality of the referent product and its place of origin. Therefore the AO definition in Article 2 of the Lisbon Agreement acknowledges that while a product's reputation may arise as a consequence of this link, the *causal link* between place and product quality is *the basis for recognition and protection*. Under TRIPS, a collectively generated *reputation becomes the basis for both recognition and protection*. Where this is likely to generate dissonances is in the requirement that a GI product's quality, characteristics or reputation is 'essentially attributable' to the place of origin.

Let us ease into this aspect, beginning with the seemingly objective connection between artefact and place, where a product's qualities or characteristics are essentially attributable to geographical origin. The drafting history of the Agreement is of little assistance. At the time of its formation there was limited experience in the interpretation or application of a link requirement at the multilateral level.[212] However, subsequent practice within the TRIPS membership is indicative, especially where *sui generis* systems utilise similar definitions and an overlapping consensus has emerged in some jurisdictions. It should be emphasised that the following paragraphs containing a descriptive account of existing practice need not be read as a normative steer, but they do illustrate the operationalisation of TRIPS language. Since Article 22.1

---

[212] R. Knaak, 'The Protection of Geographical Indications According to the TRIPS Agreement', in F-K. Beier and G. Schricker (eds.), *From GATT to TRIPS – The Agreement on Trade Related Aspects of Intellectual Property Rights*, 11C Studies, Vol. 18 (Weinheim, New York 1996), 117, 128. For experiences under the Lisbon Agreement, see Chapter 4.

refers to 'quality ... or other characteristic' there is a tendency to consider these criteria together. There is broad agreement that quality should be empirically verifiable. 'The notion of "quality" would encompass physical characteristics of the good, that is, attributes of the good that can be objectively measured'.[213] One helpful resource addressing these criteria is an applicant's guide published by France's INAO. As opposed to superior product quality, it suggests that 'the focus must be on a specific quality which differentiates the GI product from others. It must present a different quality, linked to the geographical origin (soil, climate, etc.)'.[214] This distinguishing quality should be clearly related to geographical origin, so it suggests as illustrations the colour of meat due to characteristic local animal feeds, a locally adapted plant variety or race, or particular soil or climatic features giving a product unique shape or taste. As for characteristics, Article 4(2)(b) of Regulation 510/2006, which refers to the product specification documentation, also refers to 'principal physical, chemical, microbiological or organoleptic characteristics of the product or the foodstuff'. In a similar vein, the INAO guide expands on characteristics to suggest that 'an *objective definition* can be given of the various components of the product, such as the colour, shape, texture, composition, aromas, taste, etc. For transformed products, this definition is based in part on the agricultural raw material and in part on the product after the transformation'.[215] This broader ambit includes distinctive know-how such as that relating to breeding methods or crop cycles. Characteristics would therefore include not only physical, chemical, microbiological or organoleptic product features, but also specific know-how such as cultural practices associated with livestock rearing or techniques associated with the manufacturing process. Occasionally, both requirements are combined, with references to 'characteristic qualities' or other such blended usage which blurs the boundary between the two.[216] In summation, in accordance with *terroir* logic, 'quality ... or other characteristic' is interpreted as relating to empirically verifiable aspects of the product or know-how associated with its production, which is causally related to geographical origin and which distinguishes the product in question – sometimes referred to as

---

[213] UNCTAD-ICTSD Resource Book on TRIPS, 290.

[214] INAO, 'GI Applicants' Guide' (7 October 2005), 18–19, available at www.inao.gouv.fr.

[215] Ibid., 9–10. See also Correa, *Commentary on TRIPS*, 220 (Other characteristics 'may include, for instance, taste, texture, design, appearance etc. of the goods').

[216] WIPO, *Draft Model Law for Developing Countries* (TAO/I/ INF.l), 34–40; INAO, 'Guide du Demandeur IGP – Version 2 de Février 2009', 23–24, available at www.inao.gouv.fr.

The definition of a GI: Article 22.1

specificity or typicity[217] – from others in the same general category. Various methods exist to verify this typicity, such as taste testing (e.g., classifying roasted coffee or wines) and laboratory analysis to identify chemical markers (e.g., tracing oils associated with cosmetics or cheese).[218]

Here 'essentially attributable' is clearly understood as requiring a causal connection between product quality or other distinctive features and the region of origin. As an EU Guide to PDOs and PGIs puts it: 'The link must provide an explanation of why a product is linked to one area, and not another, i.e. how far the final product is affected by the characteristics of the region in which it is produced'.[219] Regulation 607/2009,[220] which lays down detailed rules regulating the EU's wine sector designations of origin and geographical indications, illustrates this requirement. According to Articles 7(2)(c) and 7(3)(c), the product specification shall set out 'a description of the causal interaction between the' geographical area, including natural and human factors on the one hand, and details of the quality, characteristic or reputation of the product on the other. Another report notes that for 'a PGI product [defined in terms similar to TRIPS], the link with the geographical area ... has to be causal. In this sense, it is sufficient that the features or the reputation of the product are "attributable" to the geographic origin'.[221] But beyond a causal connection, should 'essentially attributable' have further prescriptive content? The notion of an 'essence' might be read as relating

---

[217] Bérard and Marchenay, *From Localized Products to Geographical Indications*, 5–6 (For such products, their 'typicity comes from the manner in which they are rooted in a particular locality and therefore culture. Historical depth, skills, knowledge, food habits and heritage are potential levers for their promotion').

[218] S. Reviron, E. Thevenod–Mottet and N. El Benni, 'Geographical Indications: Creation and Distribution of Economic Value in Developing Countries', NCCR Working Paper No 2009/14 (March 2009), 6. Cf. L. Bertozzi, 'Designation of Origin: Quality and Specification' (1995) 6 *Food Quality and Preference* 143, 145–6 (describing the formation of peptides, free amino acids and the products of their catabolism during the aging process for cheeses, which are then subject to chemometric models of analysis used to distinguish on the basis of typicality and safeguard quality); D. M. A. M. Luykx and S. M. van Ruth, 'An Overview of Analytical Methods for Determining the Geographical Origin of Food Products' (2008) 107 *Food Chemistry* 897.

[219] European Commission, Protection of Geographical Indications of Origin, Designations of Origin and Certificates of Special Character for Agricultural Products and Foodstuffs: Guide to Community Regulations 2nd edn (2004), 13.

[220] Commission Regulation (EC) No 607/2009 of 14 July 2009 Laying Down Certain Detailed Rules for the Implementation of Council Regulation (EC) No 479/2008 as regards Protected Designations of Origin and Geographical Indications, Traditional Terms, Labelling and Presentation of Certain Wine Sector Products [2009] OJ L 193/60.

[221] London Economics et al., Evaluation of the CAP Policy, 3.

234   TRIPS today

to the strength of the link between product and place.[222] Bearing in mind the EC's deliberate loosening of the link to achieve a satisfactory compromise during the Uruguay Round, an alternative reading is preferred. Carlos Correa suggests that 'essentially' may be 'understood as implying that the production of the relevant goods may partially take place outside the designated territory',[223] i.e. the product should largely or substantially originate in the region. So long as the essential or important aspects are attributable to the region in question, other aspects, such as raw material sourcing, some preparation or processing, might take place outside the region, as is the case with the EU PGI. This brings valuable flexibility to the definition while reflecting existing practice for many regional products, where certain raw materials are extraneously sourced.[224] The acknowledgment of the porosity of place also cautions us against deterministic or hermetic approaches to *terroir*. A final danger worth flagging up is the temptation to read in a loose understanding of uniqueness at this stage of causal attribution. One comes across the insistence that, for registered GIs in the EU, 'the specification must show how the characteristics of a particular region *affect a product in a way that other regions cannot*' (emphasis added).[225] In a similar vein, it is claimed that 'GIs are associated with *unique products* that embody rich cultures and history' and a 'GI confirms a link not only between a product and a specific geographic region, but usually also with *unique production methods, characteristics or qualities* that are known to exist in the region' (emphasis added).[226] Experience with the Lisbon Agreement reveals the risk associated with such loose usage. If proponents claim that GI products are literally unique, in the sense of being irreproducible elsewhere with the same fidelity, such a claim is difficult to substantiate as a matter of evidence. If this were to become a threshold requirement as part of a future international register, how would the

---

[222] See, e.g., Audier, 'Protection of Geographical Indications in France', 3 ('The link between agricultural products and foodstuffs, the goods and their originating place can be understood in different ways. The stronger the technical, historical, cultural and social link is, the more the producers will demand an efficient protection of the geographical name used to designate the product'); D. Gervais, 'The Lisbon Agreement's Misunderstood Potential' (2009) 1 *WIPO Journal* 87, 93.

[223] Correa, *Commentary on TRIPS*, 218.

[224] Two examples of EU PGIs will suffice: Spanish Sobrasada sausages of Mallorca (where the pigs are sourced from outside the region) and German Lubecker Marzipan (where almonds are sourced from outside the region).

[225] CEC, *Fact Sheet: European Policy for Quality Agricultural Products* (Luxembourg 2006) 11.

[226] Giovanucci et al., *Guide to Geographical Indications*, 1, 7.

The definition of a GI: Article 22.1

applicant prove this uniqueness? Is this viable, given the increasing sophistication of mimetic technologies?[227] Alternatively, are GI proponents claiming that it is the historic emergence of a GI product associated with a particular region – the origin stories and the socio-economic conditions of production – that is unique? Is it a reminder to pay heed to the terms of commodification for such regional products, which do circulate in the market but where the historical circumstances and location of the labour add layers to the valorisation process? Despite these outstanding issues, in practice there seems to be an overlapping consensus as regards the *terroir*-inspired link of quality and/or characteristics being essentially attributable to place.

By contrast, the requirement that a product's reputation is essentially attributable to origin remains largely unexplored. Under the national unfair competition approaches, all that is required by way of legal recognition is that a product sold under a geographical designation has an existing reputation in the marketplace, based on an assessment of consumer and trade perception. The difference in TRIPS is that reputation must somehow be anchored in or essentially attributable to place. The reputation link is usually engaged for products where the human skills are predominant.[228] In practice, it is often relied upon for textiles, toys, crafts and recipe-based products. Once again the INAO guide is a helpful starting point. It refers to three elements: the product's history, its past reputation and contemporary reputation, which may be local, national or international.[229] As part of the exploration of a product's historic origins and past reputation, socio-economic circumstances coupled with cultural practices are associated with region-specific production. This is considered relevant for the 'essentially attributable' causal link. The PGI specification for Germany's Dresdner Stollen fruit loaves and cakes helps demonstrate this, through the special dispensation which was granted for the production of cakes rich in butter.

In a document dating from 1530 and now in Dresden's city archives, 'Stollen' is referred to as 'Christstollen'. The 'butter letter' sent by Pope Innocent VIII . . . in 1490 has become particularly famous. In that letter, the 1450 ban on baking with butter during Advent (a period of fasting at the time) was lifted by papal decree for

---

[227] B. Beebe, 'Intellectual Property and the Sumptuary Code' (2010) 123 *Harvard Law Review* 809, 870 ('The problem, however, is that mimetic technology can now persuasively – and legally – simulate the material characteristics of most geographically and historically authentic goods, with the result that these material characteristics no longer reliably signal authenticity. Having lost control over the production of material signals of authenticity, traditional producers have therefore turned to . . . [GIs] to establish legal control over the production of *immaterial* signals of authenticity').

[228] UNCTAD-ICTSD, Resource Book on TRIPs, 290–1.

[229] INAO, *GI Applicants' Guide*, 18–19.

236   TRIPS today

Dresden's bakers. From 1727, 'Dresdner Stollen' was served during the Christmas period at the Saxon court of Augustus the Strong who in 1730 had Dresden's bakers bake a giant 'Stollen' weighing 1.8 tonnes for the 24 000 guests at the Zeithainer Lustlager military display. Since then, the bakers and pastry-makers in the geographical area have continually kept alive and supervised the tradition of high-quality 'Stollen' making – traditional recipes (some of them going back to the Middle Ages) are passed on within the individual businesses.[230]

Or consider the Melton Mowbray pork pie, where the enclosure of common land led to the use of hedges to delineate property entitlements. The hedges proved enticing for those of the vulpine persuasion, leading to regular fox hunting and the demand for a substantial snack which was convenient to consume for hunters on the move.[231] In other cases, the reputation link rests on skills and techniques which have developed in response to physical geography and climatic conditions, making it easier to connect the reputation to a region. Portugal's PGI for 'Alheira de Barroso – Montalegre' sausages provides us with an example. Here the Barosso region was relatively isolated, so the diet was limited to local produce coupled with a need for developing effective preservation techniques. 'The preparation of [these sausages made from indigenous breeds of pig] is the result of, and is very dependent on, the region's cold and dry climate, which forces every household to keep a fire burning at all times, thus providing unique conditions for smoking, characterised by a light and gradual smoke supply'.[232]

Building further on these insights, Bérard and Marchenay argue that *the common denominator for all GI products* is 'historical depth and shared know-how', allowing them to maintain a specific relationship with place and be considered as a distinct category.[233] They emphasise the relative importance of *savoir faire* or collectively developed and sustained skills. In their view, the notion of a place-based community collectively generating and transmitting knowledge of a particular method of production is a key aspect of *terroir*.[234] The product's history must therefore reflect this:

A product's historical depth is often seen as an abstract entity that may, where necessary, be detached from contemporary reality. In fact, historical rooting entails an identification of the skills and practices that have been developed and transmitted by successive generations. Historical depth must be linked to the collective know-how that has been passed down to the present generation – bearing in mind that the

---

[230] Dossier No. DE/PGI/0005/0704; Registered on 27/11/2010. All Dossiers can be accessed via the EU DOORS Database.

[231] Gangjee, 'Melton Mowbray and the GI Pie in the Sky'.

[232] Dossier No. PT/PGI/0005/0237; Registered on 16/02/2007.

[233] Bérard and Marchenay, *From Localized Products to Geographical Indications*, 9–10.

[234] Ibid., 17–18.

The scope of protection 237

transmission of know-how does not rule out evolution. Otherwise, history threatens to serve as a means of justifying would-be heritage products on the basis of a place's reputation – not on the specific qualities of the product concerned. Location within a historic territory area, for instance, does not entitle [GIs] to extend their boundaries unless justified by specific, up-to-date product know-how. In the event of a rupture between place and know-how, each case should be carefully considered on its merits.[235]

As opposed to commercial or marketplace reputation alone, this approach recognises continuity in the form of the inter-generational know-how sustaining the product's reputation over time, which makes it 'essentially attributable' to place. The recognition of creative/inventive effort is preferred to attempts to generate mythical or legendary product–place linkages, such as origin stories involving divine intervention or fantastical pedigrees.[236] On this basis, the reputation link could be satisfied by a composite of contemporary reputation, historic reputation, the product's history and (importantly) a record of collectively evolved production techniques arising in response to socio-economic, cultural or environmental prompts, which are responsible for sustaining the reputation over time. In conclusion, while these interpretative approaches provide us with alternatives for making sense of the language of Article 22.1, they also increasingly reveal an awareness of human investment and innovation, as opposed to physical geography alone, which connects products to places through a process of continual enactment. If the manner in which a sign is read or construed by consumers was given priority under regimes derived from unfair competition laws, these GI-specific approaches reveal a concern with recognising the labour invested in the underlying product over time. It may provide the basis for explaining why GIs are treated differently from other types of commercial signs found on products in the marketplace. We return to this theme in the next chapter.

5.   The scope of protection: one definition, yet two levels

There is no satisfactory explanation for two levels of protection contained within the drafting history of TRIPS. Nor is there any justification on record explaining why wines and spirits should be especially

---

[235] Ibid., 21–2.

[236] For examples of mythical origin stories, see Das, 'Prospects and Challenges of Geographical Indications in India', 180; S. Agarwal and M. J. Barone, 'Emerging Issues for Geographical Indication Branding Strategies', MATRIC Research Paper 05-MRP 9 (2005), 3.

238   TRIPS today

privileged.[237] Yet accounting for the scope of Article 23 is important. Echoing Article 3 of the Lisbon Agreement, it establishes a so-called 'absolute' tier of protection which cannot be sustained by unfair competition rationales. The argument that Article 23 is merely designed to prevent instances of unfair competition, such as confusion, dilution, genericide or misappropriation,[238] is therefore simply inaccurate. Its rules attempt to protect GI designations as objects, regardless of their connotations in a specific context, while this contextual approach remains the starting point for unfair competition protection. The intention seems to have been to reserve the use of GI designations solely to those entitled to use it within the home country, i.e. country of origin for the GI. Use by any outsiders is deemed unlawful. Against this backdrop, the focus remains on these unconventional provisions, since Article 22 is constructed around the standard unfair competition justifications, grounding the prohibition against false or misleading signs. For instance, the rule in Article 22.2(a) seeks to prevent uses of GIs which mislead the public as to the geographical origin of the goods, while a trade mark which consists of a GI can be invalidated under Article 22.3 where its use is likely to mislead the public as to origin. While there is clear consensus that such rules are necessary, Article 23 is harder to explain.

For a start, the negotiating record contains no normative guidance for this bifurcation. The initial EU proposal contained significantly higher levels of protection for all products.[239] The Anell Draft of 1990 also contained a bracketed proposal according to which protection was to be afforded to all products against 'any usurpation, imitation or evocation, even where the true origin of the product is indicated or the appellation or designation is used in translation or accompanied by expressions such as "kind", "type", "style", "imitation" or the like'.[240] This is similar to the present language of Article 23.1. However, the end result was two distinct levels in Articles 22 and 23. A scheme of differential treatment within an IP regime is not unusual. Well-known trade marks or those

---

[237] A. C. Lang, 'On the Need to Expand Article 23 of the TRIPS Agreement' (2006) 16 *Duke Journal of Contemporary and International Law* 487, 494 ('The hierarchy in Section 3 of the TRIPS Agreement is groundless and theoretically indefensible').

[238] Chandola, 'Basmati Rice', 176 ('The practical effect of this provision is to permit interested parties to take steps to prevent the public from being misled, without having to prove that the public is misled or that there is an act of unfair competition'); Kamperman Sanders, 'Art, Trade and Geographical Indications', 86 (Art. 23 standards 'may even be used to protect a GI against the dilution of a reputation for superior quality').

[239] GATT (MTN.GNG/NG11/W/26), [3.f].

[240] GATT, 'Status of Work in the Negotiating Group', 23 July 1990 (MTN.GNG/NG11/W/76), Section 3.2b.1.

The scope of protection 239

with repute are often granted enhanced protection, provided a certain reputational threshold is crossed. Copyright law also discriminates by granting relatively thin protection for neighbouring rights, when compared with the core categories of literary, dramatic, musical or artistic works. Nevertheless in this case special treatment for wines and spirits is the result of hard bargaining by the EU, with few attempts to articulate a principled distinction.[241] As early as 1988, wines and spirits were singled out as particularly vulnerable to unfair trade from countries which did not protect appellations and ostensibly permitted their indiscriminate use.[242] The EU's initial draft text suggested that protection should be provided for 'appellations of origin, in particular for products of the vine, to the extent that it is accorded in the country of origin'.[243] It also proposed a genericide-freeze, whereby 'appellations of origin for products of the vine shall not be susceptible to develop into generic designations'.[244] Neither of these could be pushed through, but indicate that special treatment was being considered even at the early stages. This was replicated in the EU's 1990 draft text.[245] In Part I, we have considered at length the reasons why certain agricultural products were granted special status in previous treaty negotiations, encapsulated by the *'conditions particulières de climat et de terroir'* argument. Such reasoning is conspicuously absent from the official negotiating records, yet it occasionally surfaces in the commentary. Jacques Audier concludes that special treatment 'doubtless stems from the recognition that their characteristics, identity and uniqueness are bound up with their geographical indications. Such is their link with history, culture and economic interest that general rules are difficult to apply to them'.[246] As progress reports of the negotiating groups to the trade negotiating committee indicate, the final provisions were the result of pressure from countries with an interest in stronger protection for wine, with the subsequent addition of spirits.[247] Special treatment for wines continued to be opposed and questioned throughout this process.[248] Once again

---

[241] Gervais, *TRIPS Agreement*, 305; Chandola, 'Basmati Rice', 172; H. Ilbert and M. Petit, 'Are Geographical Indications a Valid Property Right? Global Trends and Challenges' (2009) 27 *Development Policy Review* 503, 507.

[242] GATT, (MTN.GNG/NG11/W/12/Rev.1), [53].

[243] GATT, (MTN.GNG/NG11/W/26), Section III.D(3)(f).   [244] Ibid.

[245] GATT, 'Draft Agreement on Trade Related Aspects of Intellectual Property Rights', 29 March 1990 (MTN.GNG/NG11/W/68), 6–7.

[246] Audier, *TRIPS Agreement*, 26.

[247] GATT, 'Progress of Work in Negotiating Groups: Stock Taking – Market Access', 7 November 1991 (MTN.TNC/W/89/Add.1), 8–9. See also (MTN.GNG/TRIPS/1), [8].

[248] E.g. GATT, 'Meeting of the Negotiating Group of 1 November 1990', 14 November 1990 (MTN.GNG/NG11/27), [4]; GATT, (MTN.GNG/NG11/28), [7]; GATT,

240   TRIPS today

GI proponents had to settle for special rules for wine as a negotiated concession. This creates stresses for we have no official explanation for differential treatment.

Regarding the scope of Article 23, its defining feature is the absence of any requirement for misleading use and 'no need to establish confusion or deception'.[249] In fact, it applies 'even where ... there is no unfair competition'.[250] Therefore even a robust commitment to unfair competition prevention cannot account for the scope of Article 23, despite assertions along these lines during the TRIPS drafting process.

> [The EU proposal] suggested a narrow definition which did not include all geographical indications but only those where a characteristic of a product was attributable to its geographical origin. Such indications merited particular protection, since they reflected the result of important investment, financial and otherwise, over a long period by producers ... protection against consumer deception was insufficient and trade mark protection was not satisfactory due to its formal requirements such as registration and the use requirement. Since geographical indications were not always known to the public at large, the public was not necessarily deceived when such indications were used for products with different origin. But such indications were often sufficiently known in the circles concerned, especially by traders, for it not to be by mere chance that they were used. The use of such geographical indications for products not from the source indicated was always a parasitical and therefore unfair act, even when no consumer deception was involved.[251]

An act is only parasitic when it is established that the GI is known by the relevant audience. Otherwise a competitor may be innocently making use of a sign which is coincidentally similar to a protected GI, but will still get caught within the ambit of Article 23. The missing step is the need to establish a reputation (or even just awareness of the original GI) as the precondition, before suggesting that consumers will make a mental connection between the two signs. After the link is established, an additional step is to establish the harm or free riding, even if the process is aided by circumstantial evidence.

To appreciate this distinction, we need only look to the EU's pan-European Community Trade Mark (CTM) registration system,

---

'Meeting of the Negotiating Group of 16 and 22 October 1991', 18 November 1991 (MTN.GNG/TRIPS/3), [13].

[249] See *Regione autonoma Friuli-Venezia Giulia and Ors* v. *Ministero delle Politiche Agricole e Forestali* (C-347/03) [2005] ECR I-3785 (AGO), [86].

[250] Geuze, 'Protection of Geographical Indications under the TRIPS Agreement', [9]; Wasescha 'Recent Developments in the Council for TRIPS', [12]; Communication from Bulgaria et al. (WTO/IP/C/W/353), [10].

[251] GATT, 'Meeting of the Negotiating Group 30 Oct–2 Nov 1989', 4 December 1989 (MTN.GNG/NG11/16), [53].

The scope of protection 241

which provides us with illustrations of Article 23.2 being deployed.[252] A Spanish wine grower applied to register CUVÉE PALOMAR for wines, but this was refused on the basis that 'el Palomar' was the name of a local administrative area in Spain, in the Valencian sub-region Clariano, and that under the relevant law it constituted an area of production protected by the registered designation of origin 'Valencia'. Therefore the trade mark application was read as containing an impermissible 'literally false' geographical indication. The applicant objected, *inter alia*, on the basis of the obscurity of the place name, but the GC's response was that 'the fact that the name which benefits from a registered designation of origin is unknown to the general public or the relevant class of persons, or that it has many meanings which moderate its geographically indicative nature, is irrelevant for the application of [this] absolute ground for refusal'.[253] The paradoxes associated with this absolute tier of protection can be further teased out within the context of the EU–Australia Wine Agreement of 1994. It was estimated that with the exception of twenty-five generic wine designations that were to be phased out over a staggered period, thousands of EU names were reserved in Australia.[254] The treaty resulted in modifications to the Australian Wine and Brandy Corporation Act 1980. A description is deemed false under s. 40D(2)(b) if 'it includes a registered geographical indication and the wine did not originate in a country, region or locality in relation to which the geographical indication is registered'. In the *La Provence* case,[255] the respondents sold wine originating in Tasmania under the 'La Provence' label, to which the CIVC objected. While 'Provence' and 'Côtes de Provence' were registered appellations under the Wine Agreement, there was no evidence that the respondents had actual knowledge of this at the commencement of the proceeding. The evidence suggests that there was no bad faith or intention to free ride.[256] The complainants alleged that

---

[252] Art. 7(1)(j) of Council Regulation (EC) No. 40/94 of 20 December 1993 on the Community Trade Mark, [1994] OJ L 11, 1 (now Article 7(1)(j) of the similarly titled Regulation (EC) No. 207/2009 [2009] OJ L 78, 1)) (Registration shall be refused for 'trade marks for wines which contain or consist of a geographical indication identifying wines ... with respect to such wines ... not having that origin').

[253] *Abadia Retuerta, SA* v. *OHIM* (T-237/08) 11 May 2010 (GC), [131] (Unreported).

[254] S. Stern, 'Case Comment: First Test Case of the EC Australia Wine Treaty' (1997) EIPR 668.

[255] *Comité Interprofessionnel des Vins de Côtes de Provence and INAO* v. *Bryce and Another* (1996) 69 FCR 450 (Heerey J).

[256] Ibid., 452 ('The respondents' vineyard was established in 1956 by Jean Miguet, the son of a fifth generation winemaker from Provence ... It is the oldest vineyard in Tasmania. M Miguet returned to France in 1975. The vineyard had a number of other owners until it was purchased by the respondents in 1980 ... Annual production is approximately 350 to 400 cases, of which more than 90 per cent is sold in Tasmania').

242 TRIPS today

'La Provence' was a misleading description under s. 40E of the Act and that it was a false description under s. 40C. The court found that 'La Provence' was unlikely to be mistaken for the registered appellation 'Côtes de Provence', so this use was not misleading. However, the court held that this was a literally false use as per the statutory provision, regardless of its effect on consumers. On the facts of this case there is no evidence of wilful free riding and there is a finding of fact that misleading use was unlikely. Falsity in these situations suggests literal falsity – if a designation exists as a place on a map and the defendant's wine does not come from that place, the enquiry ends there. This could very well apply to any of the several hundred European designations on the register that are relatively unknown.

The difficulty associated with this approach, where words are treated as stable objects, is evident in the Australian trade mark registry's '*Feet First*' decision.[257] What happens when protected designations also have ordinary English significance, such as Wicker, First, Doctor, Sand, Wolf, Horn and Lump? Here the applicants had applied for 'Feet First' as a trade mark for wines, only to discover that First is a sub-region within the Einzellagen wine growing area of Germany and listed on the Register of Protected Names. The registry ultimately adopted a contextual approach to deciding whether ordinary English usage would be understood as falsely projecting or related to geographical origin. The applicants use therefore seemed permissible since the colloquial or ordinary English usage, as opposed to geographical usage, was the predominant impression. One also discovers attempts to reconcile absolute protection with the contextual generation of meaning, as well as established prior rights, in decisions of the EU community trade mark registry's Board of Appeals, where the existence of a registered GI is a basis for rejecting a trade mark application.[258] In these situations, decision-makers revert to an enquiry focused on the connotations of the sign as used by the defendant, raising questions about the workability of absolute protection.

Since the burden of proof is no longer on rights holders under Article 23, this presents a significant evidentiary advantage and makes it easier

---

[257] *Ross & Veronica Lawrence* [2005] ATMO 69 (21 November 2005).

[258] E.g., *Reh Kendermann GmbH Weinkellerei* (R 822/2010–2) OHIM 2nd BoA, 27 September 2010 (Unreported) (The mark being applied for, VAL DUNÁ, was insufficiently similar to the Hungarian GIs (1) Duna Borrégió, (2) Duna melléki, (3) Duna-Tisza közi); *Ivivi Pty Ltd* (R 130/2009–2) OHIM 2nd BoA, 9 June 2009 (Unreported) (considering the extent to which the status of a little-known Australian sub-region within the more famous Barossa region can prevent trade mark registration).

The scope of protection   243

for rights to be enforced.[259] It appears that the Holy Grail of strictly preventing any literally false use of the IGO, initially formulated in the early years of the Paris Convention, has at long last been (formally) achieved for wines and spirits. Subject to the exceptions in Articles 23 and 24, there is no need to prove any wrong such as misleading, diluting or misappropriating use. Nor is it compulsory for the product to have a reputation or be known in the jurisdiction where the dispute is taking place. It also prohibits 'style' or 'type' uses, translations and use with delocalising adjuncts. This absence of the need to prove wrongfulness may have led to its characterisation as 'absolute'.

It is worth reiterating that Article 23 goes beyond even generous national unfair competition regimes, which would require a threshold condition such as an existing reputation in the minds of the public, or a link being established between the claimant and defendant's signs. Here surface-level resemblance or morphological identity between two signs, coupled with their use on similar products, seems to trigger proscription but also raises the puzzles we see in *Feet First*. Similar standards are to be applied under Article 23.2 where a trade mark containing a literally false GI has been applied for or has been registered. This provision has been transposed into national trade mark laws and is the basis for refusals at present.[260] It has been applied by the OHIM Board of Appeals in relevant cases, by comparing the sign applied for with the official list of protected quality and table wines as well as spirits in the EU.[261] Here trade marks will only be refused when the trade mark application is for wines or spirits, unlike other regional agreements where marks may be refused or cancelled even when applied for on dissimilar goods.[262]

---

[259] Proposal from Bulgaria et al., 'Work on Issues Relevant to the Protection of Geographical Indications', 17 May 2001 (IP/C/W/247/Rev.1), [5] ('The burden of proof does not rest with the plaintiff of the geographical indication. Under Article 23, competitors not producing within the geographical area are simply prevented from using the corresponding denomination, and [subject to the exceptions] they may not use trade marks containing or consisting of geographical indications used to identify wines or spirits').

[260] See, e.g., *In re Bacardi & Co Ltd* 48 USPQ 2d 1031 (TTAB 1997), Fn 6 ('The amendment [to US trade mark law because of TRIPS] adds an absolute prohibition against the registration, in connection with wines or spirits, of a mark that includes a geographic indication if the wines or spirits do not originate in that geographic area').

[261] See, e.g., *René Barbier SA* v. *OHIM* (R 1220/2000–2) 2nd BoA, 11 December 2002 ('DUQUE DE VILLENA'); *Amrut Distilleries Ltd* v. *OHIM* (R 635/2005–1) 1st BoA, 26 September2005 ('OLD PORT') (Here the applicant amended the goods to exclude wine from the alcoholic beverages applied for, while successfully arguing that in this case the sign applied for along with the figurative mark of a ship would suggest a different connotation for 'port').

[262] See, e.g., the *'Saint Emilion'* decision where the French wine appellation was applied for with regard to apparel before the Colombian registry and successfully opposed on the

244 TRIPS today

This introduces an under-appreciated limitation to this otherwise broad scope. Article 23 seems to only apply in similar or identical goods situations, where the sign is used on wines or spirits not originating from the place in question. The broad language of usurpation or evocation, which was found in the early Uruguay Round proposals, in Lisbon and in Regulation 2081/92, is absent. This means that misappropriating use on *dissimilar* products or classic diluting uses are not caught by Article 23.[263] This outline of the two levels lays the groundwork for considering whether Article 23 levels of protection should be applied to all products, which we shall consider in Chapter 6.

6. Generic status

Under the TRIPS GI provisions, generic terms may remain unprotected. Article 24.6 of TRIPS provides that where 'the term [is] customary in common language as the common name for such goods or services in the territory of that Member' there is no obligation to protect it. This is further evidence of the communicative approach sustaining much of international GI protection, suggesting that these signs are protected in accordance with the message they actually convey. Yet there is little else by way of guidance in interpreting this rule. One TRIPS Council delegate has observed that 'since there were no rules on how one could make such [a] determination, it would be difficult for the relevant authority to deal with the conflict of rights between geographical indications and generic terms'.[264] This section will briefly problematise generic use in historical context. It will then set out various options for filling in the outline in Article 24.6, which remains underdeveloped in the literature.

To begin with, the rationale for unprotected status seems straightforward. A GI is a sign indicating a product's specific geographical origin and information associated with that origin. Under the communicative paradigm, legal protection rests on its ability to perform this function. An established practice for designating a broad category of product, regardless of origin, clearly negates this function.

The way in which the name of a product becomes generic is the result of an objective process, at the end of which that name, although referring to the geographical place where the product in question was originally manufactured

---

basis of the Andean Community Agreement. Editor's Note, 'The Tenth Annual International Review of Trade Mark Jurisprudence' (2003) 93 TMR 505, 567.

[263] Noted by J. Hughes, 'Champagne, Feta, and Bourbon – The Spirited Debate about Geographical Indications' (2006) 58 *Hastings Law Journal* 299, 318–19.

[264] TRIPS Council, (IP/C/M/37/Add.1), [139].

Generic terms thus 'form part of the general cultural and gastronomic stock and may, in principle, be used by any producer'.[266] Yet the process of deciding on whether a specific designation that operates as a GI in one context has become generic in another is fraught with controversy.[267] It implicates the interests of GI producers in the country of origin, competitors who have used the term generically and consumers who navigate marketplaces by relying on such signs.

This splay of interests is revealed in the aftermath of the ECJ's confirmation that Feta is not generic in the EU.[268] Producers in Denmark, Germany and France commonly used the term for a type of white cheese soaked in brine. After a transition period only producers in designated parts of Greece following specified production methods are now entitled to use Feta. Understandably, this was not to everyone's taste and Hans Bender, Director of the Danish Dairy Board, characterised the decision as 'legal nonsense' and 'a big setback for non-Greek Feta producers in the EU'.[269] A producer of 'Yorkshire feta' in the UK warned that prices may be forced up as Greece alone is unable to satisfy global demand.[270] Arguments concerning repackaging costs are often encountered in such situations, where third parties are deprived of the use of terminology they believe to be in the public domain.[271] This contrasts with the

---

[265] *Alberto Severi* v. *Regione Emilia-Romagna* (C–446/07) [2009] ECR I-8041; [2009] ETMR 64, [50]–[51] (ECJ).

[266] *Canadane Cheese Trading* v. *Hellenic Republic* (C-317/95) [1997] ECR I-4681, [28] (AG Colomer).

[267] G. E. Evans and M. Blakeney, 'The International Protection of Geographical Indications Yesterday Today And Tomorrow', in G. Westkamp (ed.), *Emerging Issues In Intellectual Property: Trade, Technology and Market Freedom – Essays in Honour of Herchel Smith* (Edward Elgar, Cheltenham 2007), 250, 283 (Today 'the issue of generic names has the potential to cause the greatest unease in negotiations for increased international protection'); TRIPS Council, 'Communication from Bangladesh et al.', 2 October 2001 (IP/C/W/308/Rev.1), [18] ('One of the key reasons for advocating extension [of GI protection] is a desire to prevent more geographical indications from becoming generic').

[268] *Federal Republic of Germany and Kingdom of Denmark* v. *Commission of the European Communities* (Joined Cases C-465/02 and C-466/02). See generally, D. Gangjee, 'Say Cheese: A Sharper Image of Generic Use through the Lens of Feta' [2007] EIPR 172.

[269] 'The EU Feta Debate Concludes' *Managing Intellectual Property - Weekly News* (31 October 2005).

[270] 'Yorkshire Feta? Hard Cheese Says European Court' *The Telegraph* (26 October 2005), available at www.telegraph.co.uk. The concern may be exaggerated as producers in non-EU states are still at liberty to use the term generically.

[271] See the statement of Michael Pellegrino, Vice-President, Kraft Cheese Division in Hearings before the Committee on Agriculture, House of Representatives on the

246   TRIPS today

vindicatory tones in the Greek Agriculture Minister's reaction, suggesting that this right to exclusive use was hard earned, developed over time and 'steeped in Greek cultural tradition'.[272] Consequently while the determination of generic status is presented as a straightforward and factually driven legal test, in practice the vortex of competing interests ensures that this is rarely the case.

For over a century, such determinations have been accompanied by allegations of artificial semantic reloading to benefit one side or another. Four examples help reveal some of the underlying issues. First, under the nineteenth century Merchandise Marks regime in Britain, the use of a false trade description, including place of origin descriptions, attracted a penalty. When faced with this charge, the party being prosecuted could raise the defence that the term was generic. Subsequently the status of Havana (or its variants) for cigars and tobacco was called into question by those wishing to use the term generically, despite the existence of a price differential for such cigars in the market.[273] This suggests the tactical deployment of the generic defence by third parties, in an attempt to take advantage of an attractive reputation. A second arena of conflict is better concealed. Within Europe, there is evidence of considerable disagreement about generic status.[274] As part of the initial implementation of Regulation 2081/92, the European Commission was required to draw up an indicative and non-exhaustive list of generic terms to be confirmed by Council Decision. The Commission's proposal began by observing that the 'issue of generic names is a sensitive one and has always met with strong reactions'.[275] This situation proved no different and the list of six cheese names proposed (Brie, Camembert, Cheddar, Edam, Emmentaler, Gouda) proved indigestible. The requisite Council

Status of the World Trade Organization Negotiations on Agriculture, (108–5) 108th Congress (2003), 325–6 (discussing Kraft having to avoid using Parmesan on non-Italian cheese in the EU).

[272] 'Greece Hails "Historic" EU Ruling on its Staple Feta Cheese' *EUBusiness – Food and Drink* (25 October2005), available at www.eubusiness.com/.

[273] Special report from the Select Committee on Merchandise Marks Act (1862) Amendment Bill (1887), 203, [2781]–[2782], [2795]–[2797], [2832]–[2835]; F. G. Underhay, *Kerly's Law of Merchandise Marks*, 3rd edn (Sweet & Maxwell, London 1909), 29–30.

[274] Apart from the *Feta* case considered above, recent litigation includes *Commission of the European Communities* v. *Federal Republic of Germany* (C-132/05) [2008] ECR-I 957; [2008] ETMR 32 (whether Parmesan is generic for a style of hard cheese); *Bavaria NV, Bavaria Italia Srl* v. *Bayerischer Brauerbund eV* (C-343/07) [2009] ECR I-5491; [2009] ETMR 61 (whether 'Bavaria' is generic for a process of beer manufacture).

[275] Proposal for a Council Decision to Establish an Indicative, Non-Exhaustive List of Names of Agricultural Products and Foodstuffs Considered Generic Names, as Referred to in Art. 3 Para. 3 of Council Regulation (EEC) No. 2081/92, COM (96) 38 final [4].

majority was never attained and the list was abandoned. A related site of disagreement concerns the existence of Article 13(3) of Regulation 2081/92, which establishes that protected names 'may not become generic'. This responds to the relative helplessness to prevent meaning erosion beyond the limits of territorial rights.[276] The Economic and Social Committee opined that such robust protection was needed since prestigious names which have been 'established through the care and hard work of certain producers must not be allowed to become generic designations simply because they are not properly protected'.[277] Yet the Committee for Consumer Protection saw this as an 'edict from the Thought Police, attempting to control the evolution of language' by legislation.[278] Once again the interests of producers in the country of origin seem to conflict with those of some consumers and competitors. For GI proponents, recognising the interests in the underlying product is desirable, but the sign proves difficult to discipline. Third, a fascinating gambit recently unfolded at the Codex Alimentarius Commission, the body established to set up internationally recognised standards relating to food production.[279] A proposal was submitted to establish an international generic standard for Parmesan cheese, which was strongly resisted by Italy and the EU. The issue has been deferred indefinitely but such a standard would considerably undermine the value of Italian Parmigiano Reggiano as a PDO under EU law.[280] It highlights the political economy dimensions of such determinations, while underlining the difficulty in achieving multilateral consensus on the status of a designation. This could be described as an attempt to internationalise generic status. Finally, one of the most derided reclamation attempts relates to the so-called EU 'claw back' list of forty-one designations that

---

[276] This is a recurring theme in the literature; see WIPO, 'The Need for a New Treaty and its Possible Contents', [8]–[9]; J. Armistead, 'Whose Cheese Is It Anyway? Correctly Slicing the European Regulation Concerning Protections for Geographic Indications' (2000) 10 *Transnational Law & Contemporary Problems* 303, 319 ('A term that has become generic is often the result of a country's inability to enforce a geographic indication because of the absence of an effective international treaty').

[277] Opinion on the proposal for a Council Regulation (EEC) on the protection of geographical indications and designations of origin for agricultural products and foodstuffs [1991] OJ C 269, 62, [1.7].

[278] Ken Collins (Chairman), Opinion of the Committee on the Environment, Public Health and Consumer Protection annexed to the Report of the Committee on Agriculture, Fisheries and Rural Development on the Commission Proposals for Council Regulations (SEC(90) 2415 final) and (SEC(90) 2414) (30 October1991; Session Document A3–0283/91), 28, 29.

[279] Codex Alimentarius Commission, Report Of The Twenty-Seventh Session (Geneva, 28 June–3 July 2004), Appendix X; Codex Alimentarius Commission, Report Of The Twenty-Eighth Session (Rome, 4–9 July 2005), [167]–[176].

[280] Dossier No. IT/PDO/0117/0016; Registered 06/09/2003.

248   TRIPS today

exist as well established generic terms in many WTO Members, which was drafted in the context of WTO negotiations. The EU was seeking to re-establish internationally protected GI status for these terms and the list included Roquefort cheese, Parma ham, Rioja wine and Feta cheese.[281] Here signs are once again treated as potentially static objects to be bartered in international negotiations. This could be described as an attempt to internationalise protected GI status.

The following elements are common to such disputes: the territorial limits of national protection (or in some cases, the non-existence of formal recognition in the home country at the initial stages); the mutability of terminology as it traverses borders and markets; the relative helplessness of home country producers in the face of this and the often legitimate claims of competitors using terminology generically. Moreover, one is left with the impression that in the past, the dichotomy found in trade mark and unfair competition doctrine whereby a sign is either distinctive of a particular trade source or descriptive/generic and open to all has operated to disadvantage GIs.[282] On an international scale, this results in islands of legal protection interspersed between the open water of generic use. Over the decades, the variable valence of Pilsner or Pilsen has often been used to illustrate this problem.[283] GI proponents respond to generic use with familiar concerns: (1) usurpation or misappropriation – why would an outsider copy the designation if it didn't already have an existing cache and recognition value; (2) harm to legitimate producers – such usage results in the erosion of meaning and distinctiveness; (3) harm to consumers in the form of inauthenticity – certain iterations of *terroir* presume inimitable products, suggesting that sellers of generic equivalents misrepresent their substitutability with

---

[281] EC Press Release, 'WTO talks: EU Steps up Bid for Better Protection for Regional Quality Products' 28 August 2003 (IP/03/1178) available at europa.eu/press_room/index_en.htm. For representative critiques, see M. Handler, 'The EU's Geographical Indications Agenda and its Potential Impact on Australia' (2004) 15 *Australian Intellectual Property Journal* 173; Goebel, 'The Road from Doha', 991–4.

[282] This is related to the political economy dimensions of such determinations. W. Notz, 'New Phases of Unfair Competition and Measures for Its Suppression National and International' (1920–1) 30 *Yale Law Journal* 384, 392 ('Before the war there was a noticeable tendency in the court decisions of most countries to regard various designations, which originally were considered distinctive and special names, as generic or conventional. Many regional appellations, names of origin, hall marks, such as Port, Madeira, Pilsen, Camembert, Solingen, Sheffield, etc., received little or no protection by the courts').

[283] Ladas, *International Protection of Industrial Property*, 1587, 1589; AIPPI Working Committee, Resolution on Question Q191, 2.

'the real thing'.[284] The counterarguments usually emerge in the context of disputed wine appellations.

[I]ndications of geographic origin used in one country began to be used in other countries, not because the indications were well known worldwide and the users sought a 'free ride', but because citizens of the first country emigrated to the second and used the same terms for their products that they had used in their home countries. Much of that emigration took place because of political, economic and other conditions from the 17th to the mid-20th centuries, in many cases before appellation of origin protection had even been established in the territories of those Members that now claim those terms.[285]

Therefore the process of terminology following technology is proffered as the long-standing and legitimate basis for such uses, usually within the context of economic migration or colonialism. It was common for people to name products after those which they had left behind, while generic usage suggested an approximate equivalence of qualities in wines and cheese, providing useful information to consumers.[286] Within the literature these opposing views lock horns in the provocatively labelled 'legitimation of past sins' debate.[287] While GI proponents concentrate on wrongful copying in generic use contexts, critics focus on the harmless audience reception of the sign. For that reason, lobbying to preserve generic usage 'must be seen as a bargaining position, not a crime and still less a sin'.[288] Yet while the generic usage of established wine GIs attracts most of the attention, comparatively newer or emerging GIs are also

---

[284] See, e.g., WIPO, (TAO/I/ 8), [30]; S. Stern, 'The Conflict between Geographical Indications and Trade Marks or Australia Once Again Heads Off Down the Garden Path', Annual Conference of the IP Society of Australia and New Zealand (September 2004), 12; R. Benson, 'Towards a New Treaty for the Protection of Geographical Indications' [1978] *Industrial Property* 127, 129 ('[T]oday's generic terms are the fossils of past consumer deception').

[285] Communication from Australia et al., 'Implications of Article 23 Extension', 26 July 2002 (IP/C/W/360), [7].

[286] A. Stern, 'The Protection of Geographical Indications in South Africa', September 1999 (WIPO/GEO/CPT/99/3a), 2; Mekis, 'Position of Chile's Vineyards', 6; B. G. Drinkwater, 'Protection and Use of Geographical Indications in Australia', November 2003 (WIPO/GEO/DEL/03/4), 2; Kazmi, 'Does It Make a Difference Where That Chablis Comes From?', 471; Lindquist, 'Champagne or Champagne?', 313; T. Unwin, *Wine and the Vine: An Historical Geography of Viticulture and the Wine Trade* (Routledge, London 1991), 300–12.

[287] For a summary, see J. M. Cortes Martin, 'The WTO TRIPS Agreement – The Battle between the Old and the New World over the Protection of Geographical Indications' (2004) 7 JWIP 287, 290, Fn13.

[288] N. Dawson, 'Locating Geographical Indications: Perspectives from English Law' (2000) 90 TMR 590, 590.

250   TRIPS today

vulnerable. Both Darjeeling tea[289] and Kobe beef[290] have been subjected to the threat of generic status. GIs from developing countries also continue to be vulnerable, since genericide is routinely raised as a defence where rights to GIs are sought to be enforced. Engaging with this argument adds considerable expense and uncertainty to litigation.[291] In an internet-enabled semiotic ecosystem, where semantic content is more open to change than ever before, it is therefore worth looking more closely at specific configurations of the formal rules, categories of admissible evidence and legal presumptions which give effect to this test in specific contexts. How should disputes about generic status *in the future* be resolved?

Since the aim is to demonstrate the considerable interpretative space within Article 24.6, it is worth illuminating some important choices which have thus far remained eclipsed. First, from whose perspective do we assess generic status? TRIPS states that the former GI must have become 'the term customary in common language as the common name for such goods'. Does this include both consumer and trade usage, along the chain of distribution? Should both constituencies be given equal weight? In response to these questions, the authorities in *Feta* considered whether the 'relevant public' understands the term to be commonly used for a type of white cheese in brine. Identifying the appropriate group to which the test is applied is an important preliminary stage and the Scientific Committee,[292] which advised the European Commission during the registration process, reasoned that since the product was

---

[289] *Tea Board of India* v. *The Republic of Tea* (2006) 80 USPQ2d 1881 (TTAB) (An applicant for 'Darjeeling Nouveau' unsuccessfully argued that the 'Darjeeling' certification mark registered by the Tea Board of India was invalid, having become generic in the US). For more successful genericide challenges in the US, see *French Republic* v. *Saratoga Vichy Co* 191 US 427 (1903) (Vichy spring water); *In re Cooperativa Produttori Latte e Fontina Valle D'Acosta* 230 USPQ 131 (TTAB 1986) (Fontina cheese); *Schweizerische Kaeseunion Bern* v. *Saul Starck Inc* 293 NYS 816 (1937) (Swiss cheese); *Institut Nat'l Des Appellations D'Origine* v. *Vinters Int'l Co.* 958 F2d 1574 (Fed Cir 1992) (Chablis for wine).

[290] D. Gangjee, *Protecting Geographical Indications as Trade Marks: Prospects and Pitfalls* (Report for the Institute of Intellectual Property, Tokyo 2006), available at www.lse.ac.uk/collections/law/staff/dev-gangjee.htm#reports.

[291] D. Rangnekar, 'The International Protection of Geographical Indications: The Asian Experience' (UNCTAD/ICTSD Regional Dialogue, Hong Kong SAR, November 2004), 20 (outlining the expense to the Tea Board of India in responding to such challenges).

[292] A committee of experts established to assist the Commission with all technical matters relating to registration of GIs, including determining generic status. See Commission Decision of 21 December 1992 Setting Up a Scientific Committee for Designations of Origin, Geographical Indications and Certificates of Specific Character (93/53/EEC) [1993] OJ L13/16.

Generic status 251

cheese the relevant public should include consumers as well as commercial purchasers such as restaurants. Here the general public across all EU Member States concerned was the target audience.[293] When it comes to trade understanding, commercial actors may be presumed to be more careful in their use of terminology. This must be balanced against the inbuilt incentives operating here – external traders often commercially benefit from generic use.[294] Other proposals have referred to the understanding of both the general public (usually consumers of the product in question) and experts.[295] Second, what is the tipping point for generic status? Put differently, what is the benchmark for deciding when this status has been achieved? In the US, where this test has developed in the context of registered trade mark law, the test is satisfied where, for the majority of consumers, the 'primary significance' of the sign is to describe a class or category of products.[296] This majoritarian approach can be contrasted with that adopted in *Feta*, where generic status is achieved 'only when there is in the relevant territory no significant part of the public concerned that still considers the indication as a geographical indication'.[297] This is a high threshold, similar to German law[298] and designed to prevent an easy slide into genericide. Those who continue to treat the sign as a GI seem to be prioritised over those who don't. This approach is once again visible in a dispute about whether 'Bavaria' had become generic for a style of beer produced via bottom fermentation. The ECJ held that since the purpose of PGI protection is

to prevent the improper use of a name by third parties seeking to profit from the reputation which it has acquired and, moreover, to prevent the disappearance of that reputation as a result of popularisation through general use ... a name becomes generic only if the direct link between, on the one hand, the geographical origin of the product and, on the other hand, a specific quality of that product, its reputation or another characteristic of the product, attributable

---

[293] Recital 23 of Commission Regulation (EC) No. 1829/2002 of 14 October 2002 Amending the Annex to Regulation (EC) No. 1107/96 with regard to the Name Feta [2002] OJ L277/10.

[294] An issue considered in the context of European trade mark law. See *Björnekulla Fruktindustrier AB* v. *Procordia Food AB* (C-371/02) [2004] ECR I-5791; [2004] ETMR 69, [AG82]–[AG83] (AG Léger).

[295] WIPO, *Draft Model Law for Developing Countries* (TAO/I/ INF.l) 30.

[296] Lanham Act § 14(3), 15 USCA § 1064(3). See also J. T. McCarthy, *McCarthy on Trademarks and Unfair Competition*, 4th edn (Thomson West, February 2011 update), § 12:6.

[297] Recital 23 of Commission Regulation (EC) No 1829/2002.

[298] H. Harte-Bavendamm, 'Ende der geographischen Herkunftsbezeichnungen? "Brüsseler Spitzen" gegen den ergänzenden nationalen Rechtsschutz' [1996] GRUR 717, 718.

252   TRIPS today

to that origin, *has disappeared*, and that the name does no more than describe a style or type of product [emphasis added].[299]

Third, how should the subject of the law be approached? Since the enquiry is predicated upon consumer understanding, the initial step is to characterise the consumer. Louis Lorvellec provocatively asks who this typical consumer is: 'Should the law, however, search for the least educated consumer from the bottom of the deepest well of ignorance to determine whether a sign deserves protection?'[300] Meanwhile Philippe Zylberg points to the increasing sophistication of consumers in the wine sector, suggesting that they are increasingly likely to be familiar with the specific origins of wines.[301] By contrast, in regimes sympathetic to GI protection, sometimes consumer understanding appears to be pro-actively warped in favour of non-generic status, through inferences drawn from product labels. This is evident from Recital 20 of the Regulation which re-recognised Feta in 2002.[302] Whilst gauging the communicative content of Feta across the EU, the Commission reasoned that because non-Greek cheese labelling (i.e., on the supposedly generic product) made references to Greek images and iconography, this continued to suggest a Greek origin associated with the product. This may be going too far. After all, there is a difference between a sign which says 'Chinese Restaurant' and the label 'Made in China'. The former is merely an allusive usage found throughout the world based on historic origins, whereas the latter communicates present-day origin more definitively. The Commission and subsequently the ECJ appear to have collapsed the distinction between the two. There are clearly choices to be made here.

Another distinction could be drawn between consumer usage and consumer understanding of terminology. To what extent can we infer the latter from the former? In the context of US trade mark law, commentators have noted that there may be a difference between everyday usage of a sign and its understanding by consumers in a commercial context.[303] Usage may be an important indicator of the manner in which consumers understand a sign, but it does not completely overlap with

---

[299] *Bavaria NV, Bavaria Italia Srl v. Bayerischer Brauerbund eV* (C-343/07) [2009] ETMR 61 (ECJ), [106]–[107].

[300] Lorvellec, 'You've Got to Fight for Your Right to Party', 72.

[301] Zylberg, 'The Lisbon Agreement', 62.

[302] Commission Regulation (EC) No. 1829/2002.

[303] See, e.g., J. B. Swann, 'The Validity of Dual Functioning Trade Marks: Genericism Tested by Consumer Understanding Rather than by Consumer Use' (1979) 69 TMR 357; R. H. Folsom and L. R. Teply, 'Trade Marked Generic Words' (1980) 89 *Yale Law Journal* 1323.

Generic status 253

understanding.[304] Here one strand of analysis focuses on the ordinary, non-commercial or everyday speech uses of trade marked terms as general descriptors.[305] The problem with current trade mark law (and potentially GI law) is that it encourages the policing of

> not only unregulated use by competitors, but also uses by *non-competitors* in *expressive* or *informative* contexts (such as newspapers or dictionaries) are taken as evidence of the death of the mark. This approach poses serious problems because it requires (or at least encourages) trade mark holders to pursue expensive and perhaps harmful if not quixotic strategies, ranging from letter campaigns to lawsuits, to attempt to control the manner in which society uses language.[306]

A symptomatic US decision concerns the use of 'Star Wars' by scientific and public interest groups to express concerns about the US Strategic Defense Initiative for orbital weaponry in space. The court held that the 'use of star wars in political propaganda, newspapers or noncommercial, non-trade references will not undermine [Lucasfilm's] exclusive property right to use in connection with goods and services'.[307] The proposed solution is to dissociate such non-trade uses from the genericide analysis, thereby easing the pressure on rights holders to develop litigious trigger fingers. Related to the distinction between use and understanding is the possibility of hybrid or dual usage, where generic or origin-specific significance varies with the context. As the court acknowledged in *British Sherry*, in 'the first place even people who are knowledgeable about wine and would expect if they asked in a bar for a glass of dry sherry to be given a wine from Spain may on other occasions use the word "sherry" to include "sherry type" wines'.[308] To what extent would any genericide determination incorporate this element of hybridity? Finally, would the decision-making process also consider the possibility that genericide is a dynamic process and may be reversible, so that a generic term can regain GI significance?[309] Fourth, which party bears the burden of proof when generic status is to be determined? Obviously this varies depending upon the nature of the dispute and the status of the GI. Is it a pending application, or is it

---

[304] I. Simonson, 'An Empirical Investigation of the Meaning and Measurement of "Genericness"' (1994) 84 TMR 199.

[305] See, e.g., D. R. Desai and S. L. Rierson, 'Confronting the Genericism Conundrum' (2007) 28 *Cardozo Law Review* 1789.

[306] Ibid., at 1791.

[307] *Lucasfilm Ltd* v. *High Frontier* 227 USPQ 967, 969 (DDC 1985).

[308] *Vine Products Ltd* v. *Mackenzie & Co Ltd (No.3)* [1967] *FSR* 402, 423 (Ch D).

[309] A possibility recognised in *Bavaria NV, Bavaria Italia Srl* v. *Bayerischer Brauerbund eV* (C-343/07) [2009] ECR I-5491; [2009] ETMR 61, [AG117] (AG Mazák).

254   TRIPS today

already registered with genericide raised as part of invalidation proceedings? Allocating this burden is a crucial consideration as much of the expense is associated with gathering the evidence to establish or rebut generic status. In a recent dispute the ECJ held that Germany, the party defensively claiming that Parmesan was generic, had not submitted sufficient evidence to discharge this burden.[310] The fifth and final issue relates to the factors or categories of evidence that decision makers refer to when deciding on this status. The limited analysis of this issue suggests the following categories: (1) evidence of everyday linguistic usage (dictionaries, press reports etc); (2) surveys of the consuming public; (3) surveys of trade opinion; (4) expert opinion; (5) the status of the designation in legislation (e.g. customs or excise categories); and (6) the rights holders' own actions or inaction.[311] Within each of these categories, there is more evaluative work to be done. For instance, what is one to make of legislation which assumes certain terms to be generic? Mentioning the US approach, which designated certain categories of wine GIs as semi-generic via administrative regulations, is apposite here.[312] Audier voices the underlying concern: 'If "generic" status stems from a government or administrative decision which fails to reflect linguistic usage, generic names will become mere bargaining chips'.[313] The issue was considered by the ECJ in *Feta* and the short answer is that, depending upon the nature of the legislation, this may not carry much evidentiary weight.[314] Legislation relating to customs tariffs would be shaped by a distinct bureaucratic interest, as would food safety regulations. The purpose of such rules would be neither to probe directly, nor reflect consumer understanding and they should not be determinative in such disputes. This review of unresolved sub-issues indicates that the general principle in Article 24.6 can be implemented in a range of ways. Despite an apparent commitment to the communicative paradigm and tracking marketplace meaning, these options suggest that the communicative paradigm itself may have enough leeway for either insulating signs or nudging them towards generic status. It also highlights the constitutive

---

[310] *Commission of the European Communities* v. *Federal Republic of Germany* (C-132/05) [2008] ECR I-957; [2008] ETMR 32 at [52]-[57] (ECJ CFI).

[311] See Gangjee, 'Say Cheese'; J. Audier, 'Generic and Semi-Generic Denominations: Determination Criteria and Methods to Reduce their Effects' (2000) 22 *AIDV Bulletin* 29.

[312] P. M. Brody, '"Semi-Generic" Geographical Wine Designations: Did Congress Trip Over TRIPS?' (1999) 89 TMR 979.

[313] Audier, *TRIPS Agreement*, 39, Fn 40.

[314] *Federal Republic of Germany and Kingdom of Denmark* v. *Commission of the European Communities* (C-465/02 and C-466/02), [88], [91]–[92] (ECJ).

aspects of some of these choices, which may invent or construct consumer understanding while claiming to measure it.

7. The relationship between GIs and trade marks

As geographical signs are potential subject matter for both trade marks and *sui generis* GI regimes, this overlap plays out along two avenues: (1) the recognition and protection of GIs within registered trade mark systems, usually as certification or collective marks; and (2) conflicts arising as a result of GI users and a trade mark proprietor making competing claims to the same sign within the same jurisdiction. The first type of overlap is considered in Chapter 6, Section 4 below. For the second, it has been proposed that the principles of priority and exclusivity should be applied. For instance, where there is a likelihood of confusion between the prior sign and a subsequent yet similar one, the rights holder for the former can object to the latter, which must yield.[315] In those jurisdictions which take the view that trade marks and GIs are functionally equivalent, a uniform rule based on prior rights trumping is projected as 'simply a matter of fairness'.[316] The formal fairness of this rule *rests on the assumption of complete functional equivalence between these two types of signs*. It is worth reconsidering, in light of the ingrained disadvantages to GI collectives when faced with a prior trade mark registration. Here, I seek to demonstrate that: (1) a considerable momentum has built up around the promotion of 'first in time, first in right' (FITFIR) as the primary rule to resolve such trade mark-GI conflicts; (2) two case studies on Parma ham illustrate the inequities of such an approach; and (3) the present doctrinal state of play is far richer and more accommodating, permitting co-existence as an alternative solution in appropriate circumstances.[317]

There is also a perception that the principle of territoriality coupled with formal equality for all applicants under trade mark regimes disadvantages regional collectives. It makes them play the game according to trade mark rules, which can be expensive and practically unrealistic. Geographical signs are accepted onto trade mark registers when they are considered arbitrary (e.g. ALASKA PINEAPPLES), or where the applicant establishes that she has taught the relevant marketplace to

---

[315] E.g., this has been incorporated into Art. 22.3 of TRIPS.

[316] TRIPS Council, 'Minutes of the Meeting on 5–7 March 2002', 22 March 2002 (IP/C/M/35), [155] (United States).

[317] This is a summary of arguments considered more extensively in D. Gangjee, 'Quibbling Siblings: Conflicts between Trade Marks and GIs' (2007) 82 *Chicago–Kent Law Review* 1253.

256   TRIPS today

perceive an otherwise geographically descriptive sign (invalid subject matter) as a badge of commercial origin (valid subject matter).[318] The dispute between the coffeehouse chain Starbucks and the Ethiopian government is a case in point. When the government attempted to register the geographical signs HARAR and SIDAMO as regular trade marks, the latter was problematic because of the existence of a prior trade mark registration by Starbucks which included Sidamo. Meanwhile HARAR was objected to on the basis that it was a generic expression.[319] Regional designations are therefore perceived as being up for grabs by the nimble. Producer groups in countries without a history of GI protection have now begun the complex process of coalescing around IGO specifications, establishing mutually acceptable production standards and defining the acceptable boundaries of production. In this period of flux, they are wide open to pre-emptive trade mark registrations in commercially significant markets. A relevant example is Kobe beef from Japan. It has already been registered as a trademark by producers based outside of Japan in the US, Australia and Canada.[320] I therefore cannot share Professor Kur's optimism that 'there is little evidence anyhow that conflicts between trade marks and GIs are likely to occur in a conspicuous number of cases'.[321] In early 2007 the International Alpaca Association, representing Peruvian breeders and those producing fibres from alpacas and llamas, objected to an application by a US farm to register ALPACAMARK[322] as a certification mark.[323] Another illustration is provided by MALABAR, recently registered for a wide range of foodstuff including pepper in the UK,[324] when Malabar Pepper has been registered in India as a GI from the state of Kerala.[325] Then there is Assam, which is a protected GI in India,[326]

---

[318] Ibid., 1259–60.

[319] Hughes plausibly argues that the Ethiopian Government's role as applicant is open to criticism. J. Hughes, 'Coffee and Chocolate – Can We Help Developing Country Farmers Through Geographical Indications?', International Intellectual Property Institute, Washington, DC (2009) 106–115. However, the point I wish to make is that further upstream in the process, trade mark registration systems are often indifferent to applications by third parties which contain geographical signs.

[320] These registrations are considered in Gangjee, *Protecting Geographical Indications as Trade Marks: The Prospects and Pitfalls*.

[321] Kur, 'Quibbling Siblings – Comments to Dev Gangjee's Presentation' 1325.

[322] US Trade Mark Serial Nos. 78425026, 78708488.

[323] 'International Alpaca Association: (IAA) Opposes U.S. Certification Mark Registration' *PIIPA Newsletter* Vol. 5 (January 2007).

[324] UK Trade Mark No. 2413954.

[325] Presently registered as Serial No. 47 with the Geographical Indications Registry, India. See www.ipindia.nic.in/girindia/.

[326] GI Serial No. 115.

The relationship between GIs and trade marks 257

while ASSAM BREEZE has been applied for in relation to tea in the US by a corporation based in Atlanta, Georgia.[327] Similarly, ASSAM has been registred as a composite (i.e. word and figurative) mark in Australia, by a registrant based in Taiwan, for tea and other beverages.[328]

These conflicts often showcase the tactical deployment of rhetoric and doctrine, emblematic of the broader politics of GIs. They also precipitate a more fundamental question. Are GIs sufficiently similar to trade marks for the principle of treating like cases alike to be engaged? If they are different, how has this difference been articulated? This final section therefore acts as a bridge, since the normative debates around why GIs deserve differential treatment are considered in Chapter 6.

7.1 The language of trumps: FITFIR

The FITFIR rule has been actively proposed as the optimal solution for such categorical conflicts.[329] The underlying reason for this is enunciated in the US Supreme Court's *United Drug* decision, where purchasers rely upon the prior mark as indicating the origin of the goods and this reliance must be protected.[330] FITFIR therefore 'is a shorthand way to refer to the combined principles of priority and exclusivity. What this means is that the sign that is protected first, whether it is a trade mark or a GI, shall take precedence over (principle of priority) and prevent the use of (principle of exclusivity) any conflicting subsequent sign. These two principles form the very heart of trade mark law'.[331] An experienced practitioner goes on to explain that preserving the '[e]xclusivity of the prior right is the equitable solution for conflicts between intellectual property. Its strict application to the specific conflict between trademarks and geographical indications is and should continue to be the international standard'.[332] The active promotion of this apparently

---

[327] US Trade Mark Serial Nos. 85146967. Exclusive use to ASSAM has been disclaimed, but this does affect the the the ability of the Assam GI to consistently signal origin in Eastern India.

[328] Australian Trade Mark No. 1000768.

[329] See generally WIPO, 'Possible Solutions for Conflicts between Trademarks and Geographical Indications and for Conflicts between Homonymous Geographical Indications', 8 June 2000 (SCT/5/3); S. Stern, 'Geographical Indications and Trade Marks: Conflicts and Possible Resolutions', 13 June 2003 (WIPO/GEO/SFO/03/13), 4.

[330] *United Drug Co* v. *Theodore Rectanus Co* 248 US 90 (1918).

[331] F. Z. Hellwig, 'Why the Principles of Priority and Exclusivity cannot be Compromised – The Trademark Owner's Perspective on Geographical Indications and First in Time, First in Right' (INTA Policy Paper).

[332] B. Goebel, 'Why Should Famous TMs Deserve Greater Protection against GIs?', AIDV Conference on TM–GI Conflicts for Wines & Spirits (Reims, 18–19 March 2004), 11.

258   TRIPS today

even-handed solution has developed in response to the EU approach. European countries 'traditionally pursue a concept of geographical indication protection which assumes a certain element of superiority of geographical indications over trade marks'.[333]

This represents the official US position on the issue, evident from the relative configuration of trade mark and GI obligations in a series of recent Free Trade Agreements (FTAs). In the context of the US–Chile FTA, the principle received a ringing endorsement:

> In general, we applaud the application of the 'first in time, first in right' principle to trade marks and geographical indications. This may serve as a useful precedent.[334]

By way of an illustration, the US–Australia FTA clearly applies this principle in Article 17.2(4). The issue remains a live one and FITFIR was proposed before the Committee on Agriculture of the US House of Representatives in 2003.[335] It is also projected with varying degrees of proselytising fervour across an assortment of international platforms, where these take the form of non-binding statements and resolutions. Some of these statements advocate an extreme position. The International Trade Mark Association (INTA) 'supports the principle of "first in time, first in right" priority when resolving conflicts between geographical indications and trademarks'.[336] The support is so emphatic that INTA 'unequivocally states that coexistence between a later GI and a prior trademark is not an acceptable alternative'.[337] Others broadly allude to the primacy of FITFIR, but are willing to consider mitigating factors to varying degrees. This includes the Resolution in 1994 of the General Assembly of the intergovernmental International Vine and Wine Office (OIV),[338] the AIPPI Resolution on Q.62 at its 37th Congress in Rio in 1998,[339] and a draft resolution of the International Wine Law Association

---

[333] Goebel, 'The Road from Doha', 973.

[334] US–Chile Free Trade Agreement, *Report of the Industry Sector Advisory Committee on Consumer Goods* (ISAC-4) February 2003, para. V(c).

[335] Hearings before the Committee on Agriculture, House of Representatives on the Status of the World Trade Organization Negotiations on Agriculture, (108–5) 108th Congress (2003), 127, 341, 361.

[336] INTA, Resolution on the Protection of Geographical Indications and Trade Marks (24 September 1997), available at www.inta.org/.

[337] INTA, 'Comments on WIPO SCT/6/3 Working Paper for the March 12–16, 2001 Conference in Geneva', [5].

[338] See Recital 5 of Resolution OIV/ECO 3/94.

[339] AIPPI, 'Question Q62: Appellations of Origin, Indications of Source and Geographical Indications – Resolution' [1998] *Annuaire* 389.

The relationship between GIs and trade marks   259

(AIDV).[340] Through this process, it is repeatedly asserted that FITFIR stands as a beacon for clarity, predictability and even-handedness when resolving such disputes but this grossly oversimplifies the issue. Its doctrinal evolution reveals that FITFIR presumes like cases (conflicts between trade marks) within a single jurisdiction. Neither of these aspects maps neatly on to the types of international disputes under consideration here.

7.2 Parma ham and the inequities of FITFIR

Two very similar disputes concerning attempts to register Parma ham as a trade mark capture the inequity arising from FITFIR, as opposed to co-existence, as a solution. In each case, the conflict arose within the registered trade mark system. The applicant in both cases was the Italian Consorzio, founded in 1963 by producers located in Parma who manufactured this distinctive air-dried ham.[341] The Consorzio attempted to register a certification or collective mark but found a similar sign already existed on the trade mark register for similar products. In both, a co-existing registration was also achieved. This is therefore not a tale of sour grapes or binary choices. These decisions are illuminating because they demonstrate the possibilities of doctrinally developed safe havens permitting coexistence within the existing law.

The *Parma Sausage* case[342] in the US showcases the legitimacy of claims on both sides. A former native of the Italian region had registered 'Parma Brand' in 1969 for a variety of meat products including prosciutto. The name was adopted in honour of his hometown but the meat was sourced from the US. Meanwhile, Italian Parma producers faced an insurmountable obstacle to their exports. Due to an outbreak of African swine flu in the late 1960s, the US Government banned the importation of pork products from Italy. This was only lifted in 1989. The prior trade mark registration proved an obstacle to the Consorzio's efforts to register similarly worded certification marks, so it had no alternative but to challenge the prior trade mark. This took the form that the registered mark was geographically deceptive within the meaning of s. 2(a) of the Lanham Act. In order to succeed, the Consorzio had to prove that:[343] (1) the registered mark was 'geographically deceptively misdescriptive',

---

[340] AIDV Draft Resolution on Trade Marks and Geographical Indications (August 2004).
[341] Dossier No. IT/PDO/0117/0067; Registered on 05/02/2008.
[342] *Consorzio del Prosciutto di Parma* v. *Parma Sausage Products* 23 USPQ 2d 1894 (1992 TTAB); 1992 WL 233379 (TTAB) 1.
[343] Ibid., 4.

260   TRIPS today

i.e., the term communicated a known and specific geographical origin, there was a goods–place association by the relevant public for this origin and the goods did not in fact originate there (making it geographically misdescriptive); and (2) the misdescription was material, i.e., likely to affect the customer's purchasing decision. The case hinged 'on the legal question of the time as to which geographic deceptiveness must be established, i.e., the date the registration issued or the time of trial.'[344] There was insufficient evidence that the Consorzio's product had established a goods–place association prior to 1989 and the Board went on to hold that the operative date to establish geographic deceptiveness should be the date registration, i.e., in 1969, when the mark was not deceptive.

The TTAB acknowledged that their reasoning could lead to 'what seems, at first, an anomalous result, namely that, even though a mark were to be proven to deceive the public at the present time, a registration of the mark cannot be cancelled by the Board'.[345] However, the legislative framework sought to balance the proprietary interests of a trade mark owner against the public interest in preventing deception. The Board's conclusion reveals the complications in trying to choose between claims in such cases:

We candidly acknowledge that this case has presented us with a difficult situation to resolve. On the one hand, petitioner has expended great efforts to promote prosciutto from Parma, and has apparently developed a worldwide reputation for this product. It also has extensively used and promoted certification marks containing the word 'Parma' and is faced with not being able to register them in the United States because of respondent's registration. Further, the absence of prosciutto di Parma from the United States market for 22 years was not petitioner's fault, and indeed was a situation which it sought vigorously to change. On the other hand, respondent has used its 'Parma Brand' mark for more than 35 years, and has owned a registration for it for more than 20 years. At the time [of registration, the mark] was neither geographically deceptively misdescriptive nor geographically deceptive.[346]

The Board concluded that, in these circumstances, it would be more equitable to favour the respondent. The postscript to this tale is that the Consorzio did manage to register their marks[347] while the respondent's mark continues to exist on the register. A comparable

---

[344] Ibid.   [345] Ibid., 6.   [346] Ibid., 11.
[347] See, e.g. 'PROSCIUTTO DI PARMA' (Reg. No. 2014629) and 'PARMA HAM' (Reg. No. 2014628). The basis was use in commerce and incontestability after a five-year period.

The relationship between GIs and trade marks 261

negotiation of co-existence occurs in the Canadian *Parma* dispute,[348] which proceeds along very similar lines.

7.3   Descriptive fair use and co-existence

Having already elaborated upon this conflict in greater detail,[349] what follows is only a brief sketch of why co-existence is possible under the ubiquitous 'descriptive use' defence in trade mark law. The affirmation for this is found in the recent WTO Panel Report on GIs.[350] The nub of this dispute between the EU and the US as well as Australia was summarised in the initial request for consultations:

Regulation 2081/92, as amended, does not provide national treatment with respect to geographical indications, and does not provide sufficient protection to pre-existing trade marks that are similar or identical to a geographical indication. This situation appears to be inconsistent with the European Communities' obligations under the TRIPS Agreement.[351]

For our purposes, it is the claim that co-existence, as embodied in Article 14(2) of Regulation 2081/92, violated the exclusive rights of trade mark owners in Article 16.1 (rights to prevent infringing uses by subsequent signs) which is of interest. The EC's response, *inter alia*, was that this provision was justified as a permissible, limited exception under Article 17 of TRIPS:

Members may provide limited exceptions to the rights conferred by a trade mark, such as fair use of descriptive terms, provided that such exceptions take account of the legitimate interests of the owner of the trademark and of third parties.

The arguments clustered around two central issues: (1) was Article 14(2) a limited exception?; (2) did the EC Regulation satisfactorily take into account the legitimate interests of trade mark owners and third parties?

---

[348] *Consorzio del Prosciutto di Parma* v. *Maple Leaf Meats Inc* [2001] 2 FC 536 (Federal Court of Canada, Trial Division). On relevant issues, the decision was upheld by the Federal Court of Appeals in *Consorzio del Prosciutto di Parma* v. *Maple Leaf Meats* [2002] FCA 169 (2 May 2002). Co-existence was made possible by recognising the Italian Consorzio as a public authority and registering the mark under S 9(1)(n)(iii) of the Canadian Trade Marks Act (RSC, 1985, c. T-13), although this route may no longer be possible for other IGO collectives. See *Maple Leaf Foods Inc* v. *Consorzio Del Prosciutto Di Parma* 2009 FC 1035 (15 October 2009).

[349] See Gangjee, 'Quibbling Siblings'.

[350] European Communities – Protection of Trademarks and Geographical Indications for Agricultural Products and Foodstuffs, 15 March 2005 (WT/DS174/R). The complainant in this dispute was the United States. As part of the same proceedings, a similar complaint by Australia resulted in Panel Report (WT/DS290/R).

[351] Request for Consultations by the United States, 7 June 1999 (WT/DS174/1), 1.

262   TRIPS today

In response to the first issue, the indispensable geographical nucleus of a GI played a significant role in establishing the descriptiveness of such signs. Here co-existence provided for a minor diminution of trade mark rights (as opposed to the alternative interpretation of a quantitatively limited group benefiting from the exception) since GIs were granted in qualified circumstances and trade mark owners retained rights against other third parties. Finally, where a risk of confusion was high, coexistence between a prior trade mark and subsequent GI was prohibited under EU law and the mark would trump.[352] In response to the second issue, the Panel developed the TRIPS notion of 'legitimate interests' as 'a normative claim calling for protection of interests that are "justifiable" in the sense that they are supported by relevant public policies or other social norms'.[353] In balancing the legitimate interests of GI users, mark owners and the consuming public, the Panel was emphatic that the fact that GIs had both a brand (distinguishing) aspect and a geographically descriptive aspect did not make the interests of GI producers illegitimate. The distinguishing function of GIs did not displace the descriptive one. Therefore coexistence was endorsed as permissible under Article 17 of TRIPS. Recent decisions of both the US Supreme Court[354] and the ECJ[355] also suggest that a brand-like or distinguishing use of the contested sign is not fatal to its ability to simultaneously be descriptive. Despite the rhetorical exhortations of FITFIR's proponents, appropriately qualified co-existence remains a viable option under TRIPS. More interestingly, conflicts between these two categories of signs compel us to think more closely about the similarities and differences between GIs and trade marks.

8.   Conclusion

The TRIPS GI regime is not quite the consolidating project or constellation of determinate rules that it's made out to be. Notwithstanding certain improvements associated with the regime, many commentators give it far too much credit. Interdisciplinary scholarship is often too deferential, crediting TRIPS GI rules with the virtues of clarity and determinacy. We need to appreciate both the extent to which these provisions remain a work in progress, as well as the interpretative leeway available. As a corrective to this tendency, a historical perspective is

---

[352] (WTO/DS174/R), 143–5.   [353] Ibid., 146.
[354] *K. P. Permanent Make-Up Inc* v. *Lasting Impression Inc* 543 US 111 (2004).
[355] *Gerolsteiner Brunnen & Co* v. *Putsch* (C-100/02) [2004] ECR I-691; [2004] ETMR 40 (ECJ).

Conclusion 263

invaluable. This chapter is offered as a counter-narrative to scholarship which presumes the TRIPS GI to be a conceptually stable entity, associated with clear rules. Nevertheless, TRIPS remains significant as a site of discursive formation. The contours of international GI protection are shaped by the influential debates and disagreements taking place within this framework, making this platform uniquely authoritative. Recognising this important function does not downplay the impact of bilateral negotiations and the ensuing free or preferential trade agreements which contain GI provisions.[356] Instead the argument here is that TRIPS continues to operate as a reference point, providing the language and conceptual resources for framing international GI protection.

This chapter has reviewed not only the extent to which TRIPS is built upon compromises, but also identified the raw materials from which these concessions have been crafted. The definition of a GI in Article 22.1 has been influenced by prior negotiations under the auspices of WIPO as well as the EU's Regulation 2081/92, where the *terroir* and reputation logics were fused together. As a result, there is considerable equivocation over central aspects of the definition, such as the methodology for delimiting the region of origin and specifying the link between product and place. Article 22.1 was designed to be flexible and accommodating, but this may be at the cost of coherence unless a more compelling normative account of the link can be developed. Here the recognition of the human dimension, of collective investment and innovation over time, has potential. Otherwise the logic of unfair competition prevention, often presumed to be the foundation for Articles 22 to 24, can only take us so far. Article 23 in particular embodies differential treatment for certain GIs, by way of 'absolute' protection. Critics of this tier of protection ask a valid question – if 'Prosciutto di Parma' and 'Pisco' are signs used in the marketplace to signal information about the associated products, then why shouldn't they be treated the same as trade marks or unregistered trade names, in accordance with established principles of unfair competition prevention and contingent upon the meaning of the sign?[357] The different approaches in Articles 22 and 23

---

[356] They remain significant for individual GIs, since the reciprocal protection of listed terms and the re-negotiation of generic status features in such agreements. See M. Handler and B. Mercurio, 'Intellectual Property', in S. Lester and B. Mercurio (eds.), *Bilateral and Regional Trade Agreements: Commentary and Analysis* (Cambridge University Press, 2009), 308, 317; D. Vivas-Eugui and C. Spennemann, 'The Treatment of Geographical Indications in Recent Regional and Bilateral Free Trade Agreements', in M. Perez Pugatch (ed.), *The Intellectual Property Debate: Perspectives from Law, Economics and Political Economy* (Edward Elgar, Cheltenham 2006), 305.

[357] For a representative critique, see K. Raustiala and S. R. Munzer, 'The Global Struggle over Geographical Indications' (2007) 18 *European Journal of International Law* 337, 340

264   TRIPS today

reflect an underlying dichotomy, between protecting signs based on their actual denotative functions and protecting products by reserving the signs associated with them. As we have seen in Chapter 1, the most prominent explanation for this differential treatment is refreshingly candid, rhetorically compelling and grounded in evidence from trade negotiations. It is alleged that since certain aspects of GI protection do not follow the conventional logic of sign protection in unfair competition law, this special treatment is simply the result of European lobbying, based on sectorial interests. There is a lingering suspicion that GIs are all about the entrenched interests of European agricultural and viticultural lobbies, seeking insulation against open competition. With these debates playing out within the context of international trade negotiations, this framing has also been dominant within IP discourse. This critique does have traction and must be taken seriously. Yet it does not exhaust the set of reasons for differential treatment. At present a broader constituency, including producers in several developing countries, have an interest in GIs while more convincing normative accounts of enhanced protection are emerging. While unfair competition doctrine cannot provide a complete explanation for the scope of protection, today's alternative explanations are driven by redistributive agendas and based on policy arguments which attend more closely to the specifics of regional products. They suggest that it may be normatively desirable to prevent the signs associated with these regional products from being copied, as opposed to a prohibition against copying the product or the process of manufacture which is found in patent or copyright law. Under this approach, the conceptualisation of GI protection takes on a hybrid form, between the creative/inventive species of IP (recognising skill, effort and innovation invested in the product) and the marketing/branding species of IP (recognising the ability of the sign to communicate something specific). We now turn to some of these arguments in the concluding chapter, asking whether they could form the basis for relocating international IGO protection.

(arguing 'that GI protection in international law is justifiable for many of the reasons that trade mark protection is justifiable: primarily, to protect consumers against confusion and to lower their search costs. We contend, however, that the current level of protection afforded by TRIPS for wine and spirits – which disallows any mention of a protected GI by a producer outside the region, even if the place of production of the product is clearly indicated – is unwarranted and goes well beyond what any existing theory of property can support').

6 TRIPS tomorrow?

1. The significance of contemporary debates

Having considered the conceptual inheritance of the past and its influence upon the present, what of the future? This penultimate chapter is more speculative and explores some of the implications for a relocation of GI law, as a hybrid encompassing both signs and certain types of regional products as its subject matter. It begins by outlining present-day debates over proposed modifications to the existing TRIPS regime, which rest upon a familiar fault line. There is entrenched disagreement between those proposing that GIs are functional isomorphs of trade marks, or other types of commercial signs protected via unfair competition rules, and those who suggest that GIs are entitled to differential treatment. The latter increasingly rely on principled or policy based arguments to support the existence of an independent regime and explain its features. The venue for these debates is the TRIPS Council, where the principal issues relate to the extension of Article 23 levels of protection to all products, as well as the establishment of a multilateral GI register, initially restricted to wines and spirits but possibly opening up to all products in the years ahead.

Given the significant numbers of new entrants on either side – those who have not actively participated in previous IGO debates – these deliberations open up the discursive space for a fundamental reconsideration of GI protection. When the object of protection is conceived of as the sign or designation ('Darjeeling'), the more conventional international rules can be explained by drawing upon familiar arguments from unfair competition doctrine. However, if an additional object of GI protection is the product (the fragrant tea collectively grown in a northern district of West Bengal) with the designation being protected as a proxy because we value such regional products, this could potentially explain the deviation from unfair competition rules. By stepping away from unfair competition rationalisations, we need alternative and independent justifications for supporting such collectively developed products under the IP umbrella.

266   TRIPS tomorrow?

This opportunity to consider an alternative or supplementary epistemology of GIs must be welcomed. These debates broaden parameters and incorporate values other than a narrowly conceived informational efficiency dynamic, which otherwise serves as the theoretical basis for protecting signs.[1] While these more recent justifications are not free from ambiguities and contradictions, some have the potential for normative guidance and they should not be dismissed without a fair hearing. These negotiations also have important consequences for the institutional form of GI protection, since the future increasingly seems to be registration-based. The bureaucratic logic of a registration system raises certain questions which have been largely ignored.

2.   Extending Article 23 to all products

At the time of writing, over a hundred WTO Members have submitted a request to extend the enhanced scope of protection available for wines and spirits under Article 23 to all products which satisfy the definition in Article 22.1.[2] For the EU, the GI extension debate has structural resonances with the WTO negotiations on agricultural reform and the withdrawal of agricultural subsidies in particular.[3] The working assumption here is that GIs signify quality as well as provenance and generate price differentials on that basis. Since consumers are willing to pay more for such goods, this encourages farmers to invest in making the transition from producing undifferentiated bulk commodities towards producing higher quality niche products. Given the global appetite for regional

---

[1] For a recent injection of such values into international IP policy making, consider the accommodation of the 'development dimension'. See WIPO General Assembly Document, 'Proposal by Argentina and Brazil for the Establishment of a Development Agenda for WIPO', 27 August 2004 (WO/GA/31/11). Cf. M. Sunder, 'The Invention of Traditional Knowledge' (2007) 70 *Law and Contemporary Problems* 97, 102 (The 'space for discussing intellectual property's distributive and social effects is expanding' beyond neo-classical price theory and a focus on economic incentives or efficiency); L. Helfer, 'Regime Shifting: The TRIPS Agreement and New Dynamics of International Intellectual Property Law Making' (2004) 29 *Yale Journal of International Law* 1 (reviewing the strategic processes by which IP issues are shifted to more receptive fora, such as the World Health Organization or the Food and Agriculture Organization, amenable to the distinct logics of biodiversity conservation, public health priorities and human rights agendas).

[2] Communication from Albania et al., 'Draft Modalities for TRIPs Related Issues', 19 July 2008 (TN/C/W/52). A full list of the 109 countries can be found in 'Groups in the TRIPS Negotiations', available at www.wto.org/english/tratop_e/trips_e/trips_groups_e.htm.

[3] The EC has linked the issue of improved market access in the agricultural negotiations to the issue of fair competition, i.e., more effective protection against usurpation for agricultural products. WTO Committee on Agriculture, 'EC Comprehensive Negotiating Proposal', 14 December 2000 (G/AG/NG/W/90), [3].

Extending Article 23 to all products 267

products and the associated willingness to pay a premium, developing countries have also been considering the export potential for their regional specialities, which could be boosted by enhanced GI protection.[4] Against this backdrop, fairly specific proposals have been submitted to the TRIPS Council, which replace the use of 'wines' or 'wines and spirits' at various points in Article 23, with the more compendious 'goods'.[5] The discussions on extension have centred on two sequentially ordered issues – the procedure and mandate, on the one hand, and the merits of extension, on the other.[6] The disagreement over the mandate for extension is particularly acute.[7] Since the procedural basis for these deliberations has proven enduringly contentious, it is unlikely that there will be progress on GI extension anytime in the near future. However, the extension debate itself is significant, since it provides us with an opportunity to reconsider the basis for GI protection. These arguments in favour of extension can be parsed under the following headings: (1) the existence of two levels of protection; (2) the inadequacy of Article 22; and (3) the benefits of Article 23. These arguments have not circulated unchallenged and the ensuing debate is well documented in the literature.[8] The analysis in this chapter is more targeted

---

[4] Communication from Bulgaria et al., 'The Extension of the Additional Protection for Geographical Indications to Products other than Wines and Spirits', 24 June 2002 (IP/C/W/353), [4]; Communication from Bulgaria et al., 'Geographical Indications – The Significance of "Extension" in the TRIPS Agreement and its Benefits for WTO Members', 9 July 2003 (TN/C/W/14), 2; Communication from Bulgaria et al., 'Doha Work Programme – The Extension of the Additional Protection for Geographical Indications to Products other than Wines and Spirits', 14 December 2004 (TN/C/W/21/Rev.1), [8].

[5] E.g., Communication from the EC, 'Geographical Indications', 14 June 2005 (TN/C/W/26).

[6] Report by the Director General, 'Issues Related to the Extension of the Protection of Geographical Indications Provided for in Article 23 of the TRIPS Agreement [and] those Related to the Relationship between the TRIPS Agreement and the Convention on Biological diversity', 9 June 2008 (TN/C/W/50), [2] ('The work continues to be characterized by different views on both the merits of GI extension and on whether it was agreed at Doha that this is part of the negotiations').

[7] Supporters base their proposals on a combination of: (1) existing TRIPS provisions, such as Art. 24.1 (aimed at increasing the protection of individual GIs under Art. 23) and Art. 24.2 (where the TRIPS Council reviews the application of GI provisions and can take action to facilitate as well as further their objectives); and (2) paragraphs 12 and 18 of the WTO Doha Ministerial Declaration. However, these readings are contested. For an overview, see A. C. Lang, 'On the Need to Expand Article 23 of the TRIPS Agreement' (2006) 16 *Duke Journal of Comparative & International Law* 487, 504.

[8] For an overview, see S. Fusco, 'Geographical Indications: A Discussion of the TRIPS Regulation after the Ministerial Conference of Hong Kong' (2008) 12 *Marquette Intellectual Property Law Review* 197; E. C. Creditt, 'Terroir vs. Trademarks: The Debate over Geographical Indications and Expansions to the TRIPS Agreement' (2009) 11 *Vanderbilt Journal of Entertainment & Technology Law* 429. For arguments in support of extension, see F. Addor and A. Grazioli, 'Geographical Indications beyond

268   TRIPS tomorrow?

and focuses on the third heading. While Article 22 does impose certain burdens on GI producers, this is an insufficiently convincing basis for enhanced protection. Many of these burdens also apply to trade mark proprietors and others using unregistered signs in the course of trade.[9] If we are to make life easier for GI rights holders as a preferred class, independent reasons must be provided for doing so.

First, there is the existence of two separate levels of protection in Article 22 and Article 23, which many find inexplicable. Why reserve the favoured treatment in Article 23 for the restricted categories of wines and spirits? Those supporting extension suggest that there 'is no systematic or logical explanation for the distinction'[10] and that there are 'no commercial, economic or legal reasons to limit effective protection only to GIs for wines and spirits or not to provide such protection also to GIs for all other products'.[11] This would recognise the interests of developing countries, enabling 'more effective protection' for a broader range of products, such as, 'rice, silk, coffee, tea, tobacco, apples, pineapples, cotton, vanilla, honey, beef, palm oil, cinnamon, carpets, ceramics, silver or wooden handicrafts'.[12] Dwijen Rangnekar points out that GI products 'tend to be from the rural, agricultural and handicraft sectors of the economy', while Aaron Lang argues that the 'disparity ... disproportionately burdens developing countries'.[13] Opponents counter

---

Wines and Spirits: A Roadmap for a Better Protection for Geographical Indications in the WTO/TRIPS Agreement' (2002) 5 JWIP 865; J. M. Cortes Martin, 'TRIPS Agreement: Towards a Better Protection for Geographical Indications?' (2004) 30 *Brooklyn Journal of International Law* 117; I. Calboli, 'Expanding the Protection of Geographical Indications of Origin under TRIPS: Old Debate or New Opportunity?' (2006) 10 *Marquette Intellectual Property Law Review* 181; M. Ritzert, 'Champagne is from Champagne: An Economic Justification for Extending Trade Mark-Level Protection to Wine-Related Geographical Indications' (2009) 37 *American Intellectual Property Law Association Quarterly Journal* 191. For critiques of extension, see T. L. Staten, 'Geographical Indications Protection under the TRIPS Agreement: Uniformity Not Extension' (2005) 87 *Journal of the Patent & Trade Mark Office Society* 221; D. L. Snyder, 'Enhanced Protections for Geographical Indications Under TRIPS: Potential Conflicts Under the U.S. Constitutional and Statutory Regimes' (2008) 18 *Fordham IP, Media & Entertainment Law Journal* 1297; M. Handler and R. Burrell, 'GI Blues: The Global Disagreement Over Geographical Indications', in K. Bowrey, M. Handler and D. Nicol (eds.), *Emerging Challenges in Intellectual Property* (Oxford University Press, Melbourne 2011).

[9] An issue also raised by Chile. See TRIPS Council, 'Minutes of the Meeting of 17–19 September 2002', 8 November 2002 (IP/C/M/37/Add.1), [144].

[10] Communication from Bulgaria et al., 'Implementation of Art 24.1', 2 December 2000 (IP/C/W/204/Rev.1), [7].

[11] Communication from Bulgaria et al., (TN/C/W/14), 1.

[12] Communication from Bulgaria et al., (TN/C/W/21/Rev.1), [4] and Fn 2.

[13] See respectively D. Rangnekar, 'The Socio-Economics of Geographical Indications – A Review of Empirical Evidence from Europe' UNCTAD-ICTSD Issue Paper No. 8 (2004), 1; Lang, 'On the Need to Expand Article 23', 497.

Extending Article 23 to all products   269

this demand for an upgrade by wielding Occam's razor. Their preferred solution would be to apply Article 22 levels of protection to all GIs and simply remove Article 23.[14] Since the TRIPS provisions took shape against the backdrop of broader trade policy agendas, additional protection was 'the result of historical negotiation and specific circumstances that were particular to the wine sector. It had been agreed as a significant concession in the Uruguay Round, not because of any belief in its inherent merits'.[15] It rapidly becomes apparent that the mere existence of two levels of protection is an insufficient basis for extension. This leads on to the second cluster of arguments, which relate to the inadequacy of Article 22 levels of protection.

Under the second heading, the concerns relate to the uncertainties and costs associated with Article 22 on the one hand, along with the narrowness of the scope of protection on the other. Under Article 22, GI rights holders have to undergo costly procedures to demonstrate that consumers are confused, which often involves the expense of opinion polls. These expenses and the associated uncertainty of outcomes are acutely felt by smaller and modestly resourced producer groups from developing countries.[16] There is some evidence to substantiate this, with the Indian Tea Board providing figures indicating that the costs for retaining monitoring agencies and litigating to protect Darjeeling run into the hundreds of thousands of dollars.[17] The extension of Article 23 'absolute' standards would eliminate legal uncertainties by requiring producers and traders 'to answer only one simple question when deciding whether to use a GI on a product: did the product come from the place and have the given quality designated by the GI in question? This was easy to examine and would not result in any additional costs'.[18] In response, opponents argue that GIs are private IP rights – once again making questionable assumptions about legal classification based on parallels with trade mark law – and those who benefit from private

[14] TRIPS Council, 'Minutes of Meeting on 25–27 June 2002', 10 September 2002 (IP/C/M/36/Add.1), [164] (Chile); TRIPS Council, 'Minutes of the Meeting on 25–27 and 29 November and 20 December 2002', 5 February 2003 (IP/C/M/38), [156] (Argentina).

[15] WTO, 'Issues Related to the Extension of the Protection of Geographical Indications Provided for in Article 23 of the TRIPS Agreement to Products Other Than Wines and Spirits', 18 May 2005 (TN/C/W/25), [9].

[16] Communication from Bulgaria et al., (IP/C/W/353), [13]; TRIPS Council, 'Minutes of the Meeting on 5–7 March 2002', 22 March 2002 (IP/C/M/35), [166] (Turkey); Addor and Grazioli, 'Geographical Indications beyond Wines and Spirits', 881.

[17] K. Das, 'Socio-economic Implications of Protecting Geographical Indications in India', Centre for WTO Studies, India (August 2009), 27–8; D. Giovannucci, E. Barham and R. Pirog, 'Defining and Marketing "Local" Foods: Geographical Indications for US Products' (2010) 13 JWIP 94, 105.

[18] TRIPS Council, (IP/C/M/38), [71] (Switzerland).

270   TRIPS tomorrow?

property must bear the expense of policing it.[19] More plausibly, they also suggest that GIs need to be first recognised domestically, while setting up a GI in the home country would involve an investment and have associated costs.[20] As for certainty, there would still need to be determinations about the scope of protection. For example, would translations such as Parmesan be caught within the scope of protection offered to Parmigiano Reggiano and more generally, what would constitute a translation?[21] Finally, they suggest that Article 22 provides sufficient protection. Its provisions need to first be implemented in the national laws of all Members and these provisions then need to be utilised.[22] Indicating an option already on the table, they suggest the adoption of certification or collective marks.[23] As we shall see in Section 4 below, there are important limitations and qualifications associated with plugging into the trade mark system. Turning to the limited scope of protection, Lang summarises the complaints about free riding, giving the example of 'Parma-style ham, made in America':

> [The] consumer confusion requirement makes legitimately labelled goods susceptible to parasitic free-riding ... This exploitative use of legitimate GIs not only unjustly enriches follow-on producers, but also '[diverts] a considerable share of the market away from legitimate producers and manufacturers'... and shortchanges those who toil to preserve the reputation and quality of the authentic goods.[24]

Similar arguments have already been reviewed while analysing Article 23 in the previous chapter. They find a mention in the submissions of several delegations.[25] An established riposte is that such usage arises on the basis of historic patterns of migration, with immigrants transporting familiar terminology along with manufacturing techniques and

---

[19]   Ibid., [78] (Australia). Interestingly, countries such as the US and Australia who make this argument are also supporters of the recently drafted Anti-Counterfeiting Trade Agreement (ACTA) which significantly engages state machinery and customs authorities in particular in order to support private parties in the protection of intangible property. See H. G. Ruse-Khan, 'A Trade Agreement Creating Barriers to International Trade? ACTA Border Measures and Goods in Transit', Max Planck Institute for Intellectual Property, Competition & Tax Law Research Paper No. 10–10.

[20]   TRIPS Council, (IP/C/M/38), [77] (Australia), [111] (Guatemala) and [113] (Chile).

[21]   Ibid., [183].

[22]   Ibid., [76] (Australia); Communication from Argentina et al., 'Implications of Article 23 Extension', 8 November 2002 (IP/C/W/386), [6]; TRIPS Council, (IP/C/M/37/Add.1), [121], [166] (New Zealand).

[23]   WTO, 'Issues Related to Extension', [38].

[24]   Lang, 'On the Need to Expand Article 23', 490–1.

[25]   E.g., TRIPS Council, (IP/C/M/37/Add.1), [115] (Bulgaria); Statement by Switzerland, 'Joint Statement by the GI-Friends Group', 13 July 2004 (TN/C/4), 2; Communication from Bulgaria et al., (IP/C/W/353), [13].

Extending Article 23 to all products

expertise.[26] While the complaints about misappropriation or free riding are directed at benefits to the allegedly undeserving, they also refer to the harmful consequences of such free riding. If external producers start using Gorgonzola in a qualified manner (French gorgonzola, gorgonzola-style cheese), this will deplete any specific semantic content and inexorably pave the way to generic usage over time.[27] Since it may be difficult to prove such delocalising or otherwise qualified usage is misleading, this conduct may not be caught by Article 22. Developing countries could find their GIs depleted of origin or quality significance before they even have a chance to begin export-orientated marketing campaigns.

The third cluster of arguments considers the advantages of extending 'absolute' protection under Article 23. Since consumers increasingly value origin as well as associated product quality, the certainty of enhanced protection will encourage producers to seek out new opportunities in export markets. Stated briefly, the organisation of collectives and promotion of GIs will be incentivised.[28] A subsidiary argument is that extension would facilitate consumer choice by allowing consumers to trust the use of geographical designations on products, as well as associated characteristics and a specific production process, rather than speculate as to whether it was a generic, qualified or merely evocative use by third parties.[29] The latter argument is questioned on the basis of whether any value is added beyond Article 22, which should be able to capture all misleading uses thereby allowing consumers to trust signs. Meanwhile extension might involve external producers being forced to re-label and a concentration of production in the hands of those from the country of origin (for instance, only Greek Feta being available on the market), which would disadvantage consumers by limiting choice.[30] The former argument is attacked on two grounds. First, enhanced legal protection may not serve as a sufficient incentive, since product specifications will need to be developed, producers will need to be organised around these specifications and a heavy investment made in the marketing of the product.[31] Legal rules by themselves are no panacea.

---

[26] Communication from Argentina et al., (IP/C/W/386), [7].

[27] E.g., Statement by Switzerland, (TN/C/4), 2; Communication from Bulgaria et al., (IP/C/W/353), [13]; Communication from Bulgaria et al., (TN/C/W/21/Rev.1), [7], [13].

[28] TRIPS Council, (IP/C/M/38), [69] (Switzerland); Communication from Bulgaria et al., (TN/C/W/21/Rev.1), [8].

[29] See, e.g., TRIPS Council, (IP/C/M/35), [166] (Turkey).

[30] WTO, 'Issues Related to Extension', [62]. However, this limited monopoly over the designation will not stop competitors from manufacturing broadly substitutable cheese produced in brine, nor retailers such as supermarkets stocking it on the same shelves.

[31] The argument is emphatically made in J. Hughes, 'Coffee and Chocolate – Can We Help Developing Country Farmers Through Geographical Indications?', International

272   TRIPS tomorrow?

This is an important caveat but it highlights the additional factors for commercial success, rather than directly addressing the merits of Article 23. Second, the existence of the exceptions in Article 24, such as generic use or the grandfathering of prior trade marks, may nullify the benefits of Article 23 for individual GIs.[32] In addition to these arguments, the costs of extension for consumers and administrative implementation costs have also been debated.[33] Yet in most of the arguments reviewed so far, a certain underlying assumption can be detected. These arguments presume a certain starting point: if we were to go ahead and extend protection, what would the practical implications be for those affected and would extension deliver certain benefits? They do not seriously engage with the question of whether such an extension is justified in principle or policy in the first place, by revisiting the normative basis for the very existence of Article 23. It is at this stage that the significance of the following arguments becomes evident. These attempts at justifying enhanced protection explicitly or implicitly subscribe to the view that it is desirable because the class of regional products satisfying Article 22.1 *ought to be treated differently* when compared with regular trade marked goods. These largely instrumental arguments have surfaced both before the TRIPS Council and in the academic scholarship in recent years. As supplementary justifications, they buttress Article 23, which otherwise extends beyond the supporting framework of unfair competition.

These additional dimensions of GI protection have been acknowledged in WTO discussions, where delegates refer to cultural heritage associated with such products, as well as the consolidated intergenerational *savoir faire* or traditional knowledge informing their creation. They surface as early as 1989, when the representative for the European Community was elaborating upon a draft proposal:

> He hoped that countries which stood to benefit from being able to exploit more fully a comparative advantage in agriculture ... would recognise the legitimacy of the Community's desire to benefit fully from its own comparative advantage, which lay particularly in the accumulation of know-how, experience and in its specific conditions of soil and climate. The essence of what the Community was seeking was adequate protection against unfair use by third parties of the results of the work, investment and goodwill generated by its peoples.[34]

Intellectual Property Institute, Washington, DC (2009). See also TRIPS Council, (IP/C/M/38), [87] (New Zealand) and [113] (Chile).

[32] Communication from Argentina et al., (IP/C/W/386), [10] (Australia).

[33] See generally WTO, 'Issues Related to Extension' (TN/C/W/25).

[34] GATT, 'Minutes of Negotiating Group of 12–14 July 1989', 12 September 1989 (MTN.GNG/NG11/14), [53].

The demand for such recognition has been amplified over the past two decades. The WTO review of national GI legislation emphasises 'human creativity and human factors' as one of the major criteria which determine eligibility for protection. Members 'have highlighted the relevance of human factors to matters such as quality, traditional methods of production, vinicultural practices and methods of production, preparation and cultivation'.[35] Switzerland notes that as opposed to private trade marks rights, GIs 'form part of the national, cantonal or communal heritage'.[36] Referring to *sui generis* GI legislation, India's position was that a GI 'is considered under the Act to be the property or heritage of all the persons engaged in the activity of creating [such] products'.[37] The representative from Thailand supported extending GI protection since 'GIs were often related to culture and ancestors' traditional knowledge'.[38] Over the course of the extension debates, a more dynamic understanding of traditional knowledge has been proposed, while countering the 'implication that the efforts invested in the reputation of any famous product in relation to its geographical origin would not be creative [since it] failed to recognize that sometimes this reputation was based on decades or even centuries of creativity, including in the development of traditional knowledge'.[39] On the other hand, such claims have also been resisted and the heritage dimension has proved controversial, with some Members highlighting that the customary usage by immigrant populations would be made subservient to an 'authentic' controlling meaning for the GI.[40] Extension proponents respond by pointing to existing safety valves, including the generic exception and grandfathering of such uses, but the fact that GI protection is being debated in these terms reveals the efforts to relocate the basis for protecting such signs, because the underlying products are considered sufficiently important.

Beyond the recognition and promotion of cultural heritage and traditional knowledge, the catalogue of inter-related policy goals extends to employment generation, rural development and biodiversity conservation.

---

[35] WTO, 'Review under Article 24.2 of the Application of the Provision of the Section of the TRIPS Agreement on Geographical Indications', 24 November 2003 (IP/C/W/253/Rev.1), [44].

[36] WTO, 'Review under Article 24.2 – Switzerland's Response to the Checklist', 16 February 1999 (IP/C/W/117/Add.13), 10, Fn11.

[37] See the response to Q.13 in TRIPS Council, 'Review of Legislation – India', 8 October 2003 (IP/Q/IND/1).

[38] TRIPS Council, (IP/C/M/38), [180].

[39] WTO, 'Issues Related to Extension', [13].   [40] Ibid., [14].

274   TRIPS tomorrow?

The benefits of 'GI-extension' and better protection of geographical indications resulting from it will foster sustainable development of local rural communities, employment in decentralised regions, support the establishment of other economic activities such as tourism, preserve traditional knowledge and biodiversity. In a time of liberalization in these sectors, 'extension' will help make geographical indications a valuable tool for the marketing and promotion of quality products and will thus offer new market opportunities.[41]

The emergence of these newer arguments at the WTO is emblematic of a more general trend, since they are also found within the context of national or regional regimes as well as being investigated within the interdisciplinary academic scholarship in this area. Present attempts to justify GI protection can therefore be categorised under the following inter-related headings, of which only the first two overlap with trade mark doctrine:[42]

(1) the consumer interest in accurate labelling and reducing search costs;
(2) the producer interest in protecting a collectively developed reputation, with the accompanying incentive to invest in quality;
(3) acknowledging that aspects of local or national cultural heritage are associated with GI production or sometimes even consumption;

---

[41] Statement by Switzerland, (TN/C/4), 2.

[42] European Commission, 'Why do Geographical Indications Matter to Us?', Brussels, 30 July 2003 (MEMO/03/160) ('GIs are key to EU and developing countries' cultural heritage, traditional methods of production and natural resources'); F. Fischler, 'Quality Food, CAP Reform and PDO/PGI', SPEECH/04/183, Siena (17 April, 2004) (GIs 'have an important role to play in the "regeneration" of the countryside since they ensure that agri-foodstuffs are produced in such a way that conserves local plant varieties, rewards local people, supports rural diversity and social cohesion, and promotes new job opportunities in production, processing and other related services. The needs of today's population are met, while natural resources and traditional skills are safeguarded for generations to come'); A. Lôrincz-Fejes, 'Protection of Geographical Indications: Point of View of the Hungarian Government', 7 July 2003 (WIPO/GEO/SFO/03/6), [13] (GIs 'form part of, and relate to, different policies: consumer protection, competition, agricultural, cultural and intellectual property policy'); D. Barjolle and E. Thévenod-Mottet, DOLPHINS Final Report: Work Programme 6 – Policies Evaluation DOLPHINS Concerted Action, Contract QLK5–2000–0593, European Commission (June 2003), 10 (GIs have a 'high heritage dimension'); FAO Committee on Commodity Problems, 'Geographical Indications for Tea', Hangzhou, 14–16 May 2008 (CCP:TE 08/5), [9] (emphasising their importance for rural environments and rural economies); J. Kuanpoth and D. Robinson, 'Protection of Geographical Indications: The Case of Jasmine Rice and Thailand' [2009] IPQ 288 (highlighting the potential for poverty alleviation and sustainable use of biological resources); D. Rangnekar, 'The Law and Economics of Geographical Indications: Introduction to Special Issue' (2010) 13 JWIP 77, 77 ('The demand [from the Global South] for stronger rights can be traced to various opportunities for endogenous rural development, protecting the rights of indigenous communities and niche marketing of culturally emblematic products').

(4) recognising the *savoir faire* or traditional knowledge which has sustained and improved these products over time;
(5) emphasising their role in achieving agricultural policy goals;
(6) environmental benefits associated with GI protection, such as the preservation of biodiversity by incentivising the use of non-mainstream plant varieties or animal breeds;
(7) stressing their potential for rural development or the economies of developing countries;
(8) responding to a growing consumer demand for regional produce which is often perceived as more desirable on a qualitative basis.

A recent study sums up the shift in perceptions: GIs 'are not exclusively commercial or legal instruments, they are multi-functional'.[43] It is to these arguments that we now turn.

3.   Normative arguments in favour of extension

While it is beyond the scope of this chapter to work through all of these supporting rationales in detail, the intention here is to assess their significance for the current legal regime. Instead of broadly embracing these arguments as further reasons in support of GI protection, they have the potential to do more specific work as they feed in to prescriptive debates about the scope and form of protection. Conventional explanations for GI protection have analogous counterparts within trade mark or unfair competition doctrine, with communicative logic explaining the protection of signs in the marketplace on the basis that uncluttered signalling is desirable. Yet Article 23 'absolute' standards of protection, or internationally applicable rules which prevent prospective generic use once a GI has been registered, cannot be explained on the basis of the semantic reception of the sign in the context of a specific dispute. How consumers in the jurisdiction of the dispute actually perceive the sign at a given point of time does not seem to matter. Even an expansive conceptualisation of unfair competition cannot account for such rules, since dilution or misappropriation prevention standards usually require that the protected sign must have an extant reputation, that the target audience is likely to make a link between the GI and the defendant's sign and that there is likely to be some harm to the GI and/or benefit to the defendant. In a nutshell, the denotative and connotative functions of the sign still matters within the communicative paradigm.

[43] D. Giovannucci, T. Josling, W. Kerr, B. O'Connor and M. Yeung, *Guide to Geographical Indications: Linking Products and their Origins* (International Trade Centre, Geneva 2009), xvii.

276   TRIPS tomorrow?

None of these prerequisites need be proved under the enhanced protection standards. Effectively, they are designed to reserve the signs in question for home country GI producers, making the rights associated with GIs far less contingent on audience perception. Of course by reserving the use of the sign, there is space for the argument that in future the GI may signal origin or quality once it is up and running in the new market, thereby re-engaging with communicative logic. However, pre-emptive protection today cannot be justified on the basis of possible future consumer understanding. While Article 23 is unusual, there are a few other context-specific situations in which signs have been given comparably broad protection, outside of the communicative logic paradigm and based on alternative rationales.[44] Since the focus is no longer on the contemporary meaning of the sign, our enquiry shifts to a consideration of the alternative explanations for why the underlying products are worth encouraging and supporting through a suitably accommodative legal regime. Three explanations have been considered in previous chapters: (1) a hermetically bounded and biophysically deterministic notion of *terroir* as the basis for the argument that if unique products come from unique places, 'outsider' use is illegitimate (Chapter 3); (2) a pragmatic and mutually beneficial bargain based on national interest, as evinced by the lists of protected terms found in bilateral agreements forming the background to the Lisbon Agreement (Chapter 4); and (3) the suspicion that enhanced GI protection is thinly veiled protectionism in international trade negotiations, which primarily benefits European producers (Chapters 1 and 5). The more recent arguments identified in the previous paragraphs, such as those based on traditional knowledge recognition or rural development, have the potential to add meaningfully to this list of explanations for why GIs should be treated differently.

To begin with, some of these justifications which are premised on the achievement of specific policy outcomes may be too context specific to

---

[44] One example is the expansive protection under Art 6*ter* of the Paris Convention, whose purpose is to protect armorial bearings, flags and other State emblems. See *American Clothing Associates NV v. OHIM* (C-202/08 P) [2009] ECR I-6933; [2010] ETMR 3 (confirming the broad protection of such state symbols, where the likelihood of confusion is not a requirement). Another is the emerging public policy debates surrounding the more controversial prevention of so called 'ambush marketing' associated with major sporting events. Here official sponsors are granted expansive rights to signs such as the Olympic symbol, in return for large sums which enable the event to take place and support the policy of promoting sports. I am grateful to Michael Handler for this example. See generally, P. Johnson, *Ambush Marketing: A Practical Guide to Protecting the Brand of a Sporting Event* (Sweet and Maxwell, London 2007); D. Cran and S. Griffiths, 'Ambush Marketing: Unsporting Behaviour or Fair Play? [2010] *Entertainment Law Review* 293.

Normative arguments in favour of extension 277

be universally applicable across the TRIPS membership. Consider the broad claim that GIs can be a useful vector to attain agricultural policy objectives. While the antecedents can be traced back to the regulation of the wine sector in the nineteenth century, the recent revitalisation of this argument is associated with structural reforms in the EU's Common Agricultural Policy (CAP). In response to trade liberalisation pressures from the WTO and the decoupling of direct subsidies to farmers for production, there has been a corresponding shift in emphasis from quantity to quality.[45] This is driven by the belief that consumers are willing to pay premiums for such regional products.[46] The European agricultural sector is particularly affected by this development, as it grapples with the challenges of restructuring a productivist model originally designed to ensure food security in the aftermath of World War II. This 'dramatic shift towards quality and marketable goods is not only promoted by public policy, but also results from growing awareness among farmers and the food industry that the market for undifferentiated commodities is declining and there is a need to react'.[47] The EU has been exploring the potential for GI products to assist with this transition, as part of a broader drive of so called Second Pillar programmes to grow the niche quality products category, including organic farming and traditional specialities.[48] A convincing rejoinder to this line of reasoning would be to bracket it as a set of uniquely European concerns, which does not affect countries committed to the productivist model, such as the agricultural exporters making up the Cairns group.[49]

[45] European Commission, 'Green Paper on Agricultural Product Quality: Product Standards, Farming Requirements and Quality Schemes', Brussels, 15 December 2008 (COM(2008) 641 final), 4 ('As globalisation spreads, products from emerging countries with low production costs are putting greater pressure on EU farmers. There is growing competition for both agricultural commodities and value-added products. Faced with these new commercial challenges, the EU farmers' most potent weapon is "quality"').

[46] CEC, *Fact Sheet: European Policy for Quality Agricultural Products* (Luxembourg 2006) ('Consumers in Europe and around the world show an increasing interest in the qualities of these foods. It is in the [EU's] interests to ensure that farmers and growers are able to make the most of the added value that their products can provide them').

[47] A. Profeta, R. Balling, R. Schoene and A. Wirsig, 'The Protection of Origins for Agricultural Products and Foods in Europe: Status Quo, Problems and Policy Recommendations for the Green Book' (2009) 12 JWIP 622, 622–3.

[48] London Economics et al., Evaluation of the CAP Policy on Protected Designations of Origin (PDO) and Protected Geographical Indications (PGI) (Final Report for the European Commission, November 2008).

[49] C. Lister, 'A Sad Story Told Sadly: The Prospects for U.S.–EU Food Trade Wars' (1996) 51 *Food & Drug Law Journal* 303, 309; H. N. Niska, 'The European Union TRIPS over the US Constitution: Can the First Amendment Save the Bologna that has a First Name?' (2004) 13 *Minnesota Journal of Global Trade* 413, 416 ('Because European countries have long made a conscious effort to avoid agricultural economies of scale that have recently characterized many other agricultural markets, European governments

278   TRIPS tomorrow?

It is trite to state that policy arguments appropriate to one specific context may not be universally applicable.

At this stage it is worth considering a related aspect of the agricultural policy debates at international trade negotiations, where recognition is sought for the 'multifunctionality' of agriculture. The concept was prominently deployed in WTO deliberations as the basis for continued agricultural subsidies or state support, where the aim was to remunerate farmers for providing non-market public goods, such as social or environmental benefits, within the broader context of trade liberalisation. 'At its simplest, [multifunctionality] acknowledges agriculture's roles beyond commodity production, including conservation, amenity, recreation, resource protection and the stability of rural landscapes; elements allegedly critical to the long-term sustainability of this sector and rural communities'.[50] The initial emphasis was on incentivising the production of non-commodity outputs via state support, as identified by the OECD in a 2001 report: 'The key elements of multifunctionality are: i) the existence of multiple commodity and non-commodity outputs that are jointly produced by agriculture; and ii) the fact that some of the non-commodity outputs exhibit the characteristics of externalities or public goods, with the result that markets for these goods do not exist or function poorly'.[51]

More recent theoretical perspectives have opened up a broader spectrum of possibilities, where the term relates to a 'multifaceted sequencing of processes, institutions and actor interactions centred upon human agency and natural/semi-natural resources that is not reducible to any single analytical perspective'.[52] While the concept and its specific applications continue to be deliberated upon, a policy debate involving the contestation of a particular neoliberal vision of agricultural commodification and productivism has relevance for a more diverse constituency beyond the EU.[53] When situated within this broader agricultural

---

claim that their farmers need either massive subsidies or stronger geographical indication protections to survive').

[50] J. Clark, 'Geographies of Multifunctional Agriculture: Developing Governance Explanations' (2010) 4 *Geography Compass* 803. See also H. Renting et al., 'Exploring Multifunctional Agriculture. A Review of Conceptual Approaches and Prospects for an Integrative Transitional Framework' (2009) 90 *Journal of Environmental Management* S112.

[51] OECD, *Multifunctionality – Towards an Analytical Framework* (Paris 2001), 13.

[52] Clark 'Geographies of Multifunctional Agriculture', 804.

[53] J. Dibden, C. Potter and C. Cocklin, 'Contesting the Neoliberal Project for Agriculture: Productivist and Multifunctional Trajectories in the European Union and Australia' (2009) 25 *Journal of Rural Studies* 299 ('There is ... evidence that the compatibility of market rule with agri-environmental (and, to a lesser extent, social) sustainability is

Normative arguments in favour of extension 279

policy milieu, GIs could be conceived of as a legal instrument with the potential to deliver on the attractive objectives of multifunctionality. Let us consider just two desirable outcomes associated with this notion – biodiversity conservation and the potential for the development of rural or impoverished regions.

Several commentators have identified the potentially synergistic relationship between the products associated with geographical indications – usually considered to be artisanally produced, often depending on agricultural raw material and therefore situated in rural regions – and the goals of biodiversity conservation.[54] It has been suggested that 'GIs provide the [market based] incentive needed to engage in the sustainable utilization of biodiversity resources'.[55] Since product specifications in registration-based GI systems pin down natural and human factors, there is optimism about their ability to 'contribute to maintaining biodiversity in general and genetic resources in particular'.[56] Philippe Marchenay teases out the further implications of *sui generis* GI protection. While genetic resources such as plant varieties are easier to conserve *ex situ*, GIs facilitate *in situ* conservation.

[They] work to preserve the resource in question by means of dynamic conservation with an economic outcome. These ethno-ecosystems not only generate well-identified, specific local products, they also perform a range of different roles, such as providing shelter for endangered species, sustaining a variety of wild flora and fauna, and landscaping, etc. Certain productions are supported by complex structures that maintain biological diversity on different levels, from whole landscapes, to local varieties or species, right down to microbial ecosystems.[57]

---

being contested in both Australia and the EU, particularly at the regional scale. The nature and terms of this contestation are different, however, given the radically divergent macro-economic and socio-political contexts in which it is being framed'); J. Dibden and C. Cocklin, '"Multifunctionality": Trade Protectionism or a New Way Forward?' (2009) 41 *Environment and Planning* 163.

[54] See generally L. Bérard, M. Cegarra, M. Djama and S. Louafi (eds.), *Biodiversity and Local Ecological Knowledge in France* (INRA-CIRAD, Paris 2005); V. Boisvert, 'From the Conservation of Genetic Diversity to the Promotion of Quality Foodstuff: Can the French Model of "*Appellation d'Origine Contrôlée*" be Exported?', CAPRi Working Paper No. 49 (April 2006).

[55] T. W. Dagne, 'Harnessing the Development Potential of Geographical Indications for Traditional Knowledge-based Agricultural Products' (2010) 5 *Journal of Intellectual Property Law and Practice* 441, 451.

[56] L. Bérard and P. Marchenay, 'Local Products and Geographical Knowledge: Taking Account of Local Knowledge and Biodiversity' (2006) 58 *International Social Science Journal* 109, 109.

[57] P. Marchenay, 'The Challenge of Conserving Local Practices, Knowledge, and the Living World', in L. Bérard, M. Cegarra, M. Djama and S. Louafi (eds.), *Biodiversity and Local Ecological Knowledge in France* (INRA-CIRAD, France 2005), 89, 94–5.

280   TRIPS tomorrow?

If there is some evidence to support the biodiversity enhancing aspects of GI protection, it must be remembered that there is no necessary correlation between the two. Environmental or ecological protection is not a primary motivation for these legal regimes. According to a recent EU evaluation:

[While] some studies have shown that certain practices under PDO-PGI specifications have some link to environmentally relevant farming practices by requiring certain animal feeding systems or maximum stocking densities [and] GI products showed positive results in reference to conservation of biodiversity and distinctive cultural landscapes ... On the other hand, there are also examples of GIs where production methods are not at all different in the sense of sustainability from standard agricultural practices, with associated environmental impacts. In some cases, farming systems and nature values may vary considerably within a PDO production area.[58]

Not only is there no indispensable connection between the desired outcome and the legal vector selected, certain features of registration-based protection may even run counter to biodiversity conservation agendas. The drafting of an official product specification results in the narrowing of practices and possibilities. 'The successful promotion of a product may result in a loss of biodiversity if some varieties or species are not included within that product's specifications'.[59] In a similar vein, Rangnekar observes: 'The adoption of a single variety of agave has given Tequila a very narrow genetic base, making agave cultivation vulnerable to pathogens and dependant on high doses of various plant protection chemicals'.[60] These qualifications help remind us that there are only so many aspirations that can be realistically heaped upon GIs. The goals and specific mechanics of GI protection regimes need to be kept in mind and we should be more discriminating while filtering through policy expectations.

There is far greater interest in the development dimension of IGO protection. Formal acknowledgement is found in Recital 2 to Regulation 510/2006,[61] which recognises that the 'diversification of agricultural

---

See also J. Larson, 'Geographical Indications, In Situ Conservation and Traditional Knowledge', ICTSD Policy Brief (October 2010).

[58] EC Staff Working Paper, Impact Assessment Report on Geographical Indications – Accompanying the Proposal for a Regulation of the European Parliament and of the Council on Agricultural Product Quality Schemes (Brussels 2010), 15.

[59] B. Roussel and F. Verdeaux, 'Natural Patrimony and Local Communities in Ethiopia: Advantages and Limitations of a System of Geographical Indications' (2007) 77 *Africa* 130, 144.

[60] D. Rangnekar, 'Geographical Indications and Localisation: A Case Study of Feni' (ESRC Report 2009), 42.

[61] Council Regulation (EC) No. 510/2006 of 20 March 2006 on the Protection of Geographical Indications and Designations of Origin for Agricultural Products and Foodstuffs [2006] OJ L93/12.

production should be encouraged' while the 'promotion of products having certain characteristics can be of considerable benefit to the rural economy, particularly in less favoured or remote areas, by improving the incomes of farmers and by retaining the rural population in these areas'. This potential is also actively being studied by international organisations such as the FAO.[62] There are two strands of analysis being pursued – the potential for GIs to improve incomes in rural and under-developed regions within developed economies, alongside an exploration of the prospects for enhanced export revenues for developing countries.[63] The interest seems to be sustained by distributive justice concerns, where disadvantaged regions and groups could benefit from this form of IP.[64] The general argument proceeds in three stages, each of which is currently being fleshed out. First, there is the hypothesis that consumers value and are willing to pay premiums for IGO labelled products. Second, this should translate into improved incomes for the relevant producers. Third, this will actually deliver on sustainable rural development by ensuring that the wealth is distributed along the chain of production, employment is generated in rural areas and this might help stem the rural exodus.

Preliminary research – largely in the context of developed country markets – suggests that there is reason for cautious optimism regarding the first two stages, while the research on the third stage paints a more

---

[62] The Food Quality and Standards Service began a programme in 2007 – The Specific Quality Linked to Origin and Traditions Programme. See www.fao.org/ag/agn/agns/projects_SQP_en.asp; see also FAO, 'Promotion of Traditional Regional Agricultural and Food Products: A Further Step towards Sustainable Rural Development', 26th FAO Regional Conference for Europe, 26–27 June 2008 (ERC/08/4).

[63] J. D. van der Ploeg, 'High Quality Products and Regional Specialities: A Promising Trajectory for Endogenous and Sustainable Development', in OECD, *The Future of Rural Policy – From Sectorial to Place-Based Policies in Rural Areas* (OECD Publications, Paris 2003), 205; European Commission, 'Geographical Indications – Background Paper to the Green Paper on Agricultural Product Quality', DG Agriculture and Rural Development Working Document (October 2008); S. Wagle, 'Geographical Indications as Trade-Related Intellectual Property: Relevance and Implications for Human Development in Asia-Pacific', UNDP Asia-Pacific Trade and Investment Initiative Discussion Paper, Colombo (2007); S. Reviron, E. Thevenod–Mottet and N. El Benni, 'Geographical Indications: Creation and Distribution of Economic Value in Developing Countries', NCCR Working Paper No. 2009/14 (March 2009); Das, 'Socio-Economic Implications of Protecting Geographical Indications in India'; D. Rangnekar and S. Kumar, 'Another Look at Basmati: Genericity and the Problems of a Transborder Geographical Indication' (2010) 13 JWIP 202.

[64] S. Bowen, 'Development from Within? The Potential for Geographical Indications in the Global South' (2010) 13 JWIP 231, 234 ('GIs are often associated with marginal or less-favoured areas in terms of productivity'); M. Vittori, 'The International Debate on Geographical Indications (GIs): The Point of View of the Global Coalition of GI Producers – oriGIn' (2010) 13 JWIP 304, 305.

282   TRIPS tomorrow?

complex picture. Beginning with the first stage, there is some evidence, predominantly from Europe, that consumers are attracted to regional products.[65] Thus:

[Two] clear trends may be identified in European food production and consumption in recent years. First, one may note a shift of demand for agricultural products and foodstuffs bearing a geographical identification and reflecting traditional methods of production, the use of local raw materials and respect for the local environment ... Secondly, there has been a shift in the demand for agricultural products that have been awarded a designated quality label in the form of [PDOs or PGIs].[66]

Origin stands out as a marker for quality and a variety of other desirable associations. Presently, attempts are being made to measure the impact of an origin signal on the marketplace. A growing body of empirical research considers the impact of PDO or PGI labels upon the consumer's willingness to pay higher prices.[67] The drivers for this demand are thought to include rising incomes, concerns about food quality and safety, a demand for superior or specific organoleptic quality, the roles of such products as symbols of cultural heritage, a desire for authenticity and to enable purchases in support of national producers.[68] Second, this consumer demand is correlated with the ability to charge a premium for the product, as several case studies have demonstrated.[69] According to one synthesis:

[65] K. van Ittersum, M. Meulenberg, H. van Trijp and M. Candel, 'Consumers' Appreciation of Regional Certification Labels: A Pan-European Study' (2007) 58 *Journal of Agricultural Economics* 1; S. Marette, 'The Collective-Quality Promotion in the Agribusiness Sector: An Overview', Centre for Agricultural and Rural Development Iowa State University, Working Paper 05-WP406 (2005).

[66] D. Skuras and E. Dimara, 'Regional Image and the Consumption of Regionally Denominated Products' (2004) 41 *Urban Studies* 801.

[67] E.g., C. Fotopoulos and A. Krystallis, 'Quality Labels as a Marketing Advantage: The Case of the "PDO Zagora" Apples in the Greek market' (2003) 37 *European Journal of Marketing* 1350; H. Resano-Ezcaray, A. I. Sanjuán-López and L. M. Albisu-Aguado, 'Combining Stated and Revealed Preferences on Typical Food Products: The Case of Dry-Cured Ham in Spain' (2010) 61 *Journal of Agricultural Economics* 480.

[68] FAO, 'Promotion of Traditional Regional Agricultural and Food Products', [12]; C. Bramley, E. Biénabe and J. Kirsten, 'The Economics of Geographical Indications: Towards a Conceptual Framework for Geographical Indication Research in Developing Countries', in WIPO (ed.), *The Economics of Intellectual Property: Suggestions for Further Research in Developing Countries and Countries with Economies in Transition* (WIPO, Geneva 2009), 109.

[69] Giovanucci et al., *Guide to Geographical Indications*, 10; EC, Impact Assessment Report, 14–15; D. Barjolle and E. Thévenod-Mottet, 'Economic Aspects of Geographical Indications', in L. Bérard, M. Cegarra, M. Djama and S. Louafi (eds.), *Biodiversity and Local Ecological Knowledge in France* (INRA-CIRAD, France 2005), at 213–215; J. Suh and A. MacPherson, 'The Impact of Geographical Indication on the Revitalisation of a Regional Economy: A Case Study of "Boseong" Green Tea' (2007) 39 *Area* 518;

Normative arguments in favour of extension 283

In 14 out of 18 cases, the price of a PDO/PGI product is higher than the price of its comparator product. The positive price premium ranges from 5% in the cases of Sitia Lasithi Kritis, Jamón de Teruel … and Turrón de Alicante/Jijona to 300% in the case of Volaille de Bresse. However, the majority of PDO/PGI products are more costly to produce than their comparators … As a result of the higher cost, a higher price does not necessarily translate into a higher margin. However, the evidence collected in the case studies shows that PDO/PGI products are generally more profitable than their comparators.[70]

Coffee is emerging as the focus of interest, for its potential to map onto *terroir* logic as well as its relevance to growers in developing countries who otherwise get to see very little of the price premium that consumers are willing to pay.[71] A strategy under consideration is the de-commodification of coffee by highlighting provenance through the use of IGOs, since single origin coffee commands a higher retail price. Yet when it comes to the third limb of the argument, the results suggest that a more context sensitive approach is required. Preliminary research has identified certain key factors that often influence the ability of IGO protection to deliver effectively on rural development targets.

In recent years, empirically informed qualitative studies have been adding layers of detail, highlighting the factors which lead to the success or failure of GIs. Questions of institutional design become important and a brace of threshold questions have been identified. To begin with, who joins these collective organisations which register and regulate GI products? And why? Modelling predicts that it is those who wish to manufacture high cost, high quality products and may not be able to compete with a price-focused retail sector. These actors are interested in quality based differentiation as a long term survival strategy. Furthermore, 'partnerships and coalitions are also a more rapid means of repositioning than internal development and are less costly, less irreversible and more successful than mergers. Networks provide a context for learning by doing. As information passes through a network, it is both freer and richer, new connections and new meanings are generated,

---

H. Vakoufaris, 'The Impact of Ladotyri Mytilinis PDO Cheese on the Rural Development of Lesvos Island, Greece' (2010) 15 *Local Environment* 27.

[70] London Economics et al., Evaluation of the CAP Policy, 258.

[71] B. Daviron and S. Ponte, *The Coffee Paradox: Commodity Trade and the Elusive Promise of Development* (Zed Books, London 2005); Hughes, 'Coffee and Chocolate – Can We Help Developing Country Farmers through Geographical Indications?'; A. Arslan and C. P. Reicher, 'The Effects of the Coffee Trade Marking Initiative and Starbucks Publicity on Export Prices of Ethiopian Coffee', Kiel Working Paper No. 1606 (March 2010); R. Teuber, 'Geographical Indications of Origin as a Tool of Product Differentiation: The Case of Coffee' (2010) 22 *Journal of International Food and Agribusiness Marketing* 277.

284 TRIPS tomorrow?

debated, and evaluated'.[72] However, risks of opportunistic behaviour arise out of this mutual dependence, prompting the need for collaboratively established control mechanisms such as a product specification and inspection structures. A case study of the Mantecoso cheese chain in Peru suggests that such vertical (e.g., between producers and processors) or horizontal (e.g., collaboration among producers) co-ordination has particular advantages for smallholders, since it allows producers to partially avoid direct cost-based competition by stressing factors such as quality, identity and trust.[73] Yet it is difficult to generalise beyond a point, since motivations and methodologies differ.

> For example, in one case (Cherry of Lari) qualification [i.e. the drafting of the product specification required for registration] is captured by multiple, but well-coordinated actors as part of a territorial strategy. In another (Culatello di Zibello), local government intervention helps to orient a supply chain strategy towards a more territorial approach. In the third case (Lancashire Cheese), one producer dominates the entire qualification process out of perceived marketing advantage, making pragmatic use of structures (a pre-existing association) and specifications (the PDO name) to achieve the desired result (an official designation that may, in future, confer marketing benefits to one product in a portfolio) ... The qualification is used as part of a marketing strategy pursued by one individual firm.[74]

The researchers tracing these three different trajectories identify factors such as the socio-economic context for each IGO application (is there a tradition of collective action and representative bodies in the region?) and the economic as well as cultural significance of the product, which help to explain the different levels of participation and motivations for registration. Another issue under consideration is the extent to which the benefits of IGO protection are distributed along the supply chain. Kasturi Das identifies the 'tricky issue' of ensuring 'that a fair share of the benefits (if any) accruing from the GI status of a product percolates down to the actual producers/artisans'.[75] As one case study of South

---

[72] Reviron et al., 'Geographical Indications: Creation and Distribution of Economic Value in Developing Countries', 18. Cf. S. O'Reilly, M. Haines and F. Arfini, 'Food SME Networks: Process and Governance – The Case of Parma Ham' (2003) 3 *Journal on Chain and Network Science* 21, 24 ('The most important factors influencing members to join the network were related to limited SME capacity to support brand development, such as product differentiation, promotion and to increase consumer demand. Market access and information were also important').

[73] P. Van de Kop, D. Sautier and A. Gerz (eds.), *Origin-Based Products: Lessons for Pro-Poor Market Development* (KIT, Amsterdam 2006), 91.

[74] A. Tregear, F. Arfinib, G. Bellettic and A. Marescottic, 'Regional Foods and Rural Development: The Role of Product Qualification' (2007) 23 *Journal of Rural Studies* 12, 19.

[75] K. Das, 'Prospects and Challenges of Geographical Indications in India' (2010) 13 JWIP 148, 149.

Africa's Rooibos tea reveals, most 'producers are not smallholders or under-privileged groups, but large-scale producers. A broad-based sectorial regulating body will thus tend to reproduce the power relations that exist within the supply chain'.[76] The study goes on to recommend that the organisation and leadership of the governance structure is crucially important, while labels such as 'Fair Trade' may be used to complement the IGO registration. The potential for influential actors within the supply chain to manipulate production standards is all too evident. Sarah Bowen illustrates this through the process of drafting specifications for Tequila. The major producing companies are internationally owned, while the Mexican state institutions responsible for regulating this product are correspondingly weak. The tensions are evident when defining quality standards for Tequila.

The history of the tequila industry is characterized by intense conflicts and deepening inequality between the agave farmers and the tequila companies ... Four key issues illustrate this loosening of [quality] standards: reductions in the minimum required proportion of blue agave sugars, the continued exportation of tequila in bulk, the recent inclusion of flavoured tequilas, and recent controversies over the definition of 'mature' agave.[77]

This exploration of assumptions about the benefits of IGO protection is particularly helpful for developing countries, where the rhetoric in favour of protection otherwise runs the risk of becoming detached from socio-economic and material realities. GI systems require time and effort to establish. If they are to be built to last, it requires an investment into institutional structures and they incur operational costs. One synthesis of lessons from the case studies suggests that four components are essential for long term success: (1) strong organisational and institutional structures to maintain, market and monitor the GI; (2) equitable participation among the producers and enterprises in a GI region, where costs, benefits and decision making is shared; (3) strong market partners committed to promote and commercialise the product over the long term; and (4) effective legal protection, beginning with a robust domestic GI regime.[78] It is encouraging to see this level of detail and nuance beginning to emerge. A broadening as well as deepening of this literature on effective institutional structures, agency-enabling approaches and

---

[76] Van de Kop et al., *Origin-Based Products*, 93–4.
[77] Bowen, 'Development from Within?', 238.
[78] Giovanucci et al., *Guide to Geographical Indications*, xviii-xix. For other such meta analyses, see Barjolle and Thévenod-Mottet, 'Economic Aspects of Geographical Indications', 213, 215–16; London Economics et al., *Evaluation of the CAP Policy*, Chapter 6.

286   TRIPS tomorrow?

appropriate market conditions should help GIs deliver the equitable distribution of value that they have the capacity for.

Finally, we conclude this survey of normative arguments with a brief appraisal of the interface between GIs and Traditional Knowledge (TK). This term of art[79] – as capitalised – has emerged in international IP discourse as a response to the blind spots within current legal doctrine, where only certain forms of creative and inventive activity are attributed to specific categories of (usually individual) rights holders. As Daniel Gervais describes it:

[IP] protection, in the form of copyrights, trade marks, designs & patents usually applies to: 'An identifiable author, inventor or other originator (who will be individually rewarded); An identifiable work, invention or other object; and Defined restricted acts'. [TK] does not fit well within these three characteristics of intellectual property rights. There are rarely well-identified authors or inventors of creations, inventions and knowledge passed on and improved from one generation to the next. The knowledge is sometimes amorphous and hard to circumscribe for the purposes of a patent application or to identify as one or more copyrighted works. Finally, the types of acts that indigenous communities want to prevent are not necessarily those that propertization provides.[80]

Several commentators have pointed out the features of registration-based GI regimes which are more advantageous for the protection of TK products, when compared to conventional forms of IP protection. GIs are a form of collective intellectual property rights. They can incorporate collectively evolved traditions; recognise a collective decision making process during the drafting of the product specification; acknowledge the intergenerational effort it takes to create goodwill; allow for production techniques to evolve by permitting amendments to the specification; are of potentially unlimited duration; cannot be transferred outside the defined region of origin; and are a market-

---

[79] A recent attempt at defining TK summarises it thus: It 'refers to the content or substance of knowledge resulting from intellectual activity in a traditional context, and includes the know-how, skills, innovations, practices and learning that form part of [TK] systems, and knowledge embodying traditional lifestyles of indigenous and local communities, or contained in codified knowledge systems passed between generations and continuously developed following any changes in the environment, geographical conditions and other factors. It is not limited to any specific technical field, and may include agricultural, environmental and medicinal knowledge, and any [TK] associated with cultural expressions and genetic resources'. See Art. 3(2) of WIPO, 'The Protection of Traditional Knowledge: Revised Objectives and Principles', 15 September 2010 (WIPO/GRTKF/IC/17/5), Annex, 33.

[80] D. Gervais, 'Traditional Knowledge & Intellectual Property: A TRIPS Compatible Approach' [2005] *Michigan State Law Review* 137, 141.

based mechanism to incentivise the continuation of artisanal or traditional production methods.[81]

The insight I wish to share here is both simple and perhaps controversial. Thus far, the literature discussing GIs in the context of TK has evaluated GIs as tools to achieve TK protection ends within the existing categories of IP. GIs have played a bit part in the TK story; they have been guests at someone else's party. By contrast, I float the idea that enhanced or 'absolute' GI protection could potentially be explained on the basis that it recognises a certain form of TK – the *savoir faire* or local knowledge identified in Chapter 3 and potentially incorporated within the TRIPS definition in Chapter 5. Enhanced GI protection can therefore be more fundamentally recast – at least for a subset of products desiring to qualify for Article 23 levels of protection – as being concerned with the recognition of this collectively generated, intergenerationally transmitted and evolving knowledge. The basis for this reconceptualisation is the historical research in this book which retraces the gradual recognition of human expertise and know how as a crucial dimension of wine appellation protection, as well as the space for such a 'human factor' requirement within the TRIPS definition. Instead of protecting the associated technical knowledge as such through a legal monopoly, in some form of patent-like or trade-secret-based regime, the alternative under Article 23 would be protecting the sign or designation by reserving its use for the 'original' producer group, regardless of audience perception. This takes advantage of the oscillation between sign and product as the object of legal regulation in *sui generis* GI regimes and works around what is otherwise perceived as a vulnerability in the TK debates. It has been noted that GI protection regimes do not protect the underlying content of the traditional knowledge. So Spanish producers of Cava can learn and utilise techniques similar to the *méthode champenoise*. However, this may not be a problem. Chapter 3 documents the porosity of place and the external influences or external raw materials which are often incorporated into GI specifications. Therefore rewarding the effort and innovation associated with geographically specific *savoir faire* by

---

[81] D. R. Downes, 'How Intellectual Property Could be a Tool to Protect Traditional Knowledge' (2000) 25 *Columbia Journal of Environmental Law* 253, 268–272; Sunder, 'The Invention of Traditional Knowledge', 114–15; Addor and Grazzioli, 'Geographical Indications Beyond Wines and Spirits', 893–5; S. Singhal, 'Geographical Indications and Traditional Knowledge' (2008) 3 *Journal of Intellectual Property Law and Practice* 732; Dagne, 'Harnessing the Development Potential of Geographical Indications for Traditional Knowledge-based Agricultural Products', 446–7; D. Zografos, 'Can Geographical Indications be a Viable Alternative for the Protection of Traditional Cultural Expressions', in F. Macmillan and K. Bowrey (eds.), *New Directions in Copyright Law*, Vol. 3 (Edward Elgar, Cheltenham 2006), 37, 55.

288   TRIPS tomorrow?

reserving the use of the sign, instead of protecting the actual knowledge itself, may strike the appropriate balance. This leaves techniques free to be borrowed, adapted and improved. For the kind of local knowledge associated with GI production, this fluidity is preferable. This would also require a threshold condition to be satisfied whereby GI products seeking Article 23 levels of protection would have to demonstrate the existence of this corpus of evolving local knowledge associated with the product. In conclusion, each of these more recent grounding arguments has the potential to explain why GIs are treated differently from trade marks under the TRIPS regime.

4.   International registration and its effects

At the time of writing, the proposed multilateral notification and registration system for wines and spirits has been unexpectedly revived. After more than a decade of moribund consultations at 'special sessions' of the TRIPS Council, a composite draft text emerged in early 2011. It is still very tentatively worded, with text options marked off in brackets.[82] Unlike the extension debate, here the mandate for negotiations is more clearly established.[83] However, both the nature of the register and the legal effects of registration continue to generate considerable disagreement. To date, three proposals have driven the discussions forward. A 'Joint Proposal' has been submitted by the US and others who are sceptical about a strengthened international regime for GI protection.[84] The EU had to modify its original 'TRIPS plus' proposal and curb its ambitions, in the process being joined by a number of countries which are collectively referred to as the 'W52' group.[85] Finally Hong Kong proposed a register pitched as a compromise between these two options.[86]

---

[82] TRIPS Council, 'Report by the Chairman to the Trade Negotiations Committee', 21 April 2011 (TN/IP/21).

[83] Initially based on the built-in mandate in Art. 23.4, spirits were added as a result of the WTO, 'Doha Ministerial Declaration', 20 November 2001 (WT/MIN(01)/DEC/1), [18].

[84] The original version of this proposal was submitted in 2005 and modified in 2008. For the latest version, see Argentina et al., 'Proposed Draft TRIPS Council Decision on the Establishment of a Multilateral System of Notification and Registration of Geographical Indications for Wines and Spirits', 31 March 2011 (TN/IP/W/10/Rev.4).

[85] Communication from the European Communities, 'Geographical Indications' 14 June 2005 (TN/IP/W/11). For previous proposals, see Fusco, 'Geographical Indications: A Discussion of the TRIPS Regulation', Fn 46.

[86] Communication from Hong Kong, China, 'Multilateral System of Notification and Registration of Geographical Indications under Article 23.4 of the TRIPS Agreement', 23 April 2003 (TN/IP/W/8).

A number of issues have arisen out of these discussions[87] but two in particular lie at the heart of the disagreement. The W52 group favour a WTO register that establishes a presumption (rebuttable on certain grounds) that the registered GI is to be protected across the entire membership of the WTO. The accompanying registration proposal is accordingly more detailed as regards the procedure for application, notification, the objection period, grounds for refusal of registration and the like. The Joint Proposal supporters would prefer the establishment of a merely informative register, as part of a voluntary system in which each Member would initially communicate the list of its protected GIs to the WTO for inclusion in a database maintained by the Secretariat. Subsequently, participating Members would have to consult the database when making GI protection decisions in accordance with their national law, whereas non-participating members would be encouraged, but not obliged, to consult the database. The disagreement therefore turns on the legal effects of registration, as well as the question of whether registration would be binding on the entire WTO Membership (*erga omnes*) or only on those who opt in to the system.[88] The Hong Kong proposal attempts to negotiate a middle path, whereby notified GIs are subjected only to a formal examination by the WTO and this establishes *prima facie* evidence of ownership, conformity to the TRIPS definition in Article 22.1 and existence of the protection in the country of origin. These presumptions may then be overcome in proceedings before national courts, tribunals or administrative bodies whose decisions would be based on domestic law, and thus, would only have territorially limited effects.

Against this backdrop, the recently developed draft text on the multilateral register follows a six-point sequence: (1) notification of the application to the WTO; (2) registration, including the nature of the WTO Secretariat's role in administering the system; (3) the more controversial aspects relating to the legal effects of registration, including the obligations imposed on Members as a result; (4) fees and costs of running the system; (5) special treatment for developing countries (special and

---

[87] For a comprehensive review, see WTO, 'Discussions on the Establishment of a Multilateral System of Notification and Registration of Geographical Indications for Wines and Spirits: Compilation of Issues and Points', 23 May 2003 (TN/IP/W/7/Rev.1).

[88] Report by the Chairman, 'Multilateral System of Notification and Registration of Geographical Indications for Wines and Spirits', 22 March 2010 (TN/IP/20), [13] (As the Chairman recently confirmed, 'the issues of legal effects/consequences of registration and participation are the stumbling block and that their resolution, in particular regarding legal effects/consequences of registration, will help progress in the other areas').

290   TRIPS tomorrow?

differential treatment); and (6) participation, which considers whether the system is entirely voluntary, or whether a term's registration would have some implications for all WTO Members.[89] While these issues are important and generate a useful discussion of the practicalities of registration-based protection, my interest in the register relates to a more fundamental transition or tipping point, which has not been sufficiently appreciated so far. These developments underline the growing commitment to a registration-based form of protection, which will define the future of international GI protection.

This book has documented and accounted for the multiple forms of IGO protection which have existed over the past century. Several of these options, especially those framed within an unfair competition regime, do not require a written specification. Instead the product details crystallise at the time of the dispute (e.g., when a judge is determining whether passing off has occurred) akin to the manner in which the boundaries of subject matter in a copyright dispute are determined. The revival of the multilateral register project must be considered alongside the gradual consolidation of the separate EU regimes for wines, spirits and foodstuffs[90] and proposals to amend the Lisbon registration system (Chapter 3). Unlike (unregistered) copyright protection or (registration-based) trade mark protection, IGO protection has existed for over a century without a corresponding widely accepted and institutionally embedded form, since signs indicating geographical origin have been regulated by a broad spectrum of civil, administrative and criminal law arrangements. While this gradual transition to a registration-based form of protection does not exclude the operation of other regimes regulating the use of signs in the marketplace, it should conceptually eclipse them over time. As we have seen in previous chapters, the necessity for flattening and pinning down production techniques onto a registration form raises a number of unresolved issues. Who makes the application and who verifies the applicant's ability to operate in a representative capacity? Whose interests and preference are embodied in the specification? How are variations in production techniques accommodated? To what extent is change and further improvement accommodated? When do new technological developments completely transform a product's 'artisanal' character? What is the algorithm for defining the boundaries of production? Should separate boundary delimitation

---

[89] The draft is annexed to the Chairman's Report (TN/IP/21).
[90] See 'Annex B: Geographical Indications', in EC Staff Working Paper, Impact Assessment Report for a Communication on Agricultural Product Quality Policy (Version 08–4–09) (2009) 44–46.

International registration and its effects 291

techniques be adopted for largely non-agricultural products, such as crafts and textiles? When it comes to definitions based on TRIPS, how are the competing logics of *terroir* and a reputation-based approach to be reconciled when determining the link between product and place? Finally, which of the two registration-based options – certification and collective trade marks or a *sui generis* regime – will prove more effective? These are open questions for future research to develop.

To underscore the need for a more wide-ranging engagement with registration systems, the last of these questions is developed a little further here. Much of the existing literature comparing a *sui generis* registration-based GI system with an alternative trade mark option (usually certification or collective marks) is unsatisfying. It is a thin compendium of points of variance, at a high level of abstraction. Cumulatively it suggests that an independent GI system is more onerous at the registration stage, subsequently involves greater monitoring but also provides for greater protection. The system is more closely involved with the creation and maintenance of the product specification.

Publicly oriented or *sui generis* systems of GI protection can be bureaucratic but tend to conceive of GIs as a public good and thus cover many of the costs associated with securing and enforcing their protection. Privately oriented systems, such as those that rely primarily on trade mark law ... can be more accessible and responsive but the responsibility and costs, especially for detection and enforcement, are borne by the GI [applicant] itself.[91]

Usually this type of comparison contrasts certification marks against GI systems. Collective marks essentially operate as clubs and the standards or pre-requisites for membership can be far more opaque. The category of persons authorised to use the mark, the conditions of membership and the conditions of use of the mark are the important aspects which must be indicated in the application. Provided they are clear, the content of these conditions is not scrutinised. Meanwhile individual trade marks remain a possibility[92] and are occasionally utilised, but these are the most opaque form of registration. They work on the basis of standard licensing agreements between the registrant and regional producers, although there may be queries about revocation for non-use. The

---

[91] Giovanucci et al., *Guide to Geographical Indications*, 14.
[92] AIPPI, 'Resolution on Q.118 – Trade and Service Marks and Geographical Indications' (1994) *Annuaire* 408 at [4.1] ('AIPPI observes, however, that in some countries where there is no legal provision for the protection of collective or certification marks or any other suitable protection, indications of source or appellations of origin are protected as individual marks'); USPTO, 'Geographical Indication Protection in the United States', 5–6 ('Finally, under the US regime, it is possible to protect geographical indications as [individual] trade marks').

292 TRIPS tomorrow?

ambiguity arises because of a question mark over use by licensees as opposed to trade mark owners and whether this alone is sufficient to sustain the individual mark. There is also the possibility of an undeserving or non-representative applicant claiming the IGO as an individual trade mark and then selectively licensing its use.[93] So drawing on the conventional literature, and primarily with certification marks in mind, a synthesis of the differences looks like this:[94]

- The information conveyed by each of these signs is different. For GIs, it is not only geographical origin but in many regimes, something is also communicated about specific product quality and objectively verified production methods. Trade marks merely signal consistent quality – this Coke will taste like the last one.
- As a related issue, the very existence of a *sui generis* GI system signals an institutional commitment to the link between product and place. The *sui generis* system is designed around a distinct set of registration concerns and policy outcomes, which only partially overlap with trade mark law. As opposed to trade mark law's neutrality or indifference, it signals that GIs are different, due to the link between product and place whereas the location of production of trade marked goods will vary with outsourcing trends, labour costs and fluctuations in taxation regimes.
- The nature of legal interests often differs. Whereas trade marks are classified as private property rights, GIs are usually asociated with the right to use the sign, based on complaince with certain collectively established production standards.
- There are procedural and bureacratic variations in the application process. Often for GIs there is no time limit, whereas for trade marks it is usually a cycle of 10-year renewals. For GI regimes, the fee structure also varies with there being no need for initial application or renewal fees in some cases, reflecting the state interest in facilitating the recognition of these signs.

---

[93] A concern recognised in the UK IPO *Manual of Trade Mark Practice* (2011), Chapter 4, Section 2.1.4.

[94] A. F. R. de Almeida, 'Key Differences between Trade Marks and Geographical Indications' (2008) EIPR 406; J. M. Cortes Martin, 'The WTO TRIPS Agreement – The Battle between the Old and the New World over the Protection of Geographical Indications' (2004) 7 JWIP 287, 309–11; Rangnekar 'Socio-Economics of Geographical Indications', 16 (Table 2); F. Gevers, 'Geographical Names and Signs Used as Trade Marks' (1990) EIPR 285, 286–7; WIPO, (SCT/9/4); I. Kireeva and B. O'Connor, 'Geographical Indications and the TRIPS Agreement: What Protection is Provided to Geographical Indications in WTO Members?' (2010) 13 JWIP 275, 288; EU–China Trade Project, *Q&A Manual: European Union Legislation on Geographical Indications* (December 2007).

International registration and its effects   293

- There is also greater variance in the scope of protection, with GIs being granted absolute protection, including the right to prevent qualified uses such as the indication of the true place of origin, or 'style'/'type' situations. While many trade mark systems offer anti-dilution protection for suitably reputed marks, there is uncertainty as to whether blurring, usually measured in terms of detriment to distinctiveness for a sign indicating a single trade source, is available when signs are collectively used by multiple parties.[95]
- Once registered, GIs are insulated against future generic use, whereas trade marks remain vulnerable to this.
- There appears to be a gradual convergence around the principle that both types of signs are open to anyone who complies with the standards and the registrant should not be allowed to unreasonably exclude those wishing to use the sign.
- Overall, there is a far greater state involvement or public/quasi-public oversight for GI systems. By contrast, under trade mark law, 'there is little public assurance that the mark is more than a private marketing device'.[96]
- On the flip side of this, certification or collective trade marks have the flexibility and adaptability associated with a system designed around private property rights and private interests. Standards can be set and modified without the need for state intervention. The fees and costs lie with the registrant and not the taxpayer. Additionally, this form of protection already exists in most countries around the world.[97]
- By the same token, IGOs registered within a trade mark system have to play by its rules. This includes being subject to the obstacle of prior trade mark registration; the need for use in that jurisdiction to sustain the registration; the necessity for acquired distinctiveness where geographical names are concerned; limits over the scope of protection and expenses associated with registration, private monitoring and proving confusion.[98]

---

[95] On the issue of reinterpreting distinctiveness for group signs, see D. Gangjee, 'The Business End of Collective and Certification Marks', in I. Simon Fhima (ed.), *Trade Mark Law and Sharing Names: Exploring Use of the Same Mark by Multiple Undertakings* (Edward Elgar, Cheltenham 2009), 79; P. M. Brody, 'Geographical Indications and Dilution: Reinterpreting "Distinctiveness" Under the Lanham Act' (2010) 100 TMR 905.

[96] R. W. Benson, 'Regulation of American Wine Labeling: In Vino Veritas?' (1978) 11 *University of California Davis Law Review* 115, 122–3.

[97] B. M. Bashaw, 'Geographical Indications in China: Why Protect GIs with Both Trade Mark Law and AOC-Type Legislation?' (2008) 17 *Pacific Rim Law and Policy Journal* 73; M. Ricolfi, 'Is the European GIs Policy in Need of Rethinking?' [2009] IIC 123.

[98] O'Connor, '10 Years Later', 12–16.

While this is descriptively useful, it does not assist us in assessing the merits of each in more specific contexts. In response to this, there are two recent developments worth highlighting. The first is a more context-ual approach to the comparison between systems. The second relates to tentative probings into the role of the state in *sui generis* GI systems. Presently there is a greater interest in the pragmatic consequences of opting for one approach over another. Therefore, adopting a more strategic approach to registration, Gail Evans considers 'not only the legal requirements for obtaining a valid GI or [trade mark], but also the degree to which differing forms of commercialization may facilitate the marketing of agricultural products under differing conditions of production and levels of economic development'.[99] She concludes that while a trade mark system 'offers producer groups the flexibility neces-sary to achieve the consumer recognition necessary to the creation of product reputation based on geographical origin, subsequently the greater breadth of protection offered by the GI system will better main-tain price premium'.[100]

Others are beginning to explore the extent to which the European *sui generis* model can be successfully transplanted. In the context of Ethopia, scholars have taken note of the institutional difficulties associated with a grass roots approach to establishing producer groups, the need to engage stakeholders and facilitate the creation of networks and reach out to the market by connecting with retailers and consumers, so that profits return to growers and farmers.[101] Research which compares the fortunes of Café de Colombia, registered as a PGI in the EU, and Ethiopian Fine Coffee which adopted the trade mark option, suggests that each regime offers mixed blessings. Therefore a strategy of cumulative protection is recommended.[102] A related nascent body of scholarship focuses on the role of state as overseer, facilitator and mediator during the process of registration.

---

[99] G. E. Evans, 'The Comparative Advantages of Geographical Indications and Community Trade Marks for the Marketing of Agricultural Products in the European Union' [2010] IIC 645, 646–7.

[100] Ibid., 647.

[101] Roussel and Verdeaux, 'Natural Patrimony and Local Communities in Ethiopia', 144–6.

[102] L. Schüßler, 'Protecting "Single-Origin Coffee" within the Global Coffee Market: The Role of Geographical Indications and Trade Marks' (2009) 10 *Estey Centre Journal of International Law & Trade Policy* 149. Several GI collectives have taken advantage of this overlap and have also registered their signs as trade marks. See WIPO, 'Technical and Procedural Aspects Relating to the Registration of Certification and Collective Marks', 15 May 2009 (SCT/21/3), Annex (These include the Ducal Crown for Parma Ham, Grana Padano, Münchner beer, Asti sparkling wine, Hilltops wine, Jamaica Blue Mountain coffee, Darjeeling tea and Pu'er tea).

Conclusion 295

The historical analysis of the French wine crisis in Chapter 3 sets out the initial reasons for public or state engagement. Even within *sui generis* systems, the initial teaching suggests that the state should facilitate and even initiate, but let stakeholders follow through during the process. While

[l]inking people, building up a structured collective marketing strategy and monitoring a collective organisation are costly ... a top-down approach is seldom a success because it may not take sufficiently into account operators' concerns and commercial risks. Regional authorities or NGOs may initiate a commercial project but they must let private operators establish and drive it because it is the latter which will have to take the commercial and investment risks.[103]

States also assist with capacity building, helping individual artisanal producers make the transition required by new product attributes geared towards wider marketing efforts, such as quality control, volumes, regularity and terms of payment etc.[104] States also have a role to play as mediators during conflicts between stakeholders. Therefore, in the case of the cured ham, Culatello di Zibello, where 'artisans [were] insisting on the long seasonal timeframe of the traditional method, whereas the intermediate institutions argued for shorter, year-round production to be allowed ... the local governments arrived at a compromise whereby two designations, with different codes of practice, were applied'.[105] Close attention also needs to be paid to the contextually sensitive borderline between state support and state interference or rent seeking. Corruption by state employees or insensitivity to producer concerns remain a real threat in many parts of the world where IGO protection has the potential to do the most good.[106] Therefore greater attention needs to be paid to the interaction between market and state within each of these registration system types, as well as to questions of institutional design.

5.   Conclusion

By juxtaposing the GI provisions in Articles 22 to 24 against those setting minimum standards for trade mark protection in Articles 15 to 21, TRIPS emphasises the differential treatment for these two categories

---

[103] Reviron et al., 'Geographical Indications: Creation and Distribution of Economic Value in Developing Countries', 19.

[104] Van de Kop et al., *Origin-Based Products: Lessons for Pro-Poor Market Development*, 90–1.

[105] Tregear et al., 'Regional Foods and Rural Development', 16.

[106] See generally, Hughes, 'Coffee and Chocolate'; Bashaw, 'Geographical Indications in China', 100–1.

of signs within IP law. Yet its negotiating history does not offer an explanation for why this is the case. This chapter has reframed the epistemic basis for differential treatment, by looking beyond the inadequacies of justifications derived from principles of unfair competition prevention. Instead it considers whether *sui generis* GI regimes implicitly recognise another kind of underlying subject matter – the products which these signs refer to. If the products – and those who produce them – are sufficiently valued or important, then the associated sign ought to be reserved for the home country producer group, regardless of the sign's reception before a given audience. This chapter has considered in greater detail some of these rationales for valuing the underlying products, particularly those related to the attainment of agricultural policy goals, biodiversity conservation, rural development strategies or benefits to developing countries. It has also considered whether a differently inflected TK argument could support enhanced GI protection. An empirically driven, insightful and interdisciplinary literature is beginning to develop as well as challenge these claims. Finally, it appears that we may be on the verge of committing to an institutional form of GI protection, by opting for registration based systems at the national level which will feed into any future international register. The chapter concludes by raising some of the questions which will need to be addressed as we make the transition towards registration-based protection in this area.

7 Conclusions – relocating geographical indications

This book set out to traverse uncharted territory. It sought an explanation for why GIs exist as a distinct category within international IP law. The reasons for embarking upon this voyage were straightforward. First, GIs are as close as it gets to an essentially contested concept within IP doctrine, despite IGOs existing in one form or another for well over a century. Second, they are also contentious within a broader political economy setting, in the context of international trade negotiations. Third, the rules governing the use and misuse of these signs are of relevance to producers of regional products, their competitors, consumers and policy makers. However, the rules – primarily those found in Articles 22 to 24 of the TRIPS Agreement – remain unclear. Fourth, and finally, the registered trade mark system has been proposed as a viable alternative. Therefore an account of the basis for their standalone status is long overdue. This account revolves around the identification of a distinctive or unique link between a certain category of products and their regions of origin. While borrowing from and being enriched by the various disciplinary perspectives which have useful and interesting things to say about this link, my objective was to retrace its recognition and reconstitution within legal discourse.

A historical perspective reveals much that is useful. To begin with, we identify a compelling answer within the legal discourse for those who question whether GIs fit within the IP canon. The IS emerged before *sui generis* appellation protection was well established. This first version of the IGO was remarkably congruent with contemporary understandings of trade marks. As described by participants during the initial Paris and Madrid negotiations and based on contemporary understandings, the IS was a sign indicating geographical origin and subsequently also capable of supporting a collectively generated reputation. The valuable intangible that we must seek at the centre of any IP regime is thus teased out. Ensuring clear channels of communication for such signs, by suppressing fraudulent or misleading uses, would benefit the general consuming public as well as honest producers. There are traces of this impulse to

298   Conclusions – relocating geographical indications

protect location-specific reputation in the formation of international norms for collective marks, as well as unfair competition prevention. However, the geographical descriptiveness of the sign and the collective interest in its use would prove obstacles to incorporation within the registered trade mark system.

The IS was therefore situated within the primordial soup of unfair competition prevention, whereby national legal systems adopted various norms to prevent third parties from misusing signs in the course of trade. It was grafted onto a range of laws organised around the prevention of false labelling, but differing greatly in institutional form and teleological aspirations. Besides the conceptual clutter this generated, origin marking was itself subject to competing fields of interests. As a result, in this version the collective reputation interest has faded from view over time. Furthermore, since international protection was the object – beyond the confines of territoriality – the IS, with its emphasis on preventing misleading uses, had inherent limitations. Since meaning was fluid and signifiers could gain new connotations over space and time (including through generic use or qualified use), such contingent protection was deemed unsatisfactory. While the IS represented a simplified link between product and place of origin, *terroir* suggested that certain products were anchored more tightly to their origins, thereby strengthening opposition to use by outsiders. At this stage the communicative logic supporting IS protection, that is shared with trade mark law, is layered over with *terroir* logic. While reputation protection remains an essential ingredient, what does change is the procedure for defining the circle of those entitled to the use of the sign, as well as the basis for defining the subject matter and scope of protection.

In contrast with the IS, AO regimes are portrayed as having distinct aims when compared with trade mark or general unfair competition rules and thus entitled to differential treatment. The conceptual underpinnings of this influential legal category were developed in the context of the legal regulation of the wine industry in France. The relevant history of this period is therefore helpful for three reasons. First, it provides us with the necessary context to better appreciate the influence, as well as limitations, of wine as the subject matter kernel for GIs in general. For wine and other broadly agricultural products, features of physical geography and *savoir faire* associated with this geography provide the resources for defining the authentic product, identifying legitimate users of the appellation as well as determining the boundaries of production. The product specification is stabilised around these criteria which, to a certain extent, can be empirically verified. The *terroir* paradigm emphasises production criteria. When it comes to 'reputational'

Conclusions – relocating geographical indications

products (crafts, toys, textiles or recipe-based products) or regionally reputed services, such as banking or massages, their inclusion within this paradigm is self-evidently more problematic. Such products have been protected an a case-by-case basis within unfair competition regimes, which prioritise consumption, i.e. consumer perception, as the vantage point from which to identify those entitled to use the sign as well as the boundaries of production. Second, it reveals a series of transformations in the legal conceptualisation of the link between product and place, through the interplay between different versions of *terroir*. These conceptual shifts within the *terroir* paradigm are carried forward into the Lisbon Agreement. The gradual recognition of the cultural element or human dimension is an important development, which simultaneously undermines a deterministic form of linkage while emphasising the performative aspects of place. Third, the history of this period brings into focus the two overlapping yet distinct epistemic frameworks which begin to operate in this area. This directly affects the scope of protection. If the initial framework had been based on truth telling or communicative logic and realised by unfair competition rules, the emerging AO regime prioritised the historic and qualitative dimensions of the link between people, products and places. What an audience would understand by the use of the sign in a given context was no longer dispositive in determining which uses were unjustified. The enquiry was realigned to focus on the gap between the imitator's product and the original, valorising place and production techniques in the process. At the national level there may have been a considerable overlap between these two regimes. *Terroir* was supposedly the basis for quality, which in turn, led to the product's reputation. However, when it came to international protection, the overlap could not be assumed, as signs because detached from specific places and regulated production techniques. This could happen in the case of genericide or where the sign was claimed as an individual trade mark in a jurisdiction where the original GI product was not yet known. Outsider use would still be deemed illicit under the *terroir* paradigm but arguably be permissible under the communicative one.

Continuing with the analysis of the AO, the Lisbon Agreement embodies this formal transition, which results in the emergence of a distinct category of subject matter. In exploring this shift, one of the principal lines of enquiry concerns the algorithm for defining suitable subject matter. In formulating the AO, the Lisbon Agreement signatories seem to implicitly acknowledge the transition from the AO to the AOC in French law. Human factors are recognised alongside natural ones, leading to an expansive subject matter category. However, a system which was originally designed with agricultural goods in mind – products of the vine, rooted to place – cannot be satisfactorily extended to products that have only a loose link to physical geography, without running the risk of incoherence. If AOs represent the socio-economic and cultural dimensions of the interaction between people and a specific place, this requires an anchor to physical geography. Otherwise geographical indications may be transformed into historic ones or cultural-geographic indications, requiring an altogether distinct foundational basis. Yet at the same time the Lisbon model did not require that such products need to be unique or inimitable. A careful study of this Agreement also helps us disentangle arguments relating to the scope of protection, separating them into norms against (1) misrepresentation, (2) dilution, and (3) misappropriation, and (4) in favour of 'absolute' protection.

It is imperative to acknowledge the full effect of 'absolute' protection, which suggests that unlike the previous international treaties or national unfair competition regimes, what the sign means to a particular audience is no longer the basis for protection. If we are deviating from a familiar cluster of justifications, then what are their replacements? One potential candidate proved unsatisfactory. We have considered the movement away from '*conditions particulières de climat et de terroir*' logic as the predominant justification for anchoring a product in a place. This is for a variety of reasons: places of origin are difficult to demarcate according to consensual criteria, innovation means that products change over time, and – as opposed to deterministic approaches to physical geography alone – human skill is increasingly acknowledged in the history of regional products. If we can no longer confidently rely on the authorship of nature and claim that clearly defined places produce (empirically verifiable) unique products, then why should we grant expansive or 'absolute' rights to prohibit the use elsewhere of identical or similar signs? Implicit in the Lisbon Agreement is the second possible explanation – accepting multilateral obligations on the basis of mutual convenience and benefit. You protect ours and we'll protect yours. This requires a certain amount of pragmatic calculus from each state, when considering whether to join. A third explanation is more blunt. Absolute protection is motivated by national interest and protectionist impulses.

These reasons are supplemented with those identified in Chapter 6, acknowledging that aspects of local or national cultural heritage are associated with GI production or sometimes even consumption; recognising the *savoir faire* or traditional knowledge which has sustained and improved these products over time; emphasising their role in achieving agricultural policy goals; highlighting environmental benefits associated with GI protection, such as the preservation of biodiversity by incentivising the use of non-mainstream plant varieties or animal breeds;

Conclusions – relocating geographical indications

stressing their potential for rural development or the economies of developing countries; and responding to a growing consumer demand for regional produce which is often perceived as more desirable on a qualitative basis. The point worth reiterating is that an unfair competition paradigm premised on communicative logic cannot account for this tier of absolute protection without being supplemented by additional arguments of policy or principle and these are the contenders.

Proponents of IGO protection wished to protect geographical signs as reified objects, closed things of actual or potential value, regardless of the contingencies of meaning before any given audience. These developments were driven by *terroir*-influenced conceptualisations of the link between product and place. Without being expressly articulated, competing epistemic frameworks have been operating in this area. Those who conceive of the regulation of *geographical signs* within the broader framework of unfair competition law (itself an unsettled category) continue to ask why proponents of greater protection desire rules which deviate from communicative logic. Meanwhile proponents of greater protection for *regional products* are beginning to explore these alternative justifications which relate to the significance or importance of regional products.

The book concludes with an in-depth analysis of the more problematic features of the TRIPS GI provisions. The TRIPS GI regime is not quite the consolidating project or constellation of determinate rules that it's made out to be. Part II is offered as a counter-narrative to scholarship which presumes the TRIPS GI to be a conceptually stable entity, associated with clear rules. Nevertheless, TRIPS remains significant as a site of discursive formation. The contours of international GI protection are shaped by the influential debates and disagreements taking place within this framework, making this platform uniquely authoritative. However, the platform is constructed from the detritus of previous compromises. The definition of a GI in Article 22.1 has been influenced by prior negotiations under the auspices of WIPO as well as the EU's Regulation 2081/92, where the *terroir* and reputation logics were fused together. As a result, there is considerable equivocation over central aspects of the definition, such as the methodology for delimiting the region of origin and specifying the link between product and place. Article 22.1 was designed to be flexible and accommodating, but this may be at the cost of coherence unless a more compelling normative account of the link can be developed. Here the recognition of the human dimension, of collective investment and innovation over time, has potential. Otherwise the logic of unfair competition prevention, often presumed to be the foundation for Articles 22 to 24, can only take us so far. Chapter 6 explores in

302   Conclusions – relocating geographical indications

greater detail some of these additional rationales for valuing the underlying products, particularly those related to the attainment of agricultural policy goals, biodiversity conservation, rural development strategies or benefits to developing countries. It has also considered whether a differently inflected TK argument could support enhanced GI protection. An empirically driven, insightful and interdisciplinary literature is beginning to develop many of these arguments. Finally, it appears that we may be on the verge of committing to an institutional form of GI protection, by opting for registration-based systems at the national level which will feed into any future international register. This chapter concludes by raising some of the questions which will need to be addressed as we make the transition towards registration-based protection in this area.

International GI protection is likely to be controversial for the foreseeable future. It is time to move beyond some of the familiar yet sterile, endlessly regurgitated legal debates and entrenched positions since there are far more interesting and important questions to pursue. The legal resolutions to these questions will affect livelihoods, impact upon consumer choice in the marketplace and – through the vectors of tradition and authenticity – engage with the politics of place. Lawyers cannot afford to ignore the significant contributions made by those from other disciplines who are exploring the issues surrounding origin-labelled products, while the latter would do well to appreciate the historical inertia as well as constraints of legal reasoning, interpretation and justification. By drawing on the past, this book has sought to explain the present, which should assist those who wish to design a better future.

Bibliography

Articles

Addor, F. and Grazioli, A., 'Geographical Indications beyond Wines and Spirits: A Roadmap for a Better Protection for Geographical Indications in the WTO/TRIPS Agreement' (2002) 5 JWIP 865.

Agdomar, M., 'Removing the Greek from Feta and Adding Korbel to Champagne: The Paradox of Geographical Indications in International Law' (2008) 18 *Fordham IP Media and Entertainment Law Journal* 541.

Akerlof, G. A., 'The Market for "Lemons": Quality Uncertainty and the Market Mechanism' (1970) 84 *Quarterly Journal of Economics* 488.

Alkin, T., 'Should there be a Tort of "Unfair Competition" in English Law?' (2008) 3 *Journal of Intellectual Property Law and Practice* 48.

Amar, M., 'Des Marques Collectives' (1901) 5 *Annuaire* 112.

Armistead, J., 'Whose Cheese Is It Anyway? Correctly Slicing the European Regulation Concerning Protections for Geographic Indications' (2000) 10 *Transnational Law & Contemporary Problems* 303.

Audier, J., 'Generic and Semi-Generic Denominations: Determination Criteria and Methods to Reduce their Effects' (2000) 22 *AIDV Bulletin* 29.

'Local, Honest and Constant Uses – Summary Contribution to a Definition' (1996) 6 *AIDV Bulletin* 5.

Aylward, D., 'Towards a Cultural Economy Paradigm for the Australian Wine Industry' (2008) 26 *Prometheus* 373.

Banks, G. and Sharpe, S., 'Wine, Regions and the Geographic Imperative: The Coonawarra Example' (2006) 62 *New Zealand Geographer* 173.

Barham, E., 'Translating Terroir: The Global Challenge of French AOC Labeling' (2003) 19 *Journal of Rural Studies* 127.

Bashaw, B. M., 'Geographical Indications in China: Why Protect GIs with Both Trade Mark Law and AOC-Type Legislation?' (2008) 17 *Pacific Rim Law and Policy Journal* 73.

Beebe, B., 'Intellectual Property and the Sumptuary Code' (2010) 123 *Harvard Law Review* 809.

'The Semiotic Analysis of Trade Mark Law' (2004) 51 *University of California Los Angeles Law Review* 621.

Beier, F-K., 'Case Comment: Court of Justice-Case No. C-3/91 "Turron"' [1994] IIC 73.

'The Need for Protection of Indications of Source and Appellations of Origin in the Common Market' [1977] *Industrial Property* 152.

304   Bibliography

Beier, F-K. and Knaak, R., 'The Protection of Direct and Indirect Geographical Indications of Source in Germany and the European Community' (1994) IIC 1.

Bendekgey, L. and Mead, C., 'International Protection of Appellations of Origin and Other Geographical Indications' (1992) 82 TMR 765.

Benson, R. W., 'Toward a New Treaty for the Protection of Geographical Indications' [1978] *Industrial Property* 127.

Bérard, L. and Marchenay, P., 'Local Products and Geographical Knowledge: Taking Account of Local Knowledge and Biodiversity' (2006) 58 *International Social Science Journal* 109.

'Localized Products in France: Definition, Protection and Value-Adding' [2007] *Anthropology of Food* S2.

Beresford, L., 'Geographical Indications: The Current Landscape' (2007) 17 *Fordham Intellectual Property Media & Entertainment Law Journal* 979.

'Trade Marks and Geographical Indications 101: What Trade Mark Owners Should Know' (2008) 1 *Landslide* 19.

Bertozzi, L., 'Designation of Origin: Quality and Specification' (1995) 6 *Food Quality and Preference* 143.

BIRPI, 'The Protection and International Registration of Appellations of Origin' [1957] *Industrial Property* 49.

Blakeney, M., 'Geographical Indications and Trade' (2000) 6 *International Trade Law and Regulation* 48.

'Proposals for the International Regulation of Geographical Indications' (2001) 4 JWIP 629.

Bohmrich, R., '*Terroir*: Competing Perspectives on the Roles of Soil, Climate and People' (1996) 7 *Journal of Wine Research* 33.

Bone, R., 'Hunting Goodwill: A History of the Concept of Goodwill in Trade Mark Law' (2006) 86 *Boston University Law Review* 547.

Bouamra-Mechemache, Z. and Chaaban, J., 'Determinants of Adoption of Protected Designation of Origin Label: Evidence from the French Brie Cheese Industry' (2010) 61 *Journal of Agricultural Economics* 225.

Bowen, S., 'Development from Within? The Potential for Geographical Indications in the Global South' (2010) 13 JWIP 231.

Bramley, C. and Kirsten, J. F., 'Exploring the Economic Rationale for Protecting Geographical Indicators in Agriculture' (2007) 46 *Agrekon* 69.

Brauneis, R. and Schechter, R. E., 'Geographic Trade Marks and the Protection of Competitor Communication' (2006) 96 TMR 782.

Brody, P. M., 'Geographical Indications and Dilution: Reinterpreting "Distinctiveness" Under the Lanham Act' (2010) 100 TMR 905.

'"Semi-Generic" Geographical Wine Designations: Did Congress Trip Over TRIPS?' (1999) 89 TMR 979.

Broude, T., 'Taking "Trade and Culture" Seriously: Geographical Indications and Cultural Protection in WTO Law' (2005) 26 *University of Pennsylvania Journal of International Economic Law* 623.

Brouwer, O., 'Community Protection of Geographical Indications and Specific Character as a Means of Enhancing Foodstuffs Quality' (1991) 28 *Common Market Law Review* 615.

Bibliography

Buchanan, J. M., 'An Economic Theory of Clubs' [1965] *Economica* 1.

Burrell, R. and Gangjee, D., 'Trade Marks and Freedom of Expression: A Call for Caution' [2010] IIC 544.

Calboli, I., 'Expanding the Protection of Geographical Indications of Origin under TRIPS: "Old" Debate or "New" Opportunity?' (2006) 10 *Marquette Intellectual Property Law Review* 181.

Carty, H., 'Dilution and Passing Off: Cause for Concern' [1996] *Law Quarterly Review* 632.

Chandola, H. V., 'Basmati Rice: Geographical Indication or Mis-Indication' (2006) 9 JWIP 166.

Chen, J., 'A Sober Second Look at Appellations of Origin: How the United States Will Crash France's Wine and Cheese Party' (1996) 5 *Minnesota Journal of Global Trade* 29.

Clark, J., 'Geographies of Multifunctional Agriculture: Developing Governance Explanations' (2010) 4 *Geography Compass* 803.

Conrad, A., 'The Protection of Geographical Indications in the TRIPS Agreement' (1996) 86 TMR 11.

Coombe, R., Schnoor, S. and Al Attar Ahmed, M., 'Bearing Cultural Distinction: Informational Capitalism and New Expectations for Intellectual Property' (2007) 40 *University of California–Davis Law Review* 891.

Cornish, W. R., 'Genevan Bootstraps' [1997] EIPR 336.

Cortes Martin, J. M., 'TRIPS Agreement: Towards a Better Protection for Geographical Indications?' (2004) 30 *Brooklyn Journal of International Law* 117.

'The WTO TRIPS Agreement – The Battle between the Old and the New World over the Protection of Geographical Indications' (2004) 7 JWIP 287.

Cotton, A. P., '123 Years at the Negotiating Table and Still No Dessert? The Case in Support of TRIPS Geographical Indication Protections' (2007) 82 *Chicago–Kent Law Review* 1295.

Cran, D. and Griffiths, S., 'Ambush Marketing: Unsporting Behaviour or Fair Play? (2010) *Entertainment Law Review* 293.

Creditt, E. C., 'Terroir vs. Trademarks: The Debate over Geographical Indications and Expansions to the TRIPS Agreement' (2009) 11 *Vanderbilt Journal of Entertainment & Technology Law* 429.

Cushing, G. D., 'On Certain Cases Analogous to Trade Marks' (1891) 4 *Harvard Law Review* 321.

Dagne, T. W., 'Harnessing the Development Potential of Geographical Indications for Traditional Knowledge-based Agricultural Products' (2010) 5 *Journal of Intellectual Property Law and Practice* 441.

Das, K., 'International Protection of India's Geographical Indications with Special Reference to "Darjeeling" Tea' (2006) 9 JWIP 459.

'Prospects and Challenges of Geographical Indications in India' (2010) 13 JWIP 148.

Dawson, N., 'Locating Geographical Indications: Perspectives from English Law' (2000) 90 TMR 590.

de Almeida, A. F. R., 'The TRIPS Agreement, the Bilateral Agreements Concerning Geographical Indications and the Philosophy of the WTO' [2005] EIPR 150.

306   Bibliography

Desai, D. R. and Rierson, S. L., 'Confronting the Genericism Conundrum' (2007) 28 *Cardozo Law Review* 1789.

Devletian, A., 'The Lisbon Agreement' [1973] *Industrial Property* 308.

'The Protection of Appellations and Indications of Origin' [1957] *Industrial Property Quarterly* 6.

'The Protection of Appellations of Origin and Indications of Source' [1968] *Industrial Property* 107.

Dibden, J. and Cocklin, C., '"Multifunctionality": Trade Protectionism or a New Way Forward?' (2009) 41 *Environment and Planning* 163.

Dibden, J., Potter, C. and Cocklin, C., 'Contesting the Neoliberal Project for Agriculture: Productivist and Multifunctional Trajectories in the European Union and Australia' (2009) 25 *Journal of Rural Studies* 299.

Dinwoodie, G., 'Trade Marks and Territory: Detaching Trade Mark Law from the Nation-State' (2004) 41 *Houston Law Review* 885.

Downes, D. R., 'How Intellectual Property Could be a Tool to Protect Traditional Knowledge' (2000) 25 *Columbia Journal of Environmental Law* 253.

Duguid, P., 'Developing the Brand: The Case of Alcohol, 1800–1880' (2003) 4 *Enterprise and Society* 405.

'French Connections: The International Propagation of Trade Marks in the Nineteenth Century' (2009) 10 *Enterprise & Society* 3.

'Networks and Knowledge: The Beginning and End of the Port Commodity Chain, 1703–1860' (2005) 78 *Business History Review* 453.

Economides, N., 'The Economics of Trade Marks' (1988) 78 TMR 523.

Editor's Note, 'The Tenth Annual International Review of Trade Mark Jurisprudence' (2003) 93 TMR 505, 567.

Études Générales, 'De la Protection Internationale des Marques d'Origine' [1896] *Propriété Industrielle* 21.

'La Marque Collective' [1934] *Propriété Industrielle* 31.

'La Marque Collective (Part II)' (1934) *Propriété Industrielle* 64.

'La Question des Fausses Indications de Provenance et l'Arrangement de Madrid' [1920] *Propriété Industrielle* 18 (Part I), 31 (Part II), 40 (Part III), 53 (Part IV).

'Un Exemple de Marque Collective la Marque «Unis-France»' [1934] *Propriété Industrielle* 191.

Evans, G. E., 'The Comparative Advantages of Geographical Indications and Community Trade Marks for the Marketing of Agricultural Products in the European Union' [2010] IIC 645.

Folsom, R. H. and Teply, L. R., 'Trade Marked Generic Words' (1980) 89 *Yale Law Journal* 1323.

Fotopoulos, C. and Krystallis, A., 'Quality Labels as a Marketing Advantage: The Case of the "PDO Zagora" Apples in the Greek Market' (2003) 37 *European Journal of Marketing* 1350.

Franklyn, D. J., 'Debunking Dilution Doctrine: Toward A Coherent Theory of the Anti-Free-Rider Principle in American Trademark Law' (2004–5) 56 *Hastings Law Journal* 117.

Fusco, S., 'Geographical Indications: A Discussion of the TRIPS Regulation after the Ministerial Conference of Hong Kong' (2008) 12 *Marquette Intellectual Property Law Review* 197.

Bibliography

Gade, D. W., 'Tradition, Territory, and Terroir in French Viniculture: Cassis, France, and Appellation Contrôlée' (2004) 94 *Annals of the Association of American Geographers* 848.

Gangjee, D., *'Melton Mowbray* and the GI Pie in the Sky: Exploring Cartographies of Protection' (2006) 3 *IPQ* 291.

'Quibbling Siblings: Conflicts between Trade Marks and Geographical Indications' (2007) 82 *Chicago–Kent Law Review* 1253.

'Say Cheese: A Sharper Image of Generic Use through the Lens of Feta' [2007] EIPR 172.

Gangjee, D. and Burrell, R., 'Because You're Worth It: *L'Oréal* and the Prohibition on Free Riding' (2010) 73 *Modern Law Review* 282.

Gervais, D., 'Reinventing Lisbon: The Case for a Protocol to the Lisbon Agreement (Geographical Indications)' (2010) 11 *Chicago Journal of International Law* 67.

'The Lisbon Agreement's Misunderstood Potential' (2009) 1 *WIPO Journal* 87.

'Traditional Knowledge & Intellectual Property: A TRIPS Compatible Approach' [2005] *Michigan State Law Review* 137.

Gevers, F., 'Geographical Names and Signs Used as Trade Marks' [1990] EIPR 285.

Gielen, C., 'WIPO and Unfair Competition' [1997] EIPR 78.

Giovannucci, D., Barham, E. and Pirog, R., 'Defining and Marketing "Local" Foods: Geographical Indications for US Products' (2010) 13 JWIP 94.

Goebel, B., 'Geographical Indications and Trade Marks – The Road from Doha' (2003) 93 TMR 964.

Goldberg, S. D., 'Who Will Raise the White Flag? The Battle between the United States and the European Union over the Protection of Geographical Indications' (2001) 22 *University of Pennsylvania Journal of International Economic Law* 107.

Haight Farley, C., 'Conflicts between U.S. Law and International Treaties Concerning Geographical Indications' (2000) 22 *Whittier Law Review* 73.

'Why We Are Confused About the Trade Mark Dilution Law' (2006) 16 *Fordham Intellectual Property Media & Entertainment Law Journal* 1175.

Hancock, D., 'Commerce and Conversation in the Eighteenth-Century Atlantic: The Invention of Madeira Wine' (1998) 29 *Journal of Interdisciplinary History* 19.

Handler, M., 'Case Comment: The WTO Geographical Indications Dispute' (2006) 69 *Modern Law Review* 70.

'The EU's Geographical Indications Agenda and its Potential Impact on Australia' (2004) 15 *Australian Intellectual Property Journal* 173.

Harte-Bavendamm, H., 'Ende der geographischen Herkunftsbezeichnungen? "Brüsseler Spitzen" gegen den ergänzenden nationalen Rechtsschutz' [1996] GRUR 717.

Heath, C., 'A Hungarian Chapter to the Budweiser Saga' [2009] IIC 328.

Helfer, L., 'Regime Shifting: The TRIPS Agreement and New Dynamics of International Intellectual Property Law Making' (2004) 29 *Yale Journal of International Law* 1.

Henning-Bodewig, F., 'A New Act against Unfair Competition in Germany' [2005] IIC 421.

308   Bibliography

Henning-Bodewig, F. and Schricker, G., 'New Initiatives for the Harmonisation of Unfair Competition Law in Europe' [2002] EIPR 271.

Higgins, D. and Gangjee, D., '"Trick or Treat?" The Misrepresentation of American Beef Exports in Britain during the Late Nineteenth Century' (2010) 11 *Enterprise and Society* 203.

Hughes, J., 'Champagne, Feta, and Bourbon – The Spirited Debate about Geographical Indications' (2006) 58 *Hastings Law Journal* 299.

Hutt, P. B., 'Government Regulation of the Integrity of the Food Supply' (1984) 4 *Annual Review of Nutrition* 1.

Hutt, P. B. and Hutt II, P. B., 'A History of Government Regulation of Adulteration and Misbranding of Food' (1984) 39 *Food, Drug, Cosmetic Law Journal* 2.

Ilbert, H. and Petit, M., 'Are Geographical Indications a Valid Property Right? Global Trends and Challenges' (2009) 27 *Development Policy Review* 503.

Iselin, J. F., 'Des Indications de Provenance' [1897] *Annuaire* 266.

Jokuti, A., 'Where is the What if the What is in Why? A Rough Guide to the Maze of Geographical Indications' [2009] EIPR 118.

Jordan, R., Zidda, P. and Lockshin, L., 'Behind the Australian Wine Industry's Success: Does Environment Matter?' (2007) 19 *International Journal of Wine Business Research* 14.

Josel, K. H., 'New Wine in Old Bottles: The Protection of France's Wine Classification System beyond Its Borders' (1994) 12 *Boston University International Law Journal* 471.

Josling, T., 'The War on *Terroir*: Geographical Indications as a Transatlantic Trade Conflict' (2006) 57 *Journal of Agricultural Economics* 337.

Kamperman Sanders, A., 'Incentives for Protection of Cultural Expression: Art, Trade and Geographical Indications' (2010) 13 JWIP 81.

Kazmi, H., 'Does it Make a Difference where that Chablis Comes From? Geographic Indications in TRIPS and NAFTA' (2001) 12 *Journal of Contemporary Legal Issues* 470.

Kireeva, I. and O'Connor, B., 'Geographical Indications and the TRIPS Agreement: What Protection is Provided to Geographical Indications in WTO Members?' (2010) 13 JWIP 275.

Knaak, R., 'Case Law of the European Court of Justice on the Protection of Geographical Indications and Designations of Origin Pursuant to EC Regulation No. 2081/92' [2001] IIC 375.

Kolia, M., 'Monopolising Names: EEC Proposals on the Protection of Trade Descriptions of Foodstuffs' [1992] EIPR, 233.

'Monopolizing Names of Foodstuffs: The New Legislation' [1992] EIPR 333.

Krieger, A., 'Revision of the Lisbon Agreement for the Protection of Appellations of Origin' [1974] *Industrial Property* 387.

Kuanpoth, J. and Robinson, D., 'Protection of Geographical Indications: The Case of Jasmine Rice and Thailand' (2009) 6 *IPQ* 288.

Kur, A., 'Quibbling Siblings – Comments to Dev Gangjee's Presentation' (2007) 82 *Chicago–Kent Law Review* 1317.

Landes, W. M. and Posner, R. A., 'Trade Mark Law: An Economic Perspective' (1987) 30 *Journal of Law and Economics* 265.

Lang, A. C., 'On the Need to Expand Article 23 of the TRIPS Agreement' (2006) 16 *Duke Journal of Contemporary and International Law* 487.

Lehman, B., 'Intellectual Property under the Clinton Administration' (1993–4) 27 *George Washington Journal of International Law and Economics* 395.

Lemley, M. A., 'Property, Intellectual Property, and Free Riding' (2005) 83 *Texas Law Review* 1031.

Lenzen, L. C., 'Bacchus in the Hinterlands: A Study of Denominations of Origin in French and American Wine-Labeling Laws' (1968) 58 TMR 145.

Lindquist, L. A., 'Champagne or Champagne? An Examination of US Failure to Comply with the Geographical Provision of the TRIPS Agreement' (1999) 27 *Georgia Journal of International and Comparative Law* 309.

Lister, C., 'A Sad Story Told Sadly: The Prospects for U.S.–EU Food Trade Wars' (1996) 51 *Food & Drug Law Journal* 303.

Lloyd, E., 'On the Law of Trade Marks: Nature of the Right to Use a Trade Mark (I)' (1860–1) 5 *Solicitor's Journal and Reporter* 486.

Long, C., 'Dilution' (2006) 106 *Columbia Law Review* 1029.

Lorvellec, L., 'You've Got to Fight for Your Right to Party: A Response to Professor Jim Chen' (1996) 5 *Minnesota Journal of Global Trade* 65.

Luykx, D. M. A. M. and van Ruth, S. M., 'An Overview of Analytical Methods for Determining the Geographical Origin of Food Products' (2008) 107 *Food Chemistry* 897.

Maher, M., 'On Vino Veritas? Clarifying the Use of Geographic References on American Wine Labels' (2001) 89 *California Law Review* 1881.

Marie-Vivien, D., 'From Plant Variety Definition to Geographical Indication Protection: A Search for the Link Between Basmati Rice and India/Pakistan' (2008) 11 JWIP 321.

'The Role of the State in the Protection of Geographical Indications: From Disengagement in France/Europe to Significant Involvement in India' (2010) 13 JWIP 121.

McCarthy, J. T. and Colby Devitt, V., 'Protection of Geographical Denominations: Domestic and International' (1979) 69 TMR 199.

McKenna, M. P., 'The Normative Foundations of Trade Mark Law' (2007) 82 *Notre Dame Law Review* 1839.

Mesneir, J., 'Semantic Analysis and Draft Definition of the Word "Terroir"' (1997) 12 *AIDV Bulletin* 4.

Misegades, K., 'The Scope of the Law of Unfair Competition' (1932) 14 *Journal of the Patent and Trademark Office Society* 763.

Mitchell, O. R., 'Unfair Competition' (1896) 10 *Harvard Law Review* 275.

Moran, W., 'Rural Space as Intellectual Property' (1993) 12 *Political Geography* 263.

'The Wine Appellation as Territory in France and California' (1993) 83 *Annals of the Association of American Geographers* 694.

Nieuwveld, L. B., 'Is This Really about What We Call Our Food or Something Else? The WTO Food Name Case over the Protection of Geographical Indications' (2007) 41 *International Lawyer* 891.

Niska, H. N., 'The European Union Trips over the US Constitution: Can the First Amendment Save the Bologna that has a First Name?' (2004) 13 *Minnesota Journal of Global Trade* 413.

Bibliography

Nguyen, X-T. N., 'Nationalizing Trade Marks: A New International Trade Mark Jurisprudence?' (2004) 39 *Wake Forest Law Review* 729.

Notz, W., 'New Phases of Unfair Competition and Measures for Its Suppression National and International' (1920–1) 30 *Yale Law Journal* 384.

Nye, J. V., 'The Myth of Free-Trade Britain and Fortress France: Tariffs and Trade in the Nineteenth Century' (1991) 51 *Journal of Economic History* 23.

O'Reilly, S., Haines, M. and Arfini, F., 'Food SME Networks: Process and Governance – The Case of Parma Ham' (2003) 3 *Journal on Chain and Network Science* 21.

Ohde, H. J., 'Zur demoskopischen Ermittlung der Verkehrsauffassung von geographischen Herkunftsangaben' [1989] *GRUR* 98.

Ostertag, M., 'International Unions for the Protection of Industrial, Literary and Artistic Property' (1926) 25 *Michigan Law Review* 107.

Paly, A., 'Organisation of the AOC Wine Industry in France' (2001) 26 *AIDV Bulletin* 2.

Pey, J., 'Protection des Marques Communales, Régionales, Nationales' [1901] *Annuaire* 119.

Phillips, J. and Simon, I., 'Geographical Indications: The Biggest Threat to Trade Marks?' (Spring 2004) *Marques Newsletter* 2.

Plaisant, R., 'The Revision of the International Treaty Provisions Dealing with Appellations of Origin and Indications of Source' [1980] *Industrial Property* 182.

Pollack, L. W., '"Roquefort" – An Example of Multiple Protection for a Designation of Regional Origin under the Lanham Act' (1962) 52 TMR 755.

Posner, R. A., 'Misappropriation: A Dirge' (2003) 40 *Houston Law Review* 621.

Prats, B., 'The Terroir is Important' (1983) 8 *Decanter* 16.

Profeta, A., Balling, R., Schoene, R. and Wirsig, A., 'The Protection of Origins for Agricultural Products and Foods in Europe: Status Quo, Problems and Policy Recommendations for the Green Book' (2009) 12 JWIP 622.

Prošek, J. and Vilimská, M., 'The Protection of Appellations of Origin in Czechoslovakia' (1975) *Industrial Property* 99.

Rangnekar, D., 'The Intellectual Properties of Geography' [2009] EIPR 537.

'The Law and Economics of Geographical Indications: Introduction to Special Issue' (2010) 13 JWIP 77.

Rangnekar, D. and Kumar, S., 'Another Look at Basmati: Genericity and the Problems of a Transborder Geographical Indication' (2010) 13 JWIP 202.

Raustiala, K. and Munzer, S. R., 'The Global Struggle over Geographical Indications' (2007) 18 *European Journal of International Law* 337.

Renaud, J. R., 'Can't Get There from Here: How NAFTA and GATT Have Reduced Protection for Geographical Trademarks' (2001) 26 *Brooklyn Journal of International Law* 1097.

Renting, H. et al., 'Exploring Multifunctional Agriculture. A Review of Conceptual Approaches and Prospects for an Integrative Transitional Framework' (2009) 90 *Journal of Environmental Management* S112.

Resano-Ezcaray, H., Sanjuán-López, A. I. and Albisu-Aguado, L. M., 'Combining Stated and Revealed Preferences on Typical Food Products: The Case of Dry-Cured Ham in Spain' (2010) 61 *Journal of Agricultural Economics* 480.

Ricolfi, M., 'Is the European GIs Policy in Need of Rethinking' [2009] IIC 123.

Ritzert, M., 'Champagne Is from Champagne: An Economic Justification for Extending Trade Mark-Level Protection to Wine-related Geographical Indications' (2009) 37 *American Intellectual Property Law Association Quarterly Journal* 191.

Rogers, E., 'Industrial Property' (1929) 27 *Michigan Law Review* 491.

'Some Historical Matters Concerning Trade Marks' (1910) 9 *Michigan Law Review* 29.

Rose, B., 'No More Whining about Geographical Indications: Assessing the 2005 Agreement between the United States and the European Community on the Trade in Wine' (2007) 29 *Houston Journal of International Law* 731.

Roussel, B. and Verdeaux, F., 'Natural Patrimony and Local Communities in Ethiopia: Advantages and Limitations of a System of Geographical Indications' (2007) 77 *Africa* 130.

Schechter, F., 'The Rational Basis of Trade Mark Protection' (1926–7) 40 *Harvard Law Review* 813.

Schricker, G., 'Protection of Indications of Source, Appellations of Origin and other Geographic Designations in the Federal Republic of Germany' [1983] IIC 307.

'The Efforts towards Harmonization of the Law of Unfair Competition in the European Economic Community' [1973] IIC 201.

Schüßler, L., 'Protecting "Single-Origin Coffee" within the Global Coffee Market: The Role of Geographical Indications and Trade Marks' (2009) 10 *Estey Centre Journal of International Law & Trade Policy* 149.

Senftleben, M., 'The Trade Mark Tower of Babel – Dilution Concepts in International, US and EC Trade Mark Law' [2009] IIC 45.

Shalov, D. B., 'Will the European Union Prove to be Lactose Intolerant?' (2004) 11 *Cardozo Journal of International and Comparative Law* 1099.

Sherman, B., 'Regulating Access and Use of Genetic Resources: Intellectual Property and Biodiscovery' [2003] EIPR 301.

Simon Fhima, I., 'Dilution by Blurring: a Conceptual Roadmap' (2010) 7 *IPQ* 44.

Simonson, I., 'An Empirical Investigation of the Meaning and Measurement of "Genericness"' (1994) 84 TMR 199.

Simpson, J., 'Cooperation and Conflicts: Institutional Innovation in France's Wine Markets, 1870–1911' (2005) 79 *Business History Review* 527.

'Selling to Reluctant Drinkers: the British Wine Market, 1860–1914' (2004) 57 *Economic History Review* 80.

Singhal, S., 'Geographical Indications and Traditional Knowledge' (2008) 3 *Journal of Intellectual Property Law and Practice* 732.

Skuras, D. and Dimara, E., 'Regional Image and the Consumption of Regionally Denominated Products' (2004) 41 *Urban Studies* 801.

Snyder, D. L., 'Enhanced Protections for Geographical Indications Under TRIPS: Potential Conflicts Under the U.S. Constitutional and Statutory Regimes' (2008) 18 *Fordham IP, Media & Entertainment Law Journal* 1297.

Stanziani, A., 'Information, Quality and Legal Rules: Wine Adulteration in Nineteenth Century France' (2009) 51 *Business History* 268.

'Wine Reputation and Quality Controls: The Origin of the AOCs in 19th Century France' (2004) 18 *European Journal of Law and Economics* 149.

Bibliography

Staten, T. L., 'Geographical Indications Protection under the TRIPS Agreement: Uniformity Not Extension' (2005) 87 *Journal of the Patent & Trade Mark Office Society* 221.

Stern, S., 'Are GIs IP' [2007] EIPR 39.

'Case Comment: First Test Case of the EC Australia Wine Treaty' [1997] EIPR 668.

Stevenson, I., 'The Diffusion of Disaster: the Phylloxera Outbreak in the *Département* of the Hérault, 1862–80' (1980) 6 *Journal of Historical Geography* 47.

Suh, J. and MacPherson, A., 'The Impact of Geographical Indication on the Revitalisation of a Regional Economy: A Case Study of "Boseong" Green Tea' (2007) 39 *Area* 518.

Sunder, M., 'The Invention of Traditional Knowledge' (2007) 70 *Law and Contemporary Problems* 97.

Swann, J. B., 'The Validity of Dual Functioning Trade Marks: Genericism Tested by Consumer Understanding Rather than by Consumer Use' (1979) 69 TMR 357.

Taubman, A., 'Thinking Locally, Acting Globally: How Trade Negotiations over Geographical Indications Improvise "Fair Trade" Rules' (2008) 5 *IPQ* 231.

Teil, G., 'The French Wine "Appellations d'Origine Contrôlée" and the Virtues of Suspicion' (2010) 13 JWIP 253.

Tessensohn, J. and Yamamoto, S., 'Japan: Trade Marks – Japan's New Regional Collective Trade Mark System will Protect Famous Goods and Services from Regional Communities' [2006] EIPR N145.

Teuber, R., 'Geographical Indications of Origin as a Tool of Product Differentiation: The Case of Coffee' (2010) 22 *Journal of International Food and Agribusiness Marketing* 277.

Thiedig, F. and Sylvander, B., 'Welcome to the Club? An Economical Approach to Geographical Indications in the European Union' (2000) 49 *Agrarwirtschaft* 428.

Tilmann, W., 'Zur Bestimmung des Kreises der an einer geographischen Herkunftsangabe Berechtigten' [1980] *GRUR* 487.

Torsen, M., 'Apples and Oranges (and Wine): Why the International Conversation Regarding Geographical Indications is at a Standstill' (2005) 87 *Journal of the Patent and Trade Mark Office Society* 31.

Tregear, A., Kuznesof, S. and Moxey, A., 'Policy Initiatives for Regional Foods: Some Insights from Consumer Research' (1998) 23 *Food Policy* 383.

Tregear, A., Arfinib, F., Bellettic, G. and Marescottic, A., 'Regional Foods and Rural Development: The Role of Product Qualification' (2007) 23 *Journal of Rural Studies* 12.

Trinchieri, T., 'Moyens d'Obtenir de Nouvelles Adhésions, Particulièrement l'Adhésion de l'Italie à l'Arrangement de Madrid sur les Fausses Indications de Provenance' [1902] *Annuaire* 17.

Trotta, G., 'The Stresa Convention on the Uses of Names of Cheeses and the WIPO Draft Treaty on the Protection of Geographical Indications' [1977] *Industrial Property* 113.

Tunc, A., 'Unfair Competition – French and European Approaches' (1974–5) 1 *Monash University Law Review* 34.

Tushnet, R., 'Copy this Essay: How Fair Use Doctrine Harms Free Speech and How Copying Serves It' (2004) 114 *Yale Law Journal* 546.

'Gone in 60 Milliseconds: Trade Mark Law and Cognitive Science' (2008) 86 *Texas Law Review* 507.

Ulin, R. C., 'Invention and Representation as Cultural Capital: Southwest French Winegrowing History' (1995) 97 *American Anthropologist* 519.

Ulmer, E., 'The Law of Unfair Competition and the Common Market' (1963) 53 TMR 625.

'Unfair Competition Law in the European Economic Community' [1973] IIC 188.

Vakoufaris, H., 'The Impact of Ladotyri Mytilinis PDO Cheese on the Rural Development of Lesvos Island, Greece' (2010) 15 *Local Environment* 27.

van Caenegem, W., 'Registered Geographical Indications: Between Rural Policy and Intellectual Property – Part I' (2003) 6 JWIP 699.

'Registered Geographical Indications: Between Rural Policy and Intellectual Property – Part II' (2003) 6 JWIP 861.

'Registered GIs: Intellectual Property, Agricultural Policy and International Trade' [2004] EIPR 170.

van Ittersum, K., Meulenberg, M., van Trijp, H. and Candel, M., 'Consumers' Appreciation of Regional Certification Labels: A Pan-European Study' (2007) 58 *Journal of Agricultural Economics* 1.

van Leeuwen, C. and Seguin, G., 'The Concept of *Terroir* in Viticulture' (2006) 17 *Journal of Wine Research* 1.

Vialard, A., 'Regulating Quality Wines in European and French Law' (1999) 19 *Northern Illinois University Law Review* 235.

Vittori, M., 'The International Debate on Geographical Indications (GIs): The Point of View of the Global Coalition of GI Producers – oriGIn' (2010) 13 JWIP 304.

Wadlow, C., 'Unfair Competition in Community Law – Part 1: The Age of the "Classical Model"' [2006] EIPR 433.

'Unfair Competition in Community Law – Part II: Harmonization becomes Gridlocked' [2006] EIPR 469.

Waldron, J., 'From Authors to Copiers: Individual Rights and Social Values in Intellectual Property' (1993) 68 *Chicago–Kent Law Review* 841.

Wang, M-C., 'The Asian Consciousness and Interests in Geographical Indications' (2006) 96 TMR 906.

Weigend, G. G., 'The Basis and Significance of Viticulture in Southwest France' (1954) 44 *Annals of the Association of American Geographers* 75.

Welkowitz, D. S., 'Re-examining Trade Mark Dilution' (1994) 44 *Vanderbilt Law Review* 531.

Whalen, P., '"A Merciless Source of Happy Memories": Gaston Roupnel and the Folklore of Burgundian Terroir' (2007) 44 *Journal of Folklore Research* 21.

'"Insofar as the Ruby Wine Seduces Them": Cultural Strategies for Selling Wine in Inter-War Burgundy' (2009) 18 *Contemporary European History* 67.

Wilf, S., 'The Making of the Post-War Paradigm in American Intellectual Property Law' (2008) 31 *Columbia Journal of Law and the Arts* 139.

314 Bibliography

Wilkof, N. and Uzrad, S., 'In the Matter of the Appellation of Origin for "Jaffa"' (2008) 3 *Journal of Intellectual Property Law and Practice* 17.

Wyatt, D., 'Free Movement of Goods and Indications of Origin' (1975) 38 *Modern Law Review* 679.

Xiaobing, W. and Kireeva, I., 'GI Protection in China: New Measures for Administration of Geographical Indications of Agricultural Products' (2010) 5 *Journal of Intellectual Property Law & Practice* 778.

Zhao, W., 'Understanding Classifications: Empirical Evidence from the American and French Wine Industries' (2005) 33 *Poetics* 179.

Zylberg, P., 'Geographical Indications v. Trade Marks: The Lisbon Agreement: A Violation of TRIPS?' (2002–3) 11 *University of Baltimore Intellectual Property Law Journal* 1.

Books and book contributions

Audier, J., *TRIPS Agreement – Geographical Indications* (EC Office for Official Publications, Luxembourg 2000).

Auriol, E., Lesourd, J.-B. and Schifizzi, S., 'France', in K. Anderson (ed.), *The World's Wine Markets: Globalization at Work* (Edward Elgar, Cheltenham 2004), 64.

Barjolle, D. and Thévenod-Mottet, E., 'Economic Aspects of Geographical Indications', in L. Bérard, M. Cegarra, M. Djama and S. Louafi (eds.), *Biodiversity and Local Ecological Knowledge in France*, (INRA-CIRAD, Paris 2005), 213.

Beier, F-K., 'The Contribution of AIPPI to the Development of International Protection against Unfair Competition', in *AIPPI – 1897–1997 Centennial Edition* (AIPPI Foundation, Basle 1997), 299.

'The Protection of Indications of Geographical Origin in the Federal Republic of Germany', in H. C. Jehoram (ed.), *Protection of Geographic Denominations of Goods and Services* (Sijthoff & Noordhoff, Netherlands 1980), 11.

Belson, J., *Certification Marks* (Sweet and Maxwell, London 2002).

Bently, L., 'From Communication to Thing: Historical Aspects of the Conceptualisation of Trade Marks as Property', in G. Dinwoodie and M. Janis (eds.), *Trade Mark Law and Theory: A Handbook of Contemporary Research* (Edward Elgar, Cheltenham 2008), 3.

'The Making of Modern Trade Marks Law: The Construction of the Legal Concept of Trade Mark (1860–80)', in L. Bently, J. C. Ginsburg and J. Davis (eds.), *Trade Marks and Brands: An Interdisciplinary Critique* (Cambridge University Press, 2008), 3.

Bérard, L., Cegarra, M., Djama, M. and Louafi, S. (eds.), *Biodiversity and Local Ecological knowledge in France* (INRA-CIRAO, Paris 2005).

Bérard, L. and Marchenay, P., 'A Market Culture: *Produits de Terroir* or the Selling of Culture', in S. Blowen, M. Demossier and J. Picasd (eds.), *Recollections of France: Memories, Identities and Heritage in Contemporary France* (Berghahn Books, New York 2000), 154.

From Localized Products to Geographical Indications: Awareness and Action (CNRS, Bourg-en-Bresse 2008).

Bibliography 315

BIRPI, *L'Union Internationale pour la Protection de la Propriété Industrielle – Sa Fondation et son Développement* (Bureau de l'Union, Berne 1933).

Biss, A. and Smith, O., *The Wines of Chablis* (Writers International, Bournemouth 2000).

Blakeney, M., *Trade Related Aspects of Intellectual Property Rights: A Concise Guide to the TRIPS Agreement* (Sweet & Maxwell, London 1996).

Bodenhausen, G. H. C., *Guide to the Application of the Paris Convention for the Protection of Industrial Property* (Bureau de l'Union, Geneva 1968).

Boon, M., *In Praise of Copying* (Harvard University Press, Cambridge MA 2010).

Bozérian, J., *La Convention Internationale du 20 mars 1883 pour la Protection de la Propriété Industrielle* (impr. de C. Pariset, Paris 1885).

Bramley, C., Biénabe, E. and Kirsten, J., 'The Economics of Geographical Indications: Towards a Conceptual Framework for Geographical Indication Research in Developing Countries', in WIPO (ed.), *The Economics of Intellectual Property: Suggestions for Further Research in Developing Countries and Countries with Economies in Transition* (WIPO, Geneva 2009), 109.

Calmels, E., *De la Propriété et de la Contrefaçon*, (Cosse, Paris 1856).

Campbell, C., *Phylloxera: How Wine was Saved for the World* (Harper Perennial, London 2004).

Capus, J., *L'Evolution de la Législation sur les Appellations d'Origine: Genèse des Appellations Contrôlées* (L. Larmat, impr. de Le Moil et Pascaly, Paris 1947).

Cegarra, M. and Verdaux, F., 'Introduction', in L. Bérard, M. Cegarra, M. Djama and S. Louah (eds.), *Biodiversity and Local Ecological Knowledge in France* (INRA-CIRAD, 2005), 19.

Coddington, C. E., *A Digest of the Law of Trade Marks* (Ward and Peloubet, New York 1878).

Correa, C. M., *Trade Related Aspects of Intellectual Property Rights: A Commentary on the TRIPS Agreement* (Oxford University Press, 2007).

Corte-Real, A., 'The Conflict Between Trade Marks and Geographical Indications – The Budweiser Case in Portugal', in C. Heath and A. Kamperman Sanders (eds.), *New Frontiers of Intellectual Property Law: IP and Cultural Heritage, Geographical Indicators, Enforcement, Overprotection*, IIC Studies, Vol. 25 (Hart, Oxford 2005), 149.

Cottier, T., 'The Agreement on Trade-Related Aspects of Intellectual Property Rights', in P. F. J. Macrory, A. E. Appleton and M. G. Plummer (eds.), *The World Trade Organization: Legal, Economic and Political Analysis*, Vol. I (Springer, New York 2005), 1041.

Daviron, B. and Ponte, S., *The Coffee Paradox: Commodity Trade and the Elusive Promise of Development* (Zed Books, London 2005).

Demossier, M., 'Culinary Heritage and *Produits de Terroir* in France: Food for Thought', in S. Blowen, M. Demossier and J. Picasd (eds.), *Recollections of France: Memories, Identities and Heritage in Contemporary France* (Berghahn Books, New York 2000), 141.

de Marafy, M., *Grand Dictionnaire International de la Propriété Industrielle*, Vol. 6 (Chevailier-Marescq et cie, Paris 1892).

de Planhol, X., *An Historical Geography of France* (Cambridge University Press, 1994).

316 Bibliography

de Vrey, R. W., *Towards a European Unfair Competition Law: A Clash between Legal Families* (Martinus Nijhoff, The Hague 2006).

Deffontaines, J-P., 'The *Terroir*, a Concept with Multiple Meanings', in L. Bérard, M. Cegarra, M. Djama and S. Louafi (eds.), *Biodiversity and Local Ecological Knowledge in France* (INRA-CIRAO, 2005), 38.

di Franco, L., *Le Indicazioni di Provenienza dei Prodotti* (Cavotta, Naples 1907).

Dinwoodie, G. B., Hennessey, W. O. and Perlmutter, S., *International Intellectual Property Law and Policy* (Lexisnexis, New Jersey 2001).

Dion, R., *Histoire de la Vigne et du Vin en France des Origines au XIXe Siècle* (Clavreuil, Paris 1959).

Donzel, L., *Commentaire et Critique de la Convention Internationale du 20 Mars 1883* (Marchal & Billard, Paris 1891).

Drahos, P., 'Introduction', in P. Drahos and R. Mayne, (eds.), *Global Intellectual Property Rights: Knowledge, Access and Development* (Palgrave MacMillan, New York 2002).

Drahos, P. and Braithwaite, J., *Information Feudalism: Who Owns the Knowledge Economy* (Earthscan, London 2002).

Dufourmantelle, M., *De la Concurrence déloyale à l'aide de fausses indications sur la provenance des produits* (impr. de Berger-Levrault, Nancy 1895).

Dunant, P., *Traité des Marques de Fabrique et de Commerce, des Indications de Provenance et des Mentions de Récompenses Industrielles en Suisse, Comprenant l'Étude du Droit Comparé et du Droit International* (Ch. Eggimann, Geneva 1898).

Echols, M., *Geographical Indications for Food Products: International Legal and Regulatory Perspectives* (Kluwer, Alphen aan den Rijn 2008).

Evans, G. E. and Blakeney, M., 'The International Protection of Geographical Indications Yesterday Today And Tomorrow', in G. Westkamp (ed.), *Emerging Issues In Intellectual Property: Trade, Technology and Market Freedom – Essays in Honour of Herchel Smith* (Edward Elgar, Cheltenham 2007), 250.

FAO and SINER-GI, *Linking People, Places and Products: A Guide for Promoting quality Linked to Geographical Origin and Sustainable Geographical Indications*, 2nd edn (FAO, Rome 2009–10).

Foulkes, C. (ed.), *Larousse Encyclopedia of Wine*, 2nd edn (Hamlyn, London 2001).

Gangjee, D., 'The Business End of Collective and Certification Marks', in I. Simon Fhima (ed.), *Trade Mark Law and Sharing Names: Exploring Use of the Same Mark by Multiple Undertakings* (Edward Elgar, Cheltenham 2009), 79.

Gastambide, A-J., *Traité Théorique et Pratique des Contrefaçons en Tous Genres* (Legrand et Descauriet, Paris 1837).

Gervais, D., *The TRIPS Agreement. Drafting History and Analysis*, 3rd edn (Sweet & Maxwell, London 2008).

Giovannucci, D., Josling, T., Kerr, W., O'Connor, B. and Yeung, M., *Guide to Geographical Indications: Linking Products and their Origins* (International Trade Centre, Geneva 2009).

Greeley, A. P., *Foreign Patent and Trade Mark Laws: A Comparative Study* (John Byrne & Co, Washington DC 1899).

Guérillon, R., *Les Appellations d'Origine: Loi du 6 Mai 1919* (Journal l'Epicier, Paris 1919).

Guy, K. M., 'Rituals of Pleasure in the Land of Treasures: Wine Consumption and the Making of French Identity in the Late Nineteenth Century', in W. J. Belasco and P. Scranton (ed.), *Food Nations: Selling Taste in Consumer Societies* (Routledge, London 2002), 34.

When Champagne Became French: Wine and the Making of a National Identity (Johns Hopkins University Press, Baltimore 2003).

Halliday, J. and Johnson, H., *The Art and Science of Wine* (Mitchell Beazley, London 1994).

Handler, M. and Burrell, R., 'GI Blues: The Global Disagreement Over Geographical Indications', in K. Bowrey, M. Handler and D. Nicol (eds.), *Emerging Challenges in Intellectual Property* (Oxford University Press, Melbourne 2011).

Handler, M. and Mercurio, B., 'Intellectual Property', in S. Lester and B. Mercurio (eds.), *Bilateral and Regional Trade Agreements: Commentary and Analysis* (Cambridge University Press, 2009), 308.

Hanson, A., *Burgundy* (Mitchell Beazley, London 2003).

Harle, R., 'AIPPI and the Appellations of Origin, Indications of Source and Geographical Indications', in *AIPPI – 1897–1997 Centennial Edition* (AIPPI Foundation, Basle 1997), 255.

Heath, C., 'Geographical Indications: International, Bilateral and Regional Agreements', in C. Heath and A. Kamperman Sanders (eds.), *New Frontiers of Intellectual Property Law: IP and Cultural Heritage, Geographical Indicators, Enforcement, Overprotection*, IIC Studies, Vol. 25 (Hart, Oxford 2005), 97.

'The Budweiser Cases – A Brewing Conflict', in C. Heath and A. Kamperman Saunders (eds.), *Landmark Intellectual Property Law Cases and their Legacy* (Kluwer Law International, Alphenaan den Rijn 2011), 181.

Heiss, M. L. and Heiss, R. J., *The Story of Tea: A Cultural History and Drinking Guide* (10 Speed Press, Berkeley 2007).

Henning-Bodewig, F., 'International Unfair Competition Law', in R. M. Hilty and F. Henning-Bodewig (eds.), *Law Against Unfair Competition: Towards a New Paradigm in Europe?* (Springer, Berlin 2007), 53.

Unfair Competition Law: European Union and Member States (Kluwer Law International, The Hague 2006).

Hermitte, M-A., 'Les appellations d'origine dans la genèse des droits de la propriété intellectuelle', in P. Moity-Maïzi, C. de Sainte Marie, P. Geslin, J. Muchnik and D. Santier (eds.), 'Systèmes Agroalimentaires Localisés: Terroirs, Savoir-faire, Innovations' (2001) 32 *Etudes et Recherches sur les Systèmes Agraires et le Développement* 195.

Hilty, R. M., 'The Law against Unfair Competition and its Interfaces', in R. M. Hilty and F. Henning-Bodewig (eds.), *Law Against Unfair Competition: Towards a New Paradigm in Europe?* (Springer, Berlin/New York 2007), 1.

Hobsbawm, E. and Ranger, T. (eds.), *The Invention of Tradition* (Cambridge University Press, 1983).

Hopperger, M. and Senftleben, M., 'Protection against Unfair Competition at the International Level – The Paris Convention, the 1996 Model Provisions

318 Bibliography

and the Current Work of WIPO', in R. M. Hilty and F. Henning-Bodewig (eds.), *Law Against Unfair Competition: Towards a New Paradigm in Europe?* (Springer, Berlin/New York 2007), 61.

Jaton, L., *La Répression des Fausses Indications de Provenance et les Conventions Internationales* (Librairie Générale de Droit & de Jurisprudence, Paris 1926).

Johnson, H., *The Story of Wine* (Mitchell Beasley, London 1989).

Johnson, P., *Ambush Marketing: A Practical Guide to Protecting the Brand of a Sporting Event* (Sweet and Maxwell, London 2007).

Kamperman Sanders, A., *Unfair Competition Law* (Clarendon Press, Oxford 1997).

Kaufmann, P. J., *Passing off and Misappropriation: An Economic and Legal Analysis of the Law of Unfair Competition in the United States and Continental Europe*, IIC Studies, Vol 9 (Max Planck, Munich 1986).

Kerly, D. M., *The Law of Trade Marks, Trade Name and Merchandise Marks* (Sweet & Maxwell, London 1894).

Knaak, R., 'The Protection of Geographical Indications According to the TRIPS Agreement', in F-K Beier and G Schricker (eds.), *From GATT to TRIPS – The Agreement on Trade-Related Aspects of Intellectual Property Rights*, IIC Studies, Vol. 18 (Weinheim, New York 1996), 117.

Kramer, M., 'The Notion of *Terroir*', in F. Allhoff (ed.), *Wine & Philisophy: A Symposium on Thinking and Drinking* (Blackwell, Oxford 2008).

Lacour, L., *Des Fausses Indications de Provenance: Contribution a L'étude de la Propriété Industrielle en Droit Français* (Rousseau, Paris 1904).

Ladas, S. P., *Patents, Trademarks and Related Rights: National and International Protection* (Harvard University Press, Cambridge MA 1975).

The International Protection of Industrial Property (Harvard University Press, Cambridge MA 1930).

Lagarde, G., 'Place of Origin: France', in H. L. Pinner (ed.), *World Unfair Competition Law: An Encyclopedia*, Vol II (Sijthoff Leyden, Holland 1965), 636.

Landes, W. M. and Posner, R. A., *The Economic Structure of Intellectual Property Law* (Harvard University Press, 2003).

Lawson, F. H. and Rudden, B., *Law of Property*, 3rd edn (Oxford University Press, 2002).

Lopez, R. A., *Crafting Mexico: Intellectuals, Artisans, and the State After the Revolution* (Duke University Press, Durham NC 2010).

Loubère, L. A., *The Wine Revolution in France – The Twentieth Century* (Princeton University Press, 1990).

P. Marchenay, 'The Challenge of Conserving Local Practices, Knowledge, and the Living World', in L. Bérard, M. Cegarra, M. Djama and S. Louafi, (eds.), *Biodiversity and Local Ecological Knowledge in France* (INRA-CIRAO, Paris 2005), 89.

Martino, T., *Trade Mark Dilution* (Oxford University Press, 1996).

McCarthy, J. T., *McCarthy on Trademarks and Unfair Competition*, 4th edn (Thomson West, February 2011 update).

Mostert, F. W., *Famous and Well-Known Marks: An International Analysis*, 2nd edn (INTA, New York 2004).

Mullins, M. G., Bouguet, A. and Williams, L. E., *The Biology of the Grapevine* (Cambridge University Press, 1992).

Nair L. R. and Kumar, R., *Geographical Indications: A Search for Identity* (Lexis Nexis, New Delhi 2005).

Nims, H. D., *The Law of Unfair Business Competition* (Baker, Voorhis & Co, New York 1909).

Nützenadel, A., 'A Green International? Food Markets and Transnational Politics, c.1850–1914', in A. Nützenadel and F. Trentmann (eds.), *Food and Globalization: Consumption, Markets and Politics in the Modern World* (Berg, Oxford and New York 2008), 153.

O'Connor, B., *The Law of Geographical Indications* (Cameron May, 2004).

Ojima, A., *Detailed Analysis of TRIPS* (Japan Machinery Center for Trade and Investment, Tokyo 1999).

Olszak, N., *Droit des Appellations d'Origine et Indications de Provenance* (TEC & DOC, Paris 2001).

Parry, B., 'Geographical Indications: Not All Champagne and Roses', in L. Bently, J. C. Ginsburg and J. Davis (eds.), *Trade Marks and Brands: An Interdisciplinary Critique* (Cambridge University Press, 2008), 361.

Paul, H. W., *Science, Vine and Wine in Modern France* (Cambridge University Press, 1996).

Pelletier, M. and Vidal-Naquet, E., *La Convention d'Union pour la Protection de la Propriété Industrielle du 20 Mars 1883* (Larose & Forcel, Paris 1902).

Pottage, A. and Sherman, B., *Figures of Invention: A History of Modern Patent Law* (Oxford University Press, 2010).

Pouillet, E., *Traité des Marques de Fabrique et de la Concurrence Déloyale en tous Genres*, 2nd edn (Marchal et Billard, Paris 1883).

Rangnekar, D., 'Protecting Indications of Geographical Origin in Asia: Legal and Practical Issues to Resolve', in R. Meléndez-Ortiz and P. Roffe (eds.), *Intellectual Property and Sustainable Development: Development Agendas in a Changing World* (Edward Elgar, Cheltenham 2009), 273.

Reddy, W. M., *The Rise of Market Culture: the Textile Trade and French Society, 1750–1900* (Cambridge University Press, 1984).

Ricketson, S., 'The *Union Label* Case: An Early Australian IP Story', in A. T. Kenyon, M. Richardson and S. Ricketson (eds.), *Landmarks in Australian Intellectual Property Law* (Cambridge University Press, Melbourne 2009), 15.

Robinson, J. (ed.), *The Oxford Companion to Wine*, 2nd edn (Oxford University Press, 1999).

Roubier, P., *Le Droit de la Propriété Industrielle*, Vol. 2 (Editions du Recueil Sirey, Paris 1954).

Schechter, F. I., *The Historical Foundations of the Law Relating to Trade Marks* (Columbia University Press, New York 1925).

Sell, S. K. *Private Power, Public Law: The Globalization of Intellectual Property* (Cambridge University Press, New York 2003).

Sherman, B. and Bently, L., *The Making of Modern Intellectual Property Law: The British Experience, 1760–1911* (Cambridge University Press, 1999).

Simon, A. L., *The History of Champagne* (Ebury Press, London 1962).

320 Bibliography

Singer, B., *Trade Mark Laws of the World and Unfair Trade* (Hammond Press, Chicago IL 1913).

Spence, M., *Intellectual Property* (Oxford University Press, 2007).

Staunch, S. and Arend, K., 'Before Articles 22–24', in P. T. Stoll, J. Busche and K. Arend (eds.), *WTO – Trade-Related Aspects of Intellectual Property Rights* (Martinus Nijhoff, Leiden and Boston 2009).

'Section 3: Geographical Indications', in P. J. Stoll, J. Busche and K. Arend (eds.), *WTO – Trade-Related Aspects of Intellectual Property Rights* (Martinus Nijhoff, Leiden and Boston 2009).

Stoll, P-T., Busche, J., and Arend, K. (eds.), *WTO – Trade-Related Aspects of Intellectual Property Rights* (Martinus Nijhoff, Leiden and Boston 2009).

Streber, A. C., *Die Internationalen Abkommen der Bundesrepublik Deutschland zum Schutz Geographischer Herkunftsangaben* (Max Planck Institute, Cologne 1994).

Taillefer, A. and Claro, C., *Traité des Marques de Fabrique et de la Concurrence Déloyale en Tous Genres, d'Eugène Pouillet*, 6th edn (Marchal et Godde, Paris 1912).

Tilmann, W., *Die Geographische Herkunftsangabe* (C.H. Beck-Verlag, Munich 1976).

UNCTAD-ICTSD *Resource Book on TRIPs and Development* (Cambridge University Press, Cambridge/New York 2005).

Underhay, F. G., *Kerly's Law of Merchandise Marks*, 3rd edn (Sweet & Maxwell, London 1909).

Unwin, T., *Wine and the Vine: An Historical Geography of Viticulture and the Wine Trade* (Routledge, London 1991).

Van de Kop, P., Sautier, D. and Gerz, A. (eds.), *Origin-Based Products: Lessons for Pro-Poor Market Development* (KIT, Amsterdam 2006).

van der Ploeg, J. D., 'High Quality Products and Regional Specialities: A Promising Trajectory for Endogenous and Sustainable Development', in OECD, *The Future of Rural Policy – From Sectorial to Place-Based Policies in Rural Areas* (OECD Publications, Paris 2003), 205.

Vidal, D., 'In Search of "Basmatisthan": Agro-nationalism and Globalisation', in J. Assayag and C.J. Fuller (eds.), *Globalising India: Perspectives from Below* (Anthem, London 2005), 47.

Vivas-Eugui, D. and Spennemann, C., 'The Treatment of Geographical Indications in Recent Regional and Bilateral Free Trade Agreements', in M. Perez Pugatch (ed.), *The Intellectual Property Debate: Perspectives from Law, Economics and Political Economy* (Edward Elgar, Cheltenham 2006), 305.

Wadlow, C., *The Law of Passing Off: Unfair Competition by Misrepresentation*, 3rd edn (Sweet & Maxwell, London 2004).

'Unfair Competition by Misappropriation: The Reception of *International News* in the Common Law World', in C. W. Ng, L. Bently and G. D.'Agostino (eds.), *The Common Law of Intellectual Property: Essays in Honour of Professor David Vaver* (Hart, Oxford 2010), 307.

Warner, C. K., *The Winegrowers of France and the Government since 1875* (Columbia University Press, New York 1960).

Watal, J., *Intellectual Property Rights in the WTO and Developing Countries* (Kluwer, The Hague 2001).

Bibliography

White, R. E., *Soils for Fine Wines* (Oxford University Press, New York 2003).

Wilson, J. E., *Terroir: The Role of Geology, Climate, and Culture in the Making of French Wines* (Mitchell Beazley, London 1998).

WIPO, *Introduction to Intellectual Property – Theory and Practice* (Kluwer Law International, London 1997).

Model Provisions on Protection against Unfair Competition: Articles and Notes (WIPO Publication No 832, Geneva 1996).

Protection against Unfair Competition: Analysis of the Present World Situation (WIPO Publication No. 725(E), Geneva 1994).

The Paris Convention for the Protection of Industrial Property From 1883–1983 (WIPO, Geneva 1983).

Zografos, D., 'Can Geographical Indications be a Viable Alternative for the Protection of Traditional Cultural Expressions', in F. Macmillan and K. Bowrey (eds.), *New Directions in Copyright Law*, Vol. 3 (Edward Elgar, Cheltenham 2006), 37.

Reports

Barjolle, D. and Thévenod-Mottet, E., DOLPHINS Final Report: Work Programme 6 – Policies Evaluation DOLPHINS Concerted Action, Contract QLK5–2000–0593, European Commission (June 2003).

Codex Alimentarius Commission, Report Of The Twenty-Seventh Session (Geneva, 28 June-3 July 2004).

Codex Alimentarius Commission, Report Of The Twenty-Eighth Session (Rome, 4–9 July 2005).

Concerted Action, DOLPHINS WP4: Final Report – Link between Origin Labelled Products and Consumers and Citizens (Key Action No. 5; July 2002).

Gangjee, D., Protecting Geographical Indications as Trade Marks: Prospects and Pitfalls (Institute of Intellectual Property, Tokyo 2006).

Hearings before the Committee on Agriculture, House of Representatives on the Status of the World Trade Organization Negotiations on Agriculture, (108–5) 108th Congress (2003).

London Economics et al., Evaluation of the CAP Policy on Protected Designations of Origin (PDO) and Protected Geographical Indications (PGI) – (Final Report for the European Commission, November 2008).

O'Connor & Co, Geographical Indications and TRIPS: 10 Years Later ... A Roadmap for EU GI Holders to Gain Protection in Other WTO Members – Part I (Report commissioned for EC (DG Trade) 2007).

Geographical Indications and TRIPS: 10 Years Later ... Part II – Protection of Geographical Indications in 160 Countries around the World (Report commissioned for European Commission (DG Trade) 2007).

OECD, Appellations of Origin and Geographical Indications in OECD Member Countries: Economic and Legal Implications (COM/AGR/APM/TD/WP (2000)15/FINAL).

Food Safety and Quality Issues: Trade Considerations (COM/AGR/CA/TD/TC (98)151/FINAL).

322   Bibliography

Multifunctionality - Towards an Analytical Framework (Paris 2001).

Papers and Correspondence relative to Conference at Brussels on Industrial Property and Merchandise Marks 92 PP 155 [C.9014], 1895.

Papers and Correspondence relative to Conference at Madrid on Industrial Property and Merchandise Marks 67 PP 725 [C.6023] 1890.

Arrangement between Great Britain, Spain, France, Switzerland and Tunisia for Prevention of False Indications of Origin on Goods, Madrid, April 1891 Treaty Series No. 13 [C.6818], 1892.

Papers relative to Conference at Rome on Industrial Property; Correspondence relating to Fraudulent Use of Trade Marks 60 PP 413 [C.4837], 1886.

Rangnekar, D., Geographical Indications and Localisation: A Case Study of Feni (ESRC Report 2009).

Reports from His Majesty's Representatives Abroad on the Laws in Force in the Principal Foreign Countries to Prevent the Sale or Importation of Goods Bearing a False Indication of Origin 86 PP 739 [Cd 5531] 1911.

Report of the Imperial Economic Committee 13 PP 799 [Cm 2493] 1925.

Report on Proceedings Concerning Brazilian Practices Affecting Trade in Cognac (EU Trade Barrier Regulations Committee, 1997).

Report on the Lack of Protection of the Wines with Geographical Indication 'Bordeaux' and 'Médoc' (EU Trade Barrier Regulations Committee, 2003).

Report on Unfair Competition, Particularly in Relation to False Marks and Indications [1922] League of Nations Official Journal 625.

Report on Unfair Competition, Particularly in Relation to False Marks and Indications Reports Relative to Legislation in Foreign Countries on the Subject of Trade Marks 54 PP 585 [C.596], 1872.

Trade Marks: Hearings before the House Committee on Patents, 72d Cong., 1st Sess 15 (1932).

Trade Marks: Special report from the Select Committee on Merchandise Marks Act (1862) Amendment Bill (1887), 203.

US–Chile Free Trade Agreement, Report of the Industry Sector Advisory Committee on Consumer Goods (ISAC-4) February 2003.

Preparatory documents and resolutions

AIDV, Draft Resolution on Trade Marks and Geographical Indications (August 2004).

AIPPI, 'Question Q62: Appellations of Origin, Indications of Source and Geographical Indications – Resolution' [1998] *Annuaire* 389.

'Resolution on Appellations of Origin at the 23rd Congress of Stockholm, 26–31 May 1958' [1958] *Annuaire* 44.

'Resolution on Q.118 – Trade and Service Marks and Geographical Indications' [1994] *Annuaire* 408.

'Resolution on Q62: International Protection of Appellations of Origin and Indications of Source' [1975] *Annuaire* 137.

AIPPI Working Committee, Resolution on Question Q191: Relationship between Trademarks and Geographical Indications (2006).

Bibliography 323

Collins, K. (Chairman), Opinion of the Committee on the Environment, Public Health and Consumer Protection annexed to the Report of the Committee on Agriculture, Fisheries and Rural Development on the Commission Proposals for Council Regulations (SEC(90) 2415 final) and (SEC(90) 2414) (30 October 1991; Session Document A3–0283/91).

EC Special Eurobarometer, European Union Citizens and Agriculture from 1995 to 2003 (September 2004).

European Commission, 'Green Paper on Agricultural Product Quality: Product Standards, Farming Requirements and Quality Schemes' *COM*(2008) 641 final (Brussels, 15 October 2008).

INTA Resolution, Protection of Geographical Indications and Trade Marks, 24 September 1997.

Opinion on the proposal for a Council Regulation (EEC) on the Protection of Geographical Indications and Designations of Origin for Agricultural Products and Foodstuffs [1991] OJ C 269/62.

Opinion of the European Economic and Social Committee on Geographical Indications and Designations [2008] OJ C 204/57.

Proposal for a Council Regulation (EEC) on the Protection of Geographical Indications and Designations of Origin for Agricultural Products and Foodstuffs (SEC (90) 2415 final; 6 February 1991) [1991] OJ C 30/9; as amended by (COM(92) 32 final; 18 March1992) [1992] OJ C 69/15.

Proposal for a Regulation of the European Parliament and of the Council on Agricultural Product Quality Schemes, COM(2010) 733 final (Brussels, 10 December 2010).

Trade Marks: Hearings before the House Committee on Patents, 72d Cong., 1st Sess. 15 (1932).

USPTO, 'Geographical Indication Protection in the United States', available at www.uspto.gov/ip/global/geographical/index.jsp.

Papers, Policy Briefs and Guides

Agarwal, S. and Barone, M. J., 'Emerging Issues for Geographical Indication Branding Strategies', *MATRIC Research Paper 05-MRP* 9 (2005).

Andrerson, K., Norman, D. and Wittwer, G., 'Globalisation and the World's Wine Markets: Overview', *CIES Discussion Paper No. 143*, Adelaide University (2002).

Arslan, A. and Reicher, C. P., 'The Effects of the Coffee Trade Marking Initiative and Starbucks Publicity on Export Prices of Ethiopian Coffee', Kiel Working Paper No. 1606 (March 2010).

Benavente, D., 'The Economics of Geographical Indications: GIs modelled as Club Assets', Graduate Institute of International and Development Studies Working Paper No. 10/2010.

Boisvert V., 'From the Conservation of Genetic Diversity to the Promotion of Quality Foodstuff: Can the French Model of "*Appellation d'Origine Contrôlée*" be Exported?', CAPRi Working Paper No. 49 (April 2006).

CEC Fact Sheet: European Policy for Quality Agricultural Products (Luxembourg 2006).

324   Bibliography

Das, K., 'Socio-economic Implications of Protecting Geographical Indications in India', Centre for WTO Studies, India (August 2009).

European Commission, 'Geographical Indications – Background Paper to the Green Paper on Agricultural Product Quality', DG Agriculture and Rural Development Working Document (October 2008).

Green Paper on Agricultural Product Quality: Product Standards, Farming Requirements and Quality Schemes (COM(2008) 641 final) (Brussels, 15 December 2008).

Protection of Geographical Indications of Origin, Designations of Origin and Certificates of Special Character for Agricultural Products and Foodstuffs: Guide to Community Regulations, 2nd edn.

Proposal for a Council Decision to Establish an Indicative, Non-Exhaustive List of Names of Agricultural Products and Foodstuffs Considered Generic Names, as Referred to in Art. 3 Para. 3 of Council Regulation (EEC) No. 2081/92, COM(96) 38 final.

'Why do Geographical Indications Matter to Us?' (MEMO/03/160) (Brussels, 30 July 2003).

EC Staff Working Paper, Impact Assessment Report on Geographical Indications – Accompanying the Proposal for a Regulation of the European Parliament and of the Council on Agricultural Product Quality Schemes (Brussels 2010).

Escudero, S., 'International Protection of Geographical Indications and Developing Countries', Working Paper No. 10, South Centre (July 2001).

FAO, 'Promotion of Traditional Regional Agricultural and Food Products: A Further Step towards Sustainable Rural Development', 26th FAO Regional Conference for Europe, 26–27 June 2008 (ERC/08/4).

FAO Committee on Commodity Problems, 'Geographical Indications for Tea', Hangzhou, 14–16 May 2008 (CCP:TE 08/5).

Fischler, F., 'Quality Food, CAP Referrs and PDO/PGI', SPEECH/04/183, Siena (17 April 2004).

Flandreau, M. and Accominotti, O., 'Does Bilateralism Promote Trade? Nineteenth Century Liberalization Revisited', CEPR Discussion Paper No. 5423 (2005).

Goebel, B., 'Why should Famous TMs Deserve Greater Protection against GIs?', AIDV Conference on TM- GI Conflicts for Wines & Spirits (Reims, 18–19 March 2004).

Hellwig, F. Z., 'Why the Principles of Priority and Exclusivity cannot be Compromised – The Trade Mark Owner's Perspective on Geographical Indications and First in Time, First in Right', INTA Policy Paper.

Hughes, J., 'Coffee and Chocolate – Can We Help Developing Country Farmers Through Geographical Indications?', International Intellectual Property Institute, Washington DC (2009).

'Notes on the Origin of Intellectual Property: Revised Conclusions and New Sources', Cardozo Legal Studies Research Paper No. 265 (11 July 2009).

INAO, 'GI Applicants' Guide', (7 October 2005).

'Guide du Demandeur d'une Appellation d'Origine (AOC/AOP)' (30 March 2009).

'Guide du Demandeur 1GP–Version 2 de Février 2009'.

Larson, J., 'Geographical Indications, In Situ Conservation and Traditional Knowledge', ICTSD Policy Brief (October 2010).

Marette, S., 'The Collective-Quality Promotion in the Agribusiness Sector: An Overview', Centre for Agricultural and Rural Development Iowa State University, Working paper 05-WP406 (2005).

Rangnekar, D., 'The Socio-Economics of Geographical Indications: A Review of the Empirical Evidence from Europe', UNCTAD–ICTSD Issue Paper No. 4 (May 2004).

'Re-Making Place: The Social Construction of Geographical Indications' (2010).

'The International Protection of Geographical Indications: The Asian Experience', *UNCTAD/ICTSD Regional Dialogue*, Hong Kong SAR (November 2004).

Reviron, S., Thevenod–Mottet, E. and El Benni, N., 'Geographical Indications: Creation and Distribution of Economic Value in Developing Countries', NCCR Working Paper No. 2009/14 (March 2009).

Ruse-Khan, H. G., 'A Trade Agreement Creating Barriers to International Trade? ACTA Border Measures and Goods in Transit', Max Planck Institute for Intellectual Property, Competition & Tax Law Research Paper No. 10–10.

Simpson, J., 'Old World versus New World: The Origins of Organizational Diversity in the International Wine Industry, 1850–1914', Universidad Carlos III de Madrid, Working Papers in Economic History (WP 09–01) (February 2009).

Stern, S., 'The Conflict between Geographical Indications and Trade Marks or Australia, Once Again Heads off Down the Garden Path', Annual Conference of the IP Society of Australia and New Zealand (September 2004).

Tregear, A., 'What is a "Typical Local Food"? An Examination of Territorial Identity in Foods Based on Development Initiatives in the Agrifood And Rural Sectors', Centre for Rural Economy, Working Paper 58 (January 2001).

USPTO, 'Geographical Indication Protection in the United States', available at www.uspto.gov/web/offices/dcom/olia/globalip/pdf/gi_system.pdf.

Wagle, S., 'Geographical Indications as Trade-Related Intellectual Property: Relevance and Implications for Human Development in Asia-Pacific', UNDP Asia-Pacific Trade and Investment Initiative Discussion Paper, Colombo (2007).

WIPO and BIRPI Documents

(Arranged Chronologically)

Actes de la Conférence Internationale pour la Protection de la Propriété Industrielle (Ministère des Affaires Etrangères, Impr. Nationale, Paris 1880).

Conférence Internationale de l'Union pour la Protection de la Propriété Industrielle (Impr. Héritiers Botta, Rome 1886).

Procès-Verbaux de la Conférence de Madrid de 1890 de l'Union pour la Protection de la Propriété Industrielle (Impr. Jent et Reinert, Berne 1892).

326 Bibliography

Actes de la Conférence de Bruxelles 1897 et 1900 (Bureau International de l'Union, Berne 1901).

Actes de la Conférence de Washington (Bureau International de l'Union, Berne 1911).

Actes de la Conférence de la Haye (Bureau International de l'Union, Berne 1926).

Actes de la Conférence Réunie à Londres (Bureau International de l'Union, Berne 1934).

Actes de la Conférence de Lisbonne (Bureau International de l'Union, Geneva 1963).

Lisbon Council, 'Report of the Second Session', December 1967 (AO/II/5).

Lisbon Council, 'Report of the Fourth Session', September 1969 (AO/IV/5).

Lisbon Council, 'Problems Arising from the Practical Application of the Lisbon Agreement', July 1970 (AO/V/5).

Lisbon Council, 'Report of the Fifth Session', September 1970 (AO/V/8).

Lisbon Council, 'Territorial Extension of the Lisbon Union', June 1971 (AO/VI/4).

Lisbon Council, 'Report on the Activities of the Lisbon Union and Financial Questions', June 1972 (AO/VII/3).

WIPO, 'Present Situation and Possible New Solutions', 28 June 1974 (TAO/I/2).

WIPO, 'Texts of International Instruments Concerning the Protection of Appellations of Origin and Other Indications of Source', 28 June 1974 (TAO/I/3).

WIPO, 'Draft of the Model Law for Developing Countries on Appellations of Origin and Indications of Source', 30 October 1974 (TAO/I/ INF.l).

WIPO, 'Report Adopted by the Committee of Experts', 15 November 1974 (TAO/I/ 8).

WIPO, 'Draft Treaty on the Protection of Geographical Indications', 25 August 1975 (TAO/II/2).

WIPO, 'Revision of the Lisbon Agreement or Conclusion of a New Treaty', 25 August 1975 (TAO/II/3).

WIPO Director General's Memorandum, 'Basic Proposals – Supplement to PR/DC/3', 30 August 1979 (PR/DC/4).

WIPO, 'The Need for a New Treaty and its Possible Contents', 9 April 1990 (GEO/CE/I/2).

WIPO, 'Report Adopted by the Committee of Experts', 1 June 1990 (GEO/CE/I/3).

Baeumer, L., 'Protection of Geographical Indications under WIPO Treaties and Questions Concerning the Relationship between those Treaties and the TRIPS Agreement', October 1997 (WIPO/GEO/EGR/97/1 Rev).

Geuze, M., 'Protection of Geographical Indications under the TRIPS Agreement and Related Work of the World Trade Organisation', October 1997 (WIPO/GEO/EGR/97/2).

Gevers, F., 'Topical Issues in the Protection of Geographical Indications', October 1997 (WIPO/GEO/EGR/97/5).

Audier, J., 'Protection of Geographical Indications in France and Protection of French Geographical Indications in Other Countries', October 1997 (WIPO/GEO/EGR/97/8 Rev).

WIPO, 'International Protection of Geographical Indications: The Present Situation and Prospects for Future Developments', 1 September 1999 (WIPO/GEO/CPT/99/1).

Bibliography 327

Tran Wasescha, T-L., 'Recent Developments in the Council for TRIPS (WTO)' 1 September 1999 (WIPO/GEO/CPT/99/2).

Stern, A., 'The Protection of Geographical Indications in South Africa', September 1999 (WIPO/GEO/CPT/99/3a).

Rademeyer, H., 'The Protection of Geographical Indications in South Africa', September 1999 (WIPO/GEO/CPT/99/3b).

Vital, F., 'Protection of Geographical Indications: The Approach of the European Union', September 1999 (WIPO/GEO/CPT/99/5).

Harte-Bavendamm, H., 'Geographical Indications and Trade Marks: Harmony or Conflict?', 1 September 1999 (WIPO/GEO/CPT/99/6).

Girardeau, J-M., 'The Use of Geographical Indications in a Collective Marketing Strategy: The Example of Cognac', September 1999 (WIPO/GEO/CPT/99/7).

van Niekerk, J., 'The Use of Geographical Indications in a Collective Marketing Strategy: The Example of the South African Wine Industry', 1 September 1999 (WIPO/GEO/CPT/99/8).

WIPO, 'Questions to be Examined With a View to the Modification of the Regulations under the Lisbon Agreement', 10 May 2000 (LI/GT/1/2).

WIPO, 'Possible Solutions for Conflicts between Trade Marks and Geographical Indications and for Conflicts between Homonymous Geographical Indications', 8 June 2000 (SCT/5/3).

WIPO, 'Notes Concerning the Proposals for Modification of the Regulations under the Lisbon Agreement', 19 January 2001 (LI/GT/2/3).

Lisbon Working Group, 'Report Adopted by the Working Group', 12 July 2000 (LI/GT/1/3).

WIPO, 'Protection of Geographical Indications: General Introduction, International Protection and Recent Developments', June 2001 (WIPO/GEO/CIS/01/1).

Wenger, F., 'The Role of National Administrations in the protection of Geographical Indications: The Example of France', June 2001 (WIPO/GEO/CIS/01/3).

Cisneros, E. R., 'The Protection of Geographical Indications in Mexico', September 2001 (WIPO/GEO/MVD/01/7).

WIPO, Report of the Second WIPO Internet Domain Name Process – The Recognition of Rights and the Use of Names in the Internet Domain System (3 September 2001).

De Sousa, D., 'Protection of Geographical Indications under the TRIPS Agreement and Related Work of the World Trade Organization (WTO)', November 2001 (WIPO/GEO/MVD/01/2).

de Javier, L., 'Appellations of Origin in the Viticultural Sector: The Vision of the Wine Producers', November 2001 (WIPO/GEO/MVD/01/3).

Mekis, F., 'Appellations of Origin, Position of Chile's Vineyards in the Concert of the New World, and in Relation to the Negotiations with the European Union', October 2001 (WIPO/GEO/MVD/01/4).

d'Imperio, G. R., 'Protection of the Geographical Indications in Latin America', November 2001 (WIPO/GEO/MVD/01/5).

328   Bibliography

García Muñoz-Nájar, A., 'Some Notes on the Protection of Appellations of Origin in Countries with Emerging Economies: the Adean Community', November 2001 (WIPO/GEO/MVD/01/6).

Taubman, A., 'The Way Ahead: Developing International Protection for Geographical Indications: Thinking Locally, Acting Globally', November 2001 (WIPO/GEO/MVD/01/9).

WIPO, 'Document SCT/6/3 Rev. on Geographical Indications: Historical Background, Nature of Rights, Existing Systems for Protection and Obtaining Protection in Other Countries', 2 April 2002 (SCT/8/4).

WIPO, 'Report to the 7th Session of the SCT', 27 May 2002 (SCT/7/4).

WIPO, 'The Definition of Geographical Indications', 1 October 2002 (SCT/9/4).

WIPO, 'Introduction to Geographical Indications and Recent Developments in WIPO', 12 June 2003 (WIPO/GEO/SFO/03/1).

Meltzer, E., 'Geographical Indications: Point of View of Governments', 30 June 2003 (WIPO/GEO/SFO/03/3).

Lôrincz-Fejes, A., 'Protection of Geographical Indications: Point of View of the Hungarian Government', 7 July 2003 (WIPO/GEO/SFO/03/6).

Das, N. K., 'Protection of Darjeeling Tea', 3 July 2003 (WIPO/GEO/SFO/03/8).

Castellucci, F., 'Geographical Indications: The Italian Scenario for the Wine Sector', 24 June 2003 (WIPO/GEO/SFO/03/10).

Stern, S., 'Geographical Indications and Trade Marks: Conflicts and Possible Resolutions', 13 June 2003 (WIPO/GEO/SFO/03/13).

Bénard, Y., 'Geographical Indication around the World', 22 July 2003 (WIPO/GEO/SFO/03/20/Rev.).

WIPO, 'Article 6ter of the Paris Convention: Legal and Administrative Aspects', 14 October 2003 (SCT/5/3).

Brand, F., 'Protection of Geographical Indications: The Experience of Switzerland', 18 November 2003 (WIPO/GEO/DEL/03/3).

Drinkwater, B. G., 'Protection and Use of Geographical Indications in Australia', November 2003 (WIPO/GEO/DEL/03/4).

Wagle, S., 'Protection of Geographical Indications and Human Development: Economic and Social Benefits to Developing Countries', November 2003 (WIPO/GEO/DEL/03/7).

Ozanam, N., 'Protection of Geographical Indications – Food Products – The Example of Champagne Industry, France', November 2003 (WIPO/GEO/DEL/03/11.rev).

WIPO General Assembly Document, 'Proposal by Argentina and Brazil for the Establishment of a Development Agenda for WIPO', 27 August 2004 (WO/GA/31/11).

WIPO, 'New Types of Marks', 1 September 2006 (SCT/16/2).

Geuze, M., 'Let's Have Another Look at the Lisbon Agreement', 18 June 2007 (WIPO/GEO/BEI/07/10).

Lisbon Assembly, 'Report of the Twenty Third Session', 29 September 2008 (LI/A/23/2).

Gurry, F., Commemoration Speech, Ceremony to Mark the 50th Anniversary of the Adoption of the Lisbon Agreement, 31 October 2008.

Ficsor, M., 'Challenges to the Lisbon System', 31 October 2008 (WIPO/GEO/LIS/08/4).

WIPO, 'Possible Improvements of the Procedures under the Lisbon Agreement', 10 February 2009 (LI/WG/DEV/1/2 Rev).

WIPO, 'The Protection of Traditional Knowledge: Revised Objectives and Principles', 22 January 2010 (WIPO/GRTKF/IC/16/5 Prov).

WIPO, 'Summary of Replies to the Questionnaire on Trade Mark Law and Practice (SCT/11/6)', 25 January 2010 (WIPO/STrad/INF/1 Rev).

WIPO, 'Technical and Procedural Aspects Relating to the Registration of Certification and Collective Marks', 15 February 2010 (SCT/23/3).

WIPO, 'Results of the Survey on the Lisbon System', 18 June 2010 (LI/WG/DEV/2/2) (Lisbon Survey).

WIPO, 'Study on the Relationship between Regional Systems for the Protection of Geographical Indications and the Lisbon System and the Conditions For, and Possibility Of, Future Accession to the Lisbon Agreement by Competent Intergovernmental Organizations', 6 August 2010 (LI/WG/DEV/2/3).

WIPO, 'The Protection of Traditional Knowledge: Revised Objectives and Principles', 15 September 2010 (WIPO/GRTKF/IC/17/5).

WTO and GATT Documents

(Arranged Chronologically)

GATT, 'Meeting of the Negotiating Group of 10 June 1987', 23 June 1987 (MTN.GNG/NG11/2).

GATT, 'Compilation of Written Submissions and Oral Statements', 5 February 1988 (MTN.GNG/NG11/W/12/Rev.1).

GATT, 'Guidelines and Objectives Proposed by the EC', 7 July 1988 (MTN.GNG/NG11/W/26).

GATT, 'Meeting of the Negotiating Group of 5–8 July 1988', 29 August 1988 (MTN.GNG/NG11/8).

GATT, 'Meeting of the Negotiating Group of 12–14 September 1988', 13 October 1988 (MTN.GNG/NG11/9).

Communication from Switzerland, 'Standards and Principles Concerning the Availability, Scope and Use of Trade Related Intellectual Property Rights', 11 July 1989 (MTN.GNG/NG11/W/38).

GATT, 'Minutes of Negotiating Group of 12–14 July 1989', 12 September 1989 (MTN.GNG/NG11/14).

GATT, 'Meeting of the Negotiating Group 30 Oct-2 Nov 1989', 4 December 1989 (MTN.GNG/NG11/16).

GATT, 'Synoptic Tables Setting Out Existing International Standards and Proposed Standards and Principles', 2 February 1990 (MTN.GNG/NG11/W/32/Rev.2).

GATT, 'Draft Agreement on Trade Related Aspects of Intellectual Property Rights', 29 March 1990 (MTN.GNG/NG11/W/68).

GATT, 'Status of Work in the Negotiating Group', 23 July 1990 (MTN.GNG/NG11/W/76).

330 Bibliography

GATT, 'Meeting of the Negotiating Group of 1 November 1990', 14 November 1990 (MTN.GNG/NG11/27).

GATT, 'Progress of Work in Negotiating Groups: Stock Taking – Market Access', 7 November 1991 (MTN.TNC/W/89/Add.1).

GATT, 'Meeting of the Negotiating Group of 16 and 22 October 1991', 18 November 1991 (MTN.GNG/TRIPS/3).

WTO, Communication from Switzerland, 'Report (1996) of Council for TRIPS', 6 November 1996 (IP/C/8).

WTO, 'Review under Article 24.2 – Switzerland's Response to the Checklist', 16 February 1999 (IP/C/W/117/Add.13).

Communication from the US, 'Suggested Method for Domestic Recognition of Geographical Indications for WTO Members', 11 March 1999 (IP/C/W/134).

EC, 'Response to the Checklist of Questions: Review under Art 24.2', 26 March 1999 (IP/C/W/117/Add.10).

Communication from New Zealand, 'Geographical Indications and the Art 24.2 Review', 18 September 2000 (IP/C/W/205).

Communication from Bulgaria et al., 'Implementation of Art 24.1', 2 December 2000 (IP/C/W/204/Rev.1).

WTO Committee on Agriculture, 'EC Comprehensive Negotiating Proposal', 14 December 2000 (G/AG/NG/W/90).

Proposal from Bulgaria et al., 'Work on Issues Relevant to the Protection of Geographical Indications', 17 May 2001 (IP/C/W/247/Rev.1).

TRIPS Council, 'Communication from Bangladesh et al.', 2 October 2001 (IP/C/W/308/Rev.1).

WTO, 'Doha Ministerial Declaration', 20 November 2001 (WT/MIN(01)/DEC/1).

TRIPS Council, 'Minutes of the Meeting on 5–7 March 2002', 22 March 2002 (IP/C/M/35).

Communication from Bulgaria et al., 'The Extension of the Additional Protection for Geographical Indications to Products other than Wines and Spirits', 24 June 2002 (IP/C/W/353).

TRIPS Council, 'Minutes of Meeting on 25–27 June 2002', 10 September 2002 (IP/C/M/36/Add.1).

Communication from Australia et al., 'Implications of Article 23 Extension', 26 July 2002 (IP/C/W/360).

TRIPS Council, 'Minutes of the Meeting on 17–19 September 2002', 8 November 2002 (IP/C/M/37/Add.1).

Communication from Argentina et al., 'Implications of Article 23 Extension', 8 November 2002 (IP/C/W/386).

TRIPS Council, 'Minutes of the Meeting on 25–27 and 29 November, and 20 December 2002', 5 February 2003 (IP/C/M/38).

Communication from Hong Kong, China, 'Multilateral System of Notification and Registration of Geographical Indications under Article 23.4 of the TRIPS Agreement', 23 April 2003 (TN/IP/W/8).

WTO, 'Discussions on the Establishment of a Multilateral System of Notification and Registration of Geographical Indications for Wines and Spirits: Compilation of Issues and Points', 23 May 2003 (TN/IP/W/7/Rev.1).

Bibliography 331

WTO, 'Main Dedicated Intellectual Property Laws and Regulations Notified under Art.63.2 of the Agreement', 7 July 2003 (IP/N/I/CHE/G/6).

Communication from Bulgaria et al., 'Geographical Indications – The Significance of "Extension" in the TRIPS Agreement and its Benefits for WTO Members', 9 July 2003 (TN/C/W/14).

TRIPS Council, 'Review of Legislation – India', 8 October 2003 (IP/Q/IND/1).

WTO, 'Review under Article 24.2 of the Application of the Provisions of the Section of the TRIPS Agreement on Geographical Indications', 24 November 2003 (IP/C/W/253/Rev.1).

Statement by Switzerland, 'Joint Statement by the GI-Friends Group', 13 July 2004 (TN/C/4).

Communication from Bulgaria et al., 'Doha Work Programme – The Extension of the Additional Protection for Geographical Indications to Products other than Wines and Spirits', 14 December 2004 (TN/C/W/21/Rev.1).

WTO, 'Issues Related to the Extension of the Protection of Geographical Indications Provided for in Article 23 of the TRIPS Agreement to Products Other Than Wines and Spirits', 18 May 2005 (TN/C/W/25).

Communication from the EC, 'Geographical Indications', 14 June 2005 (TN/C/W/26) [Also (TN/IP/W/11)].

Report by the Director General, 'Issues Related to the Extension of the Protection of Geographical Indications Provided for in Article 23 of the TRIPS Agreement [and] those Related to the Relationship between the TRIPS Agreement and the Convention on Biological Diversity', 9 June 2008 (TN/C/W/50).

Communication from Albania et al., 'Draft Modalities for TRIPs Related Issues', 19 July 2008 (TN/C/W/52).

Report by the Chairman, 'Multilateral System of Notification and Registration of Geographical Indications for Wines and Spirits', 22 March 2010 (TN/IP/20).

Argentina et al., 'Proposed Draft TRIPS Council Decision on the Establishment of a Multilateral System of Notification and Registration of Geographical Indications for Wines and Spirits', 31 March 2011 (TN/IP/W/10/Rev.4).

TRIPS Council, 'Report by the Chairman to the Trade Negotiations Committee', 21 April 2011 (TN/IP/21).

UK National Archive Documents

Meeting of a Committee of Experts on 3 December1956 to Discuss System of Registration of Appellations of Origin (BT 209/1131).

Proposed System of Registration of Appellations of Origin (BT 209/1132).

Revision at Lisbon: Preparatory Work on the Agenda (BT 209/785).

Index

absolute protection
under Berlin resolution (1937), 132
extension of TRIPS Agreement to all
products, 271
implications of, 300–1
under Lisbon Agreement, 172–7
for wines and spirits under TRIPS
Agreement, 187, 238, 243
ACTA (Anti-Counterfeiting Trade
Agreement), 270
agricultural products. *See also* specific
products, e.g. wine, cheese
Madrid Agreement proposal to
exclude from generic exception,
69–72
multifunctionality of agriculture, 278–9
Paris Convention's inclusion within
industrial property, 25–6
policy objectives and extension of GI
protections under TRIPS, 277–8
TRIPS definition of GI and, 216
WTO debates on agricultural reform and
GI extension debate, 266
AIPPI (Association Internationale pour la
Protection de la Propriété
Industrielle), 62, 74, 132, 204, 258
alcoholic beverages. *See also* specific types
of spirits, e.g. wine
definition of GI under TRIPS and, 217
enhanced protection under TRIPS
Agreement for, 187, 237–44
Iran's rejection of AOs under Lisbon
Agreement for, 152
'Alheira de Barroso – Montalegre'
sausages, 236
ALPACAMARK, 256
Amar, Moise, 62
ambush marketing associated with sporting
events, 276
American Viticultural Areas (AVAs), 205
Anti-Counterfeiting Trade Agreement
(ACTA), 270

Appellation of Origin (AO)
development of definition of, 131–7
in France, 17, 77–126. *See also* France,
Appellation of Origin (AO) in
IS, historical transition from, 21–30, 65,
69, 74–6, 97, 133–5, 177, 299
in Lisbon Agreement. *See under* Lisbon
Agreement
property rights, AOs as objects of, 149
reputation and quality under, 210
TRIPS definition of GI and, 195–8
WIPO Model Law on, 142, 159
Assam, 256
Association Internationale pour la
Protection de la Propriété
Industrielle (AIPPI), 62, 74,
132, 204, 258
Audier, Jacques, 28, 111, 239
Australia
EU–Australia Wine Agreement (1994), 241
GI extension under TRIPS, opposition
to, 115
wines in, 106–8
AVAs (American Viticultural Areas), 205

Balsamic vinegar from Modena, 210
Banks, G., 108
Barak, Justice, 155
Barham, Elizabeth, 83
Basmati rice, 221
Bavarian beer, 251
Beier, F.-K., 51, 228
Belgium, on regional marks, 61
Bender, Hans, 245
Bently, Lionel, 38, 78
Bérard, Laurence, 112, 223, 236
Berlin Resolution (International Chamber
of Commerce, 1937), 132
biodiversity conservation, 279–80
BIRPI (Bureaux Internationaux Réunis
pour la Protection de la Propriété
Intellectuelle), 24, 30

332

Index

Blakeney, Michael, 32
Bohmrich, Roger, 83, 88
Bone, Robert, 170
Bordeaux wines, 27, 82, 99, 149
Bowen, Sarah, 285
Brandeis, Louis, 55
Britain. *See* United Kingdom
Budweiser litigation, 130, 139, 144, 154, 160–1, 174, 178
Bureaux Internationaux Réunis pour la Protection de la Propriété Intellectuelle (BIRPI), 24, 30
Burgundy wines, 94

Calcide, Greek swords of, 32
Canada, generic use designations in, 189
CAP (Common Agricultural Policy), EU, 277
Capus, Joseph, 99, 104
cashew liquor (Feni), 113
Cassis wine region, 106
certification marks and collective marks
 defined, 60
 distinguished, 60
 Paris Convention (1883) on, 60–4, 201
 quality and reputation under, 208
 TRIPS Agreement
  definition of GI under, 196, 198
  international registration proposals, 291–5
  national legal responses to, 201
Chablis wine, 170
Champagne, 44, 73, 84, 95, 100–2, 105, 106, 121
cheese. *See also* specific types, e.g. Roquefort
 French regime expanded to include, 111
 generic use and, 246
 Stresa Agreement (1951) on, 130, 132
Chen, Jim, 204
CNAO (Comité National des Appellations d'Origine), 108
Codex Alimentarius Commission, 247
coffee, development potential of GI for, 283
Cognac, 207
collective know-how, regional products linked to, 87, 141–3, 221–3, 235–7, 272–5, 280–6, 300
collective marks. *See* certification marks and collective marks
Colomer, Dámaso Ruiz-Jarabo, 28, 144
Comité National des Appellations d'Origine (CNAO), 108
Common Agricultural Policy (CAP), EU, 277

communicative logic
 extension of enhanced protections under TRIPS and, 275
 generic usage under TRIPS and, 244
 in German and UK unfair competition-based regimes, 116
 Madrid Agreement and recognition of limitations of, 65
 Paris Convention's use of, 33–41
 terroir logic and, 15, 74–6, 124
 unfair competition paradigm premised on, 275, 301
Community Trade Mark (CTM) registration system, EU, 240–2
consumers
 demand for regional products by, 183, 271, 275, 282
 expenses of opinion polls demonstrating confusion of, 269
 generic use, understanding of, 252–5
 protection and concept of IS, 28
contemporary debates regarding GI, 17, 265–96, 301–2
 agricultural policy objectives, 277–8
 biodiversity conservation, 279–80
 development potential of GI, 280–6
 extension of enhanced protection under TRIPS to all products, 266–88
 international registration proposals, 288–95
 multifunctionality of agriculture, 278–9
 TK (traditional knowledge), interface between GI and, 272–5, 286–8
 unfair competition law, use of, 265, 275
copyright law, enhanced protection under, 239
Cosimo III (Grand Duke of Florence), 82
countries as regions of origin, 218–20
craft and cultural artefacts, AO applied to, 136
CTM (Community Trade Mark) registration system, EU, 240–2
cultural heritage, regional products linked to, 87, 141–3, 221–3, 235–7, 272–5, 280–6, 300
customs law and concept of IS, 28
Czechoslovakia/Czech Republic
 Budweiser litigation, 130, 139, 144, 154, 160–1, 174, 178
 Madrid negotiations, *terroir* logic used in, 71

Darjeeling tea, 163, 168, 172, 247, 269
Das, Kasturi, 284
Dawson, Norma, 3

334 Index

descriptive fair use, coexistence of trade
marks and GIs under, 261–2
Develetian, Artin, 132
developed versus developing world and
TRIPS Agreement, 191, 268,
269, 271
development potential of GI, 280–6
Dharamshala, India, Tibetan craftsmen
relocated to, 142
dilution, under Lisbon Agreement,
166–8, 170
Dion, Roger, 89
Dresdner Stollen, 235
Duguid, Paul, 81, 82
Dunant, Philippe, 39

ECJ. *See* European Court of Justice
ecological biodiversity conservation, 279–80
environmental biodiversity conservation,
279–80
Escudero, Sergio, 217
Ethiopia
producer groups, problems associated
with establishing, 294
Starbucks, dispute with, 256
Europe/European Union
agricultural reform debates at
WTO and, 266
Australia, 1994 wine agreement with, 241
CAP (Common Agricultural Policy), 277
CTM registration system, 240–2
definition of GI, use of, 214
generic use, controversy over, 68–74,
246–54
international registration proposal for
TRIPS GI designation, 288
PDOs and PGIs, 210, 211, 212,
224–31, 282
Regulation 2081/92, 224–31
TRIPS Agreement
goods included in definition of GI, 217
legal response to, 201
negotiation of, 193–5, 197–8, 239
wine labelling policy, role of *terroir* in, 88
European Court of Justice (ECJ)
on generic use, 46, 251
on GIs as private property, 202
on reputation and quality issues, 209
trade mark system, on incorporation of
GI within, 12
Evans, Gail, 294

false labelling or fraud, GI protection
via, 26, 31
Feni, 113

Feta cheese, 207, 219, 245, 247, 252
Ficsor, Mihály, 147
'first in time, first in right' (FITFIR) rule,
255, 257–61
France
EC Regulation 2081/92 reconciling
French and German approaches to
IGO protection, 224–31
fraudulent marking, penal law of 1824
on, 26, 33–4
Paris Convention (1883), French legal
influence on, 33–4
socially constitutive role of *terroir* in, 87
TRIPS Agreement, legal response to, 200
France, Appellation of Origin (AO) in,
17, 77–126
expansion of regime to products other
than wine, 111
Germany and the UK compared, 115–24
human and natural influences, interplay
of, 141
Lisbon Agreement and, 127–8, 138, 177
private property, AOs not regarded as,
204, 205
quality
origin as proxy for, 80–2, 96–7, 99, 104
product regulation and control,
introduction of, 108–11
significance of, 77–80, 124–6
terroir logic and, 17, 124–6
transition from AO (*Appellation
d'Origine*) to AOC (*Appellation
d'Origine Contrôlée*), 96–115
contemporary regime, 111–15
continuity with IS protections, 97
Law of 1905, 98–102
Law of 1919 formally adopting AO
terminology, 102–8
Law of 2 July 1990, 111
Laws of 1935 and 1947 establishing
AOC, 98–102
Lisbon Agreement recognising, 177
wine regulation
as archetypal scaffolding for *terroir*
logic and AO, 78–9
phylloxera crisis, fraudulent responses
to, 93–6
role of origin in, 80–3
terroir, concept of, 83–93
fraud or false labelling, GI protection
via, 26, 31
free riding (pure misappropriation), 170–2,
240–2, 270
'freezing' of designations after registration,
152–6, 239

Index

Gade, Daniel, 106
generic use of geographical terms
  consumer understanding and, 252–5
  France, transition from AO to AOC in, 97
  'freezing' of designations after
    registration and, 152–6, 239
  'legitimation of past sins' debate, 247
  Lisbon Agreement and, 150–6
  Madrid Agreement and, 68–74
  ordinary English usage, protected
    designations with, 242
  Paris Convention and, 43–8
  refusal of registration of product as AO
    under Lisbon Agreement, grounds
    for, 150–2
  threat of GI protections to, 10
  TRIPS Agreement and, 189, 239,
    244–55
  wine excluded from exception for,
    68–74
Geographical Indications (GI), 1–8
  competing epistemic frameworks for, 15
  consumer demand for, 183, 271
  contemporary debates regarding, 17,
    265–96, 301–2, See also
    contemporary debates regarding GI
  defined, 2
  differential treatment sought for, 2
  economic and political significance of,
    8–14, 183
  first introduction of concept, 196
  France, AO in, 17, 77–126.
    See also France, Appellation of
    Origin (AO) in
  historical methodology of approach to,
    14–18, 297–300
  historical origins of basic concept, 32–3,
    179, 298
  historical transition from IS to AO, 21–30,
    65, 69, 74–6, 97, 133–5, 177, 299
  IGO terminology, use of, 4
  importance of studying, 297
  international framework, importance of
    inclusion in, 8
  IP regime, questions about inclusion in, 7
  Lisbon Agreement, 17, 127–79.
    See also Lisbon Agreement
  Madrid Agreement, 16, 65–74.
    See also Madrid Agreement
  messiness of law regarding, 1, 2–8
  national traditions, wide variety of, 5
  new participants in debates regarding,
    9–10
  Paris Convention, 16, 23–64.
    See also Paris Convention

  progressively more specialised types of, 77
  scholarly approaches to, 6–7
  scope of protection for. *See* scope of
    protection
  sui generis models, critiques of, 10–12
  terminological diversity regarding, 2–4
  trade marks compared, 2
  TRIPS Agreement, 17, 183–264.
    See also TRIPS Agreement
  unfair competition law, origins in, 179
geographical regions of origin under
  TRIPS, 218–23
Germany
  EC Regulation 2081/92 reconciling
    French and German approaches to
    IGO protection, 224–31
  Lisbon Agreement and, 117, 147, 148
  unfair competition law for GI, reliance
    on, 77, 115–24
  wine appellations, acceptance of
    enhanced protections for, 74
Gervais, Daniel, 129, 192, 286
GI. *See* Geographical Indications
Giant White Maize (Maíz Blanco Gigante
  Cusco), 173
GMA (Grocery Manufacturer's
  Association of America), 10
goodwill, passing off injurious to,
  119–21
Gorgonzola cheese, 133
grandfathering under TRIPS Agreement,
  189
Great Britain. *See* United Kingdom
Greeley, Arthur, 40
Grocery Manufacturer's Association
  of America (GMA), 10
Guy, Kolleen M., 86

Hague Conference and Convention (1925),
  25, 26, 63, 71
'Havana' cigars and tobacco, generic
  use of, 246
Heath, C., 154, 161
historical methodology of approach to GI,
  14–18, 297–300
historical origins of basic concept of GI,
  32–3, 179, 298
historical transition from IS to AO, 21–30,
  65, 69, 74–6, 97, 133–5, 177, 299
Hoffmann, Lord, 226
Hong Kong, international registration
  proposal, 288
human factors, regional products linked to,
  87, 141–3, 221–3, 235–7, 272–5,
  280–6, 300

336   Index

IGO (Indication of Geographical Origin)
    as term, use of, 4
imitation or usurpation, Lisbon Agreement's
    general prohibition against, 162–72
INAO (Institut National des Appellations
    d'Origine), 109–10, 132, 232, 235
India
    Basmati rice, 221
    on costs of maintaining GI protections,
        269
    Dharamshala, Tibetan craftsmen
        relocated to, 142
    goods included in definition of TRIPS
        GI, 217
    socio-economic link with region of
        origin, defining, 221
Indication of Geographical Origin (IGO) as
    term, use of, 4
Indication of Source (IS)
    AO, historical transition to, 21–30, 65,
        69, 74–6, 97, 133–5, 177, 299
    in Paris Convention and Madrid
        Agreement. See Madrid Agreement,
        Paris Convention
    TRIPS definition of GI and, 195–8
indications of provenance, 37, 39
indirect indications of origin
    concept of, 66
    in Lisbon Agreement, 143–4
    TRIPS definition of GI and, 215
individualistic bias in IP law, 75
industrial property
    definition of, in Paris Convention, 25
    IP versus, 23
Institut National des Appellations
    d'Origine (INAO), 109–10, 132,
    232, 235
instrumentalist theory of
    misrepresentation, 164
INTA (International Trade Mark
    Association), 258
intellectual property (IP)
    continuing questions about inclusion
        of GI in, 7
    individualistic bias in, 75
    industrial property versus, 23
    reputation as basis for inclusion of IS in
        Paris Convention, 30–1
    rights, defined, 33
    unfair competition law and, 56
International Alpaca Association, 256
International Chamber of Commerce,
    74, 132
international law
    importance of inclusion of GI in, 8

Paris Convention, origins of international
    GI protection in, 25
international registration
    under Lisbon Agreement, 129–30,
        146–57, 178
    proposed for TRIPS GI designation,
        288–95
International Trade Mark Association
    (INTA), 258
IP. See intellectual property
Iran, rejection of AOs for alcoholic
    products in, 152
IS. See Indication of Source
Italy
    'exclusively or essentially' clause on AO
        under Lisbon Agreement, judicial
        interpretations of, 139
    Parma ham, 259–61
    Parmigiano Reggiano cheese, 133, 161,
        212, 247

Jacobs, Advocate-General, 3
Jaffa oranges, 155, 211
Japan
    European wine appellations used for
        locally made products for liquor
        tax law purposes, 193
    Kobe beef, 247, 256
    supplemental protection in, 200
Jaton, Louis, 32, 71
Johnson, Hugh, 85

Knaak, R., 230
know-how, collective, regional products
    linked to, 87, 141–3, 221–3,
    235–7, 272–5, 280–6, 300
Kobe beef, 247, 256
Kolia, Marina, 229
Kur, Anette, 206, 256

Ladas, Stephen, 24, 37, 40, 43, 73
Laddie, J., 122
Lancashire, Swedish versus British use
    of, 46
Lang, A. C., 268, 270
link between product and place
    Lisbon Agreement establishing,
        136, 231
    TRIPS on, 197–8, 223–37
Lisbon Agreement (1958), 17, 127–79
    AO under, 130–46
        definition, development of, 131–7
        'exclusively or essentially' clause,
            judicial interpretations of, 139–41
        geographical denominations, 143–4

Index

link between product and place, 136, 231
natural and human influences, interplay of, 141–3
reputation, 145–6
separate conceptual category, development as, 128, 133–5
conceptual realignments leading up to, 30
'freezing' of designations after registration, 152–6
French AOC regime and, 127–8, 138, 177
generic use under, 150–6
German abstention from, 117
Madrid Agreement and, 30, 127–8, 198, 199
Paris Convention and, 127, 162
refusal of registration of product as AO, grounds for, 150–2
regional registration systems and, 148
registration system, operationalisation of, 129–30, 146–57, 178
scope of protection, 157–77
absolute protection, 172–7
categories of prohibited uses, 158–62
contract law rather than unfair competition or IP law, resembling, 158
dilution, 166–8, 170
general prohibition against usurpation or imitation, 162–72
misappropriation, 168–72
misrepresentation, 163–6
scalability issues, 130
text of agreement regarding, 158
terroir logic and, 124, 159, 178
translations, prohibitions on, 160–2
TRIPS and. *See under* TRIPS Agreement
Lisbon Conference (1958)
on Madrid Agreement, 66
on Paris Convention, 50, 59
Lorvellec, Louis, 204, 252
Louis Vuitton, 167

Madeira wine, 92
Madrid Agreement (1891), 16, 65–74
generic use of geographical terms under, 68–74
historical transition from IS to AO and, 21–30, 65, 69, 74–6
indirect indications of origin, concept of, 66
Lisbon Agreement and, 30, 127–8, 198, 199

Paris Convention, relationship to, 65
scope of protection under, 65–8
Maíz Blanco Gigante Cusco (Giant White Maize), 173
Malabar, 256
Mantecoso cheese, 284
manufactured and natural products, distinction between, 25–6
Marchenay, Philippe, 112, 223, 236
Marx, Karl, 92
McKenna, Mark, 38
Melton Mowbray pork pies, 236
misappropriation, under Lisbon Agreement, 168–72
misrepresentation, under Lisbon Agreement, 163–6
Moran, Warren, 79
multifunctionality of agriculture, 278–9
Munson, Thomas V., 94

natural and human influences, interplay of, 141–3
natural and manufactured products, distinction between, 25–6
New World wines, 106–8
non-political geographical areas, 221

Olinalá, 136, 143
Oliveira Martins, M. De, 69, 70
Oliver, Lord, 119
Olszak, Nabert, 170

Pakistan and Basmati rice, 221
Palomar, as GI, 241
Paris Convention (1883), 16, 23–64
alternative approaches to IGO protection at, 29
on collective marks, 60–4, 201
concept of IS in, 27–41
French legal influence on, 33–4
as fundamental conceptual shift in thinking about IGOs, 33–41
generic use of geographical terms and, 43–8
historical concepts of IGOs prior to, 32–3
historical transition from IS to AO and, 21–30, 74–6
indications of provenance distinguished from IS, 37, 39
industrial property, definition of, 25
international recognition of IGOs originating with, 25
limitations of, 24
Lisbon Agreement and, 127, 162

338   Index

Paris Convention (1883) (cont.)
  Madrid Agreement stemming from, 65
  reputation as basis for inclusion
    of IS in, 30–1
  scope of protection under, 41–52
  significance of, 23
  trade mark and trade name regimes and,
    37–41
  unfair competition law and, 26, 52–9
  wide array of national responses to IS
    protection requirement in, 28–30
Parma ham, 259–61
Parmesan cheese, 247, 254
Parmigiano Reggiano cheese, 133, 161,
  212, 247
passing off and extended passing off, 29,
  119–22
PDO (Protected Designation of Origin),
  210, 211, 212, 224–31, 282
Peru
  Maíz Blanco Gigante Cusco or Giant
    White Maize, 173
  Mantecoso cheese, 284
  Pisco, 151
Pey, Joanny, 39, 62
PGI (Protected Geographical Indication),
  210, 211, 212, 224–31, 282
phylloxera crisis, 93–6
Pilsener/Pilsner/Pilsen/Pils, 139, 153,
  160–2, 246. See also Budweiser
  litigation
Pisco, 151
Portugal
  'exclusively or essentially' clause on AO
    under Lisbon Agreement, judicial
    interpretations of, 140
  translations, judicial decisions
    regarding, 161
Posner, Richard, 171
premium prices for GI products, 282
property rights
  AOs as objects of, 149
  private property, GIs as, 202–6
Protected Designation of Origin (PDO) and
  Protected Geographical Indication
  (PGI), 210, 211, 212, 224–31, 282
provenance, indications of, 37, 39
pure misappropriation (free riding), 170–2,
  240–2, 270

quality. See reputation and quality

Rangnekar, Dwijen, 113, 268, 280
regional registration systems and Lisbon
  framework, 148

registration, international
  under Lisbon Agreement, 129–30,
    146–57, 178
  proposed for TRIPS GI designation,
    288–95
reputation and quality
  France, AO in
    origin as proxy for quality, 80–2,
      96–7, 99, 104
    product regulation and control,
      introduction of, 108–11
  link between product and place under
    TRIPS, 235–7
  Lisbon Agreement and, 145–6
  Paris Convention, as basis for inclusion
    of IS in, 30–1
  in progressively more specialised types
    of GI, 77
  region of origin associated with GI under
    TRIPS, 218–23
  services, as GI under TRIPS, 218
  TRIPS Agreement and, 206–13
Rolls Royce, 167
Rome Conference (1886), 65
Rooibos tea, 284
Roquefort cheese, 32, 111, 133, 159
Roubier, Paul, 105

Schechter, Frank, 167
Schricker, Gerhard, 118
scope of protection
  absolute. See absolute protection
  Lisbon Agreement. See under Lisbon
    Agreement
  Madrid Agreement, 65–8
  Paris Convention, 41–52
  problem of defining, 4–5
  TRIPS. See two levels of protection
    under TRIPS Agreement
Scotch whisky, 44, 119, 122
Scott, Lord, 12
services, as GI under TRIPS, 217
Sharpe, Scott, 108
Sheffield cutlery, 49
Sherman, Brad, 38, 78
sherry, 253
socio-economic practices, regional
  products linked to, 87, 141–3,
  221–3, 235–7, 272–5, 280–6, 300
South Africa, Rooibos tea from, 284
Spence, Michael, 55
spirits. See alcoholic beverages, and specific
  types, e.g. wine
sporting events, ambush marketing
  associated with, 276

Index

Stanziani, Alessandro, 103
Star Wars, 253
Starbucks, 256
state emblems, protections for, 276
state's role in *sui generis* GI models, 294–5
Stern, Stephen, 7
Stresa Agreement (1951), 130, 132
sui generis GI models
  critiques of, 10–12
  international registration under
    certification or collective marks
    versus, 291–5
  reputation and quality under, 209, 211
  state, role of, 294–5
  under TRIPS Agreement, 201
Sweden
  Lancashire, Swedish versus British use
    of, 46
  translations, judicial decisions
    regarding, 161
Swiss chocolate, 122
Swiss incorporation of GI within trade
    mark system, 12

Taubman, Antony, 177, 216
Tequila, 136, 280, 285
terroir logic
  AO in France incorporating, 17, 124–6.
    See also France, Appellation
    of Origin (AO) in
  communicative logic and, 15, 74–6, 124
  countries as regions of origin and, 220
  essential attributability of qualities or
    characteristics to place of origin, 231–5
  Lisbon Agreement and, 124, 159, 178
  Madrid Agreement's use of, 69–74
  movement away from, 300
  in progressively more specialised types
    of GI, 77
  quality, origin as proxy for, 80–2,
    96–7, 99, 104
  on reputation and quality, 209
  socially constitutive role of, 87
  in viniculture, 83–93
  wine regulation as archetypal scaffolding
    for, 78–9
Tibetan craftsmen relocated to
    Dharamshala, India, 142
TK. *See* Traditional Knowledge
Tocai/Tocaj controversy, 202
trade mark and trade name regimes.
    See also certification marks and
    collective marks
  accommodation of GI within, proposals
    regarding, 11–12

comparison of GI to, 2
conflicts between GI and, 10, 255–62
CTM (Community Trade Mark)
    registration system, EU, 240–2
descriptive fair use defence, 261–2
enhanced protection under, 238
FITFIR rule, 255, 257–61
French penal law of 1824 on fraudulent
    marking, 26, 33–4
level of IS functioning analogously to, 77
misrepresentation in, 164
Paris Convention and, 37–41
private property, GIs as, 203, 205
relationship between GIs and trade
    marks, 255–62
reputation and quality under, 208
terroir logic diverging from, 78
TRIPS Agreement and, 189, 255–62
Trade Related Agreement in International
    Property Rights. *See* TRIPS
    Agreement
Traditional Knowledge (TK), 300
  defined, 286
  extension of enhanced GI protection
    under TRIPS and, 272–5, 286–8
  individualistic bias in IP law and, 75
  terroir in viniculture and, 91
translations
  extension of GI protections to all
    products and, 270
  Lisbon Agreement on, 160–2
TRIPS Agreement, 17
  absence of specific prescribed form of
    protection under, 199
  absolute protection under, 187, 238,
    243, 271
  certification marks and collective marks.
    See under certification marks and
    collective marks
  coalescence of GI debate, as site of, 1
  compromises enshrined in, instability of,
    184–5, 191–213, 224–31
  conceptual significance, overstatement
    of, 192
  consumer demand for regionally specific
    products and, 183, 271
  definition of GI in, 2, 186, 213–37
    absence of specific prescribed form of
      protection and, 199
    AO and IS, relationship to, 195–8
    essential attributability of qualities or
      characteristics to place of origin,
      231–5
    the goods, 216–18
    importance of clarity of, 213

340   Index

TRIPS Agreement (cont.)
  product and place, link between,
    197–8, 223–37
  region of origin requirements, 218–23
  the sign, 215–16
  WIPO negotiations, 195–8
developed versus developing world and,
  191, 268, 269, 271
drafting history, 191–9, 223, 238–40
exceptions under, 188–91
'freezing' of designations under, 239
generic use under, 189, 239, 244–55
grandfathering under, 189
Lisbon Agreement and
  AO definition and TRIPS definition
    of GI, 131
  indirect indications of origin, 143
  registration system, operationalisation
    of, 129–30, 178
  reputation, 145
  two levels of protection, negotiation
    of, 198
Madrid Agreement and, 198, 199
negotiations, commitment to, 188, 191
private property, GIs as, 202–6
provisions of, 185–91
reconceptualisation of GI protection
  within framework of, 184
reputation and quality, ability of GI to
  communicate or guarantee, 17
trade marks and, 189, 255–62
two levels of protection under, 186–8,
  237–44
  absolute protection, 187, 238, 243, 271
  extension of enhanced protection to all
    products, 266–88
  WIPO negotiations introducing, 198–9
unfair competition law and, 53, 186
Uruguay Round negotiations, 11, 188,
  193, 234, 244, 269
wines and spirits, enhanced protection
  for, 187, 237–44
WIPO negotiations and, 195–9

Ulin, Robert C., 83
unfair competition law
  communicative logic, premised on,
    275, 301
  contemporary debates regarding GI and,
    265, 275
  German and UK reliance on, 77, 115–24
  GI law originating in, 179, 298
  IP and, 56
  Lisbon Agreement compared, 158
  misrepresentation prohibited by, 163

Paris Convention and, 26, 52–9
quality and reputation under, 208
TRIPS and, 53, 186
uniqueness
  Lisbon Agreement, judicial
    interpretation of 'exclusively or
    essentially' clause of, 139–41
  TRIPS Agreement, essential attributability
    of qualities or characteristics to place
    of origin in, 234
United Kingdom
  collective marks, opposition to, 64
  Lancashire, Swedish versus British
    use of, 46
  Madrid Agreement, enforcement of, 67
  trade mark system, on incorporation
    of GI within, 11
  TRIPS Agreement, legal response to, 200
  unfair competition law for GI, reliance
    on, 115–24
  wine, origin-based regulation of, 81–2, 94
United States
  Budweiser litigation, 130, 139, 144, 154,
    160–1, 174, 178
  definition of GI, use of, 214
  generic use designations in, 189
  international registration proposal for
    TRIPS GI designation, 288
  Parma ham dispute, 259–61
  phylloxera crisis, role in, 93
  on private property status of GIs, 205
  trade mark system, on incorporation of
    GI within, 11
  TRIPS Agreement, legal response to, 201
  wines in, 106–8
Unwin, Tim, 95
Uruguay Round, 11, 188, 193, 234, 244, 269
usurpation or imitation, Lisbon Agreement's
  general prohibition against, 162–72

Versailles, Treaty of (1919), 74
Vialard, Antoine, 205
Vidal, Denis, 90
vodka, 220

W52 group, 288
Wadlow, Christopher, 58
Warner, Charles, 96
Washington Conference (1911), 25, 48,
  58, 62, 70
Whalen, P., 93, 98
wine. See also specific types, e.g.
  Champagne
  AO and terroir logic, as archetypal
    scaffolding for, 78–9

concept of *terroir* as applied to, 83–93
EU–Australia Wine Agreement (1994), 241
French AO and AOC regimes.
  See France, Appellation of Origin (AO) in
generic use provisions and, 68–74, 189
human and natural influences, interplay of, 142
Madrid Agreement introducing special provisions for, 66, 68–74
in New World, 106–8, 205
non-political geographical areas, defining, 221
phylloxera crisis, fraudulent responses to, 93–6
quality, origin as proxy for, 80–2, 96–7, 99, 104
rent-seeking, origin-linked reputation as means of, 82
role of origin in regulation of, 80–3
TRIPS Agreement, enhanced protection under, 187, 237–44
TRIPS definition of GI and, 217
World Intellectual Property Organization (WIPO)
  administration of Paris Convention, Madrid Agreement and Lisbon Agreement by, 22, 150, 157
BIRPI as predecessor to, 24

on collective marks, 60
on definition of GI, 214
GI, attempt at establishing, 3
human and natural influences, interplay of, 142
indirect indications of origin and, 143
legal responses to GI protection commitments, survey of, 199
Lisbon Agreement, operationalisation of registration system under, 129
Model Law on AO, 142, 159
non-political geographical areas, defining, 221
on regional registration systems and Lisbon framework, 148
on reputation and quality issues, 208
TRIPS negotiations and, 195–9
World Trade Organization (WTO)
  agricultural reform debates, 266, 278
  IGO terminology, use of, 4
  legal responses to GI protection commitments, survey of, 199
  multidimensional functions of GI protection considered by, 272–4
  Panel Report on GIs, 190, 261
  private property, survey on GIs as, 204
  survey of legal responses to GI protection commitments, 199

Zylberg, Philippe, 252

Cambridge Intellectual Property and Information Law

Titles in the series (formerly known as *Cambridge Studies in Intellectual Property Rights*)

Brad Sherman and Lionel Bently
The Making of Modern Intellectual Property Law
978 0 521 56363 5

Irini A. Stamatoudi
Copyright and Multimedia Products: A Comparative Analysis
978 0 521 80819 4

Pascal Kamina
Film Copyright in the European Union
978 0 521 77053 8

Huw Beverly-Smith
The Commercial Appropriation of Personality
978 0 521 80014 3

Mark J. Davison
The Legal Protection of Databases
978 0 521 80257 4

Robert Burrell and Allison Coleman
Copyright Exceptions: The Digital Impact
978 0 521 84726 1

Huw Beverly-Smith, Ansgar Ohly and Agnès Lucas-Schloetter
Privacy, Property and Personality: Civil Law Perspectives on Commercial Appropriation
978 0 521 82080 6

Philip Leith
Software and Patents in Europe
978 0 521 86839 6

Lionel Bently, Jennifer Davis and Jane C. Ginsburg
Trade Marks and Brands: An Interdisciplinary Critique
978 0 521 88965 0

Geertrui Van Overwalle
Gene Patents and Clearing Models
978 0 521 89673 3

Jonathan Curci
The Protection of Biodiversity and Traditional Knowledge in International Law of Intellectual Property
978 0 521 19944 5

Lionel Bently, Jennifer Davis and Jane C. Ginsburg
Copyright and Piracy: An Interdisciplinary Critique
978 0 521 19343 6

Megan Richardson and Julian Thomas
Framing Intellectual Property: Legal Constructions of Creativity and Appropriation 1840–1940
978 0 521 76756 9

Dev Gangjee
Relocating the Law of Geographical Indications
978 0 521 19202 6